VALLEY C
50690010

W9-BWO-886

Durante, Georgia,
The company she keeps /

THE COMPANY
SHE KEEPS

Additional Praise for
The Company She Keeps:

I spent a lifetime chasing gangsters out of the lives of decent people with the help of my colleagues in the FBI. Georgia Durante chased them out of her life by herself. She should have worked with us. This is an exceptionally intriguing book with eye-opening lessons for everyone.

—Bill Fleming, Special Agent (Retired)
Federal Bureau of Investigation

It's one of those stories that makes you want to write a better critique than anyone else's. But Georgia has written the best one of all. You'll agree with me tomorrow morning when you still haven't put *The Company She Keeps* to bed.

—Morton Downey, Jr.
Network Talk Show Pioneer

(Georgia Durante) has had quite a life, and the courage it takes to live it. I would never have imagined all (she's) been through. (She) hides a lot behind that lovely smile.

—Hugh O'Brian
Actor

Quite unreal, really. What a life.

—Graham Nash
Musician, Crosby, Stills, Nash & Young

Georgia Durante has great skill as an author. Her warmth, her daring and her intelligence make this book a great adventure. I couldn't put it down. Read this book! You'll be amazed, you'll be excited. You'll be grateful I made you do it.

—Buddy Hackett
Entertainer and Comedian

Once you start reading this book, you cannot put it down. It covers everything from flashy show people, to the mob, to ordinary everyday people. There's a surprise on every page and a twist and turn in every chapter.

—Dick Van Patten
Actor

(Georgia Durante) has an adventurous spirit and has led a glamorous life. She honestly shares painful experiences in this fascinating and entertaining book.

—Stella Stevens
Actress

(*The Company She Keeps*) is the high-interest, quick paced account of life in the fast lane. At the heart is the love of danger and excitement which is, for (Georgia), almost a fatal flaw. Fortunately, a love of autos and an uncanny ability to control high-horsepower cars led to an unexpected escape route. (Hers) is a story well worth reading.

—Samuel Hallock duPont, Jr.
Entrepreneur and Philanthropist

(*The Company She Keeps*) is a story of today. Women will relate to (Georgia's) inner strength that enabled her to overcome obstacles; and men will relate to (her) courage and admire (her) perseverance.

—Marty Allen
Entertainer and Comedian

(*The Company She Keeps*) is a superbly written autobiography about a lovely young woman's struggle and victory. What a struggle; what a victory; and what a woman! Georgia is one of a kind, and so is her book.

—Alan Young
Actor and Author

THE COMPANY SHE KEEPS

BY GEORGIA DURANTE

Nashville, Tennessee

Nashville, Tennessee
Copyright © 1998 by Georgia Durante

Published by Celebrity Books
1501 County Hospital Road
Nashville, Tennessee 37218

Printed in the United States of America
ISBN 1-58029-105-8

Library of Congress Cataloging-in-Publication Data:
Durante, Georgia, 1950—
The company she keeps / by Georgia Durante
p.   cm.
ISBN 1-58029-105-8 (hardcover)
1. Durante, Georgia, 1950— . 2. Mafia--United States--Case
studies. 3. Wives--United States--Biography. 4. Women automobile
drivers--United States--Biography. 5. Models (Persons)--United
States--Biography. I. Title.
HV6248.D87A3   1998
364.1'06
[b]--DC21
98-36737
CIP

DEDICATION

To my daughter Toni, whose struggle with life has set this book in motion. And my son Dustin, who has been a constant source of joy in my life.

To my parents, Tony and Angela Durante. Without your unconditional love and support, I probably wouldn't be here to be dedicating this book to anyone.

Acknowledgments

———◦——◀●▶——◦———

I would like to acknowledge:

Scott Deal, who listened to my life story over several glasses of wine in my backyard and urged me to put it down on paper. Without his encouragement, this book would not have been written.

Gail Stewart, my early copy editor, whose Radcliff education could in no way prepare her for the editing of this book. Yes, Gail, I took out all the profanity which made you cringe. Wish you were still with us to finally see the fruits of our labor. I miss you.

Buddy Hackett, whose opinion I value. You were right, Buddy, I made the changes you suggested. Sherry Hackett, my dearest of friends. Thanks for the positive attitude and for standing behind me. Your belief in this book has helped it come to be.

Barry Lund, with Lintas Cambell Ewald Advertising Agency, and Barry Meier, with Avalon Films, who put up with me writing this book "between takes" on our annual fifty-day summer shoots for Chevrolet.

Sidney Sheldon, who took time out from writing his own book to critique mine. Your kindness will not be forgotten.

Ralph Cossey, a true friend, who unselfishly gave of his time for three years, freeing me from my daily drudgery, allowing me to write without interruption. More books could be written, if everyone with a book in them had a Ralph in their life.

Jimmy Breslin, whose helpful suggestions were invaluable. I'm honored by the interest you have taken and by the guidance you have provided. It is very much appreciated.

Jim Nicole, who made me aware of Georgia Black's destruction in my personal life.

Frank Aloi, whose book, *The Hammer Conspiracies*, was helpful in jogging my memory and placing my life's events in the correct chronology.

Marty Allen and his beautiful wife Katie, thank you for your friendship and belief in me when I needed encouragement. Your unrelenting effort in helping me to bring this book together has given the word "friendship" a new meaning.

Quincy Jones, who used to think of me as "church people" until he read my book. Thanks, Q, for urging me to press forward with my dream.

A special thanks to all of my friends who took the time to read my rough drafts and point out where I fell short. There are too many of you to mention by name. You know who you are. Without you, and your encouraging faith in me, these pages would never have been turned.

I'd like to thank all of the people at Hambleton-Hill Publishing who have worked long and hard to get this book out in seven months. What a team! Thank you Van Hill, you're one heck of a businessman. Thank you Bethany Snyder, my copy editor, for all those weekends you forfeited to make our deadline. You did a superb job. And a special thanks to Sandra Laughlin, who received this manuscript on a Monday and stayed up all night reading it. (Has your husband forgiven me yet?) Tuesday we made a deal to publish. Thanks for your receptiveness and insight. Your inspiration over this project has made it come to life. I will always be indebted to you.

And finally, Jim Henderson, who in the book of my life may very well be my "Happily Ever After."

Author's Note

    This book has been written from my memory of events in my life. Although I'm amazed at my recall, there were times when I could not remember exact conversations and times of events. In these instances, I have improvised to move the story along. I have strong opinions of some of the people in this book which I do not hesitate to state. They are my own personal convictions of which I believe I have a right to express.

    There are few, but some of the names in this book have been changed to protect the innocent...as well as the guilty.

PROLOGUE

"Excuse me, are those Bugle Boy jeans you're wearing?"

If you watched television any time during the early 1990's, you saw the commercial. There was the good-looking hunk in a Jeep, heading north along the rugged Pacific Coast Highway. The raven-haired beauty in a red vintage Dino Ferrari convertible accelerates to 85 miles an hour, pulls up even with the Jeep on a spectacular hairpin turn, and inquires about the maker of the hunk's pants.

"Why, yes, they are...Bugle Boy jeans."

"Thank you," says the raven-haired beauty. She abruptly brakes, executes a perfect 180-degree turn, and heads back to wherever beautiful women in exotic sports cars go when their thirty seconds are over.

Which in this case was wheels-up on a steep bluff about a hundred feet off the highway.

The raven-haired beauty herself was safely drinking diet soda and gossiping with the crew. Her stunt double, a blonde in a wig, was trapped underneath the twisted metal of what was once a very expensive Italian sports car.

That was me.

Don't even ask what went wrong. Too much speed at the turn, a split-second miscalculation, the director's fault, the car prep crew's fault, my fault—who knows? Stuff happens.

The car fishtailed. The rear wheels squealed as they skidded off the smooth surface and caught the soft shoulder, spinning me out of control. I tried to correct, but with no power steering and no shoulder harness—damn those vintage cars—it was impossible. The Ferrari took flight and came down hard, bouncing off the highway surface and flipping over once, twice, three times.

The lack of a shoulder harness probably saved my life. While the car was still airborne, before the first point of impact, I had enough freedom of movement to pull myself sideways into the passenger seat, folding up into the cubbyhole of space beneath the glove compartment.

It was pitch dark in that little coffin. I was covered in shards of windshield glass and pretty badly banged up, but I was alive and my neck wasn't broken. I had just enough time to count my blessings before I heard a hissing sound and smelled the leaking gas. I found the walkie-talkie and screamed into it, "GET ME OUT OF HERE!"

Suddenly a dozen crew members were beside the car. They needed about thirty seconds to heave the Ferrari right side up and pull me out of my hiding place—about as long as the commercial lasts, and let me tell you that is one long, long commercial.

What did I think about all that time? My daughter? My son? My mother? No. Did I see that white light and a bunch of angels beckoning me to join them? No. Did I thank God for keeping me alive? Later. My first thought was, *"Awwww shhhhit, I smashed up a $250,000 car."* Do I have to tell you that this proved to be a turning point in my life?

The crew tracked down another identical 1973 Dino Ferrari in Los Angeles, and we managed to get the shot down the next day. The commercial ran for quite a while and earned me enough in residuals to do yet another major remodel on my house. The incident itself turned out to be a legend in the stunt driving business. To this day, people will tell me this story about an upside-down Dino Ferrari and how nobody could believe that the stunt driver got out of it alive.

There's always another Ferrari: that's the real lesson of this story.

It's also, in a way, the real lesson of my life.

If you're anything older than thirty, my face would probably be familiar to you. I was the Kodak Girl in 80,000 life-sized cutouts in drugstores and tourist shops all across America and Europe during the "Summer of Love" in 1969. That was me in that blue and white polka dot bikini—itsy-bitsy by 1960's standards, modest by today's—standing with right leg artfully bent and a come-hither expression in my eighteen-year-old brown eyes.

College boys used to steal my cutouts; I'm told that somebody ran it for homecoming queen (I nearly won) at Pepperdine University. The college girls used it in their dorms to hang their sweaters on.

You've seen me in other national media campaigns—billboards and magazine ads for More and Kent Cigarettes, Coca Cola, Las Vegas Sahara Hotel, Mattel Toys, Smirnoff Vodka, Adidas Sportswear, J.C. Penney, LA Gear, Lipton Tea, the cover of *American Woman Motor Sports*, and several catalogue covers for department stores. The list goes on and on.

As a stunt driver, you've seen me doubling for Cindy Crawford in her Pepsi commercials, driving a red Lamborghini while two little boys watch in awe as she chugs the soft drink. For Oldsmobile, I worked on several spots for "The New Generation of Olds" campaign, better known to the public as "This is Not Your Father's Oldsmobile." In one of the spots I doubled for Priscilla Presley, driving in and out of the surf on the beach with a helicopter filming in close proximity. Her daughter, Lisa Marie, was my petrified passenger. But the really tricky spot was the "007" commercial, filmed in Hawaii, where I doubled Roger Moore's daughter. The helicopter work was intense—two inches off my bumper for eight white-knuckled days. Speed had to be extremely precise or the chopper would have been in my trunk, and my head fifty feet away from the scene. We had every stunt the writers could conjure up in that spot: motorcycles crashing; explosions; bi-planes passing overhead within feet of the vehicle, expelling smoke and obstructing my vision.

Enough on the commercials. After twenty years, my résumé is eighteen pages long and I'm not pitching a job here.

I've done quite a bit of work in feature films. In *Casper*, I doubled the lead actress, crashing a car into a tree and making a high fall. It was only forty feet, but with the blue screen it looked to be two hundred. For the movie *Shattered*, I did a near miss with another vehicle at seventy miles per hour. On *Spy Hard* we did a chase scene on the city streets of downtown L.A. In Tony Danza's latest flop, *The Girl Meets Moe*, I crashed a pick-up truck through a glass solarium and did most of the car chase scenes in the film.

For television, I've worked on *Melrose Place* quite often, and I've doubled for Linda Evans on *Dynasty*. I've since moved on to *Unsolved Mysteries* and *Diagnosis Murder*. The last episode for *Diagnosis Murder* I worked on was a get-away car stunt, doubling for Piper Laurie.

There are literally hundreds of films and commercials I've worked on in past years where I do the action and the actress gets the glory, but who cares? I've had my day in the limelight. My smile isn't seen on the screen, but my teeth are sparkling all the way to the bank.

You might have seen my photograph in past years in the feature sections of some newspapers and "rag" magazines, if you read that sort of thing. "An unidentified companion." That was me. "The blonde." That was me, too. In earlier days, I was photographed by paparazzi in the company of Peter Lawford and David Janssen, both of whom died young as a result of living too fast. There I was cuddling up to O.J. (we worked together on a Hertz spot, and later I got to know him and Nicole socially in the Hollywood club scene). There I was cuddling up to actor Hugh O'Brian at a party in Aspen. There I was dining with Quincy Jones at Drai's, a hip supper club in Beverly Hills. And that recently married son of an ex-president? Well, that *could* have been me, if someone were to blow a hole in the secrecy of it all and tip off the paparazzi, but I don't make it a practice to get into a limousine (arranged by Washington's top security people) with married men, particularly when I don't know my destination. Dinner, they said. But for security reasons they couldn't tell me where. Married and divorced three times, I did manage to learn something.

A gangster's girlfriend and another's wife who spent most of her life in the shadows of the underworld, a witness to murder and unspeakable brutality, a woman whose own life had been threatened more than once. That was me too.

A wheel-woman for the Mob, which is how I wound up doing stunts for a living, that early "get-away" training. I saw the "bad guys" do good things and the "good guys" commit crimes, distorting my view of reality. My young mind was manipulated by men who held tremendous power, not only in their own dark world, but also in our own government.

The CIA has nothing on the Mob, except for the fact that no one investigates them. Back in my New York days, the CIA had a sixteen-year relationship with the Mob, starting with Carlo Gambino, working closely together in money laundering, extortion, and murder. The Mob pulled the trigger, but the CIA loaded the gun. I don't know if it still exists; I'm no longer around as a witness. It wasn't easy moving away from this world, and I suppose I will always be bound in some way.

And then there's the Georgia I was before I became Kodak's Summer Girl and got married to the Mob: the good Catholic girl in my First Communion dress, looking shy and angelic, with a circle of white daisies surrounding my veil.

———•———

After they got the Ferrari off my head and the shoot was over, I flew back home to Los Angeles and thought about my life. It struck me as odd how easily I could shrug off the face of death. Didn't I believe my life was important?

How did I get from there to here?

I discovered I'd built an entire professional persona, not in conjunction with my life as a woman, not in support of it, but in contradiction to it. My career has been a perfect avoidance technique for truths about my life I never wanted to face. As I have so often in my life when I entered a crisis, I thought only of the external, inanimate elements of that crisis, never the woman at the center. High-speed avoidance of the bad guys isn't just what I do in front of the camera, it's what I've done my entire life. Too much speed at the turns, too many split-second miscalculations, somebody else's fault, my fault—who knows? Stuff happens, I thought.

And that is when I began writing this book.

CHAPTER ONE

In a way, I was born famous. I inherited my mother's beauty along with her undeserved reputation. And like my mother and her sisters, I too never felt quite good enough. I never really understood why that was, but I vividly remember feeling that way as a child.

I also inherited my mother's spirit for adventure. She never kept a tight reign on me. She trusted me and gave me freedom to explore and open doors to the exciting, mysterious world she herself had been unable to explore, either because of financial reasons, social status, or because she was an emotional prisoner to the thought processes of a small town.

In the Little Italy section of Rochester, New York, where I grew up, my mother attracted attention early on as the most beautiful of the four Perrone sisters. All the Perrone women were well known to the gossips of this tight-knit little community.

It started with my grandmother, Rose Mazzo, who was once married to a Mafioso who beat her. Divorce was unheard of in those days, but she eventually left him and managed to escape the grip of his violence. She met my grandfather, Vincent Perrone, soon after. They fell in love and she started a new life with him. This wasn't acceptable to those who believed in the old Italian traditions. In her quest for a happier life, she accepted the punishment of being excommunicated from the church and became the main focus of the gossipmongers.

Rose and Vincent settled in East Rochester somewhere around 1920. Upstate New York was a popular settlement region for early-century Italian immigrants. There was work to be had in the factories of what was then a booming industrial area. An Italian immigrant could get by without knowing English in a place like East Rochester, which made these upstate New York communities appealing.

My grandfather went to work in the railroad car shops as a blacksmith. He worked long days in intense heat to support his growing family. I don't know how much he was paid, but it wasn't enough to buy the $300 house they lived in, so they paid the required seven dollars per month rent. Like most everyone else in East Rochester, Vincent and Rosie were poor—dirt poor. The houses in the neighborhood didn't have bathrooms, only outhouses, and even those were shared by four separate families. The neighborhood consisted of several tiny houses clustered closely together. The space between them was barely enough to park a car, for the fortunate few who owned one.

Everyone always knew what was going on in everyone else's life. On hot summer nights when all the windows were open, the sounds of those lives traveled into neighboring homes. And as it was in Italy, and all small villages, East Rochester was a community that thrived on gossip.

My mother, Angela, was one of nine Perrone children—three boys, six girls. The twins, a boy and a girl, died shortly after they were born due to lack of money for proper medical care. One of the younger girls was killed by a car while playing in front of the house when she was three years old. My grandmother, who was in her early twenties at the time, witnessed this. They say her hair turned totally white overnight, aging her by twenty years.

My uncles were hard working, decent guys who pooled their three dollars a week paychecks—earned by delivering milk and picking up odd jobs—to help support the family, but it was the Perrone girls who captured the attention of East Rochester. In the Old Country, an obedient nature and a strong back were prized among female children. In the New World, it was beauty that was most valued. A beautiful girl could attract a prosperous husband and marry above herself, thereby advancing both her own station and that of the family. But in this town no wealthy men existed. Regardless, heads turned wherever the Perrone sisters walked, and the women of yesterday, not unlike those of today, were extremely jealous of them. Of course this lead to false rumors about their promiscuity, heard enough times that they were taken as truth.

My aunt Theresa, the oldest, was a petite brunette with a dazzling smile and infectious energy. My aunt Sunda was the shy beauty who never viewed herself as beautiful. And my aunt Dolly, the youngest, was a wholesome beauty whose insecurities far surpassed those of her older sisters. But it was Angela, my mother, who really turned heads. Even as a child her devilish antics didn't detract from the obvious beauty she was becoming. In 1945, by the time she was nineteen years old, she was breathtaking.

That same year, my grandmother, whom I was never fortunate enough to know, died suddenly of a heart attack at age forty-three—while dancing the polka at a neighborhood tavern. From what I've been told, my grandmother was also a beauty with a huge heart and a loving spirit who always sought the light even in the darkest of times. This was one of the qualities she passed on to her children.

My grandfather was devastated when she died. Due to his health he could no longer work to support the family. The children's ages at the time of my grandmother's death ranged from 9 to 23. The older kids took care of the younger ones. They somehow managed to feed the whole crew on two dollars a week. The death of my grandmother left all of the siblings feeling incredibly insecure and emotionally abandoned. They only had each other to depend on, which is why, I suppose, they remain so close today.

As my grandfather's health deteriorated, he became desperate to see his family in Italy. He left for the Old Country and died there. The children, penniless and uneducated, couldn't raise the money to get his body back to the United States. Communication was a problem in those days as well, and they have no idea where his remains lay. After my grandfather's death, there wasn't any parental guidance. My mother and my aunts became prey to vicious gossip. Their insecurities lent to their helplessness to defend themselves and they subconsciously allowed themselves to believe they were as everyone said they were.

My mother married my sister's father. It was a marriage that lasted only a few years. *Ah, just like her mother, no good.* A few years later she met my father and fell madly in love. She became pregnant with me and he left town quickly with no forwarding address. No one ever heard from him again. I never knew my real father.

My mother stayed in the family home after the youngest of her siblings was grown and on their own. She worked double shifts as a waitress and sold cosmetics on the side to support my sister and me. My aunts all took turns caring for us. My sister and I were always surrounded by an abundance of love.

Tony, who would become my stepfather, came into our lives when I was six months old. I will have him as my father for the rest of my life, but in the eyes of the gossiping villagers I would always be known as the bastard child of one of the Perrone girls.

My immediate neighborhood consisted of two small blocks, Apple Street and Taft Street. Across from my house were cornfields, and directly behind it were the railroad tracks. This area of the village was called the "Northside" and this was my childhood world. Though no one in the village was wealthy, the Northside was still considered the slums. The homes were all built exactly the same; shabby and extremely tiny, they were about 900 square feet. This is where my mother was born and where my sister and I would also grow up.

Amazingly, even a few of those who lived on the wrong side of the tracks still found it in their nature to denigrate others. I remember playing on Apple Street with one of the neighborhood kids one day (I couldn't have been more than five or six at the time), when a chicken with its head cut off came running into the street. *I didn't like that. Why did they have to cut off their heads?* My playmate's grandmother came out in search of the headless chicken.

When she saw us playing together, she demanded of my friend, "Come in-na da house this-a minute. I told you I don-na want you playing with that *puttana!*" The little girl reluctantly walked to the door and her grandmother pulled her inside by her ear.

Later, at home, I sat watching my mother get ready to go out somewhere. I asked, "Mommy? What's a *puttana?*"

My mother looked at me as if I had just stuck a knife through her heart. She thought for a moment, tears filled her eyes, and she answered, "*Puttana* is the Italian word for whore."

"What's a whore?"

"A whore is a bad girl, honey."

"I'm not a bad girl, am I, Mommy?"

"No sweetheart, you're not a bad girl," my mother said. "People call me bad names too. They think I'm bad because I had you and I wasn't married. They wanted me to give you away, but I wouldn't do that. You were created from love, and I loved you too much to give you away. They can call me all the names they want, but they can never take away the joy you bring to my life."

She took me by the hand and led me to the bathroom mirror. "Look in there and tell me what you see."

"I see me."

"I see a beautiful little girl, that's what I see. That's what everyone who looks at you sees too. Because you're pretty, people will call you these names. It doesn't mean that you're bad. They're just jealous of you. They dislike people who have something they want and can't have. That's called jealousy. No matter what anyone ever says about you, always remember one thing: your real beauty is inside. If you're a good person, one day the name-calling will stop. Try to feel sorry for those people who call you names. They aren't as fortunate as you are."

I worshiped my mother. Her movements were so graceful it seemed to me that she glided rather than walked. Her high cheekbones and short, raven hair balanced her oval face to perfection. But it was her eyes that drew you in, deep brown, caring eyes filled with love and concern. She spoke softly and when she laughed the sound was like a child's giggle.

I used to love watching my mother get ready to go out on a date with my soon-to-be dad. She'd start with a clean face that needed no improvement, but when she'd finished applying her make-up she was absolutely gorgeous. I'd watch her for hours as she went through the process and I'd fantasize about being grown-up, glamorous and beautiful. She always sang to me while getting ready, making up verses that expressed her love for me. After a loving kiss she'd breeze out the door, leaving a faint trail of an Avon fragrance behind.

My mother's real beauty was within—her incredible generosity. I have never met anyone quite like her. She gives so freely from her heart, with no thought of the consequence to her own financial or emotional hardship. I remember one Thanksgiving when I was in my teens. My mother had to run to the grocery store for the cranberry sauce that she insisted we needed to complete the meal. The food was already on the table and we had just finished saying grace. She told us to start eating and she'd be right back. After forty-five minutes, dinner was over and she still had not returned.

My father went out in search of her while my sister and I started calling the local hospitals, thinking she must have had an accident. She finally showed up about two hours later. We all breathed a sigh of relief. The thought had obviously never crossed her mind that we might be worried, or that she had missed the one big meal of the year that took her days to prepare. On her way to the store she had seen a woman crying her heart out, pushing a small baby around in a shopping cart. Of course my mother had to stop and ask her what the matter was. Between sobs, the woman explained that her husband had beaten her and she was heading to her sister's house forty miles away. My mother told her to get in the car and she would take her there. Someone needed help. That was her only conscious thought. That's my mom.

— ◆ —

My mother married Tony when I was five. Everyone called him "Pooch." He got the nickname from chasing fire trucks down the road as a kid, just like a little puppy would. Poochie (as I called him) was a small guy in stature, only about 5'8", but he was a big man to me. I idolized him. Though he was quiet and soft spoken, his loving personality came through without question. He had grown up like everyone else in East Rochester. Not a rich man, but a man of integrity. I had always thought of him as my daddy. He'd been there from the beginning of my life. He was a wonderful man, a good, loving dad who supported my sister and me in every aspect of our lives. How lucky my mother was to find a man who not only loved her, but truly loved her children as well.

After they were married, my mother still had to work to make ends meet, but she didn't have to hold down three jobs anymore. She worked days while my sister and I were in school and was able to be home with us at night. We hadn't made extraordinary leaps financially, but life was a little easier for my mother.

My sister Sharon was a beautiful child. She had dark hair and a delicate, angelic face. She really was the angel of the two of us. I was more outgoing. She liked staying around the house, while I was always off in the woods or looking for whatever trouble I could get into. Sharon liked the safety of the nest. She was Mom's little helper. I was Mom's little monster, always getting into some kind of mess.

My sister and I used to laugh at the most inappropriate times. We'd giggle at funerals when everyone was wailing. Sometimes we'd really lose it in church. Every Friday after school we went to confession so our souls would be pure enough to receive Holy Communion. On Sundays, Sharon and I could always be found sitting with our friends in the balcony in St. Jerrome's Church at the 11:00 mass. We'd pick fuzzballs off our identical pink angora sweaters and have contests to see who could land the most fuzzballs on the silliest looking hats below. Then we'd start to laugh. We'd try to hold it in, but you know when you're not supposed to laugh how you just can't help it?

Once we laughed so hard we had to duck down in the pew to hide from all the sour faces peering up to see who was causing such disorder in the church. Finally the priest asked us to stand. When we stood, we burst out laughing even louder than before.

Then the entire congregation began to laugh too. The priest tried to bring some order, but it was all over after that. No one could control themselves. When things started to quiet down, Sharon and I burst into laughter again, which got everyone else going. That Sunday mass ended about twenty minutes sooner than it normally would have.

After that, Sharon and I were no longer permitted to sit together in church. And on Fridays after confession we could count on doing three entire rosaries for our penance. That's a lot of Hail Marys for a little laughing. I would have hated to see how long we'd been there if we had committed a mortal sin!

I was the little sister, the tag-along. We always fought when we were children, but we also loved each other and were protective of one another. As adults we're extremely close.

Most of my early memories of Rochester are of love and laughter and feeling very secure. Beyond the cornfields across from my house were the woods. I loved those woods. To get there I had to walk through the cornfields, which immensely irritated the farmer who owned them. I loved running through his fields and stealing tomatoes from the old buzzard's garden. I enjoyed it most when he got annoyed and chased me into the woods. They were *my* woods. I had lots of secret places to hide—he could never catch me. Sometimes darkness caught me unaware. I especially liked this because it was scary. Strange sounds from the bushes and the rustling in the underbrush heightened my curiosity. This place in the woods is where I first became aware that I was alone. That only I could protect me. At the time, it was the creatures in the forest that I sought protection from, but this awareness would come in handy when I became prey to human creatures.

Mom was the neighborhood Pied Piper. My sister and I usually walked the two miles to school with the other neighborhood kids, but the brutal winters sometimes called for a ride. It never failed—my mother stopped several times to pick up any kid walking in the cold. One day she picked up some kids who didn't have boots. She told the four of them to wait after school and she'd drive them home. She showed up at three o'clock with a brand new pair of boots for each of them. Heaven only knows how she plotted to get them. Upon discovering that this family didn't have heat, my mother paid to have it turned back on. She always did this stuff behind my father's back, and worried about how to pay for it without his finding out.

Even though we were poor, Christmas was a big deal. We looked like millionaires with the number of presents under the tree. My parents worked the whole year to pay off the Christmas debt. My sister and I were the envy of the neighborhood kids when they'd see the presents we'd gotten. I guess my mother wanted to make up for all the years that she had received only an orange in her stocking for Christmas.

One year when I was about eight years old, my mother sat my sister and me down a few weeks before Christmas.

"Do you girls realize how lucky we are?" she asked. "There are children in this world who don't have enough to eat, or a warm bed to sleep in. Can you imagine how you would feel waking up Christmas morning and not having even one present to open?"

"No," we answered.

"Well, think about it."

Sharon's delicate face tied up in a frown. "That would be pretty terrible."

"Yeah, I don't think I'd feel very good about that," I added.

"How would you girls feel about giving up some of your presents to give a special Christmas to some children who've never had one?" Mom asked.

Sharon and I were reluctant at first, but on Christmas morning my mother dressed up as Santa Claus, Sharon and I dressed as little elves with green tights and matching skirts, and we carted a car full of presents to the home of the kids with no boots. They lived about a mile down the road from us. Our house was a palace compared to their shack. The porch steps were broken and shutters were hanging half off the broken windows. The paint was peeled down to raw wood. The home looked abandoned.

We watched as they tore open the presents. There were some toys for the little kids, but our gifts consisted mostly of clothing, which was very obviously needed by this family. Their mother stood with tears streaking her face. I discovered the warmth of the spirit of Christmas that day. My mother gave my sister and me the best gift of all—the gift of giving. It's no wonder her name is Angela—she's an angel. My father never knew about our little Christmas adventure and could never figure out why it still took so long to pay off the bills when there weren't as many gifts under the tree.

I was quite the tomboy when I was a young girl. My mother always wanted to dress me up like a little princess, but I wouldn't have it. I couldn't play rough like the boys with a stupid dress on. The neighborhood boys used to fight over whose team I'd be on. I think it was because I played better than most of the boys in our circle of friends. Yeah, I'm sure that's what it was. We were too young to be thinking about other stuff. After I got the hang of how the game was played, the fighting was soon to be over. That's when I elected myself captain of the team and chose who I wanted to play with me. We played in the street for hours—football, baseball, basketball, kick the can.

I used to be pretty good at standing up for my rights, too. No one ever messed with me. If any boy tried to bully me, he'd get a surprise chop to his neck or a swift kick in the butt. I developed this "being in control" attitude at a young age, and though it lay dormant for awhile it prevailed again later in my life.

In the summertime, the nights were often sticky and sleep was hard to come by. I would lie in my bed in the tiny room I shared with my older sister Sharon and try to fall asleep. The familiar vibrating of my bed signaled a train's approach. I could feel the rumble before the distant whistle whined. Faint and far away at first, it grew increasingly louder and louder until the entire house shook. I'd peer over at Sharon, deep in a peaceful, contented sleep. Then the sounds of the train faded, and in the far-off distance that whistle sounded again. Only then could I fall asleep. I would dream about someday riding that train—going to all the faraway places it was heading.

When I was twelve, I decided, on a whim, to live out my dreams of adventure—of riding the train that raced behind our house every day. Kathy, who lived on Apple Street, was my best girlfriend. She went along with all my schemes, reluctantly sometimes, but she followed my lead. I talked her into accompanying me on this dangerous adventure and off we went. We climbed the fence between my house and the railroad tracks, and followed the tracks for quite some time before a freight train finally came by. It was traveling about twenty miles per hour when I grabbed onto the metal ladder and pulled myself up into the open boxcar. Kathy was still running alongside the train, conjuring up the courage to take hold. She finally did after I called her a coward several times, but she lost her grip and the train was dragging her, pulling her legs underneath the boxcar very close to the wheels.

Terror filled her eyes as she screamed, "Help me George! I can't hang on."

With my heart racing, I extended my hand and pulled her up, using the power of adrenaline for my strength. I knelt beside Kathy as she laid down in the boxcar breathing hard. After a minute of calm, she looked up at me and said, "Where we going?"

I stood up and faced the direction we were heading with the wind blowing my hair from my face. "Wherever it stops!" I yelled, excited by the anticipation of the unknown and the intoxicating feeling of freedom.

I didn't want to run away from home; I simply had a thirst for adventure. Kathy and I figured we'd hop off the train when we'd had enough and jump another one back home. We hadn't even made it as far as Buffalo when a conductor from a passing train spotted us. He must have radioed the conductor of our train and alerted him of his cargo. The train was stopped soon after, and a police car awaited us. Kathy was scared. Her father used to beat her for no reason, and she knew that this may be cause for a short stay in the hospital. I, on the other hand, thought it was pretty cool. I was looking forward to riding in a police car. Little did I know then, it wouldn't be my last ride in a car like that.

By the time we arrived home, my parents were frantic. I'd never seen my dad so mad. He took off his belt and gave me a few really hard whacks, leaving big welts on my back. Now I *was* scared. This was the first and only time my tolerant father ever hit me. But I didn't cry. I guess I knew I had it coming. Alone in my room, I could hear Kathy screaming from a few houses away. Suddenly I didn't hurt anymore. Sympathy for what was happening to Kathy took its place. And it was all my fault.

I was grounded for a month. This didn't deter me, however. My thirst for adventure overpowered the consequences. After my parents went to bed, I used to escape out the bathroom window from the second floor, climbing onto the shed and jumping to the ground from there. I'd meet my friends at a secret fort we'd built in the woods. We'd smoke cigarettes and think we had really pulled the wool over. Neither of my parents ever found me out. I'm still baffled as to why, but I was becoming a renegade.

———◆———

Also when I was twelve, but looking far older, my mother took me to Eastman Kodak at a photographer's request for a model test. He had seen me at Braemar Country Club, a business my parents had leased in Spencerport, about thirty miles from my hometown. We lived in an apartment above the clubhouse in the summer months. My father worked as the golf pro and grounds keeper, and my mother handled the restaurant, cooking for lunchtime crowds and big parties. Eastman Kodak was by far the dominant employer in Rochester during this time, and many of Kodak's white collar set were members of the club. They were actively in search of some local talent to use in their national advertising. It was a big honor to be chosen for Kodak's model files.

Kodak had several studios set up in different parts of the city.

The one I was taken to was their motion picture studio. The size of the place was intimidating. I walked into a huge room where several different shoots were taking place simultaneously with models being primped by stylists and photographers. What was I doing here? I wanted to hide. As the thought was taking place, a woman appeared and led me into a dressing room where a make-up person waited. As she began working on me, the wardrobe person pulled a dress from the rack and held it up to me, shook her head in disapproval, and returned to the rack for other possibilities. She finally chose a bright colored sweater and a pair of slacks. By the time they were finished, I looked like I was eighteen years old. I didn't recognize myself.

I was lead back into the studio and positioned on a stool. Totally overwhelmed, I did the testing, feeling shy and awkward in front of the camera. I had to be told where to place my hands, how I should cock my head, when to smile and when not to. I was very uncomfortable and it showed. All I kept thinking about was the baseball game I was missing. Could my team win without me? If my friends could see the way I looked, they'd probably laugh their heads off. Finally it was over and the photographer, a short, thin man with an overly pleasant face and demeanor came into the dressing room to talk to me.

Sensing I really wasn't into this, he said, "Honey, are you taking any secretarial courses in school?"

"Yes, I'm planning to."

"Good. I think you should concentrate on that, because I don't think you're going to make it as a model."

Well, that did it. Someone was telling me there was something I couldn't do! That was the wrong thing to say to me. I could do *anything* if I really wanted to. Now I was going to have to prove him wrong. What he was really saying, or the way I heard what he said was, *'You're not good enough.'* At first I felt hurt and rejected, but anger replaced that emotion fairly quickly. I thanked him nicely with the manners my mother had taught me and we left. When we got in the car I told my mother that I thought I could do better now that I knew what to expect. I asked her to find out what other studios did testing and to see if she could get me in there. When we arrived home, I washed my face, put my old clothes on, and went in search of my Apple Street gang.

Mom managed to set up another test at a different studio the following week. In the meantime, I flipped through the pages of all the teen magazines I could get my hands on. It felt kind of stupid, but I practiced posing and smiling for hours in front of the mirror when no one was home. I didn't really care about modeling, but my stubborn personality had to show that guy. I was a winner. Losing wasn't part of my program.

I was much more relaxed and self-assured for the second testing. I passed the test and was added to their files. Soon the phone began ringing on a regular basis.

In the beginning a lot of the work was testing film. It was tedious, boring work, sitting in one pose through dozens of rolls of film, but good training for what was to come.

It wasn't until I started modeling that I became aware that we were poor. The other girls all shopped at Sibley's, a fine department store. I had always gotten my clothes at Grants or J.M. Fields. I think I started out making about $80 a day. In 1962, that's what most adults I knew made in a week.

I was the youngest of the group. The other girls all seemed to be more knowledgeable about everything, and they spoke so eloquently. Because of my modeling assignments during school hours, I fell behind scholastically. I graduated high school by the skin of my teeth and college wasn't in my cards.

Being thrown into an adult world at such a young age, I grew up much faster than my peers. I looked and acted much older than I was, but underneath the facade I was still just a kid with a lot to learn. I think my level of education dictated some of the choices I would make later in life, but in the final analysis, life itself would give me an education.

The guys never asked me out in my high school. I know now they were just intimidated, but then I thought they didn't like me—an insecurity left over from the gossips of my youth. And my successes seemed to stir up even more vicious rumors. I now fully understood what my mother had endured. I hung out with my model friends and ventured more into the city, making friends away from my hometown. I seemed to be accepted more on the outside, by people who had no idea that I came from the "wrong side of the tracks."

Kodak wasn't the only game in town. Plenty of modeling assignments came from other industries in the area such as Xerox, Bausch and Lomb, French's Mustard, Champion Sportswear, Ragu, Genesee Beer, Sara Coventry Jewelry, Corningware, and Rochester Telephone, as well as several department stores and other smaller businesses that needed to advertise. By the time I turned fifteen I was making $250 to $300 per day. I really thought I'd hit the big time then—until I began working outside of the Rochester area, where my day rate rose to $1,000 per day or more, depending on the market.

During summers at the golf course before modeling became my focus, my dad was training me for the women's tour. I'd had two holes-in-one during the summer I turned eleven years old. He saw my early talent as a real possibility at the big time, but I was discovering other talents. Golf was something I did to please my father and pass the time. What I enjoyed most, after getting beyond the first hole and out of daddy's sight, was tearing down the fairway in the electric golf carts, causing my young passengers major heart palpitations.

There were little bridges, designed just wide enough for golfers who were pulling their golf bags to cross over. Those who chose to drive electric carts had another designated path to follow. My mission was to make it across these little bridges in the electric cart. (Where there's a will there's a way.) After measuring the width of the bridges and the wheel base of the cart I figured I had an inch at the most for error, but it could be done if I got the angle exact. After many attempts, landing either sideways or upside-down in the stream with minor injuries and destroying about a third of my fathers fleet, I finally got it perfect.

Due to complaints by club members and the cost of getting the electric carts repaired, my Dad finally made the carts off limits to me. He'd hide the keys, but that didn't stop me—I figured out how to hot-wire them. I'd call my friends in the area after my parents were safely asleep and we'd have drag races down the fairways. In the dense darkness we sometimes drove over the greens, causing my father some back-breaking work.

A love for driving fast developed, and it became an obsession. Eventually I went from stealing the golf carts to stealing the car for midnight joyrides. Of the many times I'd done it, I'd only gotten caught once. I took my punishment for a few weeks and then continued with my shenanigans. My father would get upset, but he loved me unconditionally and accepted his untamable wild thing. My mother threw up her hands as well, recognizing that I had inherited her free spirit. How my parents got through those years without killing me, I'll never know. I was a holy terror.

One of the waitresses who worked at the country club had a sixteen-year-old son, Mike, and a daughter, Patty, who was the same age as me, fourteen. They lived just up the road from the golf course. My parents liked these kids. They were wholesome types doing regular kinds of teenage things, or so they thought. While Patty's mother was working large parties for my mother on Friday nights, we'd be sneaking out to The 414 Club, located about ten miles down the road. We were under age, but Tom Torpey, the big bouncer at the door, used to let us in.

The 414 had the best bands in the city playing there on the weekends. We'd dance and drink beer with the older boys way past our curfew hour, and, since our parents were working, they never found out. I bonded with a whole new group of people. My world was suddenly getting bigger.

Mike and his friends used to build race cars in their garage. I started to hang out with Patty in the garage on hot summer days, sipping cold sodas and listening to the radio blaring while we watched them work. Patty was a cute little redhead with smoky eyes and soft features. She loved to laugh, flirt, and raise hell. We bonded immediately, united by our girlish mischief.

The guys were really cute, and I guess they thought I was too because they let me participate in what they were doing, explaining everything as they went along. After learning the names of all the tools, I'd hand them whatever they asked for. I felt like I was a part of it. I was beginning to become aware that boys were attracted to me and I to them. On Saturday nights, they'd haul the race car down to the local speedway for the big weekend race. Patty and I would tag along, cheering them on from the pits. Spencer Speedway became my weekend home. It wasn't long before "cheering from the pits" wasn't enough for me...

———◆———

The drag race was about to begin. My hands gripped the wheel tightly and I could hear my heart pounding loudly in my chest. I looked over at my twenty-year-old male opponent while revving up my engine. He had a cocky grin on his face as he returned my confident stare. I wasn't really confident—just gutsy and determined. The flag went down and we were off. I shifted into second gear and had him by one car length. He never caught up. The crowd cheered as I entered the pits, and my clan couldn't stop praising me. Now that I had their confidence, I raced every weekend for the rest of the season without ever losing.

Tragedy stuck that summer. My girlfriend Patty was hit by a passing car and killed. It happened as she was walking from her house to the golf course to visit me. We had been best friends in the all-too-brief time we had known each other. Becoming acquainted with death at such a young age was a shock to me. It aged me somehow, mentally. I'd lost my pal, along with the excitement that surrounded the racing life.

I didn't do much racing after that first season, not only because of the loss of my friend, but because my modeling career had began to take up more of my time in the summers. My life, like the wind, began to move in another direction, but I always thought that one day down the road I'd again find myself behind the wheel.

Chapter Two

In Rochester back in the mid 1960's, The Living Room was one of the regular stops on the Friday night club circuit. Between the Blue Gardenia Restaurant, The Fountain Blue and Ben's Cafe Society, you'd see every familiar face that made up the sinister side of Rochester's inhabitants. These places were the Mob's hangouts on the city's East Side. The drinking age was eighteen at the time, but plenty of underage girls were admitted. The club owners were not bound by fear of being busted for breaking the law and losing their liquor licenses. The law had been bought off, a fact easily recognizable when you saw the plainclothes cops hanging out in these clubs, drinking after the legal closing hour.

By the age of fifteen, while my parents thought I was at a school dance or in the safety of a friend's home on weekends, I was out with my older girlfriends dancing at The Living Room. Rochester was a small town. Not only did everyone know everyone else, most were related in some way. Since I was well known as a model, everyone knew my name. If they didn't know me personally, they acted as if they did, approaching me like long lost friends and engaging in conversation as though I had known them all my life.

The bartenders knew me and my preference in alcohol. By the time I pushed through the crowd to the bar, a glass of Scotch sat waiting, with two or three shot glasses backing it up. These guys knew how to treat a girl. It didn't matter that you could never consume all the drinks those shot glasses represented. All that mattered to the guys paying the tab is that they looked like big shots spending their dough. I was blind to this then. Being made to feel special was part of the lure of this world. In all those years, I don't ever remember buying my own drink.

To a starry-eyed teenager, being at The Living Room was almost like throwing your own party and having all your friends over. The club was open to anyone who dared to walk in. Well known as gangsters' territory, not many outsiders made it their favorite drinking hole. Set in a run-down neighborhood on Norton Street, just a few blocks from an all night diner called Skinny's, the building itself was an unassuming, plain brick structure sitting next door to an abandoned gas station. Not very inviting from the outside, but the inside held a world I was eager to explore.

The interior had an appealing, comfortable atmosphere. On each side of the entrance was a huge picture window with heavy burgundy drapes, pulled back in soft folds with thick gold ties. Some overstuffed couches covered in a muted tapestry material sat near the picture window farthest from the bar. The majority of the lounge area had tables for two with solid red tablecloths. The cheap red candle containers on the tables gave off very little light, which worked for this crowd. Discretion was preferable. The Living Room was a cesspool of out of control egos, and a constant threat of violence lingered in the air.

Opposite the other large picture window, a long bar stretched down the back wall. All twenty stools were usually taken by smoking customers, and people stood three-deep behind them in drunken conversation. Bartenders never stopped pouring, even after closing when the drapes were drawn and the music stopped playing. That's when it really got interesting.

From the bar, a small, cramped stage could be seen in the back room. Several more tables sitting on plush red carpet surrounded the thirty-square foot, gray-tiled dance floor. Other than the colored spotlights for the band, this room was also dimly lit, with a low, suspended ceiling, painted black. I'd seen this place a few times during the day with the lights on, and it looked pretty tacky.

People roamed back and forth all night between both rooms, stopping to chat and fighting to be heard over the band. All the guys were big spenders, each trying to outdo the next. And I have to admit, that impressed me. My parents struggled to put food on our table, and these guys were throwing around $100 bills like there was an endless supply. I guess there was.

I remember one night a call came in, relaying the message that someone was on their way down, gunning for Sammy G. They barricaded the place and no one could leave until an army (not from the right side of the law) showed up for back-up. I was really scared, mainly because I saw the alarm *they* were displaying. Deep concern replaced their usually confident demeanors. With guns out in full view, they paced, peering out from behind the drapes and planning who would do what if the enemy arrived before the back-up did. When the place was sufficiently surrounded with armed men, the good guys (or at least the guys who were inside the bar) escorted the women out safely.

Living through this scene would be enough to make most people jump on the first bus heading anywhere, but not me. This only served to heighten my attraction to the mysteries of their way of life.

When I first met Sammy G in 1963 he was twenty-three years old. His face had not yet been creased with the prominent signs of stress, but still, he seemed older. His medium brown hair fell casually onto his forehead and an innocent but confident expression graced his face.

I had just turned thirteen and was visiting my girlfriend Rosalie, who lived in the city. I knew her from Apple Street when she came there to see her aunt. As we usually did when I visited, we walked around the corner to Skinny's diner for a Coke. Tucked away in a rough neighborhood on the east side of town, Skinny's was a hangout for juvenile "tough guys"—a breeding ground for future hoodlums. It was a perfect place for dangerous adventure, and an intriguing lure for my endless appetite for excitement. I'd never been there at night, but I'd heard it was a favorite breakfast spot for an older version of the daytime crowd after all the bars had closed.

Rather than sit in one of the many imitation red leather booths, we shimmied up to the counter and plopped ourselves on the stools closest to the large glass windows. I looked far older than my years with white shorts that showed off my thin, tanned legs and a red paisley halter-top tied under my prematurely developed breasts. Rosalie looked her age. Her short, curly, dark hair had no particular style and her face was broken out with major pimples that she tried unsuccessfully to cover with make-up.

After ordering our Cokes we shifted our attention to the teenage boys hanging around outside, checking them out unnoticed through the big glass wall that separated us. They intrigued us, looking very continental in their tight pants and pointy, Cuban-heeled shoes. As most thirteen-year-old girls just beginning to discover boys, we thought they were way too cool with their slicked-back, shiny hair, puffing on cigarettes suspended from the sides of their mouths.

As we were drooling, two guys in their early twenties sat down beside us and began hitting on us crudely. We tried to ignore them, but they made it impossible.

"Hey doll face, whatcha want ain't out there, it's right here," said the dirty looking one as he grabbed his crotch.

"You're disgusting," I retorted and turned away from him.

His companion focused on Rosalie with a lecherous leer. She stiffened and her eyes got as big as saucers.

"C'mon, give us a little look at those luscious tits of yours," he continued, spinning my stool back around.

Sammy, sitting in a booth close by, was watching this take place. Realizing we were just babies under the piled-on make-up, he came to our defense. A heated argument ensued and ended up out in the parking lot, where Sammy proceeded to take these two guys on all by himself. Rosalie and I pressed against the glass of the big window and watched in horror as he administered his idea of fatherly advice. I'd never seen this kind of violence before and winced at every kick. Their faces were a bloody mess by the time he was finished. They scampered down the street like wounded dogs and Sammy headed back inside.

"Anybody ever treats you like that again, you just let me know. You'll be able to find me, I'm always around here, ya hear?" he said with authority.

Sammy was a young wiseguy back then, maneuvering his way quickly up the ranks in a very dark world, a world that was invisible to me then, but one which I would become all too intimate with in time.

The very first time I walked into The Living Room, Sammy G was there. He strutted over and greeted me warmly.

A little older now than when we'd first met, I was well aware men were attracted to me. I never had to go out of my way to get attention. It just always seemed to be there, as natural as brushing my teeth. I enjoyed the attention, but I was still unaware of my sexuality and how it affected men. I didn't know yet how the minds of men operated. Sammy did. He was as much aware of the evil intentions of men as he was of my naiveté. For whatever reason, he chose to protect that innocence.

During this first visit to The Living Room, we'd almost had a repeat of the first time Sammy G and I had met. As we stood at the crowded bar, a man next to me began swaying slightly. He leaned against the bar to steady himself as liquid slopped over the edge of his glass. Running his tongue across his teeth, he studied me with a half-lidded stare.

"Those are pretty nice tits you got young lady. Are they real?" he drawled.

Overhearing the remark, Sammy snapped around and silenced him with a deadly look. The man backed off, staggering out of sight, but Sammy remained agitated for several minutes. I felt a shiver of fear. After seeing him in action once before, I didn't think this was going to be the end of it, but the moment passed.

I rarely saw that side of him. The Sam I knew was kind—at least to me. He had the proverbial big heart, but he was selective about who saw it. He had to be. He had an image to protect. He was a "goodfella" who walked both sides of the street.

No, Sammy was not the typical cigar-smoking, gangster-type character. He was in a class all his own, a very handsome man, always impeccably dressed. He wasn't what you'd call tall, about 5'9", but his clothes were expensive and he wore them well. I don't think I ever saw the same diamond tiepin with matching cuff links on him twice. The same goes for the $300 shoes and custom-made shirts. He hit the streets movie star-style, surrounded by an entourage. He walked with pride, his appearance commanding attention wherever he went, but it was who he was which commanded *respect*.

Known for his generosity, Sammy left $100 tips, paid for a girl's rent if she were in a bind, and bought expensive gifts for friends for no reason. It was just his nature. For my sixteenth birthday, he organized a junket to the Bahamas. My sister Sharon and my girlfriend Vicky were invited along for the fun. With my married, older sister along as a chaperone, my mother had allowed me to go.

My most vivid memory of that trip was horseback riding on the beach. In a group of ten, we saddled up for the ride—a hysterical scene on its own. Obviously out of their element, these city boys wore dress pants and expensive Italian shoes for the occasion. Climbing onto the horse, Sammy split his tight pants and he cursed the horse excessively, as if the poor animal had anything to do with it. As Joey Tiraborelli was laughing at him, he mounted up and did the same thing!

The boys wore their buffed out shoes and hiked up their pants, displaying their designer socks and partially-exposed, hairy legs. We headed out on the sandy white beach. When the horses took off at full speed, the boys' terrified expressions would have made a great Kodak moment, but no one had a camera.

One of the guys lost his diamond pinkie ring in the panic and bitched the remainder of the way. The funniest, though, was when Sammy decided to be a big shot and run his horse into the surf. The horse got its foot caught in the coral, and, in the struggle to free itself, threw Sammy head-first into the water. We laughed like banshees when the horse finally released himself and ran away, leaving Sammy to walk all the way back to the stables, but I actually think he preferred that. When he finally arrived, looking disheveled, he snorted, "I'll take a gun pointed at my head any time compared to this shit!"

What I loved most about Sam was his sense of humor. When I think of him now, I think of all the times we laughed. Not that I was any great genius, but Sammy used to use words that made no sense. I'd always call him on it and he'd make some wisecrack that got us off on a laughing jag.

But a laugh a minute was not what most people saw. Sammy was a powerful force in Rochester. He was "The Man." He knew how to turn on the charm with his easy going manner, but underneath lurked a killer, a fact I could never bring myself to see. His strong presence was invigorating. I felt safe and untouchable when Sammy was near. The view from Sammy's world was mysterious, exciting, and seductive.

As I gained a better understanding of Sammy's lifestyle, we used to laugh about whose picture was in the paper more often, his or mine. But no matter what I read or heard, I still refused to see the reality of who he really was.

It was March 1968. Mom and Dad were preparing to leave for Myrtle Beach on their annual golf trip with members of their club. I had gone the year before. I really had a great time, but this year I had too many jobs scheduled. It was my senior year in high school and I was off for Spring Break. The photographers were taking full advantage of it with bookings for a solid week. Besides, my fiancé, Tom, was trying to get a leave the next weekend from boot camp at Fort Dix, New Jersey, and I wanted to be there to see him.

I met Tom on a humid August night in the summer of 1966 while "cruising the Main," as we called it, with my girlfriend in her new Corvair convertible. Sunday nights were always reserved for cruising down Main Street in the city. Back and forth all night long between Ben's Cafe Society and the White Tower hamburger stand. Both had large parking lots that we used to chat with anyone we thought looked deserving of our attention. Actually, it was Tom's souped up black Dodge Charger that first caught my eye. I detected the power under the hood as he peeled out from a light. We pulled up beside him in the lot and I found him to be as attractive as his car.

Tom was tall, with long, sweeping lashes and challenging brown eyes. Like most everyone else in Rochester, he was Italian. What made him unique was that he was the only Sicilian I'd met who was as innocent as his face. Tom was twenty-four and working for Kodak, while I was just about to enter my junior year in high school. We were engaged by Christmas of 1967.

The war in Vietnam was in full swing and Tom had been drafted into the Army. He'd only been gone a few months, but usually got home on the weekends. Between school and work I really hadn't had time to miss him all that much.

Before my parents had departed for Myrtle Beach, I'd promised my mother that I would sleep at Aunt Theresa's house while they were away so she could leave with peace of mind. The Monday after my parents left was one of my busiest days. I started out at nine o'clock, shooting a national ad for Kodak. At one o'clock I dashed over to Klaus Fischel's studio to shoot a cover for Sara Coventry jewelry. By six I was in the photo studio at Sibley's department store doing a series of newspaper ads for the following Sunday's paper. We wrapped by midnight and I headed home. It was one a.m. by the time I stopped home, got my wardrobe together for the following day's shoot, and arrived at Aunt Theresa's. Long day. My cheeks hurt from smiling so much.

The next day was even worse. Bathing suits on the beach for Champion Sportswear. That doesn't sound so bad, but Upstate New York is cold in March. If the temperature reached forty degrees I'd be lucky. But that's the nature of the business: swim suits in January and fur coats in July. I really crammed in the jobs. No school and all work. I even had a booking for Saturday. Friday brought a break, though—I was home by four o'clock.

Six o'clock. Tom hadn't called yet. Was he coming home? I

phoned Aunt Theresa from home to let her know I wouldn't be at her place for dinner. I assured her that if Tom wasn't coming I'd be there in an hour or two. If Tom got in, I'd be at her place by 12:30 a.m. at the latest. I had an early call the next day for Kodak and needed my beauty sleep.

Aunt Theresa lived alone with her son Keith, a cop with the Rochester Police Department. She was used to waiting up until he was safely home. The typical Italian mother. But I understood her fears. When my parents were away, I always called to let her know where I was and that no boogieman had gotten me yet.

While making myself a sandwich I heard the doorbell. Dick, my sister's husband, stood on the step. Dressed like a preppy college student, Dick's tall body slouched against the doorjamb. His youthful face was drawn and haggard, aging him.

The traditional jock-type, Dick was very all-American looking with light eyes and sandy brown hair styled in a crewcut. At twenty-five, he still played baseball and basketball with his old high school buddies on a weekly basis. His athlete's body, slender but strong, served as proof of his active sports life.

"Do you mind if I talk to you for a while?" he asked pathetically.

He looked as though he'd been crying and didn't have a friend in the world. He and Sharon had been married for about three years and had a two-year-old daughter. They'd had a tumultuous marriage from the beginning. Dick was insanely jealous of my sister and violent fights erupted often. When they did, Sharon would run home to Mom. In their three years of marriage she probably lived with us more than she did in her own home.

Recently broken up again, Sharon needed to get away and clear her head. She had taken the baby and left with my parents for Myrtle Beach. This time, I thought, she would really follow through and not reconcile again. Personally, I thought it was for the best.

"No, come on in. Do you want a sandwich?" I answered, opening the door and proceeding back to the kitchen counter.

I felt sorry for Dick. He did love my sister, but he didn't know how to control his temper. This time his apologies didn't seem to be working and he was devastated, thinking he might have lost her for good. He was always nice to me, but I wasn't the one who had to live with him.

"Yeah, sure, I am kinda hungry." He paused. "Have you heard from Sharon yet?" he asked, trying to disguise his desperation.

"Yes, they called yesterday. They'll be back on Sunday."

"Did Sharon say anything about me?" With raised eyebrows, his piercing blue eyes searched my face, anticipating my answer.

"No, Dick, to be honest...she didn't," I answered as I walked over to close the kitchen door. The evening breeze was bringing in a chill. Dick's depression was quite a contrast to the cheerful looking kitchen, with brightly colored, orange-flowered wallpaper, and a hutch filled with pictures of smiling faces.

Elbows on the table, he cupped his face in his large hands as he whined, "I don't know what to do, Georgia. I miss her so much." He looked up and connected with my eyes once again. "Do you think she'll ever come back?"

Feeling uncomfortable, I tried to ease his pain but was careful not to give false hopes. "I don't mean to hurt you, Dick, but maybe you should start thinking about what you're going to do if she doesn't come back. She seems like she may have really made up her mind this—"

"If she'd just talk to me, I know I could convince her to give me another chance," he interrupted, refusing to hear the reality of it.

"I don't know..." I answered in a doubtful voice.

"What am I gonna do, Georgia? I love her so much..." he answered defeatedly.

"Keep your mind busy," I answered, running my fingers through my long blonde hair, trying to think of some solution. "Start going out with your friends, that'll help."

"Yeah, but my friends are her friends. All we do is talk about Sharon."

That was true. Neither of them had ever left this little town. Their friends were people they'd both grown up with. Avoiding each other was almost impossible.

28

"So make new friends," I said. "Go out in the city. You can't hang around in this town and not expect to run into people who'll remind you of Sharon. There's another world out there besides East Rochester, you know."

He shook his head. "Yeah, but I'd feel funny walking into a bar where I didn't know anybody. I'm not like you, Georgia. You make friends easily. I'm not like that."

"You could make friends—if you tried," I replied sternly.

"Will you help me, Georgia? Take me to the city and introduce me to some of your friends?"

"I would, but Tom's coming home tonight."

"Oh," he said with downcast eyes.

I was such a sucker for people in pain. Even though I knew Sharon would be much happier without him, I still couldn't help feeling sorry for him. As I tried to console him, the phone rang.

"Hi, honey," Tom said. "I have some bad news. I couldn't get a pass."

"Oh, Tom, I'm so disappointed. Susie and Ralph are having a party tomorrow night, it's a farewell party. Ralph got drafted too."

"You'll have to go without me, I guess. What're you gonna do tonight?"

"I'll just make an early night of it. I have a six o'clock call tomorrow anyway."

"I'm sure I'll be able to make it next week..." He paused for a moment. "Uh, we got our orders today." We were both silent for a long moment. "They're shipping us out to Vietnam as soon as we finish boot camp."

"So soon?" I wrapped the telephone coil around my index finger. My stomach churned.

"War doesn't wait, Georgia. I've gotta go. There's a line here for the phone. I love you, honey."

"I love you, too, Tom. See you next week." I set the receiver softly in its cradle.

"He's not coming home tonight?" Dick asked.

"No, I guess not," I answered.

"Georgia?" Dick said, interrupting my thoughts. "As long as

Tom's not coming, why don't you take me to the city tonight?"

The thought of Vietnam depressed me. Four of my friends had already lost their lives in Vietnam. They were dropping like flies over there. Maybe going out would get my mind off it. A few hours wouldn't hurt, and Dick looked like he really needed some cheering up.

"Well, all right, but we'll have to take two cars. I can't stay too long."

"Nah, I really don't plan on having a good time. Let's just take one car. I'll leave whenever you're ready."

"Are you sure about that? I have to be up by four o'clock tomorrow and I really need to get to bed at a decent hour."

"I'm very sure. I could use a drink and a change of scenery, but I doubt I'll be having such a great time I won't want to leave. Whenever you say—we're gone."

"Well, okay..." I answered, half sure I'd made the right decision. I changed out of my jeans and into the black cocktail dress I'd planned on wearing for Tom and off we went.

———◆———

Friday night in the city and The Living Room lounge was hopping. I was glad I had decided to go out. As I walked through the door a Four Tops tune was blasting from the stage.

"Georgia!" someone called out cheerily above the music.

Jimmy Cristo, The Living Room's proprietor, stood at the corner of the bar, motioning me over. With him were Sammy G and Joey Tiraborelli.

Joey was the stepson of Red Russotti, a big shot mobster, and was Sammy G's best friend. They were never apart. Joey was a funny man with a crooked smile and an infectious laugh. His nose, just prominent enough to get him into trouble with a fast closing door, put a measure of Roman history in his face. He thought he was Rochester's answer to John Dillinger, shooting his mouth off way too often. He was always either insulting or throwing a punch at men who were to be respected in their world. If he had been anyone else, he'd have been found face down somewhere in a ditch with a bullet in his head. But there was safety in being Sammy G's favorite sidekick and he knew it. Dumber than shit— he'd have to take his shoes off to count past ten.

Jimmy Cristo stood out in the crowd. He *did* have a brain. Besides owning The Living Room, he had one of the most successful auto body shops in the city. He'd made a lot of money at a young age—legally—and he knew how to spend it. Without hearing him speak, you could tell he was a class act. Quiet and cautious, he spoke more with his eyes than his mouth. Dressed to perfection with a flirtatious glint in his eyes, he beckoned me over.

Jimmy gave me my very first car on my sixteenth birthday. A Studebaker, of all things, but it was a car, and I was grateful for the wheels. It was one he had hanging around the lot. Not long after, it mysteriously burned up. He'd felt so bad about it, he gave me a really neat metallic gold 1964 Buick. That car I *really* liked.

Both Joey Tiraborelli and Jimmy Cristo were on the Bahamas trip. Jimmy had broken up with his steady girlfriend, Gail, just before the trip. Attracted to each other, we hung out together the whole time, but he was ten years older than I was and he wanted an adult relationship. I wasn't even close. Besides, I was still jail-bait. He was smarter than that, but the fact was, there was a strong attraction.

As I approached the bar with Dick trailing behind I thought of walking barefoot on the beach with Jimmy. The full moon, the warm sand between our toes, the island music playing in the distance. Those soft eyes of his—God, did he have gorgeous eyes. But I was engaged now, and Jimmy was back with Gail, getting what he needed from her. So it had ended before it had really begun.

After the cheek-kissing ritual, I introduced Dick to the trio. He was obviously out of place. The Living Room catered to the city crowd. Anything other than gabardine pants and patent leather shoes was pathetically out of place. Dick's casual cream-colored pants and plaid shirt screamed to them, 'I'm an asshole!' Obviously a little intimidated, Dick looked awkwardly around the bar, avoiding eye contact with my friends.

Sammy G sized up Dick—revealing his disapproval in his mannerisms, studying Dick with a sidelong look and shaking his head. He neither liked nor trusted outsiders. Behind him, Jimmy Cristo appeared equally unimpressed.

Sammy shot me a smirk that said, 'Who the fuck is this mayonnaise-face?' I shrugged and grinned, leaving my eyes to say the rest.

"We're all going to Skinny's later, kid. Want us to save you a table?" Sammy asked, ignoring Dick.

"No thanks, Sam. I'll be long gone by that time."

The band slowed down the pace, playing a great Motown tune and Sammy dragged me off to the dance floor.

"I think Jimmy Cristo still has a crush on you. He's been eyeballin' you since you walked in," he said, shifting his gaze toward the bar.

I glanced over at Jimmy standing in his corner, looking as cool as a long drink of water. "Yeah, well, don't let Gail get wind of it. Remember what happened to the car Jimmy gave me last year? You can't convince me she wasn't the one who set it on fire."

"She did finally admit to that, ya know," he said.

"Actually, Sam, she did me a favor. The replacement car is a lot nicer."

"Just don't park it in the gas station again. If we hadn't pushed it out into the street before it blew up, it would've taken out the whole fuckin' block!" He paused and looked down at me with a lazy smile. "Did anyone ever tell you that you have an explosive personality?"

I burst out laughing.

"So who's this guy you're with?" Sammy asked as he swung me around to the music. He was an excellent dancer.

"He's my sister's husband," I answered, resting my head on his neck, taking in the musky scent of his cologne.

"So that's the jerk."

"Not for much longer, Sam. I think she's really going to go through with it this time. Hopefully he'll meet someone tonight and fall madly in love. That would solve a lot of problems," I said as the song finished and we walked back toward the lounge.

Dick had found a home at the bar. He was talking to Joey, who was going out of his way to introduce him to as many women as possible. Joey was crazy about my sister, and had been ever since the trip to the Bahamas. He would like nothing better than to see the two of them end it for good. Not that he'd ever have a chance with her—she thought he was a kick, but that's all. Dick was doing fine on his own, so I went table-hopping.

About eleven o'clock I found Dick on the same barstool where I'd left him, talking to a bottled blonde.

"I think we should be going now, Dick."

"I just ordered another beer. We'll leave as soon as I drink it, okay?"

"Okay, but make it quick," I said with a hint of an edge. I left them to resume their conversation and danced twice more with a couple of the familiar guys before going back to the bar.

"Ready?" I asked.

Another full bottle of beer sat in front of him.

"Let me just finish this one," he answered, looking as if he'd had one too many already.

I blew up. "Dick! This is why I wanted to take my own car. You said you would take me home early. If I don't get to bed soon, I'll look like crap for my job."

"Okay, okay. I'll finish this one and we'll leave."

Frustrated, I bumped into Joey on my way to the ladies' room. "What's the matter?" Joey asked, his dark eyes filled with concern.

"I can't get Dick to leave. Did you have to do such a good job, Joey? He's like a kid in a candy store!" Joey laughed. "It's not funny, Joey. I have to get up early tomorrow."

"All right, I'll see what I can do," he offered. "Meet ya back at the bar."

I came out of the ladies' room and returned to the bar. At my annoying persistence, Dick reluctantly drank his beer down and we finally got up to leave.

Sammy G huddled in the corner of the bar with some mobster

types. The conversation looked serious. He looked up as I was walking out the door and I waved. He didn't smile, he just nodded. As we pulled away I saw Sammy standing at the window watching us. I smiled and waved again. He waved back, but still no smile. *Oh boy. I wonder what's going on now?*

As we entered the expressway and headed toward East Rochester, Dick had difficulty keeping the car between the lines.

"Why don't you let me drive, Dick?" I asked, becoming concerned.

"No, I'm okay," he protested.

He passed the Linden Avenue off ramp. "Dick, where are you going? You just passed my exit."

"Oh, I wasn't thinking. I was heading home. Since we're almost to my house anyway, would you do me a big favor? Sharon's coming back Sunday. I had the guys over last night to play cards and the house is a mess. Would you help me clean it up? It won't take long. I just want to show her I'm trying," he said in a pleading voice.

I really understood his panic about the condition of the house. My sister was a nut for cleanliness. Once we got in a terrible fight when she came at me like an animal because she had just finished cleaning and I had messed up the kitchen making myself something to eat. I almost put out her eye when I threw an ashtray at her in self defense, which landed her in the hospital with fourteen stitches from her eyebrow to down the side of her nose.

"I can't, Dick, it's late. If you'd left when I wanted to I would have, but I've got to get some sleep."

"Please, Georgia, it's important to me. Look at all the times I've helped you out. Can't you just do this one little thing? Fifteen minutes. That's all it'll take if we do it together."

He exited on Fairport Road, the street where he lived, which was about a mile past my house. I let out a disgruntled sigh, realizing "no" wasn't an option. He'd been drinking and was focused only on what was important to him. The little house sat

34

about one hundred yards off the road, quite secluded, with the water department to the right and an empty lot to the left.

"Y'know, Dick, you really piss me off! If you'd planned all along to ask me to help you, then why the hell did you sit there guzzling down all those beers when you knew it was getting late? I've been telling you all night how early I have to get up!" I spouted.

"It won't take long, I promise," he said, ignoring my irritation as he pulled into his driveway.

He was right, the house was a mess. I took off my coat and immediately started to pick up the beer cans strewn everywhere. The faster I did this, the quicker I'd get home. I started on the dishes and Dick picked up a dishtowel and began to dry. He was wiping a butcher knife when suddenly he was behind me with the knife at my throat.

"Kiss me," he said in a voice that was unfamiliar to me.

"Dick, what are you doing?" I screamed.

"Just kiss me. That's all I want."

"Dick, think about what you're doing! I'm your wife's sister! Are you crazy?"

"Just one kiss—"

He yanked on my dress, and in one single motion it was ripped from my body. I tried to run for the door. He caught me and dragged me back. I kicked and screamed wildly, trying to free myself from his grip. He pinned me against the refrigerator. His slobbery mouth was all over mine. I turned my head from side to side in disgust.

"Just kiss me. That's all I want."

"Do you think you'll ever have a chance with my sister when she finds out about this?" I screamed.

"All I want is one little kiss," he said, as he bent his head to my breast and practically ripped my bra off with his teeth. His powerful hands yanked at the garment until it came loose from my body.

I kicked him between his legs. It didn't hurt him, as I was always told it would. It excited him even more. He pulled me into the living room and pushed me onto the couch. Pinning my arms over my head, he tore off my underwear.

The thought of what was coming gave me a surge of strength. I twisted violently and knocked him off balance. As he fell to the floor he hit his head on the coffee table, momentarily stunning him. I jumped from the couch and started to run. He grabbed my leg as I tried to dart past him and I fell to the floor. Kicking his face, I struggled to free myself.

"All I wanted was one little kiss!" he yelled over and over as he began hitting me with a wooden hanger.

Now I understood what my sister meant by Dick's appetite for sex. Grabbing my hair, he dragged me into the bedroom. The struggle exhilarated him. With his weight on top of me, he bit my breast viciously, leaving teeth impressions on my skin. I screamed in excruciating pain. He really enjoyed that. He tried to force himself inside me, but my legs were tightly crossed. With both his hands he persistently tried to pry my legs apart.

I grabbed a large jar of Noxema that sat on the nightstand and smashed it into his head as hard as I could. I thought it would kill him, but I didn't care. To my amazement, he looked at me and— smiled. A sick, twisted smile. He held my arms down as he used his knee to separate my legs. Feeling his penis against me, I knew I'd been defeated.

"Oh God. Please don't!" I screamed.

No! Not like this, please! This can't really be happening. Please, God. Help me.

But God did not hear my pleas, and neither could Dick. He was in a world of his own.

I screamed in pain as he violently entered me, savagely biting me at the same time. When it was over, he lay panting on top of me. I wanted to throw up. The weight of his body was crushing. Disgusted and feeling dirty, I continued to cry.

"Sharon can't find out about this," he said as he rolled off me.

"If you think no one is going to know about this, you're crazy, you bastard!" I screamed.

"You can't tell. She'll never come back," he said in a panic, suddenly feeling remorseful.

"It's a little late too think about that, isn't it? You're going to pay for what you did to me! You're not going to get away with this!" I screamed, as though I were actually talking to a rational person.

"I know, I know!" he said, as if he had just had a brilliant idea. "I'll kill you and bury you in the backyard. That's what I'll do."

At first I thought he was trying to scare me into keeping my mouth shut, but I looked into his eyes and had no recognition of the man I thought I knew. My sister had told me how he was two different people when he drank, but I had no idea what she meant until now.

He yanked me off the bed and pulled me outside, grabbing a shovel from the garage as we passed.

"Start digging!" he demanded, as he forced the shovel into my hands.

My body shook violently, both from fear and the cold.

Oh my God, he's mentally deranged! Am I really going to die? I should've never said I would tell. Will he believe me now if I tell him I won't say anything? Oh my God. Oh my God. How am I going to get out of this? Where there's a will there's a way. Think. Think!

"Dick," I said, between hysterical sobs. "You can't kill me."

"Why not?" he asked, looking disconnected from reality.

"Because the photographer I was supposed to work for today knows I was with you tonight. I told him if I was a little late it would be because I was going out with you. He knows!"

In his confused, demented state, he fell for it. "Call him! Tell him you weren't with me," he yelled, pulling me back toward the house.

This is your only chance. Think!

He picked up the receiver and shoved it into my hand. "Call!" he demanded. "Tell him!"

I took a deep breath and dialed my aunt's number. It was now four o'clock in the morning. She answered on the first ring.

"Emil?"

"Georgia! Where are you?"

"Emil, I'm sorry, but I can't work for you today," I said,

holding the receiver tightly to my ear so Dick couldn't hear the hysterical screams coming from my aunt.

"Georgia, what's wrong, where are you? Keithy, Keithy, pick up the phone! Something's wrong with Georgia!"

"Georgia, what's the matter?" Keith yelled, picking up the extension. My aunt continued to scream. "Ma!" Keith yelled. "Get off the phone! Georgia, where are you?"

"I know, Emil, I'm really sorry, but my brother-in-law is very sick and I—"

"You're at Dick's?"

"Yes!" I screamed, as Dick yanked the phone out of the wall.

"Who were you talking to?" Dick yelled, smashing my head with the phone.

"My cousin Keith! He knows where I am, and he's on his way over here!" I screamed. "You won't have to worry about my sister anymore, Dick, because you'll be behind bars!"

He began to pace like a caged animal. "What am I going to do? You've got to help me, Georgia, please."

"Helping you is what got me here in the first place, remember?"

"Oh my God...What have I done? What have I done? Sharon will never come back. What am I gonna do?" He sat on the floor, knocking his head against the wall and mumbling to himself.

I couldn't believe what I was looking at. I was numb. Unlike my normal personality, I felt no sympathy. Did he really think I would help him? Who was this person? I'd never met him before. Why hadn't I ever seen the depth of his illness? All I could think about was my poor sister. Had she lived through scenes like this all the time? Was this the reason for her constant turmoil?

Keith had run out the door partially dressed, and as he peeled out in his car he must have shouted to my aunt to call my uncle Pat, who was also a cop. They arrived at exactly the same time, just about colliding with one another as they raced down the driveway. Their squealing tires came as music to my ears.

They didn't bother knocking, just broke down the door and then stood in shock, surveying the scene. Uncle Pat looked down at Dick, huddled in the corner. His arms were over his head, bracing himself for the blows to come.

"I didn't mean it, Pat! I didn't know what I was doing. I didn't mean it."

"You sick son-of-a-bitch!" screamed my uncle as he kicked Dick in the face. Dick fell to the floor. Blood streamed from his mouth and nose. He didn't try to get up. He just lay there covering his head, pleading insanity. Uncle Pat went out of control.

Keith found a bedspread, covered my naked, bruised body, and led me to the car.

"Are you all right?" he asked, helping me into the car.

"I am now," I answered, this time crying from relief.

Keith left me for a moment and went back into the house to get in a few of his own licks. I sat in the car shivering, listening to the violent sound of breaking glass and furniture, and Dick's pleading voice.

"I didn't mean it! Don't hurt me, Pat. I didn't mean it!" he said repeatedly in a shrinking voice.

As my cousin backed out of the long, narrow driveway, I could see my Uncle Pat's silhouette through the window. The shade was pulled, but I could still see legs kicking and arms swinging as we drove away.

"I want to take a bath," I said to my aunt as we entered the house. She was on the verge of hysterics.

"Ma, you're making it worse," Keith said. "Just run the bath water for her. I have to call the police, Georgia. Are you up to giving a statement?"

"I want to take a bath," I said numbly.

Aunt Theresa took me into the bathroom. I dropped the bedspread on the floor and stepped into the tub.

"Oh, my God!" she shrieked. "What did that animal do to you?" I scrubbed my body frantically. It wouldn't come off. *He* wouldn't come off.

"Stop it, Georgia. You're going to hurt yourself!"

The police were waiting in my aunt's tiny kitchen when I finally emerged from the tub. I knew them all, and they knew me. I couldn't get through the story without crying uncontrollably.

"Why don't you get her to bed?" one of them said to my aunt. "We can come back later and make a report. Do you have any Valium?"

"Yes, I do," she answered.

"It might be a good idea if you gave her one."

My body began to relax, and my eyelids became heavy. Aunt Theresa stayed by my bedside, stroking my hair and speaking softly.

"Aunt Theresa?"

"Yes, honey?" she answered as a tear quietly rolled down her cheek.

"You have to call Emil... Tell him I can't work for him today..." I drifted off into a deep sleep.

I awoke bruised and confused in my aunt's bed. I'd thought I'd had a bad dream. But the nightmare continued.

The doctor's office, the police. The humiliation of standing naked for photographs of my bruised body. Facing my sister and my parents when they returned the next day. They were devastated. I relived the nightmare over and over and over again. My mother hovered over me, trying to take the pain from my bruised spirit. I'd never seen my normally passive father so angry, pacing the room, thinking of ways to kill Dick.

But my sister was the worst of all. She looked like she'd been speared in the heart. She agonized not only over what had been done to me but also the embarrassment she'd have to endure from the townspeople. Dick was the father of her child. Even though they had a bad marriage, she'd still clung to the love they shared as teenagers. Now there was no turning back. She not only mourned me, but the finality of the death of her marriage as well.

Tom had come home only once, the weekend after it happened. He tried to be compassionate and supportive, but I was an icicle. With no time to help me with the healing process, he shipped off to Vietnam with a heavy heart.

A long week passed. I often found myself walking down a lonely stretch of road, in search of the person I once was. Ending up in the woods for hours—a comfort zone from my childhood. The March wind blew softly across the pond as I sat on a cold rock, gazing in silence. The water's color reflected the dreariness of my heart, winter gray. Extreme depression descended upon me, not just for the loss of my virginity, but for the loss of *me*. My innocence had been taken. Blackness had entered where light had once lived.

I received a phone call a few days later. "Georgia, you okay?" asked Joey Tiraborelli.

"I'm okay, Joey."

"That bastard! Sammy G wants to see you. You feelin' up to it?"

"What does he want to see me about?" I asked apprehensively. Word spread fast in Rochester.

"He ain't happy with this situation—at all. He was like a...a...whatta ya call those crazy people?"

"Lunatics?"

"Yeah, he was like a luna...lun...one of those, when he heard what happened to you. I think ya better meet with him."

"When, Joey?" I asked, not looking forward to the predictable confrontation.

"As soon as possible."

"I guess I can't avoid it. I may as well get it over with. Where?"

"Ben's Cafe. Tomorrow, for lunch—and come alone."

"Okay, Joey, tell him I'll be there."

"Keep your chin up, kid."

Upon entering Ben's Cafe a chill settled into my bones. Spring was just a few calendar days away, but the air felt more like fall. Not crisp and refreshing, but damp and cold.

Sammy G sat alone with his back to the wall in the rear of the restaurant. His expression was somber. His lips formed a rigid line when he looked up and saw me. Nodding in recognition to a few familiar faces as I passed the tables in the bar, I headed up the three steps to the dining area where Sammy waited. He stood and pulled out my chair as I approached.

"Ya want a drink?"

"It's against the law," I said, forcing a smile.

"Don't get cute, you're with me. Now whatta ya want?" he said, smiling back at me.

I really didn't like to drink during the day, but I knew I was going to need it. "I'll have a glass of wine. Scotch is a little heavy for daytime."

He ordered a bottle, watched in silence as the waiter opened it, then looked over at me. His dark brown eyes were soft, but a hard edge encircled them. Quietly he asked, "What happened, kid?"

I had told the story so many times in the past week that I hated having to recall the details of the incident again, especially to Sammy. My uncle was acting outside of the law when he beat Dick unmercifully, but Sammy wouldn't have stopped there. I tried carefully to get through the story without getting emotional, but halfway into it I lost my composure. There was nothing I could do but plod on. Sammy sat straight in his chair, eyes alert, immaculate in a dark pinstriped suit. He shook his head silently and often.

"I had a feelin' about that guy, I just had a feelin'. I should've followed my gut," he said, almost to himself. "That cocksucker's gonna pay!" he spat.

My body became rigid with fear. "We're going to court, Sam. The law will take care of—"

"Fuck the law!" he screamed, slamming his fist on the table, spilling the wine onto the white tablecloth. We were pretty secluded, but still, heads turned from the front of the restaurant. He lowered his voice and continued.

"I'm gonna have his cock cut off and delivered to you in a box. That's the way you deal with pricks like him!"

The waiter showed up to clean the spilled wine. "Did I fucking call you?" Sammy snapped.

"No, sir."

"Then get the fuck outta here!"

The waiter evaporated. Sammy's ruggedly handsome face

was bright red, looking as if it were about to explode. The veins in his forehead were turning purple and protruding. It scared me. The way his eyebrows lowered, hooding his eyes and changing them into narrow slits, sent shivers up my spine.

"Sammy, please, calm down. I don't like seeing you like this."

"And I don't like seeing you like this either!" he retorted, slamming his fist on the table again. "Why didn't I listen to what my gut was tellin' me?"

I found myself looking straight into the hostile eyes of a cold-blooded murderer. The sort of eyes that flirt, dance—and deceive. I subconsciously knew Sammy had blood on his hands. No way he could've been in the upper echelon of the organization without bodies to count. In the past, my naive mind had chosen to deny that fact. I had never seen this side of Sammy before. For the first time in my young life, I was *aware* of looking into the face of a murderer. But it wouldn't be my last—not by a long shot. Dick would be lucky to lose only an organ. The thought of that kind of violence was beyond my comprehension.

"Please, Sammy, please, don't do that," I begged. "I couldn't live with myself. What about Sharon? And my niece? They'd never forgive me—I couldn't forgive myself! Let it go, Sam. Please. He'll get his, in time."

"You're damn right he will!"

After a long time, Sammy finally calmed down. There wasn't a hint of makeup left on my face, all erased by tears while pleading for Dick's life. But I prevailed. By the time lunch was over, it boiled down to what I wanted. I held a man's life on the tip of my tongue. Dick would have no idea how fortunate he was to only serve jail time.

"The son-of-a-bitch doesn't deserve to live after what he's done, but if that's what you want..." He shrugged.

"Yes," I said, breathing easier, "that's what I want."

Sammy had killed for lesser reasons. Could he really ignore it? An uneasy feeling said I was just being pacified, but he assured me with his intensity. The depth and consistency of his sincerity dissolved my doubts—but still, could I take that chance?

We stood in the parking lot at Ben's Cafe as Sammy gave me an affectionate hug and then turned and walked toward his car. Without breaking stride he yelled over his shoulder, "You let me know if you have a change of heart, kid."

———◆———

By the time I had to repeat the details of the rape and the events leading up to it in front of the grand jury, I was telling it as though it had happened to someone else. It *did* happen to someone else. It happened to that innocent side of me that embraced the light, believed in love, believed in trust and compassion. Another person took the stand that day, the new and sometimes frightening shadow side I came to call *Georgia Black*. The side that could hate beyond all bounds, the side that also had untold power and strength to protect me from harm. Georgia Black told the story with no emotion. Blow by blow, without a tear. She was so strong. I envied her.

Georgia Black was born the night of the rape. Her primary function was to protect my vulnerable, innocent side, the side I call *Georgia White*. I did what the human mind does naturally: I gave birth to my shadow in order to handle the trash. I sought a place to hide, as traumatized people do. Too much emotional pain will fragment anyone's personality. And if that trauma repeats itself, the fracturing will become deeper and more pronounced.

Ultimately, my Shadow emerged—a persona tailored precisely for my needs. A highly desensitized woman, impervious to pain, who could handle the disillusionment that the young Georgia White couldn't. Throughout my nightmares over the next twenty-five years, she'd whisper, telling me what to do. Sometimes my loving, vulnerable side would win the battles. But over time, my Shadow would become a monster. Eclipsing the spiritual person I was meant to be, she began to take over.

In her infancy, my Shadow might have been harmless. But as my life evolved from the time of the rape at age seventeen, she grew right along with me. I hid out in her when necessary, then emerged into the light when it was safe, leaving her to handle the poison.

Walking down the halls of East Rochester High School, it was I who heard the whispers and caught the accusing looks from my classmates. I was no longer the victim. He was the victim.

"If she hadn't teased him, and led him on, it never would've happened."

"She asked for it!"

"I know of at least five guys she's slept with."

Ah, the jealousy of a small town. Now they finally had something to say about the girl who had it all. Now there was proof she was a whore, just like all of the Perrone girls.

The court ordeal was ugly, despite all the incriminating evidence against Dick. The photographs of his handprints that had turned into bruises on my legs were not enough proof that I was not a willing participant. There I was, in black and white, and still the facts were twisted. Which was worse: the act of rape itself, or the aftermath? The entire drama consisted of me trying to prove I wasn't a whore.

My parents were more than willing to go deeper into debt for Justice, but as the painful proceedings moved along I became more depressed, taking more than the prescribed dosage of tranquilizers. I frequently thought of taking the whole bottle and ending the continuing nightmare. Recognizing my state of mind, our lawyer suggested to my parents that we let Dick plead to a lesser charge, explaining it was still an admission of guilt, with a one year sentence. My parents agreed.

In the end, Dick only served six months of his sentence in jail, but that was long enough for Sammy to simmer down. When the ordeal was over, it still wasn't over—at least not in the minds of the narrow-minded townspeople of East Rochester. And the scar was mine for keeps.

That December, I became the Kodak Summer Girl. The poster wouldn't come out until the following summer, but the news covered the story, making a big splash: "Local Girl Makes it Big." I guess it was a pretty big deal all over the country. That people still remember that poster astonishes me. In previous years, Kodak had always chosen the latest top model from New York for their Summer Girl. Cybil Shepherd took the spotlight the following year.

But even the enjoyment of that fame was tainted. Someone wrote a letter to Kodak stating that they should be ashamed of themselves. They were supposed to be such a reputable company, with a good, clean image. Using me as their Summer Girl would only tarnish that image. Didn't they know that I slept with everyone in town?

Kodak was an extremely conservative company. This was the first time they had used a model in a bikini. Before that, the Summer Girl was always in a one-piece suit. This was an important step for Kodak. If the letter had gotten to the higher-ups, the ad surely would have been pulled. That happened to the girl they used for their winter poster. Someone had mentioned that she simply *looked* quite a bit like the current Playboy centerfold and they stopped production on her cutouts.

Fortunately, the head of one of the photo departments who knew better received the letter. He showed it to me one day while I was on the set. It never went any farther than him, but I was appalled at the viciousness of the letter when I read it. It wasn't signed, but it could have been anyone of the many jealous gossips in my town.

I began to discover the meaning of the word "hate" during this time. Hate had not only started to take form in my life—it fueled my existence. I spent the next twenty-five years proving to people that I wasn't a whore. I went about it in ways that were detrimental to leading a healthy life. I set out to throw it back in their faces. If jealousy was the reason for their cruelty, then Georgia Black would give them plenty to be jealous about.

———◆———

Rochester was closing in on me. Small minds were at every turn. I not only wanted to escape, I needed to. Graduation day could not come soon enough. I would be on the first train to New York City the morning after the graduation ceremony, in June of

1968, with my model-friend Susie, and Linda, another model from Boston.

I'd leave, thinking I could leave the baggage behind and never look back.

CHAPTER THREE

The train pulled into Grand Central Station at dusk. Aboard were three young models in search of not just fame, but their own identities. New York was no longer a distant dream, but a reality. I was on my own in the city that never sleeps.

Linda, Susie, and I burst onto the scene looking like hicks. We had dressed comfortably for the train ride in shorts and t-shirts, but we now felt a little out of place. Sweat dripped from our foreheads as we dragged our luggage out to the street.

We hailed a cab and headed to the Barbizon Hotel for Women. The brochure had described both its security and stringent rules, which was the reason my reluctant mother had allowed me to go. The Barbizon was famous for attracting young women who came to New York from around the world seeking their dreams on Madison Avenue.

"Wait here till we check it out," Linda said to the cab driver.

Linda was a platinum blonde with gorgeous blue eyes, but a hardness glinted from within them as though she had lived far longer than her eighteen years. Linda and I met at a photography studio while shooting for a Sears catalogue in New York City about a year earlier. She'd been living in Boston and we'd both been flown in for the shoot. Like me, she wanted to move to New York City after finishing school, so we kept in touch until the day finally came.

We followed the matronly-looking lady from the front desk down the narrow hallway to what was supposed to be our room.

The hatchet-faced woman stood looking down her nose at us as we stared in disbelief at the tiny room.

"All the girls are quite comfortable here," she said indignantly with a clipped and very precise English accent.

"This is smaller than my bathroom at home!" Susie said, wide-eyed.

Susie was a twenty-year-old Southerner from Charleston whom I'd met, along with her gorgeous boyfriend Ralph, when I was fourteen at an after-school soda fountain called the Candy Kitchen in East Rochester. We became instant friends. She had done some modeling back in her hometown, so I took her under my wing and introduced her to the modeling scene in Rochester. She stood an inch taller than me at 5'7", and had a mane of light blonde hair almost reaching her waist. Famous for her gorgeous legs, she'd always beat out the other models whose milky thighs just didn't measure up. Although she came across as a bit of an airhead, I soon learned that this impression was primarily due to her Southern accent.

"Speaking of bathrooms, where is it?" I asked.

"It's just down the hall. You'll be sharing it with all the girls on this floor. We lock the doors at two o'clock, and there are no men allowed in the rooms," Ms. Indignant said as she paused to look at each of us with a raised eyebrow. "You can have your gentlemen friends wait for you in the lobby," she added sternly.

We looked at each other and without saying a word we turned and walked outside to our waiting cab. I'd worry about explaining this to my mother later.

"Take us to a hotel where they allow men past the lobby!" Linda commanded, and we all cracked up.

The cab driver took us to a hotel on 46th Street near Broadway. I can't remember the name of it now, but it was a real dump. The three of us stayed together in one small room, but it was cheap and we needed to economize until we could find a more permanent place to live. Little did we know the hotel was a haven for hookers.

With adventure in our hearts, we quickly rummaged through

our suitcases, pulled out our favorite bar-hopping garb, and hit the streets for our first night out in the big city.

We'd heard about a place called Fridays, which was supposed to be the "in" spot. TGI Fridays are all over the country now, but back then that was the only one in existence. We had no idea which direction to go to get there. Spotting a cop standing on the corner, we walked toward him to ask directions. He eyed us as we approached.

"What are you girls doing, working?" the cop asked before we had a chance to speak.

"We're not working yet, but we're looking for work," Susie answered innocently.

"Yeah, I know," he said looking kind of sad. "But you girls are too pretty to be working."

"Well, how are we supposed to make any money if we don't work?" I asked quizzically.

The conversation went on for a few more minutes before everybody realized we were talking about different subjects. We were right in the heart of hooker's paradise. I guess the cabby had taken Linda literally.

It started to rain. Not heavily, but enough to take the curl out of the hair-dos we had taken so long to get looking just right for the evening.

"Look, I'm gonna to be off in ten minutes," the cop said, glancing at his watch. "Why don't you girls duck under that doorway for a bit, and let me take you to Fridays? I think I need to enlighten you on some facts about life in the Big Apple."

⸺◆⸺

We entered the smoky bar and began to make our way toward the back in search of a vacant table. Imitation Tiffany lamps hung everywhere from a high tin ceiling, and the red and white checked tablecloths set an inviting atmosphere. Excited and ready for action, we pressed forward. Between the loud music and noisy patrons we practically had to yell to be heard.

I bumped into an overweight slob at the bar who obviously

had eaten too much pasta and who was smoking a cheap cigar. He swung around in his stool.

"What can I do for you, honey?" he asked with his best *'I'm a stud'* smile.

"You can refrain from calling me 'honey' for a start. After that, nothing," I answered flatly.

Linda and Susie giggled as we continued walking. Next barstool to the right of that disgusting old fart sat a pockmarked-faced youth with a wasted bleached blonde draped all over him. They both looked like they were in desperate need of a life.

The scene got better as we moved along. Pushing our way through the crowed bar area, we noticed plenty of trendy men with great physiques and lingering, hungry eyes.

Louie was a pretty nice guy for a cop. He was probably in his late thirties, and not bad looking either. Although we were skeptical at first, he really did have good intentions. Over drinks he lectured us about the many dangers for young girls living in New York. We listened the way most teenagers listen: in one ear and out the other. I wondered how he would have reacted had he known he had just bought a drink for a minor. I had a month to go before I turned eighteen, the legal drinking age. I took the innocent route, agreeing with everything that he had to say. Louie stayed long enough to finish his drink and then got up to leave.

"Well, gotta be going. You girls be careful now," he said, trying to sound authoritative.

"Thank you, Officer. Nice talking to you."

Soon after Louie departed, three men who had been eyeing us from the bar headed our way. They were exactly the kind of guys we had just been warned about.

As they approached, Linda sat up straighter, flashing a mega-watt smile and plenty of cleavage. Susie shifted in her chair, crossing her impressive legs and flipping her blonde mane behind her shoulders.

They were slick looking guys, weighted down with heavy gold chains and a bit too nicely dressed for the place we were in. I recognized the type immediately. They were Italian and exhibited the same traits as my Rochester friends. With the way they talked and carried themselves, I felt as if I hadn't left home. I had seen the tough guy syndrome many times before. The familiarity of these fellas made me immediately at ease with their presence. If nothing else, I knew they'd be amusing.

"Mind if we join you?" asked the big man with the squashed nose as he shook a cigarette loose from a pack of Lucky Strikes.

"Not at all!" Linda answered quickly, pushing her chair aside to make room.

As they squeezed into the tight space around the table I got a whiff of their potent cologne and immediately got a headache.

The man with the squashed nose said his name was Vic and introduced his sidekicks as Chippy and Billy.

"Whatcha girls drinkin'?" Vic asked, lighting up his cigarette.

After stating our preferences, Linda immediately went into her act, engaging Chippy in small talk. She laughed flirtatiously, her huge blue eyes sparkling, capturing his undivided attention. Trouble was emblazoned on her forehead in big red letters. She had an incandescent presence that made men drool.

"So where'ya girls from?" Chippy asked while attracting the attention of the waitress. "Bring us all a Dewars and water and put it on my tab."

"Rochester. We just arrived today," I answered.

"Huh? You girls don't look like country bumpkins to me," he said, eyeing us even more closely. I wondered if he would've had this thought had he seen us earlier at the train station.

"So this is your first night out in the land of fruits and nuts?"

"Yeah, it is," Susie answered shyly.

"Well'ya ran into the right guys. You're in for a good time," he said as he picked up a handful of peanuts and tossed them into his mouth one at a time.

As I'd expected, the guys turned out to be funny and kept us laughing from the moment they sat down. It didn't take much to amuse girls our age, and these three had their bar act down to perfection.

Chippy, I thought, could have been a professional comedian.

He had a quirky, off-beat kind of presence. A short, stocky guy, dressed in a yellow sweater over a navy blue shirt and gray dress pants, he looked too refined to act like such a nut. He kept us in stitches, twisting his face by doing imitations, sticking cigarettes up his nose, and other silly antics. When he laughed, he cried, which made everyone laugh even harder.

Acting more like twelve than thirty, they'd all burst out laughing at nothing. Watching them together was like having our own entertainment channel.

Vic didn't have to try to be funny, he just was. His mannerisms were what made him comical. He had a habit of waving his hands in the air when he got excited, and couldn't speak a sentence without some contortion of his face or body.

Baby-faced Billy was the most handsome of the three in a subtle, been-around-the-block sort of way. Although the quiet type, and more serious than the others, he didn't hesitate to partake in the laughter.

Susie and Linda both vied for Billy's attention, but I was immune. Vic had his eye on me, but I wasn't interested in him either. They apparently lived under the impression that they were irresistible to woman. Wrong. These guys were fun, but fatigue was beginning to set in. It was three-thirty in the morning and no one seemed to want the night to end.

Billy's eyes glittered dangerously when he spotted a short, rotund man with bulging eyes, hairy hands, and no chin approaching our table. Oblivious to the agitation of our companions, the man asked me if I cared to dance.

Vic took a long pull on his cigarette and inhaled deeply. His whole demeanor changed, exhibiting an anger so dark and overwhelming that he couldn't control it. It seemed to go a lot deeper than male pride to me. Squashing out his cigarette, he stood slowly, stifling what appeared to be a murderous urge to smash this guy in his fat red face. Towering above him, he put his bulk in the man's face and they exchanged long, chilling looks.

Vic poked his thick index finger repeatedly into the man's chest as he growled, "Don'tcha have no brains in that pea brain of a head? Can't y'see these girls are busy? Get the fuck outta here while ya can still walk, ya fuckin' moron."

Everyone in proximity pretended not to watch the intense confrontation. One look at the size of Vic was enough to quicken anyone's pace in the opposite direction. His nose, broken more than once, exhibited untold tales of a violent past. The bug-eyed man shot out of there in a big hurry.

"Fuckin' jerk," Vic murmured under his breath as he sat back down, adjusting his collar and resuming his composure.

Ooh, the temperature's changing. Maybe it's time to leave. I wanted to say something to ease the tension, but no flip remark came to mind.

Chippy squinted while dragging hungrily on his cigarette. "This place is gettin' boring. Whatta ya say we all go over to an after-hours club," he said, while expelling a stream of nauseating smoke in my direction which only served to increase the intensity of my headache. I'd had my fill. All I wanted to do was sleep.

"Hell yes!" Linda answered without hesitation.

"Linda, why don't we go back to the hotel and go to bed? It's been a long day," I interjected, knowing I'd be defeated.

"Yeah, maybe we should call it a night," Susie added.

"C'mon girls, tomorrow's Saturday. Whatta ya hafta get up early for? You're in New York. Gotta start livin' like New Yorkers, y'know what I mean?" Vic persisted.

"Yeah, sleep tomorrow. Give it a shot, you'll have a good time," echoed Billy.

Linda was determined to go. Susie and I looked at each other and rolled our eyes. Afraid to let her go off by herself with these guys, we all left for the after-hours club. Like it or not, it was going to be a long night.

The six of us drove down 2nd Avenue in Billy's banged-up black Buick. The fresh night air was a pleasant change from the smoke-filled bar. "Hey Jude" blasted on the radio as a soft breeze flowed through the open windows. The streets were empty at three-thirty in the morning. No horns honked. No people hustled forward to their destinations. The nine-to-fivers had already fled for their weekend retreats. We made a right turn onto East 23rd Street and pulled into an empty parking space. We finished listening to "Hey Jude" before Billy turned off the ignition.

Rain had fallen earlier. The pavement was a little wet, drying in spots from the warm summer air. I took a deep, sleepy breath as we crossed the street. The clean smell after the recent downpour reminded me of country mornings when I was a kid.

The guys started up a flight of narrow wooden steps, taking them two at a time. We followed. A dim light emanated through a peephole in the second floor door when Vic knocked lightly three times. A water buffalo in a light blue suit opened the door, blocking the entry with his imposing bulk. A stubby cigar hung from the side of his mouth as his fat eyes gave us the once over. He nodded and allowed us to enter.

Above the bar a sign read: "The Sundowner." Music of the Four Seasons played quietly from the back room. A black material covered the walls, giving me a closed-in feeling I didn't like. Other than a few suspicious looking guys in dark raincoats, the place was deserted.

"This looks like a really fun place," I chided Linda.

"It's not even four o'clock yet," Linda retorted. "This is an after-hours club, Georgia. It won't start jumping for another half hour," she retaliated.

"Oh, great. I'd rather be sleeping."

Flip, a short man resembling a Leprechaun, was sweeping the floor and chatting with his partner, Frankie, who nursed a Scotch and water at the other end of the bar. We'd learned that the two of them had recently opened this club and had high hopes for its success.

It was Frankie's penetrating black eyes that first drew my attention. He was a handsome man with dark olive skin, which I assumed he'd inherited from his Sicilian ancestors. I liked the way he stood: self-assured, with a hint of arrogance.

"When we gonna get a porter?" Flip asked Frankie. They

both burst out laughing.

"The guy from Harlem called, said he'd be down tonight," Flip added in a more serious tone.

"Good," Frankie answered. "We'll find out what he wants."

"Hey, Chippy, Vic, and Billy just walked in with three knockout blondes," Flip announced, setting down the broom and turning his attention toward us.

We started to walk in their direction. Frankie looked up.

The closer I got, the more his face came together. He wore a cobra's smile as he watched me approach. His slicked-back black hair heightened the intensity of his deep-set, hooded Valentino eyes. His medium-size frame was casually dressed in a dark, opened-collar shirt and a light-colored sports coat. A sparkle from his pinkie ring caught my eye as he lifted his glass in slow motion to his mouth. His intense dark eyes never blinked.

"She's the most beautiful girl I've ever seen, Flip," I heard him say. "Look at that face...a porcelain face." Silky long blonde hair rested loosely on my shoulders. Just a little blush of color, thick lashes, pale shade of lipstick. No expression graced my face, except maybe boredom. Frankie seemed awestruck, stunned by his perception of beauty.

But I was oblivious to him. My head was throbbing and I was more than ready to go home. Not once did my eyes linger on his. I stopped two bar stools away from where he stood, sat down, curled my arms on the bar, laid my head down—and tried to fall asleep. In a dreamy state, I occasionally opened my eyes and saw him reflected in the mirror. He stood watching me until Vic appeared at his side.

"Frankie, how's it goin'?"

Irritated by the intrusion, Frankie looked up at Vic and reluctantly came back to reality.

"Where did you find her?" Frankie asked.

Vic thrust his chin out with pride. "Fridays. They arrived on the train today from upstate," he answered.

"She's beautiful..." Frankie's voice trailed off as he shifted his gaze back to me.

"Beautiful, young, and naive, the best kind," Vic replied in a voice he thought I couldn't hear. Frankie shot a disgusted look at Vic, who studied Frankie's face as he stared at me.

"Oh no you don't, Frankie, this one's mine. I found her, so put it back in your pants."

"This one's different, Vic. I'm not asking your permission."

"C'mon, Frankie, I can't compete against your charm. Let's play it clean."

"Back off, Vic. I'm not kidding, really—she's the one."

"Y'know, Frankie, it just ain't fair. Why didn't God make *me* look like Tyrone Power instead of you?"

"Got nothin' to do with God, Vic. You just stayed in the ring a few fights too long. It's amazing you can even breathe outta that thing you call a nose, not to mention what those punches did to your brain. You don't have a chance with this one, my man."

Vic threw his hands in the air. "Okay, you win."

In a twilight sleep, just two feet away, I was only half-aware of my destiny being decided. Little did I know that this was the beginning of a journey that would last a lifetime. Throughout the years I'd remain haunted by the memory of this moment in time.

<hr />

We had no idea how expensive it was to live in New York until we started looking around at different places. Shocked at the money it cost for so little space, we settled for a shabby little place called The Claridon Hotel on East 31st Street between Madison and 5th. The damage was six hundred a month. None of us were thrilled with the place, but we excitedly shopped around, buying throw pillows and pictures and things that gave it a homier, cozy feeling.

The place had one bedroom with dirty walls and a queen-size bed, and a living room with a pull-out couch. The living room window faced the street with a neon sign that kept me awake most nights. In between the two rooms was a sort of kitchenette. In reality, it was a small counter with a few little cupboards and a pint-sized fridge. Not that we would have cooked, but it had no stove and microwave ovens hadn't yet been invented.

Next on our list: find an agent. That wasn't as easy as we'd thought either. None of us were giants in stature. We lacked two inches to make the cut with Willamina and Ford, the top agencies. We weren't the high-fashion *Vogue* types. We possessed what was called a "commercial" look, the all-American, girl-next-door kind of physiognomy.

After two weeks of unsuccessful attempts at securing an agent, Chippy offered us a job tending bar at The Sundowner. With the rent due in two weeks, we accepted. Frankie was delighted. We'd all been out on the town together almost every night since the first night we'd met. They'd taken us to the Play Lounge, Vic's bar in Queens, and out to dinner numerous times. Bino's Tavern was one of the favorite restaurants, with its homemade Italian food cooked with love by the mother of a neighborhood pal of theirs.

Though we hadn't spent any time alone together, Frankie was making it clear that he was more than a little interested in me. I fought it at first, being engaged, but he had an addicting sort of charm that I found irresistible.

Not long after we started working at The Sundowner we managed to find agents. If one of us had an early audition the other would fill in so we could be rested enough to look good and hopefully land the job.

The best times were when we all worked together at The Sundowner. Playing off each other, we brought life into the joint. Kidding with the customers increased business, but it wasn't always fun and games. A lot of shady business was being done in this place. Serious stuff. And these guys weren't always wearing smiles. We learned fast when to stop joking around and fade into the background.

The Sundowner operated as if it were a private club. No money ever passed over the bar. We had cards with code names on them to keep track of who owed what. Frankie's favorite spot to stand was at the end of the bar next to the entrance, not just so he could greet everyone, but so he'd get a jump on trouble coming through the door—and I don't mean from cops. He put on a good show, but he was always on edge.

At times when it would've served him better to be paying attention to business, he'd be staring at me. The heat of his gaze had the required effect. Whenever I looked his way, he'd return my glance with a wink or a steamy smile that made me melt.

Although he had an extremely seductive, easygoing manner, he sometimes displayed a temper. Being very protective of me in the club, he'd be in the face of any guy who got out of line in an instant. Against my will and my better judgment, I was falling deeply in love with Frankie.

By day, we girls pounded the pavement going from one "go-see" to another, vying for modeling jobs. We dragged our heavy portfolios in and out of cabs, up and down countless flights of stairs, and into dirty elevators. By night, we poured drinks for the "wiseguys," who left us huge tips. Georgie Girl, Suzy Q, and Linda Bird were the nicknames they gave us. We only worked three hours a night—from three-thirty till six-thirty in the morning—but always walked out with three to four hundred dollars in tips a night. That we didn't know what we were doing didn't seem to matter. The guys just liked looking at us. Besides, we were like The Three Stooges, a comedy act of our own. Mostly they were Scotch and water drinkers, but if a request ever came for anything really complicated, Frankie or Flip stepped in and helped us.

After closing the bar we'd head for breakfast either somewhere in the neighborhood or in Chinatown. It became a ritual. Our little group: Frankie and me, Billy and Susie Q, Chippy and Linda Bird, and Flip and Vic. Sometimes Tommy Red would join us if he could last that long. Tommy was the only mayonnaise face in the group. A tall, thin Irish guy with curly red hair, jail-pale skin, and a quick wit. He'd grown up with this crew and understood the unspoken language of the streets.

All having the same adventurous spirits, we became inseparable. Sometimes after breakfast, if we didn't have modeling obligations, we'd pile in the car and go to Palisades

Park, or drive to Queens, rent horses, and ride them on the city streets. We hit Aqueduct race track at least once a week, where I acquired my addiction for betting on the horses. Frankie laid down fifty dollars on a horse of my choice. I liked the name. He hated the odds—sixty to one, but he went for it. The horse ran wire-to-wire, paying me about $3,000. You couldn't keep me away from the track after that, and Frankie was convinced I was his good luck charm.

Once we stopped by a laundromat we happened to pass and the guys entertained us by getting into the huge dryers and pretending to do TV commercials. All of the guys were in their late twenties or early thirties, and we were in our teens. Hard to tell at times who acted more their age. Staying up all night and trying to find time to sleep so we could look good for casting calls became a real balancing act.

When we weren't laughing, we were singing. When we weren't singing, we were laughing. We had a favorite song we sang all the time. Growing up together in the harsh city streets, the guys related heavily to the lyrics, and now so did we.

> *Down on the East Side of 33rd and 3rd...*
> *That's my home, sweet, home...*
> *Some people call it the home of black eyes...*
> *That's because guys don't wear collars and ties...*
> *God help collectors when they come to call...*
> *Three flights of stairs is a hell of a fall...*
> *They'd give you their shirts, only they ain't got none...*
> *Down on 33rd and 3rd...*

I was settling quite nicely into my new life. My agent sent me on a go-see for the cover of *Bride's Magazine*. He said I was the preferred model from my composite.

I had taken the night off from the club so I could look fresh for the following day. I arrived on time only to find the elevators on the blink. After hurrying up twelve flights of stairs, I was not only late, but frazzled. *Gotta lighten up on that smoking.*

To my surprise, I was the only model there. The photographer was pleasant, ignoring my tardiness, but his cold, flat eyes were unsettling. He was a powerful looking man: over six feet tall, with a shock of unruly gray hair, craggy features, and a deeply lined face. I felt more comfortable when he turned on the stereo. The vast empty space had an eerie feel to it when it was filled with silence.

He showed me to the dressing room where a magnificent wedding gown hung. He looked amused as I pulled the curtain closed, blocking his view. Models are notorious for stripping down wherever—on an open set, even on a crowded street. No stranger to that behavior, I was still very modest. He busied himself lighting the background while I dressed.

Because it was a test, no money was allotted for hair and make-up, but I preferred it that way. Having had years of practice, I did a pretty good job of it myself. I walked out of the dressing room looking like the picture of purity and stood on the seamless paper waiting for direction.

"You look lovely in that gown," he said, flashing yellow teeth in approval. He snapped a Polaroid and handed me the artwork to view while he waited for the picture to develop. "Here's the layout for the cover, but give it to me the way you feel it."

After inspecting the Polaroid he loaded his Hasselblad and began shooting. I moved in front of him with the mood of the upbeat music, gliding on the paper with pure virginal grace. I felt like an angel in that exquisite gown and gave the camera all the angelic looks I could muster. After walking up twelve flights of stairs with a ten-pound portfolio, it took some imagination.

"Great!" he said. He loaded another roll of film and changed the music on the stereo. "I knew you were the one for this job as soon as your picture crossed my desk. It shoots Tuesday. I've already cleared your schedule with your agent. Let's shoot a few more rolls to satisfy the client, but as far as I'm concerned, you've got the job, honey."

Quietly excited, I acted as though this was an everyday event, but I wanted to jump up and down. I hadn't been in New York for long and I had landed a juicy cover. *Not good enough, huh? I'll show those gossips back home who I am.*

He played with the lighting for a few more minutes and we began to shoot again, but the music wasn't conducive to the mood I was trying to convey. The pace had changed to a slower, more seductive feel.

"Give me something a little more sultry. Pucker your lips and tease me with your eyes," he prompted.

I gave him what he asked for, but it didn't seem to fit. He put his camera down and walked behind me, fluffing my sleeve and smoothing out the wrinkles. He stood back and eyed his work. Shaking his head, he stepped behind me and parochially unzipped the dress, pulling the sleeve off my shoulder. I didn't think this was unusual; stylists always made these kinds of adjustments, but the expressions he requested didn't portray the image for *Bride's Magazine*, I was sure.

My discomfort grew. I felt a tenseness in my stomach, a knife-like feeling of doom. Something was wrong with this picture. I made an excuse that I had another go-see on the other side of town and we'd have to wrap this up soon. He finished the roll and I hurried into the dressing room, pretending to be running late.

"Can I help you undress?" he asked. He pulled open the drape and entered the dressing room, catching me half disrobed.

"No, no thank you. I can manage," I answered, pulling the gown up and holding it tightly to my body.

He creased his forehead, genuinely puzzled. "How about a glass of wine? It'll help you relax."

"I don't have time, I'll be late."

"I think you can miss your next audition for the cover of *Bride's Magazine*. We're paying you enough, aren't we?" he said with a nasty attitude.

"What are you saying?" I fired back.

He threw me a penetrating stare. "Come on, you may look as innocent as apple pie in front of the camera, but you know what's going on here."

I must have looked shocked or maybe I *was* in shock. Realizing I was as innocent as I looked, he became angry and insulting. My heart started beating faster. Feeling trapped, I looked around the room for something I could hurt him with if it came to that.

"Do you really think we pay an outrageous amount of money to you models just for your face? You've got a lot to learn, honey. Five thousand dollars is a lot of money for most hungry women. Now why don't you just relax, take off your clothes, and have some fun," he said, his stupid grin firmly in place.

Oh my God, not again.

Panic set in. My entire body shook as I grabbed for my purse. Reaching inside, I frantically felt around for my nail file. *Oh, God, let it be there.* Finally feeling the thin metal in my hand, I yanked it out and held it inches from the dress, threatening to shred it. My innocent-looking face suddenly changed into the snarl of a vicious animal readying for the kill. "If you don't leave this room right now you're gonna have a lot of explaining to do to your client," I shouted forcefully.

Don't be ridiculous, White! Stab the son-of-a-bitch in the eye! That'll get his attention.

Luckily for me, he backed off. I quickly changed into my street clothes and flew down the twelve flights of stairs in a lot less time than it took to climb up them.

Still trembling, I got to the street and called my agent, blurting out what had happened between deep breaths. At first he was appalled and determined to get to the bottom of it, but later, after speaking to the photographer, he acted as though I had over-dramatized. I vividly recalled that kind of attitude. I'd lived through it before, in a courtroom, just a few months earlier. He was even pissed at me for the loss of his commission! *Damn him!* It infuriated me. I was helpless to do anything about it. What could I do? The photographer hadn't actually done anything, except deepen the trepidation of my already fragile psyche. Reporting him to the police was futile. No one really gave a damn. I just let it go and became more cautious, but I did find another agent.

In all the years I'd been modeling, I had never encountered the casting couch, but the disillusionment stayed with me for a long time. With every booking I wondered if strings were attached. I didn't know if this was just an isolated incident or if these were really the rules in New York.

It didn't take too long to get educated in the Big Apple. As it turned out, it was an isolated incident. Once I shed my naive face I never encountered anything like that again.

I didn't tell Frankie what had happened. Somehow the event would be misconstrued and end up looking like my fault, just like the last time.

My sexual phobias, born from my rape, became more extreme. But the time came when the laughter gave way to a more serious tone, a time when a relationship requires intimacy in order to grow. I was far from the woman my exterior displayed. Sex terrified me. Losing my virginity to a rapist made the idea of sex a dirty, disgusting act.

I panicked when Frankie tried to get closer to me. My body stiffened and I'd pretend to busy myself with something. Like a scared child, I wanted to run away when we were alone together. I did run once, and then felt stupid for doing so. It happened shortly after I started working at The Sundowner. We were sitting in Bino's Tavern and without warning, Frankie pulled me toward him and kissed me. The unexpected force of his hands as he held my shoulders hostage caught me off guard.

Run, run!

My heart rate soared and I literally ran the five blocks back to my apartment, leaving Frankie bewildered and confused. Frankie was the first man to kiss me since I'd been raped. The incident left me questioning my fear. I did like him. In fact, I thought I may even love him. So why was I acting like this? I felt like such a child. In reality, I was.

I showed up at Frankie's apartment an hour later with a bottle of Old Spice cologne and an apology. (I found out later he hated Old Spice.) In the process of trying to explain my actions, I began to recognize the depth of my fear. To his credit, once he became aware, he was sensitive about my unspoken fears. Slowly, he began to gain my trust.

The meaning of love eluded me in my early years. I thought I loved Tom, but I didn't know what it was supposed to feel like. I hadn't yet experienced intimacy—that beautiful experience between two people who care for each other. No, I couldn't be convinced that something so vile was meant to be enjoyed. I wasn't afraid of men. I loved their company. It was the getting naked together part that scared the hell out of me, and I avoided it like the plague.

Frankie and I were about six weeks into a steady relationship. We'd all been out on the town and wound up back at Frankie's apartment. The place was the same kind of set up as we had: a dreary hotel/apartment, but his was even worse than ours. Being there normally depressed me.

Billy was so slouched he had to raise his eyebrows to focus. Then Chippy lit a sweet smelling cigarette. I watched it being passed around and realized it was marijuana. Pot had become quite popular in the past few years, but I had never been around anyone who smoked it. I was afraid at first, but Frankie was assuring, so I watched how it was done and took a few hits.

Everything was so much funnier than before. I started laughing at the craziest things. Of course, Chippy was laughing and crying at the same time, he did that normally. But now he was crawling on the floor. Tears rolled from his eyes as he tried to talk, but nothing but laughter came out. None of us could stop. The night was a blur of laughter.

All of a sudden everyone was gone. I didn't spend much time wondering where they all went. Instead, I shifted my attention to the nightstand, which held five or six burned-out cigarettes balancing on their filters. They looked like little rockets waiting to be launched. I stared at them for a long time, off on a space trip.

Frankie led me to the bare, soot-covered window. We climbed

out onto the fire escape, where we sat for what seemed like hours and gazed at the stars. He called them diamonds in the sky, and every one of them had a story.

Whether due to Frankie or the drug, I felt a new world opening before my eyes. He had an extraordinary way of telling a story—even when I wasn't high. He made me look at everything so differently. Frankie, being nine years older, had a lot more knowledge about the world than I did. Having incredible insights, he looked at things more deeply than most people, or at least I saw it that way. There was a great deal of color to the world he viewed, and he taught me how to see it clearly. I was as wide open and as eager to learn as he was to teach me. Almost like a child being told a fairy tale, I'd be captivated for hours listening to him. He'd lead me through a detailed story, painting pictures in my mind, heightening my awareness of the world around me.

I saw a Frankie rarely seen by his peers, and learned a lot about the man himself through his stories. With every story he told, I fell more in love. I came to the conclusion he was a good man in a bad world. Deep in his core he was a gentle, decent man with an enormous love and appreciation for life, but he was caught in a darkness for which he had no escape. Having little choice, he accepted this life and learned to survive there.

While I gazed at the stars, Frankie nibbled at my neck. Turning my face, I kissed him. My sense of touch was heightened. I wasn't afraid. Rather than sickening me, his hands on my breast felt unusually natural.

I was in a daydream state as he carried me to the bed. Tracing his face lightly with my fingers, I traveled with wonder in the limitless depth of his intense brown eyes. I felt as though he was familiar, as if I'd known the taste and feel of him from a dimension I'd never before explored. Closing my eyes, I blindly let his gentle hands explore the soft curves of my body. The world went still with his touch as we got lost in the ecstasy of making love. With none of the usual fears, I gave of myself in a way I never thought possible. Love in the purest form.

Afterward I had to sort out the half-realized desires and

denials that churned within me. *Did this mean I was a whore now? Had I just validated what the gossips had been saying all along? What must Frankie think?* Guys didn't respect girls who weren't virgins before they got married.

Sexual demons still play in my mind, but for that brief moment I was aware of how intimacy is supposed to be. After that night I knew what I felt for Tom wasn't love. I could not marry him, but I would wait until he was out of Vietnam before I told him. To tell him now would be too cruel. I continued to write him, but my letters became less frequent.

As Frankie and I became closer he became more of a mystery. I wasn't as naive to his lifestyle as he perceived me to be. I'd been around it before. But I didn't fully understand how it all worked, and Frankie gave no clues. In his constant secrecy, he separated me from that side of his life, causing a huge gap in our relationship. I needed to be intimate with the whole man, not just the face he chose for me to see. He disappeared from time to time, sometimes hours, sometimes days, and danced around my questions. My prodding produced vague answers. When I pushed, he resorted to some lame silliness or just stopped speaking altogether.

On a modeling assignment one day, the make-up person did a great job. I usually hated how they made me up, but it was just one of those days when I looked and felt good about myself. I didn't want to waste this make-up job without having Frankie appreciate it. I called him from the studio and we made plans to meet at Bino's for dinner. He sounded as if he couldn't wait to see me. I loved being with him. He was always so complimentary and proud to be with me, making me feel so special.

After my photo session I rushed to the restaurant, only to sit there for three hours staring at the door. He never showed. Disappointed? You bet. Rosa, Bino's mom, tried to make me understand in her broken English that this behavior was normal with all of her son's friends and I shouldn't worry.

Later, Susie Q and I sat on the floor of our apartment flicking through the pages of *Vogue* while Linda Bird got dressed for a date. "Where're you going tonight, tramp?" Susie Q asked kiddingly.

"To dinner with that rich hunk I met last week. He's not as much fun as traipsing around with you girls, but at least I'll eat a good meal. How do I look?" she asked, brushing a lock of hair from her forehead as she checked herself out in the mirror.

"You look great," I said with just the right amount of sincerity. My mind was still on Frankie. My frustration had eased, but my curiosity was getting the better of me. When the phone rang, I pounced on it.

"Hi, baby."

"Frankie, damn you! I waited three hours for you today. Where were you?"

"I know, baby, I'm sorry. I got tied up."

"Doing what?"

Susie Q stirred her tea vigorously, totally engrossed in the confrontation. She wanted to know too.

"Pass the dice, baby. You know better than to ask questions."

"Why does everything have to be such a secret, Frankie?" I asked, feeling excluded from his life. He tried to gloss over it with his easygoing manner.

"C'mon, Georgie Girl, somethin' came up. I'm sorry I had to leave you hangin', but it couldn't be helped." Changing the subject, he added in a playful tone, "Flip's gonna sing with the band at the Play Lounge tonight. Why don't you see if the girls want to go?"

"Frankie, I can't stand this anymore. I need to know who you are. Every time I—"

"Look, Georgie Girl," he interrupted, suddenly becoming serious, "I'm a man of two faces, honey. There's things I gotta do I have no say about. I *can't* discuss it, and I *won't*. You're not blind, baby. You've been around me long enough t'get a sense of who I am, so please, stop asking questions that can't be answered," he said coolly. After a long pause, he added, "Now c'mon, let's just go out tonight and have a good time, okay?"

Although I tried to abide by his rule, my irritation over the secrecy was evident. To appease me, he started taking me with him to some of his meetings during the day. He called them *sit-downs*. I waited at the bar while he huddled in smoky booths with men of Italian descent. I was finally getting a look at the mysterious life he led.

At one meeting it looked like a federation of gangsters. A few were dressed casually in sport shirts and slacks, but most wore suits, starched shirts, and jewelry the average hood wouldn't hesitate to kill for. Becoming invisible, I chatted with the bartender as I inconspicuously watched them, fascinated.

A thin, gray-haired man with beady eyes and a big nose made an entrance with a newspaper tucked under his arm. He was a small man, only weighing about 130 pounds, but he was apparently a big man to everyone there. They practically bowed to him. He didn't look like a king, dressed casually in a dark blue button down sweater with a collared shirt fastened at the neck, but if there was a chain of command, he was at the top. He sat silently, shifting his steely gaze often, speaking without saying a word.

The others were more animated than the mysterious gray-haired man. Many spoke Italian, others, broken English. The majority, though, spoke in the familiar New York "tough guy" slang I'd come to know. Only fragments of conversation could be heard, but the language created with their hands revealed a lot, especially the forefinger sliding across the throat. It didn't take a rocket scientist to figure that one out. And the gray-haired man just nodded.

I watched as the conversation got heated, but when they got up to leave they acted as though they were great friends, hugging and patting each other with affection. However, common sense said that one wrong move could easily turn them into treacherous enemies devoid of conscience. Their presence exuded a power that was undeniable.

As strange as it sounds, they intrigued me. They played into my enormous appetite for adventure of the unknown, along with the natural curiosity that integrates with youth. After the meeting I quizzed Frankie about the men.

"Who was that little guy with the gray hair, Frankie?"

"Nobody, baby," he answered.

"He didn't look like *nobody* to me," I said, trying to prompt an honest answer.

"Georgie Girl...C'mon now, you promised you wouldn't ask questions if I took you with me," he reminded.

I wanted to know everything about Frankie because I loved him. And I hated the secrecy. But a side to his life existed that he had no choice but to keep secret.

My afternoon outings ended the day he took me along to meet with two men.They were not the typical kind of characters he usually met with. These two guys were in suits obviously bought off the rack, with pens in their pockets and dime store shades. Clean-cut, respectable sorts. Respectable was questionable. Even I could spot a cop in plain clothes. They were the Commissioner's men.

Frankie had somehow managed to go above the Division, above the Bureau, as high as you could go—the Police Commissioner. Just about any cop in New York could be bought, that was a given, but at that level of the law, secrecy was essential.

The two suits looked at each other in astonishment when we walked through the door of the 23rd Street Bar & Grill on the West Side. Frankie immediately knew he'd made a stupid move. He hurried me to a corner booth out of view and approached them. I was out of view, but not out of earshot. I peeked through the plastic plants and watched as they confronted him.

"What's with the broad?" said the heavy-set man, demanding an answer.

"She's just a kid, she doesn't know anything," Frankie said.

Standing up, the taller one spouted, "You want protection, make another appointment! Another time, another place." As they walked out the door they both looked back, glaring disgustedly, leaving Frankie unprotected—at least for the moment.

After-hours clubs in Manhattan were big business, and everyone had their hands out. Police protection did not mean safety from the wiseguys, either. Frankie had to contend with their demands as well, and they demanded a great deal more than a fair share. Fortunately, Frankie had some heavy people behind him. But staying a step ahead of the discontented enemy was a constant struggle. He was always looking over his shoulder. Moving against the grain, he rubbed some bad people the wrong way. Frankie stood firm, giving them a generous cut, but also realizing that greed rules in the underworld.

———◆———

A quiet night in the club, unusual for a Saturday. Many unoccupied stools lined the long bar, and with no one feeding the jukebox the back room remained quiet and dark. It was kind of lonesome without the usual customers. Even little Flip wasn't there, and he hardly ever missed a night. His smiling face and constant teasing was greatly missed. Susie Q had gone home for the weekend, and Linda Bird had a hangover and had taken the night off. I was alone behind the bar, and it wasn't much fun without my sidekicks. No one seemed to be in a laughing mood. The florescent lighting under the bar cast an illuminating coldness in direct contrast to the dim red light that filled the rest of the room.

Small groups of men huddled together in heavy conversation. Something was brewing. The atmosphere had felt tense from the moment I'd arrived. I couldn't put my finger on it, but a strangeness hovered.

The wiseguy from Harlem came through the door. Sensing trouble, Frankie immediately approached him. They were having heated words, but I was too far away to hear what was being said. The Harlem hood thrust out his jaw, ready for battle. Frankie retorted, determined to get the upper hand. Irritated, the big man walked away from Frankie and bellied up to the bar, pushing the stool back to make room for his protruding gut. His left eye twitched as he ran a hand over his balding head, a sure sign he was severely angry.

"Gimme a drink," he demanded, treating me to his insane expression.

I knew this guy was an irritant to Frankie, but I had no idea why. I didn't like him for my own reasons. He gave me the creeps. His eyes were as cold as an Arctic winter and he was never very pleasant, throwing his weight around and demanding respect. I poured him his usual, V.O. and soda. I set it in front of him and moved down the bar, giving him privacy for an ensuing argument with the man sitting beside him. The next thing I knew, he pulled out a gun and aimed it at the man. My mind registered the sight, but I couldn't move. I couldn't scream. I couldn't even get out of the way. All I could do was stand there, paralyzed with fear.

One shot, two...The man fell, but my focus was on the gun. So fast. *What? What happened?* Stunned, I stood frozen in place, not fully realizing what was happening. My mind couldn't grasp the reality.

Suddenly I was being pulled. Frankie was practically dragging me out the door. Another shot sounded as we reached the stairs. On the street, we headed for the corner and made the turn. Halfway down the block we ducked into a doorway. He trembled as he held me.

The wiseguy turned and slowly walked out of the club, silently warning anyone who made eye contact to keep their mouths shut if they knew what was good for them. As soon as he left the building, everyone fled.

"Holy shit!" Frankie uttered.

I started to turn, but he grabbed my head with both his hands, holding it inches from his face. Terror reflected in his eyes as he shielded my vision.

"Just kiss me. It's him. He still has the gun," he whispered. "Whatever you do, *don't* look at him."

My heartbeat soared. I closed my eyes and kissed Frankie as if it were our last kiss. It could have been. But the man rushed past us, not taking much notice. When he was clearly out of view, we raced back to the club.

Billy was hunched over the body when we walked in. The color had gone from his face as he looked up with a desperate expression.

"Fuck! We should've seen this coming, Frankie."

Frankie bent down to take the man's pulse.

"Oh my God! Frankie, is he dead?" I cried, trying to keep in control, but my entire body was shaking. I'd seen dead bodies before, but not from this kind of violence.

"I think he's still alive," he answered, frantically searching his pockets for his car keys. "You okay to drive?"

"Yeah, I...I think so," I answered, still trembling.

"Get the car. Pull it up front. Make it fast, Georgie Girl. The cops will be here any minute. C'mon, Billy, help me get him outta here."

"What about the blood, Frankie, shouldn't we—"

"No time, Billy. Let's just get 'em the hell out." Frankie grabbed under his arms, and Billy grabbed his legs. They struggled to get him down the stairs.

Five-thirty in the morning—not long before the sun came up. Remaining anonymous was crucial, no question. They finally got him into Frankie's borrowed car and we sped off to Bellevue Hospital. Georgia Black came to the rescue. I wasn't allowed to think of the life draining from the man in the back seat. We had a job to do.

Get to the hospital—fast! There's a cop! Turn left. Slowly now, don't blow it. Okay, good. Coast is clear. Hit it.

"You're doin' good, baby, you're doin' good. Take it easy now, we don't wanna attract attention," Frankie said, trying to act calm as he glanced back at Billy and the wounded man.

I drove brusquely, handling the car as though it needed to be taught a lesson, getting us there without incident. When we arrived at the hospital's emergency entrance, Billy and Frankie dragged the man from the car and left him lying lifeless on the sidewalk. We didn't know if he was still living or not. Frankie leaned on the horn for a short time, hoping to bring attention to the man and not to us.

"Step on it, baby!" Frankie shouted.

I drove swiftly away from the scene. "Do you think he's going to live, Frankie?" I asked, on the verge of tears. Georgia Black had retreated. Job done.

"You better hope so, or I'm in deep shit. Drive by the club."

I turned on East 23rd. From two blocks away we saw the red lights flashing in front of the building.

"Shit," Frankie muttered.

"Drop me off at Bino's, Georgie Girl," Billy said. "Christ, Frank, we needed this like we need a hole in our heads." I pulled in front of Bino's Tavern on 2nd Avenue and Billy exited the car. "Call me when you hear something," he said, slamming the door and heading up the stairs from the Tavern to Bino's apartment.

"Get a hold of Flip," Frankie instructed. "Tell him I'll meet him at the Abbey at nine o'clock."

"Frankie, you drive," I said, when Billy shut the car door.

"Why, baby? You're a natural behind the wheel. Good enough to make a career of it. Pays good, too."

"It's all a blank. I have no idea how I got there."

"Well, you did. And in record time!"

Frankie fell silent as we drove down Madison Avenue toward my apartment on East 31st Street. I pulled in front of my building, put the car in park, took a deep breath and expelled it with a deep sigh.

"That bastard!" Frankie spat, slamming his fist on the dash.

"Who, Frankie?"

"The wiseguy from Harlem, who else? The son-of-a-bitch probably did this so the cops would shut me down. I wouldn't put it past 'em—those bastards. You've gotta get out of here, Georgie Girl. Pack your clothes, I'm taking you to the airport."

"I don't want to leave you, Frankie."

"I don't want you involved. They're gonna question all witnesses. You are a witness. I want you outta here."

"I didn't see a thing."

"You're goin'. Don't argue. I'll have to take the heat any way you look at it, but there's no need to drag you into this mess. I don't know what you're doing with a guy like me anyway."

"Frankie, what are you talking about?"

"This is no kind of life for you, Georgie Girl. You deserve a lot more than I can ever give you. This is my world, honey. Always was, always will be. It's the only world I know. I don't have the right to bring you into it."

"Frankie, what are you saying?"

"Go home, honey. Stay there if you know what's good for you."

"Frankie, I know you love me. How can you say that?"

"*Because* I love you," he said, wanting me to understand.

"You're just upset over what happened. You don't mean that, I know you don't."

He looked at me and didn't say anything. His mind was somewhere else. I wanted to be with him, but it was out of the question. Knowing what he was facing, worrying about me was a burden he didn't need. I packed my clothes, but had every intention of returning. He just wasn't thinking clearly, I knew that.

Before my flight had landed in Rochester, Frankie was in custody. Flip and Billy called to keep me posted. The charge was attempted murder. The police confiscated the cards we used to keep track of the bar tabs. They had a mug shot to go with every code name we had. They obviously knew who came and went; it wasn't that they weren't aware the club existed. They brought in a stream of potential witnesses, but nobody was talking. The cops on the beat were uptight, but not as much as the Commissioner's men, who were afraid the investigation would blow their cover. Every day Frankie was led from his cell and questioned for hours. They knew he didn't do it, but they were sure he knew who did.

CHAPTER FOUR

---<o>---◀●▶---<o>---

"Jerry Vale's at the Copa tomorrow night," said the voice on the phone. It was eleven in the morning but I was still asleep when the phone rang. "I'll take you if you wear that white dress."

"Frankie!" I hadn't heard his voice in two weeks.

"Hi, baby. I'm out."

"Oh, Frankie, are you all right?" I asked, concerned.

"Of course. 'A horse is a horse, of course, of course...' I need to see you, baby. Can you get here faster than a speeding bullet?"

"Let's not talk about bullets, Frankie." The victim of The Sundowner shooting still remained on the critical list, but it looked as though he was going to live. "I can be there on the 8 a.m. plane."

"Lots of things for me to do, so hop in a cab to 502," he said as though he were reciting a poem. 502 was Frankie's apartment on East 26th Street.

My mother and father had been ecstatic to have me home, but they knew I'd fly off again soon. They worried about me constantly. They didn't know about the shooting, but they knew the dangers for a young girl alone in New York. Like most parents, they wanted to cloak me in protection.

After hearing from Frankie I was so relieved. I couldn't sleep all night thinking about seeing him. Getting up extra early, I spent a long time in front of the mirror, making sure my make-up was perfect before getting on the plane.

Exiting the cab in front of Frankie's building, I bumped into an old man shuffling his feet, inching his cane along the sidewalk. "Watch where you're going, stupid broad," he sneered.

Tin cans and spilled garbage littered the curb. A derelict with skin the color of bruised parchment huddled in a doorway, speaking grandly to the sky. Ah, New York. It was good to be back.

The elevator was broken again, forcing me to walk the five flights lugging my bags. If I had been any more out of breath, I'd have been dead. In the lightless hallway a broken TV leaned against the wall. I could smell a lingering odor of deli food as I turned the key and pushed open the door.

Inside, the sparsely furnished room depressed me. White plaster showed through the dirt-streaked yellow paint on the ceiling. No plants. No signs of life. Dingy. Dark. If Frankie had to disappear in a hurry, he'd have no problem. Or maybe this was the place he would disappear to.

Minutes turned into hours. I waited. I busied myself cleaning up the diminutive place, emptying ashtrays loaded with stale cigarettes and hanging up clothes that had been haphazardly strewn around the room. He finally arrived, looking pale and exhausted. No need for words. His lengthy hug told me how much he'd missed me. But then he became distant.

"Where were you, Frankie?"

"I had to do somethin'."

"Something? That's all you can say? Couldn't you at least call? It's been so long since I've seen you. Weren't you anxious to see—"

"Georgie Girl, I couldn't call. Please, don't question me, okay?"

Hurt and disappointed, I gnawed like a dog on a bone. "I don't understand why you're always so secretive. Why can't you—"

"Drop it," he said in a tone that stopped me cold.

Obviously on edge about something, he walked out of the room. He'd never spoken to me with this tone before. I watched his reflection in the bedroom mirror as he took a gun from inside his jacket and placed it in a drawer.

"C'mon," he said, "I wanna take you somewhere."

He was aware of his cranky attitude and was making an effort to change his mood. I had a sinking sensation in my stomach, never having seen him with a gun before. I thought I knew something about his secret life, but the reality of this sight made me aware of how much I didn't know.

We walked to Saks Fifth Avenue, where he bought me an outfit he had seen in the window and said I *must* have. I didn't argue. Shopping was my favorite activity. But this time was different. Frankie didn't seem to be on the same planet as me. As much as he smiled, I could tell he was deeply troubled.

"You're not going to believe what those rat bastards did to the club," he said in a resentful tone as we got to the street.

"What did they do?"

"You'll see," he answered, extending his arm to hail a cab.

As we walked up the dimly lit stairs to the club, I didn't know what I was expecting to see, but it wasn't what I saw, that's for sure. My mouth hung open as I scanned the room. I still had a lot to learn about cops. They had taken the liquor and most of the tables and chairs, probably to furnish their basements, but what they had left was completely destroyed. They'd used an ax to tear down the bar. Shattered glass lay strewn from the smashed cigarette machine and the jukebox. The few remaining barstools were slashed, stuffing covering the floor like a blanket of snow. The drapery material was pulled from the walls, exposing the decaying brick. Total destruction. I glanced at Frankie's disgusted face. He looked so lost and defeated.

"What are you going to do?" I asked, feeling sick as my eyes focused on the large brown spot on the floor.

"I guess I'll just do...what I do."

"What *is* it that you do, Frankie?"

"Don't start that, Georgie Girl. C'mon, let's get out of here."

"No, Frankie, I need some answers. I'm tired of the guessing games. You need to let me into your life or this relationship is going to die."

He stared at me in silence for a long time before he spoke.

"There ain't no easy way t'say this, so I'll try an' give it t'you straight. Y'know what I was doin' when you were flying here from Rochester? I was pullin' a robbery! And I came damn close to killin' a guy. Is that the kind of man you want to spend the rest of your life with, Georgie Girl? Even if you think it is, you deserve better than me. I got nothin' to offer you, honey. I'm not proud of who I am, but these pricks leave me no choice. None of 'em will let me make an honest buck!"

I didn't care; I was too much in love at this point to shut down my feelings. *He'll get over this. Everything will be like it was before.*

Later that night, the line outside the Copa Cabana was unusually long. Spotted by the doorman, we were lead to a side entrance and through the kitchen to a waiting table. Waiters respectfully acknowledged Frankie as they hurried past us with heavy trays. Frankie discreetly stuck a $50 bill in the doorman's palm and the man disappeared. Jerry Vale joined our table for a few minutes before he went on.

"Sing my girl's favorite song, Jerr," Frankie instructed as Jerry was being announced.

For a short time the old Frankie was present, but the more Scotch we consumed the more distant he became. I hoped he would soon return to his normal self.

<hr/>

After calling my agent and telling him I was back, I quickly fell back into my New York routine, running all day from go-see to go-see, lugging my portfolio.

Susie Q had gone to see Ralph where he was stationed in California after the shooting. They eloped while she was there and she never returned to New York. Linda Bird had been seeing some rich guy and stayed at his place through all the turmoil. She decided she liked being taken care of and moved in with him permanently. I was on my own. Everything had changed so drastically.

I still kept the apartment, and I spent most of my time with Frankie. But Frankie was different. The Sundowner was now gone, along with the "good-time charlie" with whom I'd fallen in love. Frankie looked at life from a different perspective now.

Facing the reality of his life, he battled with himself constantly. He said I had a bright future ahead of me and he wanted me to taste all the good things that were surely in store for me.

Thinking about it now, it took a lot of strength on his part to do what he thought was honorable. But I didn't see it then. I thought that I was the one who wasn't good enough. I didn't understand that he was protecting me from a life that was too dark. He constantly reminded me that he was no good for me.

We still laughed and did silly things, like go to the top of the Empire State building and fall into hysterics when I tried to talk him into bonking old ladies on the top of their heads with quarters.

"If we bonk old ladies from here, baby, those rat bastards *will* make a murder charge stick. We'd better hang with bonking from the Ferris Wheel."

When he'd catch himself giving in to his heart, he'd pull back. I could feel him distance himself from me, yet I sensed that behind the facade he really loved me. Feeling this way, I was reluctant to let go.

After a few months of mental torture I decided to return to Rochester, hoping Frankie would miss me and ask me to come back.

"Frankie, I'm going home," I blurted out, hoping to get some sort of positive reaction.

He stared at me in mournful silence. It's what he ultimately wanted, but he couldn't bring himself to force the issue.

"I guess we both knew this day was comin'," he finally said.

Tears streaked both of our faces as we embraced.

"I do love you, Georgie Girl," he said, holding me firmly with his head resting against mine.

"I know," I answered, my heart breaking. "But I need all of you, Frankie."

The following day he borrowed his cousin's car and drove me to the airport. Hanging on desperately to our final minutes together, I waited for the very last passenger to board the plane. My blood pumped hard when the announcement came.

"This is the final boarding call for flight #67 to Rochester."

Trying to exhibit strength, Frankie squeezed my hand and

encouraged me to pick up life where I had left it before I met him. Fighting tears, we kissed for one last time before I walked down the long narrow walkway. I turned back one final time before disappearing into the plane. The sight of his face pierced my heart and I could no longer hold back my tears.

"See ya when I see ya, baby," he said, forcing a smile.

I hadn't been gone from Rochester all that long, but I was light years away from the innocent little girl who'd boarded that train such a short time ago. It seemed like an eternity had passed. I tried hard to adjust.

New York City was on another planet. Rochester was like a recurring nightmare. Nothing had changed. Eight months had passed since the rape, yet it was as if it had happened yesterday in these townspeople's minds. Heartbroken over my shattered love affair and dealing with the simple minds of the gossips, my depression became severe.

Upon walking into Woods Drug Store I noticed people staring at me, whispering. When they saw me looking they got quiet. I knew the difference between the stares of admiration and the gossiping stares. These were the vicious kind. People who smiled to my face and then danced around the flames while they burned me at the stake in the village square.

My sister Sharon was barely coping with all the rumors that had followed the rape. Maybe it was just my imagination, but I sensed she held me responsible for what she'd had to face.

Even through all the ugliness, Sharon loved this town. If her thoughts ever strayed beyond the boundaries of home, they only reinforced the feeling that she wanted to lay within them. But the walls that were so comforting to her were the same walls I desperately needed to escape.

I was once again subjected to the same things I had defended myself from since childhood, only now I was beginning to convince myself there might be some truth to these rumors. I wasn't the pure, innocent child I had been when they first had such cruel things to say. Maybe they were right. Maybe that's why Frankie didn't want me. Maybe no one ever would. Maybe I wasn't good enough anymore.

I continued to seek friendship in the city, where I was accepted, away from the whispers of a small town. The dark people of the underworld had become my friends because they opened the door—and allowed me entry. But even *they* weren't helping my depression.

I stopped eating and began sleeping a lot. Facing the long days was almost intolerable. I thought of ways to end my life, but that would only make *them* the winners, wouldn't it? I wrote letters to Tom describing the anxiety of what I was experiencing. He wrote back, professing his love and apologizing for not being there to comfort me. Nothing he could say would cheer me up. My mother and father thought I might be suicidal. They watched me sink rapidly into a deep depression. Although they tried the best they could to help, nothing worked.

On a gray Saturday morning in December the doorbell rang, awakening me from a heavy sleep. I looked at the clock next to my bed. It was 1 p.m. Still hung over from a late night at The Living Room, I stumbled down the stairs in my flannel nightgown. Rubbing the sleep from my puffy eyes I opened the door. To my amazement, Tom was standing on the other side, handsomely dressed in his Army uniform.

The war hadn't hardened his boyish face. His normally thick black hair that had clung to his head in soft waves was now short, accentuating his perfect features.

"Tom? What are you doing home?" I stood there in shock, not believing what I was seeing.

"I came home to marry you and take you away from all this."

"What? I don't understand. How did you—"

"Are you going to let me in, or do I have to stand out here and freeze my ass off?"

Scooping me up in his muscular arms, he kissed me passionately. Still stunned, I didn't quite know how to respond, but I felt uncommonly safe and secure in his arms. I'd forgotten how handsome he was. His soft doe eyes spoke volumes about his feelings.

"Marry me, Georgia," he said, looking deeply into my eyes.

"Uh...When?" Panicked, I looked away, my heart racing with mixed emotions. I didn't think I loved him. How could I? I loved Frankie. *But Frankie doesn't want me. Will anyone ever want me?*

"Well, I've only got two weeks."

"I...It's so—"

"Just say yes," he said, not understanding my hesitation. He knew nothing about my real life in New York. I needed to talk to Frankie. I had to hear him say that he didn't want me. I couldn't give Tom an answer without knowing for sure.

"We don't have a lot of time, Georgia," he said, pulling me back into his arms. "I want to protect you and love you, honey. We were going to get married anyway after I got home, so why not now?"

"Just give me a day to think about this."

Tom didn't detect anything strange about my reaction. He explained that he had shown my letters to his commanding officer and he had been given a compassionate leave. I hadn't realized just how depressed I'd become, but according to Tom, his superiors thought my mental condition was serious enough to grant him a leave.

That night I called Frankie. We still talked frequently, but his lifestyle hadn't changed. A future with him didn't look promising, but I still hadn't lost hope.

"Hi, Frankie," I said, not sure how to begin.

"Hi, baby."

"Frankie, Tom's home."

"Did he get shot?"

"No. He came home to...to marry me."

Minutes passed before he spoke. All I could hear was the distant wail of sirens from the city street.

Finally he said, "Well...maybe it's for the best, baby."

We both got quiet. I imagined Frankie looking out his window, listening as the December wind funneled icily up the canyon of buildings. Through the silence I could almost feel the hollow sadness that filled his heart. I laid on my bed, staring at our picture from the evening at the Copa Cabana and quietly wondering why it had all fallen apart.

"Frankie, do you love me?"

"Baby...I love you more than I ever loved anybody. That's not true—I never was in love till I met you, but Georgie Girl, what kind of life can you have with me? I've never been able to explain it to you right, 'cause there's so many things I can't talk about, but you gotta just trust me on this, okay? Marry him, honey. Have kids, be happy. I'll always love you. What we have together can never be taken away."

"Frankie, tell me something—truthfully. Does it have anything to do with my not being a virgin when we met?"

"C'mon, Georgie Girl, will you stop that? It's got nothin' to do with the way I feel about us. Those people in that town of yours really got your head screwed up. It's about what you deserve out of life—and I'm sure as hell not it. You can't see it now, honey, but someday you'll understand. It hurts me just as bad to let you go, but I gotta do it."

"I don't get it, Frankie. How can you tell me to get married if you say you love me? There *has* to be another reason."

"It's not because I *don't* love you, baby, it's because I *do*. Can't you see that?" he said, sounding melancholy. "You're making it very hard for me, Georgie Girl. All I want is for you to be happy."

Four days later, Tom and I were married by a Justice of the Peace. We drove to a honeymoon resort in the Poconos. Set in a romantic, woodsy atmosphere tailored for honeymooners, the rooms all had heart-shaped bathtubs and a bottle of cheap champagne.

Everywhere I looked I saw recently married couples in love. They depressed me. Watching them together made me realize how I'd gotten married for all the wrong reasons. I loved Tom, but not the way I once thought I had. Grateful for the cheap champagne, I made it through the week and resigned myself to making the best of it. Maybe it would get better.

When we returned from the Poconos, my mother and father

had planned the big wedding. Amazing how they pulled it together in such a short time. We got married again in a church with all the trimmings. The reception was at Braemar Country Club, the place Mom and Dad had been running. My mother did all the cooking. She was used to putting on large parties. With the help of all my aunts, it came off beautifully.

Both my mother and father were happy about the marriage. They had watched me sink deeper and deeper into depression and thought this was the answer to snapping me out of it.

Two days after the second wedding, Tom returned to Vietnam. One month after he left, I discovered that I was pregnant. Just what I needed. The gossips had a field day.

Sammy G stopped by my new apartment on Empire Boulevard in Webster at least once a week with his arms full of groceries. The suburb of Webster was only fifteen minutes from East Rochester, but my parents still thought I was too far away. My mother was so excited about a new grandchild she found it hard to contain herself. I had continued to work for as long as possible before I began to show, but by the sixth month I had to stop. I spent the days visiting my family in East Rochester. Sharon came over quite a bit, which was a real show of love. To her, leaving East Rochester was like leaving the country.

"Sammy, I'm okay, really, you don't need to buy me food. Besides, I'm too fat already!"

"Ah, shut up. Break out the cannolis and put the coffee on. You got this place lookin' like it belongs in a magazine," he said, eyeing my new, ultra-modern furniture.

Since I could no longer spend my money on clothes, I emptied my account on an apartment, furniture, and a new car. When the money stopped coming in, I relied on the one hundred and twenty-two dollars a month the government allotted for military wives.

"Why don't you go into the decoratin' business? You got an eye for it, kid," Sammy said, touching one of the several stands of hanging crystal balls that separated the brightly furnished living room from the dining area.

"What I'd like to do someday is go to college, Sammy. Really get a good education."

He took a sip of coffee. "Ah, whatta ya need that for? You got street smarts. You can't buy that kind of education. Besides, if you get too book smart, you won't want nothin' to do with us guys anymore. You don't need to be smart for your modeling, just beautiful, and you ain't got a problem in that department," he said, setting his coffee cup down on the glass table.

"I *don't* have a problem, Sam, not ain't."

"See what I mean? You get educated, and before you know it, I won't understand a damn thing you're sayin'."

"Well, Sam, I don't think you have anything to worry about," I said, looking down at my protruding stomach.

"It's gonna be a girl, I can feel it," he said, gently placing his hand on my belly.

"I think so, too."

"God help me if she takes after her mother. I got enough problems just watchin' out for you. The last thing I need is *two* of you." He paused and pressed his hand over mine. Staring at me with his intense eyes, he gently asked, "Are you happy, kid?"

No, I wasn't happy. I was miserable. Stuck in a boring life in a boring city. I hated Rochester. Now that I knew there was more, I couldn't see living this existence forever.

The phone rang before I could answer him, saving me from a lie. Evidently Sammy had told someone where he'd be; the call was for him. While Sam was on the phone I busied myself putting the groceries away and thought about the talk I had with Tom on our honeymoon. His plan was to go back to Kodak and work in their factory.

The thought of being stuck in Rochester for the rest of my life depressed me, and the news of my pregnancy put the lid on my coffin. There was no escape.

After Sam hung up, his mood became serious. "I want you to do me a favor, kid."

"Sure, Sam, what do you need?"

"You go to Nicky's place a lot, don't you?"

Nicky owned The Overlook, a bar and restaurant next door to my apartment complex. It was another of the many Mob hangouts in the outer areas of the city.

"Well, yeah, it's right next door. Great hamburgers. I have lunch there frequently, why?"

"You ever see Tommy DiDio there?"

Tommy DiDio was one of Valenti's boys, the current boss of the Rochester Syndicate.

"Once in a while. He's usually there at night, though. I've seen him there a few times when I've run in to pick up an order. They have great baked ziti, too, ever try it?"

He ignored the question. Pulling back the pale yellow sheered curtains, he gazed out my picture window. "You have a perfect view of the Overlook from here."

"Yeah, I've seen some pretty nasty fights from that window a few times."

"If you happen to see DiDio pull in, casually walk over there and keep your eyes an' ears open. I want to know who he's meetin' with, and if you can get close enough without being conspicuous, find out what they're talkin' about."

"Conspicuous? That's a good word."

"This is serious, Georgia. I need a little help here."

Sammy had never asked a favor like this before, so I knew it had to be important, but I felt uneasy about it.

"That guy gives me the creeps, Sammy. I hate the way he looks at me with that demented glare. Just the sight of him makes me go cold inside. He looks like the type of man that could stab his own mother and watch a football game while she bled to death. I avoid him, and he knows it. He might get suspicious if I suddenly sit near him, and besides, how do I not look conspicuous with this stomach?"

"What'd I just get through sayin', kid? You got street smarts—you'll handle it. Georgia...It's important."

Three days later I spotted Tommy DiDio's car in the parking lot of The Overlook. I waddled over and sat at a table as close to

the bar as I could get. I ordered a double cheeseburger, French fries, and onion rings. To top it off, I had a chocolate milk shake that Nicky threw in on the house. It was so thick I could feel my face turn purple as I tried to sip it through the straw. I finally gave up and used a spoon. I still had a few months to go and I'd already gained close to forty pounds. Nicky watched with amusement as I eagerly stuffed myself. My appetite was enormous—so was I.

I only got fragments of the conversation, but apparently they were the key words Sammy needed to hear. Something about Frank Valenti and the boys in Utica, and something about money that wasn't accounted for. None of it made any sense to me, but when I repeated it to Sammy he didn't look happy. He pulled an envelope from his pocket and handed it me. It contained five crisp $100 bills.

"What's this for?" I asked.

"Buy somethin' for the kid, or put it away for the schoolin' you never got."

He kissed my forehead and walked out the door.

————◆————

In October of 1969, few months after my nineteenth birthday, I gave birth to my daughter, Toni. Tom had returned from Vietnam shortly before she was due. At eighty miles per hour, he sped me to the hospital at three o'clock in the morning. I continuously cursed him for driving so slow. Less than an hour after we arrived, Toni was born.

Everyone thought she was beautiful. I thought she looked like Mr. Magoo. But she did get cuter. Her full head of pitch-black hair fell out and grew back in platinum blonde, but her eyebrows and thick, long lashes remained black. It was the oddest thing. Within a month's time she became strikingly beautiful.

A child myself, grasping the reality of the responsibility of motherhood didn't come as natural as my mother had said it would, but this little girl brought with her a joy that had never touched my heart before. For hours I would watch her sleep, touching her fingers and toes, like a kid with a new doll.

Even with the miracle of a child, I still felt trapped and robbed of my youth. I struggled with my selfish thoughts, but so much of the life I'd envisioned had been painfully lost. I had missed out on the publicity tours that went along with the title of Kodak's Summer Girl. By the time the poster came out I was so fat that I could stand directly next to the cut out and no one could recognize me. Everyone said I had that radiant glow that expectant mothers get, but the truth was, I was a tub. It really didn't bother me—I actually loved being pregnant.

Marriage was another story. I wasn't adjusting well to the blandness of routine. The only thing I liked about being married was the amount of safety it provided from the advances of men. Not that I couldn't handle them, it just got old.

I started back to work six days after Toni's birth. Since I was still a bit heavy, they only shot me from the shoulders up, but it didn't take long before I was working as much as I had before my pregnancy. Toni worked, too. Kodak loved to take mother and baby photos. We shot department store ads and a number of other assignments together. In a flash, Toni became Rochester's most photographed child.

Two months after Toni's birth, I got a booking in New York City. I'd been looking forward to escaping Rochester and tasting New York once again, especially at this time of year. I loved 5th Avenue at Christmas time; the Santas ringing their bells on every corner, the store windows so beautifully dressed with holiday decor. It put me in the spirit.

While I was away, Tom decided to visit his brother, who lived out of town. Toni wasn't a problem—my mother was more than willing to take her while I worked. The problem was tearing Toni away from my mother once she got her hands on her!

I happened to mention the job to Sammy G over lunch at a diner near my apartment. Sam seemed distant; he was bothered by something. He tried to look interested.

"Really," he said, looking gloomily over his coffee cup at the rows of snow-crusted cars parked outside the diner. Turning back to me, he said with a little more enthusiasm, "This may be good timing. You could do something for me while you're there, Georgia. Is it possible for you to leave a day earlier?" he asked.

"I don't see why not," I answered.

"Good. I'll set up a meeting. I can't discuss anything on the phone. You'll need to personally sit down with these guys and deliver a message. I'll make your reservations and arrange to have you picked up at the airport."

"Oh, that's okay, I can have the studio take care of that."

"I said I'd do it," he retorted with authority. "Georgia, this is heavy information I'm trusting you with. No one—and I mean no one—is to know about this, you understand? As far as anyone knows you're going to New York to work. Trust no one."

"Of course I understand. Why would you even question that?"

"If word about this gets out, they'll be dredging my body out of the Genesee River. I'm trusting you with my life here—"

"Okay, okay. Don't worry," I assured.

Not many women were allowed in this world, and it gave me a sort of sick fascination to be trusted at this level. In some strange way I felt connected to fear, but the thought never crossed my mind that I may be in any kind of danger. I was too engrossed in the intrigue.

A man waited at the airport, holding a sign with my name on it. He led me to a black limousine. I tried to conceal a surge of excitement. I'd never ridden in a limousine before. Power. The chauffeur opened the door and I slid in. The slender man inside leaned forward, extending a diamond-clad hand. His white, starched cuff bore the embroidered initials S.J.R. He was even more polished than Sammy G, not a hair out of place or a single crease in his obviously expensive European suit.

"Hello. I'm Salvatore Reale," he said with no expression.

"I'm—"

"I already know who you are," he said in a deep, raspy voice.

With the tinted windows and his dark sunglasses, I couldn't really see his eyes. We sat silently as he studied me. I found his shadowed gaze unsettling.

"Were you ever called Georgie Girl?" he asked, breaking the silence.

"Yes, when I lived here," I answered.

"Didn't you work at The Sundowner on 23rd Street?"

"Yes..."

"Yeah, right, you're Frank Conti's girl. Never forget a face."

"Was—I'm married now," I answered.

"Yeah, yeah, it's coming back, you're the girl that saved that Harlem slime-ball from getting his due. He got it anyway, didn't matter," he said disguising a smile.

"What happened to him?"

"He passed away in his sleep one night from natural causes. His heart stopped beating when two men slipped into his room and stuck knives into it," he answered without a hint of compassion. "But I remember the talk about your driving that night. You're regarded as a pretty good wheel-man."

"I am? Well, I don't do that for a living," I replied, still not feeling at ease.

"You ought-a think about it then," he answered, searching my face for a receptive glint. He must have seen the thought take shape in my eyes, but I didn't want to endorse it.

"Where're we going?" I asked.

"You'll find out when we get there," he answered with a perfectly straight face. Asking no more questions, I transferred my gaze straight ahead through the rain-streaked windshield, wondering what dark and tangled path lay ahead as the limousine inched silently forward in the congested traffic.

The sleek stretch limo crawled to a stop a block away from our destination, an Italian restaurant somewhere in Brooklyn. Four men waited in a quiet corner in the rear of the dining area. It wasn't as fancy a place as I'd expected, but more of a neighborhood hangout.

The men eyed me suspiciously as Salvatore and I approached. I remembered seeing the gray-haired man with the cold, beady eyes before on one of my outings with Frankie, but I thought it

THE COMPANY SHE KEEPS

wise not to make reference to it. I didn't know his name, but I knew he was important. The heavyset guy dressed in a dark green pullover sweater eyed me nonchalantly while poking at his gums with a toothpick. The place wasn't brightly lit, but the other two guys wore dark sunglasses and no expressions. I couldn't get an immediate sense of them.

Salvatore Reale introduced me as Georgie Girl, Frank Conti's ex-girlfriend. The gray-haired man lifted an eyebrow and nodded in recognition. Seemingly more comfortable now, feeling as though I weren't a total stranger, he began to speak.

"I understand you have a message for me?" he asked, fixing me with his steely gaze.

"Yes, I do," I answered, handing him the letter in a sealed envelope.

He took the envelope and examined it suspiciously. I got the distinct feeling that he didn't trust that I hadn't read it. As he opened the letter and read its contents he shifted in his chair with obvious agitation. His eyebrows arched more than once as his eyes moved down the page. He was clearly not happy with what he was reading. Passing it on to the guy with the sunglasses, he waited for his reaction. The man raised his blacker-than-black shades and stared at me in disbelief. My curiosity was piqued.

"Hey," I said. "I'm just the messenger here. I have no idea what this is all about."

The guy with the green sweater let out a small laugh, but quickly contained it when the gray-haired man shot him a disapproving look.

"Tell Mr. Gingello he's gonna hafta discuss this in person. I'll arrange a meeting in Utica for next week. How long you gonna be stayin' in New York?"

"A few days," I answered.

"You'll be contacted with a time and place."

The meeting was over and Salvatore Reale escorted me to my hotel via taxi. I later understood why he had dismissed the limo. It attracted too much attention.

"The old man liked you, Georgia. I could tell."

"Which one? They were all old," I replied.

He laughed loudly, displaying a warm personality that had been absent on the ride in. "Carlo Gambino, the one with the beak and the gray hair."

"*That was Carlo Gambino?*" I asked, genuinely impressed.

"The one and only," he answered, amused by my ignorance. "Y'know, I wasn't kidding about what I said on the way in from the airport. You've got a style, a certain way you handle yourself that could be an asset t'me. An' from all I've heard, you're not bad behind the wheel. If you're interested in making some real money, maybe we should talk."

I left the meeting never knowing what resulted from it, but what eventually came out of this adventure in New York was my official indoctrination into the workings of the underworld and the groundwork for my future involvement. I was cast in a part that I would play throughout my life in one form or another.

It began as an innocent side job, delivering messages and packages. As their comfort level with me increased, so did the seriousness of the job. I wasn't just a dumb kid anymore, I was a dumb kid who could be trusted.

Taken in by the intrigue, my curious nature sailed into this world without much thought of consequence. Number one rule: never ask questions. That only served to fuel my attraction. With my thirst for adventure, I'd join a posse going in any direction, especially if it was heading away from Rochester.

Over time I began traveling to the city a couple of times a month on so-called, "modeling jobs," leaving my daughter in my mother's care. Many of the jobs I performed for the Gambino crime family were dropping off and picking up money from cargo planes at John F. Kennedy Airport. Millions of dollars, I was later told. Not that I knew this at the time or gave it much thought, but the path had been cleared by the CIA. Our government was setting up bank accounts for the Mob in Switzerland, among other countries, and getting paid quite handsomely for their involvement—not only in the form of money.

Part of my duties were to drive some "goodfellas" around to

make pick-ups, or so they called it. The money I made was just as good as standing under hot lights all day, and it was a lot more exciting, that's for sure.

Though I was never really told any details, I had my suspicions. The day came when my unvoiced questions were finally answered. I waited around the corner from a construction site with the engine running, as usual, while my two passengers were inside collecting money. I assumed they were probably breaking legs or whatever they do when people don't pay the "vig," interest paid to loan sharks.

Watching in my rear-view mirror, I saw them charging toward the car. Out of breath, they flung open the doors and yelled at me to floor it. In my naive mind I thought maybe the men inside had outnumbered them and they themselves were running from a beating. But that thought quickly disappeared when I heard the sirens. My adrenaline shot into orbit when I saw they had pulled out their guns. The desperation in their faces left no doubt they were prepared to shoot.

If Academy Awards were given for driving performances, I would have won hands down that day. I drove at high speeds through traffic, up and over sidewalks, and between cars a bicycle couldn't squeeze through—or it least it seemed that way. It played in my mind like watching a video in fast-forward. My only thought was to create distance between us and those cops or someone was going to get killed. Squealing around corners at dangerous speeds, we lost sight of the flashing red lights on 1st Avenue. Hanging a quick right on 76th Street, I sped down to East End Avenue and ducked into an alley near the park until it was clear to pull out.

Only then did I have time to think about what had just happened. I was getting in way over my head. This was a serious game, one I didn't think I wanted to play anymore.

Later that evening we met some other men in the back room of a dark and dingy after-hours club. I still hadn't stopped shaking from the robbery I had participated in earlier, but they were all exuberant. They lifted their glasses, toasted me for escaping the law, and presented me with an envelope stuffed with one hundred-dollar bills for a job well done. I accepted the three thousand dollars and the praise, but not without guilt.

Of course greed always plays a part in corruption, but for me it was the adrenaline rush. Hooked on that high, I spent the rest of my life in pursuit of it. The exhilarating feeling of defying death. Why? I have no idea. But as far back as I can remember I've been seduced by danger and the mystery of the unknown.

—◆—

That I would see Frankie again was inevitable. All I had to do was walk into Bino's Tavern on the corner of 2nd Avenue and 30th Street. The spicy-sweet aroma of sauce cooking filled my nostrils from a block away.

Bino's mom was in her usual place—the kitchen. She was a short old woman with a concerned, round face. Wearing a flowered print dress, her body showed evidence that she thoroughly enjoyed her own cooking. Dining at Bino's took me instantly to my own mother's kitchen, to the warmth always surrounding her. The richness of that world. The safety.

The guys were all sitting on the same bar stools where I had left them a long year ago. All except Frankie. We'd spoken off and on, but I hadn't seen him since I'd gotten married.

"Hey, Ma, look who's here, Georgie Girl! Cook up her favorite macaroni. Make enough for all the boys. We're gonna have a celebration!" Bino yelled gaily, as he began pushing tables together.

Bino was pure Italian, but he looked more Scandinavian. Being from northern Italy, that wasn't uncommon. He stood 6'1", and had kind blue eyes and light brown hair. He could be counted on as a friend, but he wasn't one to be crossed. Underneath his unassuming looks and tranquil demeanor he was a tough guy who'd learned how to survive, just as most of his friends in the neighborhood had.

Rosa came out of the kitchen with a wide grin on her face and her gray hair pulled back in a loose bun, wiping her hands on her soiled apron as she approached.

"Its-a no the same without you, *bella*," she said, kissing my cheeks. "You got a bambino now, no?"

"Yes, Rosa, I named her Toni. She's beautiful," I answered.

"Like-a her mama. Toni...thats-a good Italian name. Sit, I go cook for you. You look-a too skinny."

She turned and hurried her plump body toward the kitchen, hitting Bino on the head with the spatula as she passed. "Bring-a the olives and the bread!"

"Okay, Ma, I'm coming, I'm coming." Bino affectionately rolled his eyes and followed his mother into the kitchen.

"Does Frankie know you're here, Georgie Girl?" Flip asked.

Flip. What a perfect name. I towered over him and I wasn't what you'd call tall. He was an exact replica of Leo Gorsy from the old TV movies of the "Dead End Kids." All he needed was a cap turned sideways on his head to finish off the look.

"No, Flip, I thought I'd surprise him."

"He should be walking in any minute," he said, glancing out the fogged-up window.

"How is he, Flip?"

"He's fine. You know Frankie...To be honest with you, Georgie Girl, he's been a bear since you left."

Frankie waltzed in the door before I had a chance to ask Flip what he meant. His eyes lit up when he saw me. Mine did too.

"Georgie Girl? What a surprise, baby! What are you doing in the city?" he said, unzipping his worn leather jacket.

"I'm here for a modeling job."

"How long ya here for?"

"I'm leaving tonight."

"Tonight? You gotta be kiddin', you just got here."

"I know, but I—"

"I'm not taking no for an answer, baby. Y'can leave tomorrow. We're going to the Play Lounge tonight. Our favorite band is still playing. We'll get Flip on the stage to sing us a few songs. It'll be just like old times."

The food was served family-style. Rosa came out of the

kitchen, eyeing everyone's plates.

"*Mangia, mangia,*" Rosa said, encouraging us all to eat. "How you let dis-a-one go, Frankie? Whats-a matter wit you, huh?" Rosa scolded, slapping Frankie on the back of the head.

"The question, Rosa, is how do you *keep* one like this?" Frankie answered, shielding his head in anticipation of the next blow.

"You a man, no? You no tink of someting? Ah, you *stonato!*" she said, waving her arms as she waddled back into the kitchen.

Time had stood still here. The whole gang was at the Play Lounge: Billy, Chippy, Flip, Tommy Red, and Vic, of course, who still owned the place. We drank and danced the Lindy until four o'clock in the morning. I had not laughed like this since I'd left New York the year before. It seemed to me that I could step in and out of time, picking up in each world exactly where I had left off.

Soon I'd come to realize from my own endeavors why secrecy had to be a priority in the underworld. I'd keep the same kinds of secrets from Frankie that he had once kept from me. It would all make perfect sense.

I flew back to Rochester the following day, only to become even more frustrated with my life. Tired of living a lie, I told Tom about my previous affair with Frankie.

"Tom, when I was living in New York...I had an affair," I blurted out, hoping to bring an end to a marriage that had no hope of making it.

"I know, Georgia. Do you really think I'm that stupid?" he said passively.

"If you knew, why didn't you ever say anything?" I asked, amazed that he could hold that in.

"Because I was afraid of losing you," he answered, looking pained. "Did you see Frankie in New York this week?"

"How do you know his name?" I asked, stunned.

"I found a letter he wrote you. You're not too good at covering your tracks. So, did you see him?" he asked, still calm.

"Yes," I answered, feeling guilty.

"At least you're honest." He paused to study my face. "I followed you from your hotel...and I also know you came back alone. So does this mean it's over?"

"You were in New York?" I asked, wondering if he'd seen where I went when I'd landed. But then I realized he couldn't have, since he had dropped me off at the airport.

"Georgia, I love you very much. I'm willing to forget this and try to make our marriage work. Will you please try...for Toni's sake?"

Again I voiced the reasons for my discontent, and again he made concessions. I knew our marriage would ultimately end, but I felt so bad for him that I couldn't bring myself to hurt him any more that night than I already had. Putting his happiness before my own, we continued to live the lie. Although Tom had never met him, Frankie would always be an irritant in his subconscious.

Life with Tom was mere existing. Even if Frankie had never come into the picture, it never would have worked. I couldn't stand staying home all the time, so I started doing things with my girlfriend Susie and my sister Sharon on the weekends, leaving Tom contentedly sitting in front of the TV with Toni and his popcorn. Fortunately, Toni was a good baby. She quietly amused herself without interrupting Tom's television programs, although he was an attentive father. Tom was really a good person and I loved him in my own way, but I wasn't *in* love with him. My friends and I went bowling or played cards—anything to break the monotony—but that got old too.

I had paid Tom's tuition to the Rochester Institute of Technology. RIT is considered one of the best schools in the country for photography. He lasted for six months before he quit, an occurrence that validated my dismal outlook for our future. Tom didn't have much going for him in the ambition department. The only time we ever went out was to visit his family, all of whom I liked very much, especially his brother, Babe, and Babe's wife, Billie. But I needed a little more excitement than I was getting. I was bored to tears. On the other hand, Tom was disgustingly content.

My daughter wasn't even a year old when I concluded I couldn't live this way. The humdrum pace made me crazy. Life had to hold more than this. Stifled, I wanted to learn more, to expand my horizons. I was a curious cat with a mate who didn't want to explore. I was adventurous, with a ferocious appetite for whatever was on the other side, just out of my reach. But Tom would never change. He was happy just the way he was. I had to get out. Breaking his heart wasn't something I looked forward to.

The phone rang, interrupting my thoughts about the future.

"Georgia? This is Don Maggio, your favorite photographer."

"Hi, Don, thanks for announcing yourself. I tell them all they're my favorite, you know. What's up?" I asked, laughing.

"We finally got approval to go ahead with that job in Puerto Rico."

"No kidding. I thought that was pretty much dead."

"No, it looks like Kodak got American Airlines, Samsonite Luggage, and the Puerto Rican government to all go in on the deal. It'll be a longer schedule, but I think we can handle a few more days of sunshine, don't you?"

"Sounds great," I said. "When do we leave?"

"On the tenth, two weeks from now. Are you clear?"

"I've got some catalog work booked for that week, but I'm sure they'll let Susie replace me."

"Wait'll you hear this," Don said. "Jim Alquist is trying to get out of his other bookings, but it looks like he's pretty locked in. What do you think about using your husband as the male model?"

Tom was perfect model material. If you can call a man beautiful, he was. His facial features were delicate for a man. Though he was of Sicilian descent, his heritage wasn't obvious.

I hesitated. "Well...it would put a damper on the reason I want the job."

"What do you mean? Aren't you two getting along?"

"Well, we're not fighting or anything, but I've been thinking about telling him I want a divorce and I could use some space right now to think this over."

"Jesus, after all I went through to pull this off! Do you think you could hold off telling him until the job is over?" I sensed his blood pressure rising. "You're supposed to be a honeymoon couple on vacation in Puerto Rico. I sold the client on the money we could save on the room, and how real the photographs would look because you're really married. They flipped over the idea. Do you think you could—"

"Don, I get paid to pretend. I do a pretty good job of it in real life too. Don't worry, your shoot will come out just fine. They'll never know. Have I ever let you down before?"

"No..." he said, taking a deep breath.

Putting down the receiver, I sighed. But then, this was exactly the vehicle I needed to send Tom out into the world on his own. He wasn't working and depended on my income. My persistence in hounding him to better himself caused him to quit Kodak, and he hadn't been able to hold on to a job since then. The money from this assignment would give him a nice cushion with which to embark on a new life for himself.

⋘⬥⋙

The first night in Puerto Rico the Governor threw a party on his yacht in our honor. The guests made a big fuss over the loving couple who would soon grace their brochures. I put on my professional mask and fooled them all. Little did I know, this was a mask I would wear for years to come. I could have won an Oscar for my performance that evening and throughout the shoot.

Our final sunset had finally come. A week of conjuring up heart-felt, loving looks was wearing on me. Tom had no idea that it was just pretend. In a romantic setting, we posed on a steep cliff under a picturesque tree. The orange glow of the sun sank slowly in the background into the angry sea below. My long chiffon dress blew softly in the evening breeze in silhouette as Tom and I exchanged tender expressions of love.

"You're doing great, guys," Don yelled out, feverishly clicking his Nikon.

"I love you, Georgia," Tom said with genuine sincerity as we gracefully posed for the camera.

I continued to reflect the illusory mood.

"Okay, we've lost the light. I think we've got it, kids. It's a wrap everyone," Don announced.

I stood on the edge of the cliff, deep in thought, watching the sun's final radiance before it disappeared into the ocean. I yearned to be as free as the wind that gently blew my long blonde hair against my face. Turning back to Tom, I engaged him with my eyes and revealed my agonizing thoughts.

"Tom, I want a divorce."

Chapter Five

It took a while for my eyes to become accustomed to the darkness as I walked into Caesars II, the latest happening place on the West Side. Low ceilings covered in red burlap disguised the musty smell of what had formerly been a cellar. Rooms partitioned by hanging beads left over from the sixties lent a cozy feeling to the vast, soulless space. Spotting Sammy G and Joey Tiraborelli sitting at the front table near the band, I walked over to join them.

"Hey, kid, how ya doin'?" Sammy asked as he stood and kissed each of my cheeks. The two women sitting with them didn't seem as pleased to see me.

"Whatta ya drinkin'?"

"I'll have a Scotch, Sammy. In fact, make it a double."

"Bea!" he yelled to the waitress as Jimmy Cristo came through the door. "Bring us another round and a double Chivas for the lady. And take care of Jimmy's table. Line up another shot for our proprietor, too, while you're at it."

"Sure thing, Sam," she said as she whisked away, fighting her way through the crowd.

The band took a break, making it possible to hear.

"A double, huh? What's going on with you, kid?"

"I left Tom, Sammy. He's not taking it very well."

"Yeah, well I knew that would happen sooner or later. You're goin' places, kid. I knew that the day I laid eyes on you. What were you then, thirteen, fourteen years old? I've watched you blossom into a beauty. You deserve better anyway."

A man appeared from behind, pulling the back of a chair up to the table and straddling it. I continued my conversation with Sammy, sensing the man hanging on my every word. Finally, I turned and looked at him for the first time.

Seated with a straight back, he appeared a little over six feet, weighing approximately 165 pounds. Mystery peered out from his unwavering dark brown eyes. He didn't smile, nor did he introduce himself. He just stared at me with a truly piercing look.

"I'm going to marry you," said the stranger.

I laughed at him. "Get serious," I said, looking over at Sammy, my eyes asking, 'Who *is* this jerk?' With a crooked half smile, Sammy shook his head in disbelief.

"I am. You'll see," he said with unfettered confidence.

Well, if I hadn't heard it all. A little egotistical for my taste, although he was unusually handsome, with olive skin, a sharply etched jaw line, and a perfectly straight nose. Arrogant, to say the least, but he had an enticing allure. A curl from his thick, jet-black hair fell softly onto his forehead as he lifted his glass in Sammy's direction.

"Thanks for the drink, Sam."

"*Salud*," said Sammy, raising his glass and taking a swig.

"Well, is anyone going to introduce me to this gorgeous girl?"

No one looked too eager to make the first move. Finally, Joey Tiraborelli spoke up. "Joe, this is Georgia Durante. You've probably seen her on TV and in the newspapers," he announced proudly.

In an attempt at regaining some attention, the sexy looking redhead seated at the table cleared her throat as she crossed her legs, exhibiting a suggestive amount of creamy thigh.

"Yeah," Joe said. "Weren't you on the cover of *Upstate Magazine* last Sunday?"

"Yes, I was."

"That was a great article."

"Thank you," I responded, allowing myself a small smile.

"Georgia, this is Joe Lamendola, the owner of this joint. He's turned it into one hell of a gold mine."

"I can see that," I said, looking around at the people pouring in. "This is my first time here." I hadn't been out in the club scene much since I'd been married.

"I know," Joe said. "You never could've gotten by without me noticing you before."

I ignored the compliment, convinced it was a line he'd rehearsed many times before. "I like your choice of bands."

As he began to respond, someone tapped him on the shoulder. "Joe, I think we have a problem in the back room."

He excused himself and disappeared into the crowd. Joey Tiraborelli watched me as my eyes followed him until he was out of my view. Something about him intrigued me.

"Hey, Sammy," Joey Tiraborelli yelled above the music. "Looks like our little Alice in Wonderland has eyes for Casanova."

"Beauty and the Beast is more like it," Sammy said under his breath.

Obviously no great love existed between them. An unspoken rivalry always simmered between the Eastsiders and the Westsiders. I chalked it up to that being the case here. As I pondered this conflict, the waitress appeared with a tray filled with drinks.

"These are on Joe Lamendola," she said, unloading her bounty.

"Bring me my tab on your next pass, Bea," Sammy ordered.

"Coming right up, Sammy."

"We're going to Ben's Cafe from here, Georgia. Would you like to join us?"

"Sure, why not?" I answered, noticing hostile glances from the two girls at the table.

Bea returned with the check and Sammy paid it, leaving her a $100 tip. "Give these ladies whatever they want and put it on my tab," Sammy instructed as we stood to leave.

I was surprised the girls weren't joining us, but evidently not as surprised as they were. Their venomous stares undoubtedly followed us even after we passed through the door.

"Why aren't they coming with us?" I asked as we climbed the flight of cement stairs leading out of the club.

"Why bring a ham sandwich to a smorgasbord?" Sammy answered, and we all burst out laughing.

Two days later I received a call from Joe Lamendola. "Hey, pretty lady. Where'd you run off to the other night?"

"Oh, we just did the Friday night ritual. The Blue Gardenia, Ben's, and breakfast."

"Listen, I have to go to Buffalo Wednesday night to see a group I'm thinking of booking. Would you like to come with me? I'd really like your opinion."

"Well...are you planning on returning the same night?"

"No, but you'll have your own room if that's what you're worried about."

"In that case, I'd love to go."

He picked me up in his 1970 Stingray—my kind of car. We drove the ninety miles to Buffalo, learning a little history about each other along the way.

"You know," I said, "your brother Ronny is a friend of mine."

"I know, how do you think I got your number?"

"Oh...well, I assumed you got it from Sammy."

"I tried that route, but he basically told me you were unlisted."

"He's overprotective of me sometimes."

"That's an understatement."

"I didn't know Ronny even had an older brother," I said. "Why haven't I ever met you before?"

"I've been in Boston for the last six years. I'm sort of the black sheep of the family. The one no one ever talks about," he said with a nervous laugh. "How do you know my brother?"

"I used to date a friend of his, Sammy Sapienza. I was about fourteen or fifteen at the time. Ronny was the bouncer at a club Sammy took me to. He got me past the door without having to show my ID. We just became friends over time."

We arrived at the Executive Hotel about six-thirty. Jimmy Constintino had the red carpet rolled out upon our arrival. Champagne was in Joe's suite and flowers were in mine. The note he left read: *Relax and enjoy. The limo will pick you up at seven-thirty for dinner. Looking forward to seeing you.*

I had heard about this powerhouse, Jimmy Constintino. He was a young, good-looking guy, the owner of one of the largest hotels in Buffalo. I had to admit I was curious about him and he seemed interesting. But like so many of Joe's praiseworthy acquaintances, I would meet him once, never to encounter him again.

Joe and I had a wonderful dinner at a quaint Italian restaurant, compliments of Jimmy. Songs from Italy, played on a harp, added charm to the atmosphere and set the stage for a romantic evening. After dinner the limousine took us back to the hotel. We went into the lounge to hear the new group. Joe asked the female singer if she knew the song "What Are You Doing the Rest of Your Life." She did. We danced like we'd been together for years.

"You are going to marry me, y'know," he said as we danced.

"I'm already married."

"We'll just have to do something about that, won't we?"

"I'm only six days into a separation, and I'm not ready to jump into the fire quite yet. Besides, it's bad enough being married, having a child, and getting a divorce all before I'm twenty," I said, laughing.

"How old is your baby?"

"Eight months," I answered.

"We'll be married by the time she's three. Is that long enough?"

He held me close for the remainder of the song. I felt that tingle in my vulnerable young heart—the kind of feeling that only seems to happen in youth, the first stage of falling in love.

The evening was wonderful, but as we walked from the lounge toward our rooms, apprehension surged through me—the dread of the sexual advances that were sure to come. I knew Joe wouldn't be satisfied with a simple kiss at the door. I was determined to handle the situation as an adult, but how? How does a young girl handle a dilemma like this without adult experience?

Being married young had furnished me with a cloak of safety.

Now I was single again and fair game. Conventional myth said divorcées, having had a steady diet of sex, were easy marks. Except I was maybe as difficult as they came. With a month to go before I turned twenty, being married and having a child didn't automatically make me an adult. My instincts said run. I never did perfect the handling of sexual encounters. Even today, though I no longer physically break track records, I still hold the gold medal in my head for running the fastest.

I worked myself into a frenzy thinking about it. Sensing my extreme discomfort, Joe acted like a perfect gentleman. He was probably intrigued that a woman wouldn't sleep with him on the first date—a problem I was sure he had *not* encountered often.

Frankie came to Rochester a few times after the break-up with Tom, and I saw him when I traveled to New York on my little side jobs. On one of his visits, I packed a lunch and we went on a picnic with Toni. Frankie had a wonderful way with children. He would have been a good father.

Somehow we wound up in the cemetery—not really so unusual for our peculiar relationship. Sitting under a willow tree, we ate our lunch and watched as Toni climbed on the tombstones. We wrote a letter professing our love for one another, wrapped it in the plastic from our sandwich, and buried it under the tree. We made a promise we would come back in twenty years to read it again. We knew, barring death, we would always be in contact. I actually did go back twenty years later, but with the natural growth of the trees I couldn't remember which one the letter was buried beneath.

We still harbored strong feelings, but life was a little different now. Having a baby changes everything. Life in New York was harsh enough for an adult; with a child it was out of the question. New York City and my life there with Frankie became only fond memories.

Joe and I were soon an item. Just as he predicted, we ultimately were married. As unhappy as I was with Tom, I was still scared and insecure about what the future held for a young woman with a year-old infant. Intuitively understanding my fears, Joe used this apprehension as a vehicle to lure me in, making my daughter as big a part of his life as he made me. Never having any children of his own, Joe seemed to enjoy the little pleasures kids can bring into one's life. He had little trouble converting from his bachelor lifestyle to instant family man.

Caught off guard by love, I was grateful I'd found someone who loved my daughter and was willing to take us both as a package. Determined to be the only father Toni would ever know, Joe wanted Tom out of her life. For some reason, Tom really wasn't a major problem. I'm sure Joe's reputation had something to do with it, but Tom was as lax about Toni as he was about himself. Toni, just being a baby, didn't know the difference. She enjoyed the attention from wherever it came.

The beginning of our relationship was a whirlwind of excitement. But then again, any kind of social life, much less life in the fast lane, would have been exciting compared to living with Tom. Joe was a flashy nightclub owner and always dressed the part. Drawn by his thousand-watt charm and good looks, women threw themselves at his feet—which, of course, made men secretly hate him. But he had chosen me, and I felt proud to be his woman.

Joe knew how to spend money and doors opened wherever we went. Maître d's greeted him as though he were a king. Only the best table in the house was good enough for Mr. Joe. When he walked into a room, people were immediately intimidated by his presence. He carried an undeniable aura of power. I fell madly in love, dazzled by the *illusion* of Joe Lamendola.

We connected beyond anything we could relate to on an earthly plain. Our strong desire for one another felt as if it were a continuation from another lifetime. We didn't need to speak to understand each other's thoughts. We were happy together and utterly miserable when apart.

Once we were separated by a snowstorm. I was stuck in a photography studio only seven miles from home, but the streets were impassable. The night on a cold studio floor promised to be long. But Joe wouldn't give up. He searched until he found a kid with a snowmobile and paid him $100 to bring me home. When I got there, he had a candlelight dinner and wine waiting. We spent a warm, snowed-in, romantic evening together.

Joe took me out frequently, even on Fridays, which had always been deemed "boys" night out. On Saturdays, everyone took out their wives, but Fridays were reserved for girlfriends. We truly enjoyed each other's company, always finding something to giggle about. This is what I had missed when I was married to Tom.

We took many short trips to Toronto and New York, usually in search of good bands to book for the nightclub. In anticipation of our arrival, other club owners made sure we were treated like royalty. We were an envied couple by the women who vied for Joe's attention. I had captured the heart of one of the most desirable bachelors in town, and he had *captured* me.

––––◆––––

Once I was under his spell, and hopelessly in love, Joe's jealously began to intensify. He wanted to shield me from any external influences. I became his property. Men couldn't even look in my direction without a violent reaction from Joe. I started to change my own personality, careful not to attract attention from the opposite sex, but it didn't work. To eliminate the problem, Joe started to make me stay at home. At my age, with the world to explore, his restricting conduct was like a death sentence.

Life with Joe soon became twisted. He began to dominate and control me. Over time, in subtle ways, the frequency of his dominant behavior became more pronounced. At first his caring seemed genuine, guiding me in ways that appeared to be in my best interest. Eventually, though, he made all my decisions and my independence completely crumbled. I wasn't allowed to associate with my friends—for my own good, of course—and eventually I even had restrictions on my own family. He forbade me to have contact with anyone who might open my eyes to the destruction of his domination. My opinions had no value. His opinions were law.

When my mother sensed what was happening, she offered

me refuge. Refuge didn't mean safety, however, so I camouflaged my unhappiness. The more aware Joe became of my parents' feelings, the less contact I was allowed to have with them. I tried my best to balance it all with harmony, but resentment grew on both sides.

We lived in an apartment above Caesars II. There wasn't anyplace where Toni could go out to play—no trees, no park, just pavement. I started to feel as if I had traded one prison, my marriage to Tom, for another. And from the new one there seemed no escape.

I loved Joe, or so I thought. His flashy club-owner status and the attention from other women made him seem quite a catch. As a result, I put up with his behavior. In Joe's world, women did what they were told. He knew that my sense of self was shaky, despite my successful modeling career. His put-downs became vicious and cruel. I began to believe that I was lucky to have found him. Who else would want me, especially with a child? I actually began to participate in my own subjugation.

Because of Joe, my modeling assignments became limited to the Rochester area. Even nearby Buffalo was considered too far out of town. I could only work at a distant location if he traveled with me. Having Joe on the set, not surprisingly, was propelling me into early retirement.

Joe never said much—he didn't have to. His expressions said it all. His presence made everyone extremely uncomfortable, including me. My side trips to New York were impossible now, but at least I had a good excuse to turn down the frequent requests for my services.

Industry parties often demanded my presence, but I could never go to these affairs alone. If Joe didn't accompany me, then I'd have to stay home. I recall one party we attended and, as usual, he made me a nervous wreck. It was obvious to my colleagues that Joe was from a different world, and my business friends caught the change in my personality with him around. I could feel that my conversations were impaired and strained. I knew what the evening would hold even before we arrived, as Joe always became irritated whenever I enjoyed the spotlight. I hoped against hope that he'd conduct himself with dignity and show respect.

A male model, Jim Alquist, approached us at the party. "Hi, Georgia. Great party, huh?" he remarked, innocently resting one hand on my shoulder while sipping his drink with the other.

"Yes, the studio doesn't look quite the same with all these people in it. Jim, this is Joe."

"Good to meet you, Joe," Jim said, holding out his hand.

"You touch my wife like that again, you'll be missing a hand," Joe retorted.

Jim stood, stupefied, with his arm still outstretched.

Here he goes. Let's leave now, White. It's only gonna get worse.

Joe took my arm and abruptly led me through the crowd. He was seething.

"Joe, please don't embarrass me," I pleaded, forcing a nervous smile at familiar faces as we passed.

"Embarrass *you*? Quite the opposite, my dear. How can you allow yourself to be touched like that and expect me to stand there like a fuckin' idiot?"

"Jim was just being friendly, he didn't mean anything by it."

"Yeah, I know how friendly he'd like to be."

"You're ridiculous, Joe. That's his wife right over there. Look at her. She's gorgeous! What would he want with me? We all work together—we're friends!"

"Not anymore you're not. Get your coat. We're leaving."

"I can't leave yet. They haven't started the slide show. I'm being featured—it's why we're here!"

"Get your coat."

You may as well leave. People are beginning to stare. Next time, pretend you're visiting your mother—and go alone!

I said whatever it took to appease Joe, while never agreeing with the way he thought. When, against my better judgment, I occasionally attempted to demonstrate that I had a mind of my own, he became infuriated. The result was never worth my effort.

I learned very quickly how to sneak. I took jobs out of town and drove ninety miles an hour to get back home at a reasonable time. I even had Toni lying for me: "Tell Daddy we stopped for an ice cream. Don't say we visited with Susie. If he asks, say we were at Grandma's." Only now do I realize how sick it was, putting that type of pressure on a child. But then I was so terrified, I'd do anything to escape his wrath. I still find it difficult to think about the normal life I deprived my daughter of because of my own chaos.

Toni practically lived with my parents. They were wonderful, loving grandparents, but they weren't what she needed the most. She needed me. My parents took care of her when I worked and when I played, both of which I did a lot. I wanted to taste the life of my youth that early motherhood had stolen from me. Mom and Dad lovingly afforded me that opportunity.

Other reasons surfaced for my frequent absences from Toni's life. As time went on, Joe graduated from emotionally destroying things that were precious to me to punching holes in walls—and, finally, to physically abusing me. He never laid a hand on Toni, but the mental abuse she endured during his outbursts took a significant toll on her psyche.

When Joe became physically abusive, which happened often, I'd take Toni to stay with my mother. I desperately attempted to avoid her being subjected to Joe's violent behavior. I would lie to my parents, but they suspected something was wrong. They eagerly opened their door and sheltered my little girl. Although Toni missed me, she was more relaxed and happy in the safety of my parents' loving home. Absorbed in my own pain, my mind was scarcely free to mourn her absence, but I took comfort in knowing she was receiving the attention she needed.

Toni played as quietly as a mouse around Joe. She never

knew quite what to expect from him. She gradually became timid and withdrawn, fading into the background whenever he raised his voice.

One day Joe and Toni were playing in the kitchen while I was preparing breakfast. Toni climbed onto the counter and jumped into his arms. Delighted with the attention, she actively pursued the game. I placed the pan on the stove and turned to survey them, enjoying their laughter. Toni repeatedly climbed back up and jumped. On her sixth jump, Joe moved away, letting her fall to the floor.

"There—that'll teach you never to trust anybody."

I ran to her and picked her up, wiping the tears from her eyes. "That was sick, Joe! How could you do that to her?"

"Don't challenge me on how to bring up a kid! Maybe if someone did that to you when you were younger, you'd never have gotten raped. She's not going to grow up to be as stupid as her mother."

You're not stupid! He's trying to confuse you by turning it all around—so he looks right. He's wrong! Don't give in, you have nothing to apologize for.

Joe's dominant behavior persisted. I loved him and hated him in equal measure. My will became the only thing that sustained me. My reluctance to let go of what belief I still had in myself just increased his insecurity. His lack of self-control became more overt. The blame always flowed in my direction, and, after a time, I came to accept it. Through it all, I persistently and paradoxically believed I loved him.

In the beginning, I saw the possessive side of Joe as proof of his love. But time showed it to be a sickness. The signs were there from the start, but love has a celebrated myopia. Yes, Joe was certainly suave. Although I had been around enough to know the kind of character he was, I was still just a babe in the woods, young and impressionable. Joe was thirty-five when we met— and a master of mind manipulation. The fifteen years of experience he had on me made his molding me into the person I would become that much easier. Joe was tall, dark, and handsome, but the dark was much darker than I had bargained for. Once I entered that darkness, escape would take years.

I still managed to keep in touch with Tom's brother and his family. *Another broken rule.* I would occasionally sneak over to visit my ex-sister-in-law, Billie, for coffee. She was always happy to see me pulling into the driveway. A simple housewife, she was stuck at home with four children, all less than nine years of age. She loved hearing my stories of the outside world.

Billie was becoming increasingly discontent with her existence, and she often vented her frustrations over coffee during our visits. As I had also felt when I was married to Tom, Billie wanted more from life than a humdrum existence. Now, my life was anything *but* humdrum. There *had* to be something in between.

The only time Billie and Babe ever went out was to church socials. They took no vacations, and there were no dinners away from the kids. Determined to start getting out, she joined a women's bowling league—an act of independence which I could readily understand. Babe, being the typical possessive Sicilian, didn't agree with this sudden show of independence. In his view, a woman's place was barefoot, pregnant, and chained to the stove. Billie reluctantly dropped out of the league.

Only twenty-eight years old, she looked closer to forty. Her dark hair sported a plethora of gray, quite a bit more than you would have expected for a woman her age. She wanted to color it, but Babe refused to let her. His fear was that the effect would make her more attractive to the opposite sex. It was simply out of the question. Although miniskirts were in fashion, Billie could only wear her skirts below the knee. If Babe had allowed her to wear make-up, she could have been a truly attractive woman.

Over time, Billie's resentment continued to grow. After all, she wasn't asking for the moon. She definitely didn't want any more children, but birth control was against the Catholic religion and Babe opposed it. She took the Pill anyway and hid the containers in her drawer. When Babe stumbled upon them one day, he became convinced Billie was having an affair. He started popping up at home at all hours to check on her.

An obedient wife from the beginning, Billie eventually began to rebel. This confused Babe. The only explanation could be that she was being unfaithful. He became obsessed with the thought and their marriage started to go downhill fast.

Babe became so depressed he took an overdose of sleeping pills. Barely found in time, he was rushed to the hospital. Billie begged the doctors to keep him for psychiatric observation, telling them that the next time he would kill them all. They said they didn't have enough beds and sent him home.

How could this be happening? This was not the happy-go-lucky Babe I remembered. In her kitchen, not long after Babe came home from the hospital, Billie told me in a prosaic tone, "He's going to kill me, Georgia."

Emotionally drained, her eyes appeared dull, and the dark bags under them were big enough to pack clothes in. Her sparkle was gone. She was giving in to her belief of the inevitable.

"What are you saying, Billie?"

"You don't know what it's like, Georgia. Every time I have to run to the store for a quart of milk or a loaf of bread, I have to pile all the kids into the car. I'm terrified to leave them home alone with Babe. I'm afraid he'll kill them."

"Oh, Billie, come on. He would never kill his own children. Remember how he tore down your pool when David almost drowned? Babe loves those kids! He wouldn't hurt them."

"Something is very wrong with his mind, Georgia. You don't believe me, the doctors don't believe me, *no one believes me.*"

Babe arrived home unexpectedly just then, interrupting our conversation. Billie began to twitch and nervously bite her lower lip, fearing that Babe had overheard us.

He seems pretty normal. Billie must be paranoid. Joe has threatened me too, but Babe is not like Joe. Babe is compassionate. He could never do anything like that.

"How are you, Georgia? It's been a while," Babe said, kissing me hello. He acted like the same old Babe, but his face showed signs of stress. The playfulness that normally shone in his eyes was absent.

Babe was only about 5'6", with tight, curly hair and an outgoing personality. Always the teaser, he never stopped kidding around. I'd always enjoyed his company. He constantly went out of his way to do you a favor. He was my favorite of Tom's two brothers. Tom had even been jealous of our rapport.

"I'm fine, Babe."

"Saw Toni outside playing with the kids. She's getting big." He looked down at the table and paused. His face flushed red with rage. "Why aren't you using the china?" he shrieked. He picked up a half-filled coffee mug and threw it against the wall. Billie shrank in her chair as the mug shattered.

God, could Billie be right? I'd never seen Babe behave this way.

He stormed out the door, slamming it so hard that the pictures rattled on the wall.

Billie looked at me wide-eyed. "Do you believe me now?"

"Geez, Billie. What's happened to him?"

She ran to the front window to be sure he'd really left while I picked up the broken mug and wiped up the mess.

"I don't know what to do, Georgia. I have to get out of here." Her hand shook uncontrollably as she pushed her dark, tangled hair from her face. "I'm going to my sister's in Pennsylvania tomorrow after he leaves for work. I can't take this anymore. I've got to get away from him for a while."

"Does Babe know you're going?" I said, comforting her with an arm around her shoulder.

"No, I'll leave him a note. You can do something for me, if you would," she said with pleading eyes.

"Sure, Billie, anything."

"Call him after I'm gone. See if you can get him to go to your nightclub. Try to talk to him for me. Please," she said, desperation dripping from her voice. "Convince him there's no one else, that it's just his behavior that's driving me away. Will you do that for me, Georgia?"

"Consider it done," I answered. "I'll help in any way I can. You know that."

"Oh, thank you. I'm so scared," she said, bursting into tears.

Deeply troubled, I drove home, considering Billie's fears. Was Babe possibly capable of fulfilling Billie's prediction? They were just going through a tough period. Babe was acting a little irrational, but time would eventually heal that. Surely, this was true.

To keep my promise to Billie, I had to admit to Joe that I had done something against his wishes. I had committed the sin of visiting with my ex-in-laws. This would not sit well, but I had pledged myself to help.

"You sneaky little bitch!"

"Joe, they have a right to see Toni, she's their niece. Why is that so hard for you to understand?" I yelled back in my defense.

"They're not your family anymore! You divorced that fuckin' guy. Now divorce the family," he said heatedly.

"I gave Billie my word I would try to talk to Babe. I can't go back on it now. I think I can help," I insisted. "Babe listens to me."

"You actually think you have anything intelligent to say?" he said, laughing.

"Yes," I said defiantly, "I do."

"Stay out of it! It's none of your business," he demanded in a booming voice.

"You say you hate it when I lie, but you *make* me lie. I'm being honest with you now. I'm going to try to talk to him," I retorted, standing up to him.

He flashed me one of those don't-fuck-with-me stares. "Go ahead. Try it. You'll see what fuckin' happens. Get me a lighter," he ordered, brushing off my brazen attempts to get my way.

Frustrated, I picked up a pack of matches and threw them at him. "Here! Light yourself on fire!"

That did it. Joe grabbed my neck and shoved me against the wall, his thumbs pressed hard into my throat. "Don't you *dare* defy me. If I hear you've talked to those people again or anyone I've forbid you to, you'll fuckin' live to regret it. Do you understand?"

I couldn't answer. Couldn't even nod. The only way he knew I understood was from the tears streaming down my cheeks. When he finally let go of my neck, I gasped for breath.

"Okay, okay...I won't call," I answered, backing away.

Satisfied, he went downstairs to the club to prepare for the evening. Anger festered inside of me.

Follow your heart, White. You're surrendering again.

I can't...

Why was I letting him take control of me? I was afraid. Fear of the pain that he would inflict on me overpowered my will. It made me a coward. And he was a *master* at this game.

No one could ignore Joe's presence in a room. The false confidence in his demeanor made everyone aware of his domineering sense of superiority. Mr. Authority, he got off on holding court, expounding his theories, and daring anyone to challenge him. If they did, he'd pounce. He had an uncanny way of knowing others' secret fears, never passing up an opportunity to point out their shortcomings. Joe enjoyed mentally mutilating people, stripping them of their own self-confidence. He squashed them like insects, without a hint of compassion. He was downright cruel.

One night after hours, a cop showed up at the club. New on the beat, he stated confidently, "It's after two. Lock it up or I'm going to have to close you down."

Joe laughed at him. "Who the hell do you think you are, Gunga Din?"

I couldn't believe he had spoken to a uniform like that. But such was Joe. He respected no one. When the cop got angry and cited him, Joe ripped the citation up in his face and showed him the door. The next day the officer was reprimanded and transferred out of the division.

It wasn't just strangers who Joe treated this way. He even

bedeviled his own family. I recall him belittling his younger brother Jimmy in front of customers while Jimmy worked behind the bar. Jimmy walked out, leaving Joe stranded without a bartender on a Friday night, the busiest night of the week.

Later that night, after closing, Joe went to his mother's house and woke his brother from a sound sleep by choking him. Joe told Jimmy that he if he wasn't out of their mother's house by morning, he was going to burn all his clothes. The next day Joe found Jimmy's clothes still hanging in the closet. He loaded them into his car, drove to the nearest dump, and set them on fire. Jimmy came back to work the next night. This is the man I lived with.

During these times I was slowly being brainwashed, and continually being convinced that I was worthless, just as Joe said. Joe constantly confirmed all of my self-fears. He was a real pro.

Somehow, ever so slowly, my inner Shadow began to extend a hand and pull me out when I was in trouble. She grudgingly encouraged me and told me I deserved more. I was too scared to listen most of the time, but she had obviously never completely given up. To grow strong would take time, but she would, eventually.

———◆———

Breaking my promise to Billie bothered me. Every day I thought of calling Babe, but I could not summon the courage to openly disobey Joe again. The night Billie was due to return home, Joe and I went to an opening of a new dinner club in Billie's and Babe's neighborhood. I couldn't stop thinking of them. Were they all right? I should've done more. But how? I struggled with my guilt. An uncanny heaviness gnawed at me all evening.

Call her, White. She needs you.

Spotting a pay phone outside the ladies' room, I dialed their number. It rang twice before Joe became suspicious and sauntered over. I hung up quickly.

"Who you calling?" he asked.

"I was just checking on Toni," I answered casually.

Babe had kept himself busy while Billie was away. He'd gone to a nursery and bought grass seed for the lawn, then he had stopped at a gun shop where he purchased a shotgun and ammunition. On the day of Billie's return, he busied himself making a giant sign that read "WELCOME HOME" and he hung it over the kitchen door entrance from the garage. He'd apparently planned for it to be the first thing Billie would see when she opened the door and saw his dead body sprawled under it. But he changed his mind.

As soon as Joe left home the following day, I called Billie. The phone rang and rang—no answer. I tried again later that day, and still there was no answer. That feeling again...*something's wrong*. Joe returned and I couldn't make any more calls. I wanted to discuss my fears with him, but it was out of the question.

Then the phone rang.

"Georgia," my sister Sharon said, "are you alone?"

"No, Joe's here, why?"

"I have to tell you something and you shouldn't be alone."

"What's the matter, Sharon?" I asked, but I already knew. The feelings were too strong to doubt them. I felt a thousand invisible pins piercing my skin as I waited for her to confirm my premonition.

"It's Babe. Georgia, he killed himself."

"Oh my God! I knew it, I felt it...Oh God, Sharon—"

"Georgia, that's not all. He killed Billie, too."

"Oh, no...oh God...she told me he was going to do it. I didn't believe her. Oh my God."

"Georgia..." she hesitated. "He killed the kids, too."

"Please, God, no. No...No, not the kids."

"What happened?" Joe kept repeating.

I handed him the phone and began crying uncontrollably. After Joe hung up, he tried to comfort me. "I'm sorry, honey," he said putting his arms around me.

I abruptly pulled away from him. "I'll never forgive you for this, Joe! If I hadn't listened to you, they might still be alive. I hate you!"

I'm the one you need to hear, White. Start listening.

I had never been to a funeral with six caskets in one room. Not many people have. I sat numbly looking at the pictures on top of the caskets, remembering.

Billie's body was found on the bed, severed in half from two .12-gauge shotgun blasts to the abdomen and chest. Michelle, the oldest child, was found on the floor of her bedroom. A bullet from a .22-caliber rifle had gone through her hand first, then into her head. She must have been awakened from the sound of the shotgun blast that killed her mother. My heart ached for that child. She was old enough to realize what was happening.

Then there was Karen, only seven, found in her own bed with a bullet in her head and one in her stomach. And four-year-old David, the only boy in the family, Babe's pride and joy. He was found lying on the living room couch, one bullet in his head. Why had he shot David only once? The baby, just a year old, was found in the family room on the couch, one bullet in her skull and another in her tiny torso. They found Babe next to Billie in their bedroom with his brains splattered against the walls. Babe had been determined to keep his family together, one way or another.

Gradually, the shock wore off, but the reality of how closely I was walking that same line haunted me as I tiptoed through my own *mind* fields in the years that followed.

CHAPTER SIX

A cry in the night jolted me from a sound sleep. I sat on the edge of the bed, my face moist with sweat. *A nightmare?* Yes, I was awake, but I kept hearing that pathetic cry for help. No, it wasn't a dream. The real nightmare was outside, just below my window.

I looked out of my window from the second floor at the parking lot below. Joe glanced up at the same moment. He stiffened. The lights were out, but the drapes were slightly parted. He knew I was there. Quickly, he returned his attention to the boys, so as not to let on they might have been seen.

A man lay on the asphalt, groaning, begging for his life. Every time he'd make a move, they'd kick him. They viciously kicked him in the head and body simultaneously. They couldn't seem to get enough. I stood in the shadows, frozen with fear for this man's life. What could I do to stop the madness forty feet beneath me? Nothing.

"Whatta ya wanna do with him, Joe?"

"I don't give a shit. Just get him the hell out of here."

They tossed him in the trunk with seemingly little effort, and the two men drove away. Joe watched as they disappeared into the damp, drizzly night, then peered up at the window once more before heading down the cement steps into the bar. I ran to the bathroom and hung my head over the toilet bowl, taking deep breaths, trying not to gag.

In the darkened room, I lay shaking, fighting to expel the images from my mind. Mental pictures of that man being continually kicked long after he had ceased to move wouldn't leave my head. At five a.m., the door opened and I heard Joe's footsteps shuffle up the stairs.

He knows you saw what happened, White. Pretend you're sleeping.

How do I lie? He's going to know I'm lying, he always does.

Scared, I started crying before he even opened the bedroom door. He'd been drinking heavily.

"Why, Joe? Why? What did that poor guy do to deserve that? Is he dead?"

Leave it alone! Don't question him, not now. He's been drinking.

"What did you see?" Joe demanded.

"Enough."

He slapped me so hard my head slammed against the headboard, dazing me for a moment.

"I said, what did you see?"

"Nothing! I didn't see anything!" He slapped me again.

"That's right, honey. You didn't see anything and don't you *ever* forget it. Stop that fucking crying before I really give you something to cry about," he yelled as he stormed out of the room.

Minutes passed in silence. I lay there in the dark, my mind racing and my head hurting, fighting hard to keep my hysterical gasps from being heard.

The door burst open, and Joe climbed on top of me. He wrapped his hands around my neck and began choking me. I started to feel lightheaded. My eyes felt as if they were going to pop out of their sockets.

"Don't you ever, *ever* fucking question me! Who the hell are you to question me?"

He released the pressure on my throat when I started

slipping into unconsciousness. I lay there half in and half out of consciousness as I felt him enter me. He moved inside me like a crazed animal as I lay limp as a rag doll. The smell of alcohol filled my nostrils as I drifted into a dreamlike state. Then he passed out. So did I.

When I first awoke I didn't remember what had happened the night before. That is, not until I tripped over Joe's shoes, now crusty with dried blood. I struggled to drive the images out of my head. Joe's lack of compassion repulsed and terrified me. He had become a stranger. I felt as a mouse must feel stuck in a trap, half-dead, half-alive.

I stumbled into the kitchen, still not fully awake, and made coffee. The slow tick of the wall clock, which I normally found comforting, seemed almost unbearable. Lighting a cigarette, I sat at the table and stared at the black and white tiled floor.

No natural light graced the room to brighten my shattered spirit. The entire apartment had only three windows: the one in our bedroom overlooked the parking lot, the one in Toni's bedroom faced a brick wall across the alley, and the living room window had the most beautiful view of garbage cans housed between buildings.

I walked into the living room with my coffee mug and idly studied the red and black flocked wallpaper. My attention lingered on the heavy Spanish furnishings. The stink of stale cigarette butts in an astray on the wooden coffee table suddenly made me feel like throwing up. The dreariness of my surroundings was suffocating.

Pulling back the thick red drapes, I hoped to bring in some desperately needed light, not only into the room, but also into my soul. But as luck would have it, the sky was gray and threatening rain. I stood with my coffee and stared through the barred window at the empty trashcans below. This place was a prison, and I was its prisoner.

Joe emerged from the bedroom, interrupting my thoughts of escape. He looked like death. I didn't dare bring up the incident, and he acted as if nothing had happened.

"Oh, honey, did I do that to you?"

"Do what?" I asked.

"Your face."

I ran to the bathroom and looked in the mirror. The right side of my face was swollen and bruised. *Damn it! You son-of-a-bitch!* No way make-up could cover it. I'd have to be confined to the house again until it faded. If my friends and family saw me, I'd only have more restrictions placed on my contact with them. Joe couldn't tolerate the contemptuous ridicule.

I swallowed hard. "This is the third time in the last two months I'll have to cancel a shoot. I *hate* you, Joe, I hate you!"

How did you get here? You can't let this happen anymore, White.

"I'm sorry, honey," Joe said. "I'm really sorry. You know I love you. I don't mean to hurt you. I don't know what happens to me when I drink."

Don't fall for his bullshit. Get the hell out the first chance you can.

"Then *please*, Joe, stop drinking."

"How can I stop drinking, Georgia? Don't be ridiculous. You know how the shots line up downstairs. If I don't drink, the guys get insulted. It's not good for business."

"Then have the bartender pour yours from a watered-down bottle, I don't know, but you can't keep doing this to me, Joe. I can't take it anymore."

"I love you, Georgia. You're the only one who understands me; you're the only one who cares. Oh God, please don't ever leave me, Georgia. I'd be a dead man without you."

"I'll be a dead woman if I stay."

Stop threatening—do something about it.

"Let's not start that again. You're not going anywhere."

The phone rang. I picked it up and Joe jerked it from my hand.

"Hello," he said sharply. "No, she's not here." He slammed down the phone and pulled it out of the wall.

"Who was that?"

"That was that long-haired blonde bitch you think is your friend. I thought I told you I don't want you talking to her. Don't you ever fucking listen to a word I say? She's jealous of you, Georgia. Wake up! I'm not gonna tell you again: if that bitch calls here one more time, or I find out you called her, you won't be able to work for a fucking month! How many black eyes is it going to take before you learn?"

"Susie's been my friend for a long time, Joe. You hate her because she lets me know what she thinks of you. Let's be honest," I retaliated.

"Keep it up, Georgia," he yelled, looking as if ready to pounce.

Toni entered the kitchen, awakened by the noise. She inched around the screaming monster that was her step-father and ran into my arms. She hid her face under my chin, clinging to me with one hand and pressing the other against her ear.

"It's okay, baby, it's okay," I whispered softly into her ear. Her tiny body trembled as I stroked her hair, trying to calm the fear.

Defeated again. Not wanting to subject Toni to Joe's escalating temper, I agreed to his terms and avoided another confrontation I could never win. But, someday...someday...

The image of the man in the parking lot wouldn't go away. I couldn't talk about it to Joe—or to anyone for that matter. Had he lived or died? I checked the papers every day but didn't see anything that gave an indication. I had difficulty looking at Joe without replaying the scene of that night in my head. Why had Joe become such an angry man? This was *not* the person I had fallen in love with.

Joe had changed in many ways. Of course it was my fault, but what had I done that made him so cruel? Was it because I wouldn't go along with his sexual fantasies? He'd get angry and hold a grudge, punishing me in little stupid ways that made me crazy. He beat me with silence. But I just couldn't do the things he desired. His sexual demands became overwhelming, perverted. I was his wife, and according to him my duty was to make him happy. When I refused, he would force me, leaving me dreading the next encounter. I went to a priest for counseling, and was urged to stay and try to work it out. I didn't think this could be fixed.

This is insane, the way you're living. Get out of it now. He's never going to change. You don't deserve it and neither does Toni. You want a miracle.

———◆———

I finally summoned the courage to leave Joe. He left to check out a band in Toronto, and when he returned I was gone. Surprisingly, he didn't put up a fight. The reality was, he now had a good excuse to carry out a fantasy. In all likelihood, he was already carrying out the fantasy, since he wasn't making his usual scene. I knew about Roxanne. She was the beautiful red-haired sex kitten I had seen making eyes at him in the club. After a very short time, I'd heard he bought her a horse. Not much got past the gossips in Rochester. It hurt, but the pain came from the memories of the old Joe. Moving forward, I avoided thinking about it. It felt good to have the needed space without harassment or the threat of violence.

Quite by accident, I met someone too: Gino Provenzano. I felt as if struck by lightning. We were instantly attracted to each other. He was the spark I needed to lift my sunken spirit. Knowing it wasn't the smartest thing to do, I accepted a date with him.

Gino was tall, about 6'4". A mass of curly hair worn in an Afro suited him. Stylish in his dress, his height and slenderness made everything he wore look as if it were tailor-made. I'd always been attracted to men who took pride in the way they dressed. Gino's inviting eyes were soft and genuine, and they had a seductive invitation to mischief. His overall appearance was gentle, yet rugged. The chemistry between us was electrifying.

I hadn't anticipated this happening. The timing wasn't right. I couldn't date Gino publicly; not enough time had passed. Joe would go nuts. I was taking a big risk seeing Gino, but I couldn't help it. I'd been suffocated for so long.

Our first date was to a concert in Toronto, a three-hour drive out of Rochester, but even there I ran into people who knew me. The next weekend we went camping with three other couples in Letchworth State Park. Eight of us huddled in the tent while rain pounded down on the thick canvas. The constant crackle of thunder and lightning was frightening, but that's what I found most exciting. I fell in love with Gino that weekend—or at least the idea of Gino. He made me feel alive, the way I used to feel with Frankie—the way I *wasn't* feeling with Joe.

I couldn't help but compare my life with Joe to this new feeling. There was no comparison. Joe was once fun too, but as much as I wished he could be that person again, he couldn't, at least with consistency. I was bursting with spontaneous happiness. But Gino was nervous about Joe. I couldn't blame him. So was I.

Joe enjoyed his freedom until he heard I was seeing someone. He called.

"I want to talk to you," he said casually.

This freedom couldn't last, but why make him angry by refusing to see him?

Stand firm. You haven't been this enthusiastic about life in a long time. This is the way it's supposed to be. Don't let it go.

"Come to the club at closing time. There's something I want to say to you."

Hmm...Maybe you don't have to say a thing. Maybe he's crazy about this girl and he's going to tell you it's over. This could be easier than we thought. Just be careful what you say.

I drove to Caesars II at two o'clock in the morning. I sat at the bar and waited until he finished closing out the cash register.

"Come on, let's go have breakfast," he said as he locked the door. We drove in silence to a 24 hour diner—not the one nearest the club. Why had he chosen this particular place? Inside I spotted Gino sitting with a few of his friends. Coincidence? He saw me at the same time. We just looked at each other, both in quiet shock. I could tell by his quizzical expression that he was wondering why I was there with Joe, but he wasn't about to ask.

We sat two tables away. Joe's back was to Gino and I faced him. Not looking at him was hard. Our eyes locked a few times and I forced myself to look away. His face expressed hurt and confusion. I wanted to shout out, 'It's not the way it looks!'

"Hey, Gino, how you doing?" said a man passing by.

Joe swung around in his seat, his eyes flashed wildly, then turned back to me. I sat there frozen, trying my hardest to act normal. He studied my face briefly before he spoke.

"So, I understand you're seeing someone, is that true?"

"Who told you that?" I answered calmly. My heart was racing.

"Never mind who told me. Is it true?"

"No, it's not true," I answered, staring into my coffee cup. I couldn't look at him. He'd know I wasn't being truthful.

"Why are you lying, Georgia? You know it'll be worse if you lie."

My gaze rose from the coffee cup to meet his eyes, but instead drifted over his shoulder to meet Gino's. I quickly looked back down at my coffee and struggled for something to say.

"What about Roxanne?" I asked finally, lacking something more intelligent to say.

He tried to hide his surprised expression. "Roxanne's just a piece of ass," he answered, as if it was of no consequence.

"I'm amazed you're not broke by now if you make it a practice to buy a horse for everyone who's *just* a piece of ass."

Annoyed that the focus was now on his behavior, he leaned over the table and raised his voice. "We're not talking about Roxanne now, we're talking about *Gino Provenzano*," he snapped.

His hooded eyes bore into mine, waiting for a reaction. I clutched my purse and looked away uncomfortably. Pressure pounded in my ears. *Does he know what Gino looks like? Does he know he's here? Did he bring me here for a reason?*

"So it *is* true, isn't it?"

"I have to go to the ladies' room," I said, and started to get up.

He grabbed my arm and pushed me back into the seat. "Sit down!" he demanded. "You haven't answered me yet."

Gino started to rise. I knew Joe was packing a gun inside his jacket. I looked at Gino and told him all was okay with my eyes. He relaxed. I wanted to get out of there. *What did Joe know?* I feared for Gino.

"I don't think this is the place to have this discussion Joe. Let's go home."

"I don't think there's going to be much of a discussion, do you?" He rose and threw a $20 bill on the table.

We walked by Gino's table on the way out. He and his friends stood after we passed and followed us out the door. I was too terrified to look back to see which direction they were headed.

As we approached our car, someone yelled out from the parking lot, "Hey, Provenzano, don't you return your phone calls anymore, or what?"

Joe stopped dead in his tracks. He pivoted around to see Gino, who returned his icy stare. The air was thick with tension. They stood facing each other like pacing pit bulls for what seemed like an eternity.

"Get in the car, Joe," I said as calmly as I could.

They continued to stand in their frozen positions and glare at each other. Joe slowly raised his arm toward his jacket.

"Joe!" I screamed. "Please, let's go. Come on. Please get in the car."

He lowered his arm, but never broke eye contact. The Provenzano name rang a bell. Joe wasn't quite sure what family connections there might be. The only connection to the name as far as I knew was Gino's uncle, a prominent judge in the city. But Joe wasn't sure. Anyway, four to one weren't good odds—and only I knew that Joe had his six little friends hiding under that coat.

"Joe, if you don't get in the car right now I'm gonna call a cab."

Gino broke contact first. Joe turned to me with a twisted smile and finally got in the car. My fear for Gino had been so great that I'd forgotten what I had to look forward to.

"Where the hell's your taste?" he asked sarcastically.

I didn't answer.

"Did you sleep with him, Georgia?" he asked accusingly.

"No." I hadn't—yet.

"Liar!" he shouted, slapping me.

When we arrived back at the apartment I was still crying from the abuse in the car.

"I'll teach you to embarrass me, you no good whore!" he screamed as he dragged me to the window. "You're going to leave me? I'll show you the way out if that's what you want!"

My upper body was hanging out the window as I pleaded for my life. He shoved me all the way out, holding me by my ankles. The blood rushed to my head as I tried to assure him I'd stay and never see Gino again. When he was convinced, he pulled me inside. His entire personality changed instantly and he became loving and apologetic. I was grateful to be alive and somehow managed to forgive him his bizarre behavior.

The tragedy of my sister-in-law and her children was proof that threats do get carried out. Clearly I'd been caught up in a phenomenon known as Stockholm Syndrome, where a hostage eventually bonds with her captor. When the warden locked the door to my invisible cell, I obediently stayed to finish out my sentence—till death do us part.

Little did Joe know that Gino, having heard about Joe's reputation, had already decided it wasn't in his best interest to see me anymore. And that was that.

⎯⎯◆⎯⎯

I pushed open the office door in our apartment above the club. Joe shifted nervously in his high back leather chair, trying hard not to laugh. The shyster accountant's back was to me. He spoke in a business-like fashion as Joe sat across from him, facing in my direction. In a playful mood, I lifted my shirt and exposed my breast to Joe. Toni wandered in and imitated me. The two of us stood there for several minutes, practically giving Joe a nervous breakdown.

"Do something about it! I'm not paying it," Joe demanded, trying to focus on the business of the day.

Badly in need of a shave, Carl the accountant rubbed his stubby fingers back and forth across his chin as he sifted through the papers strewn on the desk. His eyeglasses were as thick as windshields, and I seriously doubted he could see us even if he did look our way. Fighting a smile, Joe sneaked another look at us. Without a sound, he mouthed, "Stop that. He'll see you."

We quietly smiled back and continued to hold up our shirts. Joe lost his concentration but continued to babble, keeping the accountant's attention on him. A return smile in our direction would surely cause Carl to turn his head, catching the children at play.

The game was over at the sound of the doorbell, at least for me. Toni continued to play.

"Get the door, honey," Joe said, grateful for the intrusion.

I bounced down the stairs and opened the door. My good mood faded when I saw Frank Valenti and Gene DeFrancesco standing outside.

"Hello, Georgia, is Joe around?" Frank asked in his gentlemanly voice. Always dressed like an elegant statesman, he walked with the grace of royalty. Only his stone-cold eyes gave a hint of the darkness which lived inside.

"Yeah, come on up." The bounce in my step disappeared as I led them up the stairs.

I knew this was not a visit Joe was expecting. Frank rarely made personal appearances.

"Hey, Frank...Gene," Joe said. "Carl, can we continue this tomorrow?"

"Ah, sure, Joe," Carl answered, quickly gathering his papers.

"Honey, why don't you and Toni go out and have a nice lunch," Joe said, handing me a $100 bill.

Hmm, Frank should stop by more often.

I took Toni to McDonald's and then headed for the

shopping mall. When I returned, Joe was in the office leaning back in the chair. A bottle of Scotch sat on the desk. He wasn't in a good mood.

"What was that all about?" I asked, not expecting to get an answer.

"Who the fuck does he think he is?"

"He is who he is, Joe. I don't know what the problem is, but I think you'd better keep that in mind."

He threw the glass at me and missed. It shattered against the wall. Toni grimaced and ran to her room.

I turned back to Joe, exasperated. "Jesus, what the hell did I say that was so bad?"

"Who's side are you on, anyway?"

"Joe, I don't even know what the hell is going on. All I'm saying is, don't act before you think. You're playing with fire with that guy. In the end, he'll have it his way anyway."

"They already have a piece of my action—and that's all they're getting!"

Any look at the Rochester rackets had to focus heavily on Frank Valenti, "made" in the Mob by Joseph "Joe Bananas" Bonanno in the 1950's. A delegate to the Appalachian Crime Convention in 1957, he had been arrested with 57 of his cohorts when the state police pulled their surprise raid on the home of host Joe Barbara. Frank served jail time when he refused to talk about the Appalachian agenda. His silence earned him control of Rochester when Upstate crime czar Stefano Magaddino of Niagara Falls decided it was time for a change in the Flower City.

After returning from prison, Frank settled into the Rochester rackets as Magaddino's handpicked Capo. Frank Valenti began playing Godfather with a classic flair. The files of the Rochester Police Department swelled during his years at the top. Death awaited anyone who refused to play the game his way.

With the help of his old-time pal Joe Colombo in New York City, Valenti opened a Rochester chapter of the Italian-American

Civil Rights League. He effectively used the office both as a Mob front and to pursue the cause of anti-defamation for his ethnic kinsmen. I attended many of the fund-raisers. After the dinners, Joe Colombo would return with us to the club and the parties continued. But it wouldn't be long before the party would end for all of them.

Two weeks had passed since Frank Valenti had darkened our doorstep. Joe didn't mention him after that day, and I didn't ask. My parents had taken Toni on a trip for the weekend, affording me the opportunity to enjoy the nightlife at Caesars II for a change. Without Toni as an excuse for Joe to keep me locked up, I dressed conservatively in an elegant pantsuit and walked downstairs into a din of noise and the bustle of activity.

Friday night and business as usual. Through a growing crowd that threatened to exceed the club's 300-seat capacity, I spotted Joe trying to accommodate the steady stream of high rollers.

I sat at a vacant table and quietly took in the room, which resembled the decor of our home upstairs: the dismal colors of red and black. Although the apartment didn't have the heavy stone and brick walls, they both had a dusky, cave-like atmosphere.

The cocktail waitress hurried over to take my order. "Hi, hon."

"Hi, Bea."

"Your usual?"

I nodded. "Say, where's the hostess tonight?"

Bea Massaro shrugged. "Beats me. Hasn't shown up."

"On a Friday night? Is she sick?"

"Could be I suppose, but as far as I know she hasn't called in. It's not the first time she's pulled this either. I don't know why Joe hasn't fired her. It's not like him to tolerate that from an employee."

I know why, White, he's sleeping with the bitch.

I caught a glimpse of Joe across the room, beaming as he charmed a pretty brunette. Even at a distance I could see the nervousness in him when he had to play host and couldn't keep an eye on me. Or was it more about *me* keeping an eye on *him*? *Maybe I should show up unannounced more often.*

Company joined me—unwanted company, as usual. I tried to force a smile as he sat down, but the expression failed to appear.

"How's it going with you tonight, Georgia?" Jimmy Massaro asked.

"Just fine, till *you* showed up."

"What the fuck is that supposed to mean?"

"I don't like being treated like a child, that's what. Why aren't you babysitting Frank Valenti? He needs a bodyguard. I don't."

"What the fuck's gotten into you tonight, ya got your period or somethin'?" Shifting his focus from me, he called out to Bea, "How fucking long does it take to get a drink around this joint?"

"I have customers, Jimmy. I'm moving as fast as I can," Bea answered as she hurried past us.

Agitated, Jimmy turned his attention to the band until Bea arrived with his drink. He grabbed Bea's wrist and pulled her face-to-face with him. "I don't give a shit about your customers. I'm your husband, goddamnit. You serve me first! You got that?" he growled, applying pressure to her wrist.

"Yes, Jimmy," she responded peevishly. "I'm sorry."

Appalled by his behavior, I just had to get in my digs. "You may not care about the customers, Jimmy, but I'm sure Joe feels differently. Bea is working for us, you know. Who do you think you are anyway, King Farouk?"

His eyes hooded over. "Y'know, I think I've had about enough of that mouth of yours tonight, Georgia. I'm not in the mood." He stiffened and leaned over the table. "So lay off."

God, how I despised him. Bea was such a sweet woman. She didn't deserve this treatment. Besides, they were separated. Even though Jimmy was living with another woman, he still controlled Bea's every move. She still loved him. Even if she wanted to make another life for herself, she knew it could never happen. His last girlfriend had tried that...

Word had it that Jimmy followed her one night when her date picked her up. He killed them both—shot 'em in the head, cold turkey. Then he blatantly bragged about it. He had no fear of the law, or of the Mob, for that matter. No, Jimmy "The Hammer" was not the kind of guy one crossed. Only about 5'4", he was a wiry little hothead. He'd rather shoot than argue. And to set him afire didn't take much.

I left for the ladies' room. On the fifty-foot walk, I was asked to dance several times and offered just as many drinks. I ignored them all. Not even a "no, thank you." I learned to alter my personality in the club. Too many innocent people under the influence of alcohol did not walk out the same way they had walked in.

When I returned, Joe was standing at his usual place at the end of the bar. His suspicious eyes shot daggers at everyone who dared to let their look linger for too long. At my table, yet another undesirable, Gene DeFrancesco, joined me. His broad, owl-like face showed years of a hard life. Big Gene and Jimmy were both Frank Valenti's part-time bodyguards.

"Who's guarding Frank tonight?" I asked as he sat down.

Big Gene frowned and gave me a cockeyed expression.

"Don't mind her, she's got the rag on tonight," Jimmy said, shooting me a disgusted look which I returned.

"Hi, Gene," I said with a forced smile.

"Hi, Georgia," he said without one.

"You know what, Gene?" I ventured. "I don't think I've ever seen you smile. Do you...ever?"

"Yeah, I smile."

Yeah, I bet. A friendly pat on the back was just Big Gene's way of looking for a soft spot to stick the knife in.

"When? I've never seen it."

"When I *hurt* someone," he answered, devoid of feeling or compassion—just the cold, dark eyes of a shark.

His thick glasses magnified the lurking evil. I felt as if he were sucking me into the depths of his demented mind, as if toying with me to enter. I turned away from his frosty glare. If this was a mind game we were playing, he was winning.

Big Gene was completely the opposite of Jimmy, but only in stature. He towered over Jimmy by at least a foot. His large frame housed over 250 pounds of solid muscle.

Jimmy cleared his throat and asked, "When'd you get back from Boston, Gene?"

"Yesterday," Gene answered, adjusting his glasses with thick fingers resembling Italian sausages. "Mike 'the Fink' is a memory now."

"Yeah?"

"Yeah. He dropped dead while being strangled." They burst into laughter. I rolled my eyes and looked away. Big Gene's face became serious again. Rubbing a hand over his patent-leather hair, he said, "Jimmy, we got business to discuss."

That was usually my cue to leave, but I had just returned from the ladies' room, and besides, this was *my* table! If they wanted to talk, *they* could leave. They did just that. Good! I sat alone and listened to the band, but not for long.

"Would you like to dance?" a man asked.

Looking over my shoulder I simply replied, "No, thank you."

Joe was watching, of course. He never missed much. Within seconds he stood behind my chair.

"It's time to go upstairs," he said.

"I don't want to go upstairs."

"I'm too busy to watch you, get your ass upstairs."

"I'm a big girl, Joe, you don't need to watch me. I'm not going anywhere," I retorted defiantly.

Atta-girl, White. Don't let him push you around.

He discreetly pulled my head back by my hair. "You heard me."

Sammy G appeared from out of nowhere. "This table open?" he asked.

"For you it is, Sammy, sit down." Sammy slipped casually into the seat and unbuttoned his coat. Raising my head to Joe I whispered mockingly, "I have a baby-sitter now. I think I'll be safe."

"Hey, Sam," Joe said, extending his hand. "How's it going?"

"Could be better," Sammy answered, not offering his hand in return.

Joe left to defuse an argument at the bar.

"What was that all about?" Sam asked.

"What was what?"

"Georgia, don't play dumb, you know what I'm talking about."

"It was nothing, Sammy, really. He just doesn't like it when I exercise my brain."

"How's he been treating you lately?"

"Okay," I answered, avoiding looking at him.

He squared his shoulders and confronted me. "Then what's that bruise on your arm?"

"What bruise?" I questioned, peering down at my arm. "Oh, I must have done that on the car door yesterday."

His doubting eyes pierced mine. He smirked and looked away. He knew I was lying.

"Where's Joey Tiraborelli?" I asked, wanting to change the subject.

"He's around here somewhere."

I turned to survey the room. Joe stood at the bar with three women hovering around him, enjoying the attention.

Who does he think he's kidding, White—you or me?

"Do you ever wish you had stayed with Tom?" Sammy asked, recognizing my wounded expression.

"No, Sam, never. Whatever made you ask that?"

"Just wondering."

"I don't even know why I married him."

"I do."

"You do?"

"Yeah, I think I got you pegged. You married him because you thought you were spoiled goods. Right?"

"Well, I don't know, maybe..."

"You sold yourself short then, kid, and you're selling yourself short now. You don't need to take the shit this asshole gives you. You're a special lady, Georgia. Everyone seems to know that but you."

"I love him, Sam, but there are times..."

He shook his head and looked through the partition of red hanging beads just in time to catch Joe depositing the brunette's phone number in his pocket. Something in Sammy's expression was unsettling.

"Are you going to the after-hours club tonight?" Sam asked after a moment of silence.

"Oh, I don't think so. If you hadn't come along when you did, I'd already be upstairs. All dressed up, entertaining myself by staring out the window at the parking lot, watching who's cheating on who. It's shocking what I see from that window." I bit my tongue, hoping he didn't pick up on it.

"I'll bet it is. Isn't that your cousin at the bar?"

"Oh, yeah, she said she might stop in tonight."

I left Sammy and joined my cousin Debbie at the bar. When we returned to the table, Sammy was gone.

———◦———

We cashed out at three in the morning and headed for the after-hours club on Lyell Avenue, just a few blocks down the street from Caesars. Joe knew I had watched him in action with the ladies all night, and he felt he needed to appease me. The after-hours club was an old, run down house in a commercial area, converted into a meeting place where swarthy business was usually conducted. The boys were all there, except for Sammy G. Joey Tiraborelli surfaced through the parade of faces.

"What are you doing here?" he asked, looking perplexed.

"What do you mean, what am I doing here?"

"Well, Sam said you weren't coming tonight. I'm just surprised to see you, that's all," he said. His eyes darted around the room. The left side of his cheek twitched as he lit a cigarette, shifting his weight from one leg to the other.

"Joey, you remember my cousin Debbie, don't you?"

"Sure, I remember Debbie. How are you, Deb? You guys want a drink?" he asked, looking nervously over his shoulder.

"Of course we want a drink, Joey, why the hell else do you come to an after-hours club? The question is, what do we *want* to drink?" I replied with a throaty laugh.

He didn't laugh. That wasn't like Joey. He was always good for a laugh. He bought us a drink and disappeared.

"Seemed kind of edgy, didn't he?" Debbie asked.

"Who knows what weirdness goes on in their world, Deb. I've learned not to question it," I answered, looking down at the worn linoleum floor.

Joe was busy at the other end of the bar, instructing the bartender as to whom to give drinks. It was Debbie's first time in an after-hours club. She glanced over her shoulder continuously, worried about being caught in a raid.

"Relax, Deb. The cops are well taken care of."

Just when she started to get comfortable, the all-too-familiar sounds of a fight broke out. I immediately looked for Joe. I couldn't see him anywhere. Panicking, I pushed my way through the crowd to the kitchen, dreading what I would see. My fears were validated.

It was five on one. Joe didn't have a chance. Joey Tiraborelli, *my friend*, was doing most of the damage. Every time Joe went down, Tiraborelli smashed a foot in his face. I broke through the crowd and jumped on Joey Tiraborelli.

"No! You'll kill him!" I screamed. "You bastard! How could you do this?"

Tom Torpey grabbed me and pulled me off Joey, throwing me against the coffee machine. Then I was blocked, forced to watch as they beat Joe to a bloody pulp.

"Please, please," I begged Torpey.

Behind his dark glasses his eyes widened, his mouth became set. "Please what? The motherfucker's got it coming!"

Tom Torpey was treating me as though I were the enemy! I was shocked and powerless. Nothing I could say could make them stop their brutality.

The kitchen door window steamed over, shielding them from any outside interference. "Kill 'em!" Torpey shouted as he held me hostage.

These were no ordinary men doing this damage. These were

Rochester's fiercest, men who made their living killing and mutilating. Some men killed for money, others for family business...and then there were those who killed for pleasure. They were the guys who slithered around town collecting debts for the Mob, living for the poor dummies who couldn't pay.

I had seen their wrath many times over the years at clubs throughout the city. At the age of fourteen, I witnessed Tom Torpey's brutality in front of The 414 Club on Ridge Road, where he worked as a bouncer. I watched in horror as he bit off a guy's ear. He'd graduated from those days. Tom was my friend and my protector; I'd known him since I was a kid. I loved all these guys, and assumed the feelings were mutual. Why were they doing this to me? I was terrified for Joe's life.

"Stay down! Stay down!" I kept yelling, but Joe was dazed. He kept getting up and the punishment was severe.

I finally broke through the human barricade and ran outside into the cold winter air, my tangled hair covering my face. Gasping for air, I spotted a police car patrolling the alley. I wasn't thinking about the rules—never call the cops. I was hysterical, sure they'd kill Joe if I didn't get help. The cop stopped. I knew him, he was a regular at the club.

Eyebrows raised, eyes afire, I screamed, "John! They're killing Joe in there! Help me. They're killing him!"

John took both of my hands in his and squeezed them tightly. Appearing genuinely sympathetic, he said, "I can't help you, Georgia, I'm sorry."

"But they're—"

He let go of my hands, looked straight ahead and drove down the alley to the street. I stood with my mouth open as the patrol car made a right-hand turn onto Lyell Avenue and disappeared. Feeling totally helpless, I ran back inside.

Joe lay motionless on the floor. Joey Tiraborelli was crouched over him, making the sign of the cross on Joe's forehead—with his own blood. I thought he was dead. Frozen in place, I screamed. Tiraborelli turned, and seeing me, he rose slowly. His face showed remorse as he approached. I resisted as he pulled me outside.

"Joey, how could you?" I yelled, punching him.

"I had to, Georgia!" he shouted, shaking me to bring me out of my hysteria. "I didn't have a choice. I'm sorry. But the asshole deserved it, the way he treats you."

"Oh no! Oh my God! You didn't do that because of me? Please say you didn't do that for me! Not because of me..." I cried.

"Let's just put it this way: he's stepped out of line one too many times."

Joe's friend, Butch Marionette, stood in the doorway with Joe's dead weight leaning against him. Everyone had scattered—the club had emptied out.

"Georgia, get the car. Hurry!" Butch yelled. "We've gotta get him to a hospital."

I ran to the street, jumped into the car, made a 180 degree turn and tore down the alley, screeching my tires as I came to a stop. I sprang from the car and helped Butch get Joe inside. Butch then ran around and got in the driver's seat.

"Stay here," Joe said, his voice barely audible.

"No, I'm going with you."

"I don't want you to," he said, still dazed.

"Don't argue with him, Georgia. Close the door. We gotta go. Now, goddamnit! I'll call you as soon as I know anything."

Alone in a frightening atmosphere, I stood in the alley and watched as they sped off.

"Come on, Georgia, get in, I'll give you a ride home," Debbie said.

I'd forgotten all about Debbie. She was pretty shaken, unaccustomed to this world. Joey Tiraborelli stood in the doorway, head hung low as we drove off.

The phone finally rang. "He's got five broken ribs, and some internal bleeding. They're keeping him here for awhile."

"When can I see him, Butch?"

"He...he doesn't want to see you, Georgia. Not right now."

"I don't care, I'm coming anyway."

"I wouldn't do that if I were you."

"How did it happen, Butch? How did it start?"

"You'll have to ask Joe about that, but I think you'd better think about whose side you're on, lady." The phone went dead.

The purpose of that beating was never made clear to me. I'd always thought Frank Valenti had his hand in it. Then again, for months after the incident, Joe refrained from using physical violence with me. But as his bruises faded, so did his memory.

By the turn of the decade and into the 1970's, Frank Valenti had soared to his peak. The years 1971 and 1972 saw the beginnings of legal problems that would cut short Valenti's reign. His underlings were not anxious to tolerate his continued rule from behind bars. The time had come. Sammy G was strategically moving into the long-awaited position. Sammy killed one of Frank's bodyguards with a shotgun blast to the face. Valenti understood the message and went quietly to serve his prison sentence of twenty years to life.

Sammy Gingello, Red Russotti, and Rene Piccarreto were the trio that inherited the empire Frank Valenti had built under Stefano Magaddino. Sam was the one with the flamboyance. Red and Rene stayed quietly in the background—well, in the background anyway. The life and times of Frank Valenti were a thing of the past by mid-1972. The new regime took over. The shifting of power produced a wave of murders.

They found him in his trunk. Six bullets in his head. Five days had elapsed since he had disappeared. The cool November air had kept his body from decomposing. I knew he didn't have long. He just couldn't keep his mouth shut. Jimmy "The Hammer" Massaro was a memory now, and a bad one at that. Thanksgiving Day 1973 would be the last holiday Jimmy would live to see. I shudder to think how he got his nickname.

I didn't want to go the funeral. I only went to comfort Bea. She was really a gentle soul. She couldn't help that she loved him, any more than I could help loving Joe. Now she was free to live without dread. She would realize that in time and find peace.

The room had a chokingly-sweet smell of roses. Old ladies

with rosary beads twisted in their wrinkled hands took turns wailing as we moved through the horde toward Bea. We sat in the front row, Joe and I on her left, her family on the right. I held her hand and stared at the picture on top of the casket. There were no tears in *my* eyes. I had no fond memories; only dark pictures developed in my head. I couldn't burn the negatives, no matter how I tried.

The entire Rochester Mob filed in before the night was over. The absence of color was the traditional attire for an Italian funeral. When Sammy G showed up wearing a cream-colored raincoat, he made his point. The level of murmur in the room attested to his rank as he arrogantly strutted to the widow's side.

He took Bea's hand gently in his own. "I'm sorry, Bea," Sammy said with unbelievable sincerity.

Bea snatched her hand back and pierced him with a freezing glare. Sam looked away, unremorseful. He nodded in my direction, ignored Joe, then turned and walked to the casket. His bodyguards followed, making a solid wall of human flesh and muscle behind him as he stood with head bent for a brief moment. When he turned to leave, I thought I caught a hint of a smirk on his lips.

Rose Rotundi, Jimmy's live-in girlfriend, sat across from us in the row of chairs against the wall. She was visibly shaken. She had a lot to be shaken about. It was she who had answered the phone call that had sent Jimmy busting out the door, in a rage, to his death. She knew whose voice was on the other end of the line, but she wasn't talking. Now, her body stiffened, and the little color she had drained from her face. I followed her frigid stare to see Gene DeFrancesco making his entrance.

"Big Gene" was the name used when referring to him, but I had my own name for him: "The Accountant." He could not only pass for one, but according to the talk, he could personally account for a number of bodies found floating in the Genesee River. He was one mean son-of-a-bitch. He and Jimmy were tied on that score. But Big Gene knew how to keep his cool, and Jimmy didn't. That made him easy to set up for the kill.

Rose was holding her hands tightly in her lap, trying to keep them from shaking. Could Big Gene have been the triggerman? I watched him, and the interaction when their eyes met as he passed in front of her. That's when I knew that he had done it. And he knew that *she* knew. And she knew that *he* knew. Now, I knew too. Maybe others sensed it, but nobody was talking. They had been very tight and Jimmy trusted Big Gene. They say it's always the one closest to you, the one you could trust with your life.

"Bea, I'm so sorry," said the Accountant.

"Oh Gene, he's gone...he's gone," she said, a spurt of emotion escaping her.

"I know, honey, I know..." he said, hugging her tenderly.

I stifled my scorn. What a wonderful display of compassion. Something I had never seen in him before. Maybe he missed his calling—he should have been an actor.

"Jesus, Joe, can we get out of here now?" I whispered. "I think we've overstayed our show of respect, don't you? Bea has her family, she doesn't need us."

I waited alone while Joe disappeared into the jammed parking lot. The silent air was brisk. I pulled my coat collar up over my neck and tucked my chin into my chest. A fine snow was falling now, the kind that accumulated fast. The ground would be covered with a soft white blanket by morning. Trudging through the snow to an open grave in the cemetery was not where I would be tomorrow. I'd had enough of this charade.

Suddenly, a chill surged through my body, and it wasn't from the cold air.

"Hi there," said a voice that sounded like a rusty car muffler.

I turned to see the Accountant hunched inside his coat. "Hello, Gene," I said coldly, but he didn't seem to notice.

"I wouldn't want to die in the winter, would you?" he asked, trying to make small talk—I think.

Shoving my cold hands deeper inside my coat pockets, I answered, "Not if I had a choice, Gene, but unfortunately, I doubt I'll have that luxury. With your connections, why don't you put the word in that I prefer the fall."

146

That was a pretty stupid thing to say to a guy like that, but it was spontaneous. The silence that followed made it worse. I looked everywhere except at him. Joe finally pulled up, and Big Gene opened my door. *What a gentleman!*

"See ya around," he said with a curious expression as he shut the door.

Hope not too soon, I thought to myself with a shiver.

I never voiced my observations to Joe. I perceived a lot, but I never talked much. Life was easier that way.

Four years passed before the truth was known, but Gene DeFrancesco was ultimately charged with the murder of Jimmy Massaro. And life in the underworld went on.

CHAPTER SEVEN

Gunshots woke me again. I knew they weren't in my imagination as Joe had suggested the last time I heard them. I listened. There was only silence. I fell back to sleep. Voices in the distance woke me again. *The stragglers are leaving. Joe will be up shortly...* I drifted back into a sound sleep.

"I heard that sound again last night. I swear it sounds like gunshots," I said at breakfast the next morning.

"It was. The boys got a little rowdy last night. Wanna go to the track today?" Joe asked, changing the subject.

"Sure, who's going?"

"Chris Fiorito, Butch, and some of the guys in the band. A friend of mine has a horse running in the seventh race and the jockey is a friend of Chris's. It's a sure bet."

"What's the number of the horse?" I excitedly asked. I loved the horse races.

"Seven."

"It's going to win, I just know it. Seven is my lucky number."

"You won't need any luck."

He was right. We won, and we won big. Joe was in a good mood. Driving home from the track, he had an idea on how to spend some of this newfound money.

"Ya know, honey, I really need a bigger office. I think I'll convert our bedroom into an office."

"What will we use as a bedroom?"

"We'll build one, and I'll even let you design it."

The plan went into effect immediately. We took a townhouse two blocks away until the construction was completed. The problem with the new bedroom was the absence of light. And there was no place to knock out a window. Not having any natural light depressed me, but Joe was satisfied. Darkness suited him.

I hated staying at the townhouse alone. Joe worked late and sometimes he would crash at the apartment. I got bad vibes from the place. I wasn't the kind of person who scared easily, but being there by myself made me strangely uncomfortable.

"Joe, I want to sleep at the apartment tonight. I don't like it at the townhouse alone."

"Stop being so silly."

"Really, Joe, that superintendent gives me the creeps. I don't like the way he looks at me. Sometimes I get the feeling he's out there watching me."

Suddenly he was interested. He sat upright. "Did you ever see him snooping around?"

"No. I just feel it. The hair on the back of my neck stands up and I *know* he's out there, somewhere in the dark. He scares me."

He stood up and began pacing the floor like a bull. "If I catch that creep watching you, I'll make him a new asshole! You and Toni sleep at the apartment tonight, I'll be home early," he said, kissing me good-bye.

I woke up in Toni's room at three o'clock in the morning. I walked into the office and peered out the window at the dark, echoing emptiness of the parking lot. Hungry, I tried calling Joe's favorite late-night haunts to ask him to bring me something to eat. He was nowhere to be found. My heart sank, suspecting the worst. How he begged me not to leave the last time this happened, promising never to do it again. And I believed him. The flowers, the romantic dinners—all a sham.

Show him you're not going to put up with this, White! Don't be here when he gets back. You let him get away with too much. Stop being such a fool!

My stomach churned. I bundled up my daughter and left for the townhouse.

Joe's car sat in my parking space. I began to tremble. My suspicions were correct. I turned my key in the door, only to be stopped by the chain lock. Setting Toni down on the sidewalk, I threw my weight against the door with unbelievable force. The chain lock broke, taking the entire doorjamb with it.

I scooped Toni into my arms and ran up the stairs. I hastily put her in her room and closed her door. Adrenaline rushed through me. I pushed open the door to my bedroom and turned on the light. I was shocked. The woman in my bed was Joe's *cousin*!

Joe shouted, "Are you gonna believe what you see, or are you gonna believe what I tell you?"

"You sick bastard!" I screamed as I ripped the decorative sword off the wall. "In *my* bed! You son-of-a-bitch."

I was out of control. All the times he'd beaten me, I'd let him convince me that I was to blame, that I had done something to set him off. But this time was different. And he was going to pay.

Kill the no-good bastard! He doesn't deserve you—he doesn't deserve to live!

I swung the sword with a deranged vengeance, slashing the bedspread and everything in its path. Joe's cousin jumped from the bed totally nude and ran out of the house. Joe pulled the thick polar bear bedspread over his head for protection, but I managed to wound him anyway, just missing the real culprit by inches. The thickness of the bedspread saved his life, and mine too. I would have killed him if he hadn't managed to grab the sword. He tried to slap me back into reality, but my rage continued.

Toni cried loudly, but I was in no condition to calm her. Still out of my mind, even the sight of his blood wasn't satisfying enough. I ran down the stairs, threw open the cupboards, and began smashing glasses against the brick wall. It was a pretty senseless thing to do, but I needed to vent the incredible anger. Joe came down the stairs fully dressed, but his once cream-colored pants were now blood red. Dodging glass, he grabbed me and pulled me into the living room, shaking me violently to stop my insane behavior. He sat me on the couch, holding my arms hostage. He waited impatiently until I stopped convulsing. He didn't dare hit me; he was too afraid of losing me after what I'd seen.

"This wasn't planned, Georgia. She was depressed and wanted to talk, so we came here—just to talk."

"Yeah, that's what it looked like to me—talking. You cocksucker! Let go of my arms!"

"After we got here...she seduced me," he continued, speaking calmly.

"In *my* bed! Your own cousin! You're sick, and she's even sicker. Let go of my arms, you son-of-a-bitch!"

"Georgia, it wasn't that way...Hey! What was that?" He gestured toward the sliding glass doors onto the fenced-in courtyard.

"What?" I said, looking outside, thinking he was just trying to divert my attention.

"I just saw something move behind the fence," he said, letting go of my arms and moving toward the window with concern.

Joe slid the door open. A trail of blood followed the path from his badly wounded leg.

"Who's out there?" Joe yelled.

"It's the superintendent," answered a meek voice from the shadows.

"What the fuck do you think you're doing out there, you fuckin' degenerate? Show your face, you sorry excuse for a man!" Joe yelled in his perfected belittling voice.

"I was just checking out the noise, that's all..."

His shadow passed by the spaces between the fence and he was gone. Joe closed the door and turned back to me.

"You were right about that pervert," he said, putting a calming hand on my shoulder. I shrugged it off violently.

"Look who's calling who a pervert!" I mocked.

With not much he could say in his defense, he walked into the kitchen, ripped up a dishtowel, and put a tourniquet on his leg. I was smoking a cigarette when he returned. My hands were still shaking, but I was slowly regaining my composure.

"You did a pretty good job on this leg."

"You're lucky to have a leg at all, let alone a penis, you bastard!"

"I'm going to get some stitches. Go back to the apartment, I don't want you here alone. We'll discuss this later."

"There's nothing to discuss, Joe. I won't stay here, but don't expect to see me at the apartment."

"Georgia, I love you. I know how hurt you are; I'm hurting too. Please, just be there when I get back." He walked down the narrow path between the buildings to the parking lot.

When he was out of sight I started to close the door, but movement caught my eye. I opened the door wider. At the end of the walkway the superintendent was crouched, pointing a gun in Joe's direction.

"Joe! Watch out—he's got a gun!" I screamed.

He fired twice, then got up and ran toward Joe, out of my view. I ran to the end of the walkway to see Joe slumped over in the car. Backing out at high speed, his tires squealed as he shifted his Corvette into first gear and floored it out of the parking lot. Had he been hit or was he just dodging the bullets? The man ran out to the middle of the street and began firing after the speeding car.

Thank God a patrol car was cruising down the street. (It was the first time I'd ever seen a cop when I needed one—at least one who could help). I ran into the street to flag the car down, although I don't see how they could have missed this nut in the middle of the road firing a gun. They screeched to a stop, flung open their car doors, and pulled out their guns, using the doors as shields.

"Drop the gun!" they yelled, pointing their weapons at the superintendent.

The man turned and began to fire at the police. I stood in the middle.

"Get the hell out of there, lady!" screamed a cop.

Three more police cars came charging up. I ran back to the townhouse and grabbed Toni, still crying, from her bed. I held her tightly and waited.

The bizarre incident was quickly under control, and the police were soon at my door. In the meantime, Joe had gone back to the apartment to get his gun. When he returned to see the police apprehending the lunatic, he went to a pay phone. I still had no way of knowing if he had been shot.

"What happened here, lady?" one of the officers asked, taking in the broken glass and the trail of blood on the floor.

Where do I start? Just then the phone rang.

"You all right?" Joe asked.

"Yes, we're fine...are you?"

"Yes," he answered, sounding relieved. "Are the cops in the house?"

"Yes."

"Don't tell them what went on...with us."

"Why? You embarrassed?"

"Christ, Georgia, you stabbed me, for God's sake. They'll take you in."

Hadn't thought about that.

The night's surreal events were catching up with me. I was totally drained. I hung up and told the police I was going to put my daughter back to bed. The bedspread was drenched with blood. It looked as if a murder had been committed. Close, but no cigar. I discreetly closed my bedroom door and returned downstairs. Three more policemen had entered the house.

"Whose blood is that?" one of the new cops asked.

"It's my husband's. He cut himself on the broken glass."

"Where is he now?"

"I don't know."

"What went on here tonight?"

"My husband and I were having an argument when—"

"Must have been some argument," the cop said.

"—we noticed that weirdo, the superintendent, watching us through the back fence, over there," I pointed. One of them walked into the living room to check. "Joe opened the patio door and—"

"What's his last name?"

"I don't know."

"You don't know your husband's last name?"

"Oh, I thought you meant the other guy. It's Lamendola."

"Isn't he the guy who owns Caesars II?"

"Yes."

"Okay, then what happened?"

"Joe yelled at him, called him a degenerate, among other things, and the guy went away. Obviously insulted, he got a gun and waited outside for Joe to leave. He started shooting at him, and then you guys showed up."

"What were you arguing about?"

"That's none of your business."

"We'd like to talk to your husband. When will he be back?"

"Never, I hope."

"Here's my card. Have him give me a call when you talk to him. If we don't hear from him, we'll drop by the club."

"What are you going to do with that nut case?" I asked.

"You won't have to worry about him for a while. We don't like it much when people shoot at us. But I do suggest you look for another place to live—and I wouldn't leave a forwarding address. We may need to talk to you again. We'll be in touch."

Their suspicious eyes swept the house one last time and they were gone. I made a few long-distance phone calls and packed my suitcase. The sun was peeking over the horizon as I turned down Lake Avenue, heading for my mother's house.

Toni was more confused than I was. I smiled down at her sleepy face. Peace for her was just a few more miles away. Mine was a little further. I left Toni with my mother and boarded the first plane to Miami.

"Georgie Girl, baby, what a surprise," Frankie said in his usual casual manner. His tone changed as he lifted my suitcase into the trunk. "What's wrong now, baby?" Without answering, I opened the car door and got in. "C'mon, baby, I know when something's eating at you. This is Frankie."

"I don't want to talk about it right now, okay?" I snapped.

"Okay, okay, baby, that's fine, you'll tell me when you're ready. But I do have to know one thing right now."

"What, Frankie?"

"Is he keeping his hands off you?"

"Yes."

"Any guy who can push a woman around ain't a fuckin' man. If I'd known you was gonna end up with an asshole like him, I would've married you myself."

"Frankie, please, can we talk about something else?"

We drove without saying a word. I turned on the radio to fill the gap in the silence.

"You hungry?" he finally asked, turning onto Collins Avenue.

"That's a stupid question."

He smiled and ruffled my hair. "That's my Georgie Girl. It's good to see you, baby."

As we drove, I took a good look at Frankie. A few years had passed since I'd seen him, although we had talked on the phone and kept up with each other's lives. He looked good—better than I remembered. Ah, I'd never seen him with a tan before. The color of his skin somehow made his deep brown eyes more vivid.

"So what brought you to Miami, Frankie?"

"I got a call about three months ago to come down and take over the Dream Bar. There wasn't much happening in Manhattan, so here I am."

Frankie made us a salami sandwich at the Dream Bar. We sat alone in the deserted bar, listening to Frank Sinatra on the jukebox and reminiscing about New York. Frankie didn't discuss the present. I was grateful for that.

"I've gotta set up the bar for tonight. Why don't you throw on your suit and relax on the beach? I'll join you when I'm done."

"That's a good idea."

I walked out the back door onto the beach. The transition from the dark atmosphere of the bar into the bright sun instantly gave me a headache. I hadn't slept at all since the craziness of the night before, and my muscles made their vivid complaints known. I sat on the warm white sand and stared out at the ocean. The sound of the waves made my problems seem distant. Not gone by any means, just further away. The tension began to drift from my body.

Little children were building sandcastles about twenty feet away. When was life that simple? Watching them made me miss Toni. Why hadn't I brought her with me? Then again, attending to her needs when overwhelmed with my troubles was an emotional feat. How could I ever make this up to my child?

Feeling depressed, I sat for what seemed like hours. Frankie joined me eventually. He came up from behind, saying something funny. I wasn't in a laughing mood.

Defeated, he sat down facing me. "I've lost you, haven't I?"

Looking beyond him to the sea, I answered, "You lost me, Frankie, the day you let me go."

"But I always thought, no matter what, or who you were with, you'd always be there."

My hair blew softly around my face as I turned to him. "Well, you weren't wrong, here I am."

"Yeah, but your head's not here, baby."

"I know, Frankie, and I don't know where the hell it is either." I transferred my sight out toward the ocean again and fought to keep from crying.

By the next morning, Joe had gotten a message to me through my girlfriend Susie that if I wasn't home the following day he was going to burn my portfolio. To build up my pictures again would take years. Modeling was all I had left of my independence. I couldn't work without my portfolio. I went home.

❖

Reluctantly, I climbed the stairs to the apartment over the club. Joe was sitting at the kitchen table when I walked in, looking as though his last few days had been as bad as mine.

"Where were you?"

I didn't answer. His eyes bore into mine. I looked away and shifted uncomfortably in my chair, losing my temporary belief of having the upper hand. He waited. An awkward silence ensued. He put a finger to his lips and ran it back and fourth across his mouth. My heart began to pound, sensing his simmering hostility.

Punctuating the silence, he slammed his fist on the table. "Where were you?" he screamed, demanding an answer.

I grimaced, but quickly regained my confidence. "Some place wonderful, until you called," I retorted.

Oh, aren't we brave. I'm proud of you, White.

"Answer me, goddamnit!"

Well, you got away with it so far—Go for it.

"No, *you* answer *me*. What gives you the right to question me after what you did?"

"I'm not going to ask you again. Where were you, and who were you with?"

"Where's my portfolio?"

"You little bitch," he screamed, lunging at me.

I dodged him and ran into the bathroom, locking the door just in time. *Trapped again.*

"Open this door or I'll fuckin' break it down!"

"I haven't done anything. You did. Why are you acting crazy?"

"I won't hurt you, Georgia, now open this goddamn door!"

"You promise?"

Don't believe him.

"I said I wouldn't," he answered, trying to sound convincing.

He'd break the door down if I didn't open it, only making it worse. I unlocked the door and opened it cautiously.

"Where were you?" he asked again, trying to control his temper. Arms stiffly at his side, he clenched his fists, taking deep breaths as he paced.

"I went to Florida."

"With who?"

"Myself."

"Who do you know in Florida?"

"No one."

"Don't lie to me! Who did you sleep with?" he screamed, pulling my hair.

"I'm not lying! I'd never stoop to that level just to get back at you. Although I can't think of anyone having more of a reason."

You're pushing it now, White. Quit while you're ahead.

"So, you *were* thinking of it, weren't you?"

"No, I've got too much class for that."

"If I ever catch you screwing around on me, Georgia, I'll kill you," he yelled, pointing his index finger in my face.

"Oh, and what's your punishment to be? I'm just supposed to forget what happened? Sorry, I don't have that kind of power over my mind," I retorted, backing away, but determined to get my point across.

"It wasn't a big deal."

"What? I can't believe you said that! Why would it carry a death sentence for me and not for you? I don't see where it's so different."

"I'm a man."

"You're a sick man."

"What was I supposed to do, Georgia? She took her damn clothes off. She seduced me, for Christ's sake—"

"She's your cousin, Joe."

"She came on to me, Georgia, I was just trying to help her."

I laughed. "Give me some credit for once, Joe. Do you really expect me to believe that? Why didn't you bring her *here* if you just wanted to talk?"

"Honey, I'm sorry. I can't undo it now. Whatta you want me to do? I'll be reminded of it every time I look at my leg. You got your licks in pretty good."

"How many stitches?"

"Too many to count, but Clyde's still attached, that's all that matters."

"If you want it to stay attached, you'd better think twice the next time."

"I love you, Georgia."

He pulled me toward him, but I jerked away.

"Don't. I can't get that picture out of my head. I just can't."

His frustration was building. I didn't want to get him angry again. He was calm now, we were talking. Expressing my feelings was an uncommon occurrence.

"Where's my portfolio, Joe?" I asked, changing the subject.

"It's in the bedroom. I didn't do anything to it."

"Thank you."

"How long is it going to take, Georgia?"

"How long is what going to take?"

"How long is it going to take before you're over this?"

"I don't know. I don't know if I'll ever be. Knowing you've cheated is one thing, but seeing it with my own eyes is quite another. I don't think I could ever sleep with you again without seeing that picture in my mind. I just don't know."

"I understand. I'll give you time. Why don't you pick up Toni and I'll take you out to dinner?"

He wasn't getting it.

"Joe, I think I want to stay at my mother's for awhile. You really didn't give me much time to think this through. I'm too angry to stay here right now. I need time."

"A week, Georgia, you got a week."

"I better go," I said as I walked out of the bedroom with my portfolio.

"Where you going with that?"

"I might need it."

"Leave it."

"What if I need it?"

He reached out and took the portfolio. "You won't. I'll call you later. And Georgia—be there."

I suppressed my own anger countless times in order to avoid

his. All throughout our turbulent marriage, Joe danced with his demons. Whenever I wasn't silently hating and resenting him, I was feeling sorry for him. He was truly a tormented soul. As twisted as our relationship was, he had a strong hold on my heart. Somewhere in the depths of his darkness, there was a man that I loved.

Nurturing by nature (a gift from my mother), I sometimes felt I was the single thin thread that held his fragile life together. He needed me. What would become of him if I were no longer around to supervise his happiness? This responsibility weighed heavily on my heart. It would prove to be my downfall with Joe.

In future years, this caring quality, among others I possessed, would meet an untimely end. As a result, other deserving men who passed through my life had no possible access to my heart. Georgia Black stood guard.

I left the apartment knowing I would not be returning. But I couldn't break it to him face to face. One couldn't talk to Joe like an ordinary person. He had already given me gonorrhea and actually had me half-believing I'd gotten it from a toilet seat. No, I could never forget the sight in my bed that night. Even if I could forgive, I would never forget.

There had been good times in the beginning, but the laughter isn't what I remember. We had such an intense love, but somehow it all changed. Fear kept me there, but it also pushed me away.

Gathering the courage, I finally called Joe and told him I wasn't coming back. I knew what would follow. Not a day went by that he didn't call. He cried and begged. I held firm. When the pleading didn't work, he resorted to threats. Forced to stay one step ahead of him, I moved around, staying with different friends, hiding, hoping time would solve the problem.

———◆———

After awhile I ventured out. I went to Greenstreets, a bar that was highly competitive with Caesars II. The owner, Tony Sapienza, was a friend of mine. I had worked for him part time in his hot-dog stand when I was fourteen. Tony had come a long way from those days at Willow Point Amusement Park. He developed into one of the city's most prominent restaurateurs. Wherever he opened, the crowd would follow. Greenstreets was the current addition to the night club scene in Rochester.

Being imprisoned for quite some time, I was enjoying myself for a change. I was sitting at the bar talking to some of my modeling friends when Tony approached me.

"Georgia," Tony said nervously, "Joe just walked in. He's asking people if they've seen you."

"Oh shit, Tony, I never expected him to leave Caesars on a Friday night. Does he look mad?"

"He doesn't look happy. Here's the key to my office. Go downstairs and wait there until I come for you."

"He's probably seen my car, Tony."

"Just go. Now!"

I hurried down the spiral stairs and through the downstairs lounge. In a panic, I bumped into Sammy G as I rushed toward the office.

"Hey, kid, where you goin' in such a hurry? Join us for a drink."

"I can't, Sam. Joe's looking for me. I have to hide. He'll kill me if he finds me here."

"We'll see about that," he said, taking my arm and leading me to his table. "Sit down," he demanded. He signaled the waitress and ordered me a double Scotch and water.

"Please, Sammy, I don't want a scene," I pleaded, as I reluctantly slid into the booth and tried to become invisible.

Seated at a table with six of the most notorious gangsters in the Rochester Syndicate, I was uncomfortable, but couldn't have been safer. Something sinister was brewing. Judging by their frowns and focused stares, they certainly weren't in the mood for Joe Lamendola using physical or verbal force on a 114-pound woman.

"How ya doin', Georgia? Haven't seen much of you these days," said Donny Paone, reaching across the table to light my cigarette.

My hand shook as I took my first drag, hoping it would help to calm me. "I've been okay, Donny," I answered, nervously searching the crowd for signs of Joe.

The waitress arrived with my drink and I immediately gulped it as if it were water. I hated scenes, and this one in particular would not be one I wanted to live through. Joe spotted me and started over. My forehead creased with worry.

Please, Joe, keep your cool.

Rene Piccarreto's deceivingly kind eyes were half closed as he blew out a puff of smoke, "This ain't gonna fly, Sammy," he said, tapping his lighter on the table.

Oh God, why did Sammy make me sit here?

They watched Joe in agitated silence as he approached the table. Tony Sapienza paced nervously in the background. Joe was cool. He had to be. He wasn't stupid. He looked directly at me, avoiding the explosive personalities that cloaked me like a second skin.

"Can I talk to you?" he asked like a perfect gentleman.

"Sure, you can talk to her. What is it you'd like to say?" Sammy asked with fire in his eyes.

"I'd like to talk to my wife, Sammy—alone," Joe retorted, breathing deeply, trying to keep his fragile temper under control.

He's gonna lose it. Oh God, Joe...please, just go away.

"You got anything you want to talk to him about, Georgia?" Sammy asked.

Their focus was all on me now. I looked at all the faces before raising my eyes to meet Joe's. "No," I answered, lowering my head and staring into my half-filled glass of Scotch.

"Well, there you have it. Guess she doesn't want to talk to you, Joe," Sammy interjected.

I was cringing in my seat. *Please don't let this escalate, for Joe's sake, please.* He was hurting, but I knew how it would end if I left with him.

"I'll call you later, Joe," I said to give him an out, and hopefully to defuse the tempers beginning to flare.

Ignoring the men, Joe shot me a penetrating look, turned, and walked out of the bar. I took a deep breath, gulped the rest of my drink, and silently thanked God.

"Fuckin' asshole," Rene Piccarreto said under his breath.

"What do you see in that guy, Georgia?" Donny Paone asked

while twisting a napkin.

Adrenaline flowed like wine at the table. Their combined negative energies shot through my body like a series of lightning bolts. The intensity bore down on my shoulders. Joe was a renegade; he didn't always follow the rules. These guys didn't need much of an excuse to take him out, but I didn't want to be the reason.

"Leave the kid alone, she'll work it out in her own time," Sammy G said.

I stayed and had a few more drinks. I'd won the battle, but the war was long from over. I wasn't anxious to leave; Joe could be out there somewhere waiting for me. This could even be worse for me than if I had called the police. I knew the pride Joe took in his manhood—his ego had to be shattered. I wasn't going to get off easily.

I rose to leave. "I think I better be going. Thanks for the drinks."

"I'm gonna call it a night, too," Sammy said. "I'll walk you out."

Sammy inconspicuously scanned the surrounding area as we walked toward the parking lot. "He's across the street, parked near the bank. I'll follow you home," he said, trying not to alarm me.

"Thanks, Sammy."

I wasn't home long before my phone rang. I snatched it up on the first ring, hoping my parents weren't awakened by the noise.

"You're pretty brave with your friends around, aren't you?"

"I'm sorry, Joe, I didn't plan for that to happen."

"Making me look like a jerk, huh? What'd I tell you I would do if I found you out?"

"Joe, I'm not coming back. You can't dictate my life forever," I answered bravely.

Infuriated, he screamed, "You're *still* my fucking wife! You're not gonna make me look like a fool! You—"

"Joe, I'm not doing anything wrong. I just wanted to get out and see my friends. There's nothing I'm doing that makes you look like a fool," I said, trying to calm him.

"What the fuck do you think you just did? You just remember one thing, you no-good whore: your friends can't always be around when you need them. Just keep that thought in mind, little girl." With a bitter, mocking laugh, he hung up on me.

———◆———

My informants told me Joe was planning to take a date to the racetrack on Sunday. I wasn't as interested in this information as in knowing he would be gone from the apartment long enough for me to get my portfolio and my clothes out.

I heard the door open as I reached the top of the stairs with another armful of clothes. *Oh my God!* There was only one exit—and he was blocking it. I froze. My fast-beating heart pounded loudly in my ears.

He raced up the stairs. "When are you gonna stop being such a fuckin' liar?" he screamed, jerking the clothes from my arms and throwing them down the narrow stairway. "When?" he shouted. He clutched my face with both his hands and pushed me to the floor.

"I didn't lie. I didn't lie!" I cried, covering my head.

"You said you'd be back in a week, and I *believed* you. I let you go because I believed you. You lied to me again, you fuckin' whore!"

"I never said that. You *told* me to be back in a week, I never said I would. I didn't lie!"

He kicked me in my side, knocking the wind out of me, and dragged me into the bedroom. Frantically, I struggled to breathe.

"I'll show you!" he screamed, kicking me again.

I still hadn't recovered from the last blow. I lay helplessly doubled up on the floor. Wide-eyed, I watched him take the gun from the drawer. He grabbed me by my hair and knocked my head against the dresser.

"Where are your friends now, dear?" was the last thing I heard.

I don't know how long I was out, but upon waking I was wet, my hair was wet. Had he shot me? No—just the water he threw on me to bring me back, only to torture me some more. He was taking the bullets out of the gun now.

Maybe he's coming to his senses.

"You didn't answer me...I said, where are your friends now?"

He placed one bullet back in the chamber and gave it a whirl. He then placed the gun at my temple.

"What are you doing?" I cried.

"I'm gonna find out once and for all how badly you really want to leave," he snarled.

"Please, Joe...don't."

He brought his face within inches of mine. All I could see were his eyes. I watched in horror as demonic possession took place. In a voice that I didn't recognize, he spewed, "Are you sure you want to leave?"

Paralyzed with fear, I couldn't talk. He pulled the trigger. *Click.* My life passed before my eyes. I saw my daughter, my parents, Babe and Billie.

I'm going to die.

"Do you remember now what I said I'd do if you ever left me? Well, the time has come." He was crying, too.

"I won't leave! I'll stay! Please don't kill me. What about Toni? Oh my God..."

He considered this for a moment, then dismissed it. "You're lying again. I don't believe you." He pulled the trigger again. *Click.*

You know what to say, White. You've been here before.

"I love you, Joe. I was just hurt. I had to punish you for hurting me. I was going to come back after you learned a lesson. I love you too much to stay away from you forever. You know that!"

He hesitated. Relief surged across his face, and then slowly he removed the gun from my head. Pulling me to my feet, he gently picked me up and lowered me onto the bed.

"You do love me, don't you?" he asked, wanting to believe.

"If I didn't love you, why would I be so angry over what you did?"

The demon evaporated. "Yeah, I guess you do love me, but you've got to forget about that now. It won't happen again, I promise you that. I can't live without you, Georgia. Promise you'll never leave me...promise."

"I promise."

The violent Joe was nowhere to be found as he tenderly undressed me and made love to me. Grateful for my life, I cried silent tears and pretended to enjoy it. It was all too painful to cope with, so I did what had become a common practice—I plunged into nothingness.

During this time, I had no idea that I was a classic example of a battered woman. We were all in the Stone Age then. There were no safe houses. To see a therapist was to admit that something was wrong with you. The church turned its back on women. Police were notorious for siding with the man, leaving a frightened woman with no safe place to turn. There were no books to educate you on the subject, or at least none of which I was aware. I didn't even know a name existed for what I was experiencing.

Shame and embarrassment kept me from reaching out. Society pointed the finger at women and blamed them for men's behavior. This only served to immobilize me even more. I was psychologically paralyzed—virtually left on my own to wade through the confusion in my adolescent mind. And the vicious cycle continued.

In the months that followed, Joe was exceedingly nice. Of course I didn't know this was typical batterer behavior after an extremely abusive act. It is called the "honeymoon cycle," a time of flowers and remorse in an attempt to restore the woman's positive feeling for her attacker. It worked.

Joe went out of his way to do romantic things. He took me out more often, and kept his temper under control. His actions showed his remorse. Soon the incident faded from my mind, replaced by all the reasons I had fallen in love. We could be so good together. I wished he could be consistent, but I subconsciously knew the demons would eventually overpower him. The pattern was becoming evident, but I was still in denial. I felt as if there was no way out and I resigned myself to my fate. Maybe Joe would change this time.

During the peace before the next storm, Joe laughed a lot more. Laughing was rare for him. The only time he laughed hardily was when someone made a fool of themselves, or did something stupid like falling and getting hurt. In any event, the fact that we laughed more often was a refreshing change.

Winter turned into spring and we planned a trip to the Adirondack Mountains with four other couples. The cast of characters was a strange combination: the typical gangster types, sprinkled with a couple of detectives, one of them being Sal Ruvio. I'd always liked Sal's company. His warm personality and soothing nature made me feel safe. The peculiar mix promised a colorful trip.

It was the off-season in the mountains. The nearby reservation Indians being restless, we were warned not to go. *Right.* A few blood-thirsty Indians couldn't deter *this* mighty crew.

Together in a large, rustic cabin with the lake outside our door, we barbecued our dinner and laughed non-stop. Everyone had a story to tell, the cops describing their exploits and the others sharing their crime adventures. To see these guys outside their normal environment was more than comical. No signs of macho men were present. They were sillier than a bunch of kids.

The old Joe was present; he was loving and attentive. We took a long hike in the woods, away from the others. He stopped, took my hand in his, and leaned against the thick trunk of a Maple tree. Its newly-sprouted green leaves shadowed his face as he spoke. "I don't know why I'm such a jerk sometimes," he said softly.

"I don't know why either, Joe. It could be so good with us— if you'd just control your temper. Every time you act violently, you push me further away from you."

"There's gotta be something wrong with me. Every guy here thinks I'm the luckiest son-of-a-bitch alive. I don't know why I treat you the way I do. I don't want to lose you, honey. When I think I might, I don't know, something snaps. I want to kick myself in the ass afterwards, but when you get me so goddamn hot, I just don't know what I'm doing."

"Maybe you should get some help," I replied cautiously.

"I'm not gonna tell some fuckin' quack my life story. Whatta you, fuckin' nuts?"

"Well, I just thought—"

"Honey, don't think."

We were silent as we continued to hike. The air was still and the mood was serene as we walked quietly, listening to the sounds of the dried brush crunching beneath our feet. Joe took my hand and helped me up an incline and we continued, both in our private thoughts.

"Yep, I've decided," he said, breaking the silence.

"Decided what?"

"We'll go out to dinner at least twice a week, like we used to. We've gotta get the romance back. But I get to pick the restaurants."

"Screw you, you selfish creep."

"All right, we'll take turns."

"That's better."

He slowed his pace and turned to me. With soft, loving eyes, he looked deeply into my mine. "Georgia, I love you very much. Please forgive me for being such a fool. I really don't want to hurt you, honey."

"Why don't we use a code word?" I suggested. "When I see you starting to lose it, I'll say the word, and you'll know to stop, okay?"

"Okay. What's the code word?"

"Help."

"That's easy to remember. I just hope I don't get it confused."

Suddenly he became mischievous. "Hey, there's a sandy beach over there...You wanna make love?" he asked, taking my hand and leading me through the trees.

Night had fallen. While we sat on the water's edge looking at the moon's reflection on the still, dark water, I silently wished we had more times like this. So loving and peaceful. We walked past the smoldering fire, across the cool sand toward the cabin. Our porch light, the only light for miles, guided us home.

Maybe there was hope.

In the summer of 1974, Joe decided we should move to Las Vegas on a temporary basis. He had sold Caesars II to Jimmy Massaro's brother, and the money was burning a hole in his pocket.

Well, why not? It's only for a few months. A change might be good for us both. Toni wasn't in school, and it would give my Nevada relatives a chance to know her. Eight months had passed since Jimmy Massaro's murder. The city had been quiet, but things were simmering since Bill Mahoney had taken over as the new chief of detectives. Maybe the timing was right.

Las Vegas turned out to be another prison. Not having my mother to run to when Joe lost control was a frightening experience. Away from my roots, I was suddenly alone with Joe in unfamiliar territory. I attained an agent, but there really wasn't any substantial work. With neither of us employed, we spent considerable time together in our small apartment. Like caged animals, we had vicious fights. It was the same old pattern and my hope was gone. I got some relief by visiting my relatives, but Joe put time limits on my visits. He wanted me around to cook and wait on him—and do whatever else he desired.

My cousin Mickey instantly recognized my situation. He was a burly guy with a deep, booming voice, contrary to his teddy bear personality.

"Leave him, Georgia," Mickey urged. "We'll help you."

"I can't involve you, Mick."

"I'm not afraid of that asshole. When he leaves for the casino, I'll come over and help you get your clothes out. Just leave him a note and tell him you went to Los Angeles." Adjusting his glasses, he waited for my reply. "We'll put your car in my garage. After he realizes you've gone for good, he'll probably go back to New York."

"I don't know, Mick, I'm scared. He'll just find me and it'll only be worse."

"What time does he leave for the casino?" he pushed, dismissing my fear.

"It's always different; he's not punching a clock."

"This is bullshit. I'm not taking no for an answer this time. I can't believe you live like this. I'm off tomorrow. I'll stay home and wait for your call. How long does he usually stay out?"

"Two, three hours. Depends if he's winning or losing," I answered, feeling pressured.

"Is that enough time to get your things out?

"Yeah, but—"

"Just call me the minute he leaves," he insisted, giving me a big bear hug. "What's family for?"

"Mickey, if I leave, I can't go back to Rochester. He'll find me and kill me for doing this."

"You can stay with us for as long as you need to."

⸻

The liquid surface in the glass pot trembled as I poured Joe's morning coffee. He noticed.

"Okay, what's the problem, Georgia?" he asked, raising a suspicious eye from the pot.

"There's no problem," I answered, trying to sound staid.

"You're awfully jumpy this morning. Don't tell me there's no problem. I know you better. I can read you like a book." His eyes searched my face. "You're not thinking of doing anything stupid, are you?" he asked suspiciously.

How does he always know what I'm thinking?

"If you are—don't!"

"What are you talking about? I'm not thinking of anything," I answered, failing miserably in my conviction.

"You know what I'm talking about. It's not like we haven't been through this before." He got up from the table.

"I, um, need to get some groceries. Could you leave me some money?"

"I'll stop at the store on my way home, whatta we need?"

Damn! He must have some money stashed in here somewhere.

He stopped at the door, as if just remembering something. He went into the bedroom and came back out again.

"How would you like to go out to dinner tonight?" he asked.

"That'd be nice. I'll see if one of my cousins can baby-sit."

"I love you, Georgia," he said, giving me a heartfelt kiss.

"I love you too, Joe," I responded, and he walked out the door.

I can't do this. I'll wait till he hits me again. Then I'll have a better excuse. He won't be so angry when he catches up with me.

There isn't a right time, White. Just put your fear aside and go for it! You're gonna have to do it someday, ya know. You may as well face it sooner, rather than later.

The phone rang and I hesitated, but the ringing persisted until I finally picked it up.

"Did he leave yet?"

"He just walked out."

"I'll be right over."

"Mick—"

He hung up. I was committed now. I gathered a handful of clothes and quickly took them down to the car. My keys were gone!

"Toni, did you see Mommy's keys?" I asked, distracting her from her favorite cartoon.

"No, Mommy," she answered, unconcerned.

That's why he went in the bedroom! He took my keys, but I had another set hidden. Mickey showed up ten minutes later and we were gone within half an hour.

At four o'clock that afternoon, Mickey's phone rang.

"No, she's not here. I talked to her yesterday and she said something about a modeling job in Los Angeles. Sure, I'll let you know if I hear from her."

Mickey hung up with a satisfied smirk.

———

Two weeks passed. I caught sight of Joe driving by the house a few times late at night. I was beginning to feel trapped.

"Mickey, I don't have any money. I need to get a job. I can't expect you and Gloria to keep feeding us," I announced.

"I don't know, do you think it's wise at this point?" he asked.

"I'm getting a little stir-crazy. I think it'll be okay," I answered as I glanced through the French doors and watched the kids splashing each other in the pool.

Mickey sat in his brightly-lit kitchen, squeezing his lower lip as he contemplated my need. "I know the Cashman brothers who own the camera concession at the Sahara. One of them owes me a favor. I'm sure I can get you in there as a camera girl. Maybe I can even get you into the showroom. You won't be as visible there."

Three days later I was confined to the showroom at the Sahara Hotel. I actually liked the job. Just being around people, regaining my independence, and loving the ambiance of my freedom felt good. A month went by. The heaviness which I usually carried was gone. I had opportunities to date, but survival was my only concern. I did my job and just went home.

After a few weeks at the Sahara, I finished work at two a.m. as usual and walked out to the deserted employee parking area. Putting my key in the door lock, I felt fingers sink deep into my shoulders.

Into my ear he whispered, "Did you *really* think you could get away from me?"

Like a captured bird, my heart started beating so rapidly I thought it would burst.

"Get in," he ordered, jerking the door open and shoving me into the driver's seat.

I climbed over the seat to the passenger's side. My mind raced. *How can I escape?* He started the car and began to drive.

"Where are we going?"

"Home. Where you belong," he answered shortly.

"I don't want to go home," I cried.

He hit me with the back of his hand, bouncing my head off the side window. Blood filled my mouth. But I didn't cry.

Let me handle this, the voice inside of me said with steely calm.

"I'm happy, Joe. Why can't you just let me go?"

"The last words out of your mouth were 'I love you,' and then you disappeared. You're not going to get away with that, Georgia!"

"I won't stay! I'll leave the first chance I get," I said boldly.

"Okay," he said, as he made a radical U-turn and headed toward an uninhabited desert road.

"Where are you going?" I screamed.

"You've made up your mind. You're not coming back, so I'm going to do something to you I'll probably end up doing time for. You're not going to get away with it this time, Georgia."

"Joe, please—"

"I'll be a motherfucker! You no good—You're not gonna make a fool out of me! You love me? You're a fucking liar. You're no good. Who is it, Georgia? Who have you been seeing—and don't lie to me!"

"There isn't anyone else, Joe. I just wanted to be happy."

He took hold of my face with his hand and squeezed it with damaging force. "Who is it, I said!" He pushed my face into the glass again. This time I did cry.

"Why do you always think there has to be someone else? Can't you understand the real reason is because of what you're doing right now?"

"I've been following you. You better be honest."

"If you've been following me, then you know I'm not lying."

Don't panic now. I'll get you out of this. But just don't panic! In the meantime, tell him what he wants to hear.

He slowed for a light. I thought about jumping, but he read my mind again. He grabbed my leg and applied pressure.

"Don't even *think* about it."

The light changed to green and he sped up. I'd lost the opportunity to jump and prayed I'd get another, but the road was becoming more desolate.

"Joe, I do love you, but I just can't live like this anymore."

"You won't have to honey, 'cause you're going to die—and so is the motherfucker you've been seeing!"

A traffic light glared in the distance. *Please be red when we get there.* It was, and luckily there was another car stopped there.

Joe slowed to about twenty miles per hour. My last chance.

The door swung open and I jumped out. I landed on my shoulder and rolled on the pavement. The car started coming at me in reverse. He missed me by inches. I ran to the car still parked at the light, tore open the door, and jumped in. The driver was a woman.

"Please, take me where there are people!" I pleaded.

"Does he have a gun?" she asked, her eyes as big as saucers.

"No," I answered, looking back to see how close he was.

She made a U-turn and sped down the deserted street, back toward the Strip. Joe caught up to us and tried to force us off the road. This gal had guts. No time for conversation, but I sensed that she had known this kind of terror in her own life. Why else would anyone take a chance and get involved? Thank God she was the one sitting behind the wheel at that light, or who knows what the outcome would've been. On the Strip, four police cars were sitting in front of the Stardust Hotel.

"There's some cops, do you want me to pull in here?"

Then I knew for sure. Any ordinary woman would naturally seek the help of the police if she were in trouble. The fact that she asked indicated that she knew "the rules."

"Yes! Pull in, pull in!"

She dropped me off and took off in a flash. I never even got her name. Joe pulled in, too. He got out of the car and I ran to the cop, trying to regain my composure so I could speak.

That was a close one, but you're safe now.

Taking deep, steady breaths, I said, "Officer, that car over there belongs to me. I just want my car and I want to go home."

I was a mess. My clothes were torn, my legs and arms were all scraped, and my lip was bleeding. Joe walked toward us, calm, cool, and confident. He had the walk of someone used to being obeyed. He darted a look at me, a warning. Dressed tastefully in a dark, pin-striped suit, just enough gold not to be gaudy. Not a hair out of place. He looked as if he had just stepped off the cover of *GQ* magazine. He stood across from me, controlling my words with his eyes.

"What's the problem here, lady?" the cop asked.

I looked at Joe. His face gave the answer; it was all I needed. "I don't want to press charges, I just want my car and I want to leave."

"Officer, this is my wife," Joe said smoothly. "We came here from New York because her psychiatrist thought a change might be good for her, but obviously this isn't working either."

What? Dear God! Did this cop actually believe him?

"What are you talking about? I don't have a psychiatrist!" I began to get hysterical again. He put a hand on the cops' shoulder and led him aside, saying something I couldn't hear.

The cop turned back to me impatiently said. "Lady, take your problems and go home."

No! This cop wanted me to get back in that car, like an obedient wife and just go home? Except home wasn't the direction we were going. No way was I getting back in that car with Joe, especially now, since I had violated "the rules."

Sorry to do this to you, White, but there's no other way...

"What kind of a cop are you anyway?" I screamed as I ripped his nametag off his shirt. "Your job is to protect the public, not send them to the desert to be killed!" I shouted. I spit in his face, then kicked him like a wild woman.

Four cops were on me in two seconds flat. They threw me against the police car and handcuffed me. The cop I kicked was beyond rage. To satisfy his own anger, he handcuffed Joe as well, though he had no legal reason to do it. Joe glared at me, but kept his mouth shut. I took a deep breath and let it out slowly. Georgia Black had accomplished what she had set out to do. He couldn't hurt me—at least not that night.

————◆————

They shoved us roughly into one of the police cars, Joe in the front seat and me in the back. They slammed the door, then proceeded to tear my car apart. Joe turned around to look at me. The flashing red light splashed eerily across his face. His hypnotic stare made me feel as though I was confronting the soul of the devil himself.

"That wasn't a good move. What if I'd had a gun on me?"

"Then I guess I'd already be dead, and there wouldn't be any need to be having this conversation, would there?"

"Drop the attitude, Georgia! You haven't had too much experience dealing with these pricks, but you're about to see it firsthand. Just keep your mouth shut. I'll get us out of this."

"I don't want to get out of this," I shot back, feeling brave. This was actually the first time I could say anything to him without him cutting my words short with his attacking hands.

The battered cop opened the door and got in.

"Officer," Joe said, "I'd like to know exactly what I'm being arrested for."

"Vagrancy, public intoxication, and possession of a dangerous weapon," he answered sarcastically.

"What dangerous weapon? Whatta you talking about?" Joe cocked his head toward me with disgust. "*Here it comes*," he said in a low voice.

The cop produced a billy club from underneath the seat of my car. Joe had put it there a year earlier so I'd have some protection. I'd forgotten it was even there.

"That's not mine," Joe said. "That's not even my car!"

The cop twisted the billy club to expose the name that was freshly printed in black marker. The aroma of new ink assaulted my nostrils.

"J. LAMENDOLA. That sounds like your name to me," the cop said with a smile, but his eyes had no connection with his lips.

Joe's face was a study in controlled rage. His teeth began to grind back and forth inside his tight jaw, a look that would paralyze me under any other circumstance, but he understood all too well the consequences of releasing his anger.

"I've got over $3,000 in my pocket. You can hardly call that vagrancy," Joe hissed. "And I haven't had a drink all night. I want a sobriety test!" he demanded.

Without a word, the cop smiled cockily and got out of the car. Joe never got that test. He couldn't prove that he hadn't been drinking, but then again, they couldn't prove that he had.

"Do you see what I mean? They're a bunch of pricks!"

I did see what he meant. I couldn't believe they would go as far as forging his name on that billy club. They had no legal ground to arrest him in the first place! I was the one who kicked the cop. The jerk should have helped me. Joe always told me never to trust a cop. Now I believed him. They were all *bad guys* in disguise.

The cop returned a few minutes later. As we pulled out of the parking lot, he called the dispatcher and gave our location and our destination: Clark County Jail. We drove in silence. I sat in the middle of the back seat. The handcuffs were tighter than necessary, but I wasn't going to complain. Somehow I knew it wouldn't matter. The cop glanced in his rear-view mirror and our eyes locked. He looked to be a little calmer now.

"Officer?" I said in the softest, sweetest voice I could conjure.

"Yeah?" he said with a lighter tone.

"Did I tell you that you're a asshole!" I screamed.

Joe snapped his head around and glared at me in steely silence. If looks could kill, I'd surely be dead. Thank God he was handcuffed and there was a cage between us. The cop slammed on the brakes and got back on the radio.

"Send a paddy wagon down to Sahara and Maryland Parkway or these clowns aren't going to make it." He got out of the car, lit a cigarette, and began to pace.

"You've really done it now, Georgia. You never listen to me! They're gonna throw the book at us. What the hell made you say that?"

"I couldn't help it."

"You couldn't *help* it? Don't you think I'd like nothing better than to blow the motherfucker's brains out? Christ! Shut up!"

"I think you're forgetting something here, Joe. We wouldn't be in this situation if it weren't for you."

The paddy wagon arrived and the cop took great pleasure in removing me from his vehicle. He took my arm and jerked me out of the seat.

"Hey!" Joe yelled. "Be careful how you handle her!"

"I don't need any lessons from *you* on how to handle a woman, mister, especially one like this!"

—◦—

The paddy wagon carved its way through the strip. Apparently we had to make a stop before arriving at the station. Whatever had given me the idea this would be a non-stop trip? It turned out to be an interesting journey.

Our destination: Caesar's Palace, where we had the pleasure of meeting some high society folks—Vegas style. A hooker, dressed in a very low-cut top, made the first entrance. With her hands cuffed behind her back, her large breasts were accentuated. Joe couldn't take his eyes off them. He saw me watching him and looked away. The hooker sat behind me. Then a guy who seemed to be suffering from malnutrition got in. He sat next to me.

On the drive to the county jail, I learned that Mr. Bones had stolen $50,000 off the baccarat table and tried to make a run for it. He even had chains hidden in the bushes outside to hold the door while he got a head start. Unfortunately, the dealer he had chosen to hit was a high school track star.

When we reached our final destination, the door slid open and I followed the others out, but not before I quietly slid my oversized purse under the seat with my foot. That was back in the days when I used to smoke pot. I had an ounce of it in my purse— a felony back then. If they found it, I could always say the purse was not in my possession at all times, and anyone could've put it in there. I wouldn't put it past these cops to plant evidence anyway. In any event, the fact that others had access to my purse would create reasonable doubt.

They led the men down one hall and the women down another. As we headed in separate directions, Joe looked back and said, "Don't call anyone, I'll get us out of here. We'll be out in a few hours."

The hooker was first in line to be booked. They took her purse, emptied it on the counter, and proceeded to mark down its contents. Thank God I had made the right move. They put the articles in a plastic bag and shoved it under the counter.

"Name?" said the female cop behind the counter. She gave her name.

"Address? She gave her address.

"Occupation?"

"I'm a model," was her answer.

Great! Now what am I going to say?

Fine mess I got you into this time, White. Sorry...

I didn't want to embarrass Mickey by saying I worked at the Sahara in case it made the papers. Not wanting to tarnish my name either, I gave them Joe's last name. I never took his name when we got married. What a stir that had caused. No one did that back then. Women had just begun burning their bras about that time, but we all still had a long way to go.

When my turn came, I gave them all the information and explained I had lost my purse. They led me to a room to be fingerprinted and have a mug shot taken. The man placed a number around my neck and went behind the camera. As he readied to squeeze the shutter, I smiled.

"No, no, no, you don't smile for this type of picture," he said. "One more time now." He squeezed the shutter again, and again I smiled. "Look, sweetheart, you can't smile."

"Excuse me," I said, "you don't know me well enough to call me sweetheart! And for your information, mister, people pay a lot of money for this smile. I refuse to look like a criminal."

"You *are* a criminal, honey, or you wouldn't be here. Lose the smile."

He took another picture, and he got another smile.

"You'd better accept it. You're not getting it any other way.

You've got three of them now. I'll autograph one for you if you'd like. It may be worth something someday."

"Smart-ass," he muttered as the matron led me away.

I don't know where they took the hooker with the big boobs, but I never saw her again. At six o'clock in the morning I finally settled into my temporary home with two very nice roommates. One was a Lady of the Night, and the other was a young girl who was picked up for hitchhiking—she said. She was allowed one phone call and made the mistake of calling her boyfriend, who was the reason she was getting out of town in the first place. Still upset that she'd left him, he'd never made the call to her father to bail her out. Going on her third week, she was exchanging favors with the matron for use of the phone. The Lady of the Night told some wild stories, giving me an unsolicited education.

How did I get here?

I couldn't imagine spending more than a day in that hole. The room was about a 10x10 cell with four bunk beds. The toilet was in between the beds in the middle of the room—out in the open!

There's no way I'm using that thing. I can wait. I'll be out of here in a few hours—at least, I think I will.

After listening to the young girl's story, I began to wonder.

What if Joe decides to teach me a lesson? I should've called Mickey. Why didn't I call when I had the chance?

I banged on the bars in an effort to get the matron's attention. She finally sauntered down the hall.

"I'd like to make a phone call, please."

She laughed. "Where do you think you are, honey, in a hotel?"

"I'm supposed to get one phone call. I have a little girl at home, and no one knows where I am. I have a right to make a call!"

She smirked at me. "I have to clear it first. Right now it's time for breakfast."

She unlocked the cell door, and we walked single file down the hall to the cafeteria. Some women wore blue dresses and others didn't. The girls slopping the powdered eggs on the plates were all wearing blue dresses. I was curious.

"Are you girls prisoners or employees?" I asked innocently.

"Hey!" shouted the one I had questioned. The room fell silent. "Did you hear this broad? She wants to know if we're prisoners or employees!"

The entire cafeteria exploded with laughter, which took several minutes to subside. Even Old Sourpuss cracked a smile. I took my powdered eggs and sheepishly followed my new roommates to a table. I was unfamiliar with the rules of the house, and I wasn't anxious to learn them.

"You'd better hope you get bailed outta here soon," said the Lady of the Night. "They're never gonna let you live that down."

"I think I'll be out of here in a few hours, but I have to make a phone call to be sure."

"Good luck," said the young girl, blankly staring down at her gourmet eggs.

I put the fork to my mouth, raising my eyes to sneak a quick look around the room. I was curious to see if the focus was still on me. To my relief, they had all gone back to their own private worlds.

"Oh my God! How can you guys eat this shit?" I exclaimed after tasting the eggs.

"You get used to it," said the Lady of the Night.

"How long have you been here anyway?" I asked, thinking it must take years to acquire such a taste.

"Two weeks—this time. I called my pimp, but he didn't know about the trick that got me in here. Figured I was pulling a scam on him. He'll get me out when he thinks I learned my lesson."

Breakfast was over and we were led back to the cell. Three more hours had gone by and I still hadn't gotten my phone call. I didn't know how much longer I could go without using the bathroom.

"Georgia Lamendola?"

The matron was standing on the other side of the bars with that wicked smile on her face. "They found your purse," she said.

I froze. *That was all? 'They found your purse?' Did they find what was in it?*

She gave no other information, but that face indicated she knew more. Withholding was a game she liked to play. She turned and walked away.

"Hey, wait a minute! What about my phone call?"

"Haven't gotten clearance yet..."

Two more hours passed. I was convinced I wasn't leaving anytime soon. *They must have found the grass.* A short time later Old Sourpuss showed up again.

"Your partner-in-crime is out on the streets now. It seems the name you gave and the name on your license are not one and the same. They're in the process of checking you out in other states to see if you're wanted. You may as well get comfortable, it could take a while," she said with satisfaction.

"How long?"

Of course she didn't answer. She just gave me a silly smirk as she walked away.

"Why'd you kick the cop?" asked the Lady of the Night.

"Because he was an asshole, that's why!" I responded sharply.

"*Excuse* me. I was just asking a simple question."

"I'm sorry, I didn't mean to snap at you. That bitch just gets under my skin."

"If you're here for awhile, just keep that attitude up, girl, and you'll do just fine," my cellmate said approvingly.

Another hour passed before Old Sourpuss showed up again.

"Georgia Lamendola—a.k.a. Georgia Durante—you're out," she announced as she reluctantly opened the cell door.

"I never did get that call," I said as we walked down the hall.

Old Sourpuss smirked. "I never did get that clearance."

"So, where'd you get that face anyway?" I asked as we approached the door to freedom. Her forehead creased and her eyes narrowed. "Did a truck run over it when you were a kid, or what?"

"You sassy little bitch!" she cursed under her breath.

I gave her the same sick smile I'd been looking at for the last eight hours.

"Hope to see you soon," I heard her say before the steel door shut with a loud clank.

Joe and Butch Marionette were waiting for me. Butch had been living in Vegas for the last six months. He was Joe's "eyes," I was sure. I didn't say hello.

"Come on, the car's outside," Joe said nonchalantly.

"I'm not going with you."

He looked around, then casually took my wrist. Applying pressure, he whispered, "Don't start in here. I'm not going to hurt you. Now put a smile on your face and just walk out that door."

I did what I was told. I obviously couldn't count on the police for help.

"Aren't you going to thank Butch for bailing us out?" Joe asked as we got into Butch's car.

"No, *you* thank him, he's your friend."

Butch turned in my direction and our eyes locked. He finally looked away.

"I was in the same cell as the guy who stole the money at Caesars," Joe said. "You know what his bail was? Nine hundred dollars. You know what ours was? Five thousand—apiece! You wouldn't listen to me, Georgia. You had to shoot off that mouth of yours. That mouth is gonna get you killed one day, you know that?"

I ignored him and rummaged through my purse. The pot was still there. I couldn't believe my luck. That purse was so crammed with junk that they probably only went as far as finding the identification and stuffed it under the shelf. They'd still be writing if they had to list all the contents—and I'd probably still be in there.

"Where's my car?"

"The pricks impounded it. We're on our way to pick it up now."

"I have to go to the bathroom. Can we stop somewhere?"

"We can stop if you promise not to run."

Whenever I got the courage to stand up to Joe and threaten to leave, he would always say in a mocking voice, 'Where you going?' So I used those famous words, except I said, "Where am I going?" in a defeated tone.

"Finally figured it out, huh?"

"Yeah, Joe, I'm not going anywhere."

We stopped at a Denny's restaurant, he with his crumpled suit and me with my torn clothes, fat lip, and scraped-up body. What a pair. But this was Las Vegas—nothing was out of place. He waited by the bathroom door until I came out. Butch was seated at a table. His pale face looked drawn and his sandy colored hair was messy.

"We're gonna eat something before we get the car," Joe informed me. "You must be starving. I know you didn't eat that food, just like I knew you wouldn't go to the bathroom in there. I worried about you."

"You *worried* about me? Last night you were going to *kill* me and today you worried about me? You need help, Joe. Order me some eggs. I'm going to make a phone call."

Joe escorted me to the phone by the door. I was hungry and tired and every inch of my body ached. I called Mickey and briefly explained what happened. I told him I'd be home in a few hours.

"Is Toni okay?"

"She's fine, she's playing in the pool with the girls. Are you sure you don't want me to pick you up?"

"No, it's okay, Mick. Really, I'll be fine. Could you call the Sahara though, and tell them I won't be in tonight?" I hung up the phone.

"So, it was Mickey's you've been staying at—that lying bastard."

"Joe, it wasn't his fault. I asked him if I could stay. What'd you expect him to do, turn me in? We're blood." I turned and walked to the table.

"You should have seen her, Butch. That cop won't be forgetting her for a few weeks—especially when he takes a shower. She's one feisty little chick! That's why I love her, I guess," he said, tenderly squeezing my hand.

I pulled my hand away. "It wasn't funny, Joe."

"Aw, c'mon, my little jailbird. We'll laugh about this in years to come."

"Maybe so, but right now I don't see the humor."

<hr>

Butch dropped us off at the impound. They released my car after a lengthy delay, which I'm sure was done intentionally to increase our aggravation. I was too tired to be a smart alec, so I just sat patiently until the paperwork was done. Joe took the car keys and got into the driver's seat. He drove in silence to our apartment on Sahara Boulevard. When we arrived, he took the keys from the ignition and placed them in his pocket as if they were a prized possession.

"Joe, I told Mickey I'd be there in an hour or so. It's been well over that now. I have to go."

"Just come in for ten minutes. I want to talk to you. Then you can go."

Not really having a choice, I walked up the two flights of stairs. Joe followed close behind and put the key in the lock.

"Let's talk out by the pool," I said, feeling anxious.

"I'm not going to hurt you, Georgia, I just want to talk to you." He pushed opened the door and I reluctantly stepped inside. The door closed. His body leaned against it like a human barrier.

"What am I going to do with you?" he said softly.

"Let me go, Joe."

"I'll *never* let you go, Georgia. I love you too much to let you walk out of my life. You'll leave over my dead body, but until then, you belong to me, body, mind, and—"

"Don't say it, Joe. Don't say spirit, because you've broken that. I'm dead inside. Can't you see that? You've taken my body. You've managed to twist my mind. And now you've killed what was left of me—my spirit. I'm afraid to say what I feel, so I try not to feel anything. I can't remember the last time I laughed. Do you think that what you did last night just goes away? It doesn't. I try to push it out of my mind, but I can't."

"You love me, Georgia, I know you do."

"Yes, I love you, but I hate you just as much. I'm sad all the time, and I want to be happy. I don't want to live like this anymore, and I don't think this is any kind of life for Toni either. Children are supposed to laugh, and that child rarely does. We tiptoe around you, never knowing if we're going to say or do something to set you off. You would have killed me last night. There's just no stopping you when you get into a rage. You've got to let me go, Joe."

"Who is he, Georgia?"

"Who's who?"

"The cocksucker you're seeing. Don't play stupid."

"Oh, Jesus, I'm not seeing anyone, Joe. Why won't you listen to me?"

"You wouldn't be talking like this if you weren't seeing someone."

"Why can't we talk like normal people, Joe? Why is it impossible to say what I feel? Why can't you ever *hear* what I'm saying?"

"If you're lying to me, I swear...I'll kill you. I'll kill anyone that touches you. You belong to me."

"I'm not lying."

"Honey, please—don't leave me," he begged, pulling me to him. "I can't go through this again. You tear my fuckin' heart out when you do this. I can't live without you, Georgia. Please...say you'll never leave me. Say it."

"Can you say you'll never hurt me?"

"I'm so sorry about last night. I know I scared you."

"Scared me? Joe—you were going to kill me! You tried to run me over with the car, for Christ's sake!"

"I know, I know, but you were gone for so long. I didn't know where you were. I thought I'd lost you for good. I just couldn't stand the thought of you never coming back. I love you so much, Georgia. You're all I have, you and Toni. You're my life. Please say you love me, just say it."

Honesty was impossible. He didn't want to hear the truth. He didn't want to know how I felt. He only wanted it to be all right.

You'll never win, White. Just tell him what he wants to hear, what he needs to hear, or you know how this will end. You know how he is. Be careful how you talk to him, he's on the edge now.

But I want to get off the merry-go-round.

He can't hear you, White. He won't hear you.

My family, my friends, no one understands why I stay, why I go back. All they can see is the tough guy, the "in control" Joe, never the tears, the insecurity, the Dr. Jekyll and Mr. Hyde. How can anyone understand? How do I get out—and be free from harm?

He pressed my body tightly against his, moving his hands down my back and onto my buttocks. His breathing became hard as his right hand moved to my breast. "I love you, Georgia." Kissing my neck, his pace quickened. Then he violently ripped off my blouse and pushed me to the floor.

"You're mine," he said. "No one will ever have you but me. Tell me you love me."

"Stop it, Joe!"

"Tell me you love me!"

Dick's face flashed in my mind; the memory of being raped became vivid.

Kiss me. Just one little kiss, that's all I want.

"You're hurting me, Joe, please, stop."

"Don't fight me honey, just let me love you."

"You're not loving me, Joe, you're fucking me. You're hurting me—let me go!"

"I'll kill anyone who ever touches you like this. You belong to me."

My shoulder hurt and I was exhausted. I had no strength or will left. He took me, as he had so many times before.

"Can I go now?" I asked when it was over.

"Will you come back?"

"Not tonight."

"But you *are* coming back?"

"Yes, I'll be back in the morning," I promised. That was the easiest and fastest way to leave.

Slipping silently into my cousin's house, I climbed the stairs. I peeked into Toni's room and found her in a peaceful sleep. Tears welled in my eyes as I stood looking down at her in the darkened room. Pulling the covers softly over her shoulders, I studied her angelic face as she slept unaware. *God, I never meant for your life to get messed up like this, my precious angel. Somehow Mommy will make it better*, I promised. My hands trembled as I pulled the door closed.

Blotting away the tears, I tiptoed down the stairs, hoping Mickey had fallen asleep. No such luck. He looked up from the couch as I entered the room.

"Jesus," he said, inspecting my appearance and shaking his head. "You're going back with him, aren't you?"

"No, Mick, not this time. I got a taste of freedom—I'm leaving in the morning for New York. I'll take what I can fit in the car; you can ship me the rest. I'm exhausted, Mickey. I'm going to bed. I want to be out of here as early as possible ."

—◦—

"Mommy, Mommy," Toni yelled, jumping on the bed. "Can we go with Cousin Mickey and the kids on the boat today?"

I opened my eyes and struggled to push myself up against the headboard. My body winced with every movement.

"No, baby girl. We're going to take a trip in the car today, just you and me. Won't that be fun?"

Her eyes flashed with excitement, "Oh goodie!" Blonde hair cascaded to her shoulders in a mass of curls as she bounced out of the room.

I waited until I was out of the state of Nevada before I called him. His tone was none too friendly.

"I trusted you, Georgia."

"The problem is, Joe, I don't trust you. I'm going home."

"Don't do this to me, Georgia, I'm warning you, don't do this," he said in a cold, hostile voice.

Fearful, I thought of the consequences and didn't answer.

"Georgia, did you fall asleep, or are your ears underwater? If you don't—"

"You don't have the slightest inkling of how I feel!" I retorted angrily. "I'm giving you the courtesy of a phone call so you won't worry about me, but I'm not coming back. I tried to make you understand how I felt last night, but you refused to hear me, as usual."

"You can't leave. You have to be in court in a few days."

"You handle it, Joe. You got us into it, you can get us out."

"If you jump bail, I'll be out five grand."

"It costs you more than money every time you do what you do to me, Joe. Maybe if you have to reach in your pocket you'll think twice next time. I'll call you when I get home to let you know I got there safely. Good-bye Joe."

Chapter Eight

Upon my return to Upstate New York, I moved into the garage behind my mother's house and began the process of renovation. Joe left Nevada as soon as he got the mess with the court straightened out. He lost the bail money and I had a warrant out for my arrest. Fortunately, the computer age wasn't in full swing then. They never did catch me, but for years after that I had to tiptoe through the state of Nevada. Three days after he hit the road, Joe was back in New York with his usual pocketful of promises. For the hundredth time, he said he'd finally learned his lesson and was really going to clean up his act.

To hide in Rochester was impossible—too visible there. And the ensuing battles beat me down emotionally. I surrendered. Nothing really changed. Joe and I picked up our life where we had left it. Just another botched escape. I still daydreamed about the time I would actually get the courage to go through with my quest for happiness and sanity. Until that day, the merry-go-round continued in an endless cycle.

Over a year had passed since Caesars II had been sold and Joe and I had returned to Rochester. I turned the garage into a beautiful carriage house, with light streaming through in every room. The knotty pine walls and light-colored, contemporary furnishings gave my spirits a needed lift. The work was both extensive and expensive. Finally, every little nook and cranny was exactly the way I wanted it. Although our old apartment over the club was considered a showpiece, it was dark and depressing. Everything was black and red, even the walls. Joe wouldn't let me make any changes; he liked the bachelor's pad ambiance. I was never happy in that atmosphere.

With Joe not drinking nearly as much as he did when working at the club, we argued less. He played tennis every day with Sal Ruvio, and we socialized a lot more, with *his* friends, of course. We still had our knock-down-drag-out fights, but not as often. I didn't put a lot of stock in his current behavior, but I was grateful for the calm.

Something was going on. Joe began acting like a rat in a corner. I didn't know exactly what was eating at him, but I had my suspicions.

"Why don't we move to California?" he suggested from out of nowhere.

"What? Are you crazy? Why would I want to move after just getting this place the way I want it?"

I couldn't conceive of leaving the state with him after the last episode. If Las Vegas taught me anything, it was never to be out of driving distance from my family and friends. I was too vulnerable without a safety net.

"This place will always be here. We'll come back someday."

"No, I won't go," I said adamantly.

"Georgia, I have to go—and I want you with me."

"Why do you *have* to go?"

"Don't ask questions, Georgia, we just gotta go."

"*We?*"

"You're going, and that's all there is to it."

"What about my work?"

"You can work out there."

"I'm established here. I'm booked all the time. They don't know who Georgia Durante is in California. I'll have to start all over. Are you willing to support my clothes habit until I start making some money?"

"You'll always have food on the table and a roof over your

head, but I'm not making any promises about buying your clothes. You still have price tags on half the shit in your closet. I don't even think you know what the hell you've got in there. Your closet is like a fucking department store with all the money you spend."

"It's my money, Joe. I'll spend it the way I want to. Besides, I need an extensive wardrobe for work."

"You make a goddamn fortune, Georgia, and what do you have to show for it?" he spewed.

"This house for one thing—and I'm not leaving!"

"Look, Georgia, I'm not giving you a choice. I'll stay with my brother Jimmy until I find us a place. That should give you enough time to take care of things here. When I settle in, I'll send for you."

I agreed. However, I had no intention of going. I flew to San Diego to visit Joe four times during the last three months of 1975. Each time I gave a different excuse as to why the move was taking so long: my work, Toni, whatever I could think of. Nevertheless, Joe was determined to have me with him in San Diego—permanently. His reasons for leaving New York must have been serious, because he was too afraid to come back and drag me by my hair. He called every night and pleaded with me to speed up my move. I was always there to answer his calls. He seemed too afraid of losing me again to resort to violence. When I'd visit, he was gentle and loving, the man I'd fallen in love with. But my past experiences were still vivid and I wouldn't give in.

The death of Jimmy "The Hammer" Massaro was the beginning of the end for organized crime in Rochester. Well, at least it was the end of an era that had been a part of my life for a long time. There aren't many left alive today to reminisce when I think of the "good old days."

It all started with a crooked cop. Bill Mahoney had the bad guys on the run. No one knew who to trust anymore. Mahoney was playing them all against each other. He even had *me* picked up for questioning. When I was led into Mahoney's office, Al DeCanzio, a local gangster, was sitting with his feet up on

Mahoney's desk, talking on the telephone as though he owned the place! Well, he practically did—he owned Mahoney.

Al had the goods on everybody, and he was feeding Mahoney a little at a time. Al's wish was Bill's command. Al was awaiting trial for murdering his accomplice in a heist that they had pulled off together a few months earlier. He was obviously trading information for his freedom.

Al DeCanzio could be characterized on the same level as Jimmy "The Hammer" and Big Gene, the Accountant: he was a "strong arm" for the mob. When Frank Valenti was in power, Al had acted as one of his bodyguards.

After Valenti's unfortunate departure, Sammy Gingello took control of the city's underworld activities. Yes, he still had people to answer to, but the glory was his. This was the position for which Sammy had striven his entire life. He had managed to gain his standing by the age of 33. Blood flowed during that takeover, but nothing like during the war that was to come. No, Sam would not let go of what he had worked so hard for. The only way his position would be taken was over his dead body.

The detectives left me alone in Bill Mahoney's office with Al, closing the door behind them as they departed. Al hung up the phone, put both his arms behind his thick neck, and leaned back in Mahoney's overstuffed chair. His muscle-bound legs were still comfortably outstretched on top of the desk.

"Hi, Georgia. It's good t'see you. You're lookin' good," he said with a sick smirk, which was his normal facial expression.

I wished I could return the compliment. Dark circles encased his eyes, revealing the strain he'd obviously been living with. His hairline had receded since I had seen him last, and his straight brown hair looked a bit greasy.

I fixed him with my accusing brown eyes. "What the hell are you doing here, Al?"

This special treatment could only mean one thing: he was spilling his guts. I hadn't heard anything about him ratting, so I assumed no one was aware of it yet.

"Bill wants to remodel his office, so he gets me out a few days a week to pound some nails. It's cheap labor for the city and I get to use the phone and stretch my legs a bit," he said. "So what's going on in the streets?"

I nonchalantly searched the room for recording devices. "What are you asking *me* for, Al? You probably have more information than I do, and you're inside. With all those phone calls you make, you must have enough information to write a book."

"That I do...that I do. How's Joe?"

"He's fine," I answered curtly.

"Where is he these days?"

"He's around," I lied. He had been gone for four months.

"Seen Sammy or any of the boys around lately?"

I had enough of this cat-and-mouse game. "Al, what's the deal? Why are you here, and why am *I* here?"

He laughed out loud. "Well, I know why *I'm* here—"

I was irritated with the position these dirty detectives had put me in. "Why am I here, Al?"

"If you don't know, then I sure don't," he answered offhandedly.

I leaned forward and laid both hands flat on Mahoney's desk, arresting him with a penetrating glare. "Since you have unlimited use of the phone, Al, why don't you call me a cab." I stood to leave. They couldn't hold me. This was a setup if I ever saw one, or maybe it was Mahoney's way of unnerving a few people. He was a master at that.

Opening the office door, I turned back to Al, who was regarding me with hooded eyes. "You know what, Al? You're nothing but scum," I spouted, refusing to be intimidated. "You can tell those two-faced bastards that I said to drop dead! If they have a problem with that, tell 'em to call my lawyer." I slammed the door behind me as I left.

I marched down the corridor, buzzed the elevator, and waited impatiently. When the door opened, a man in a suit exited. In my haste to get out of there, I smacked right into him. It was Sal Ruvio, one of the cleaner detectives.

"Georgia? What are you doing here?"

"You tell me, Sal! Give Mahoney a message for me: tell him that the next time he wants to speak with me, he's going to need a warrant. Cops—they're all alike!" I stormed into the elevator and pressed the desired button, leaving Sal looking baffled and confused as the door closed between us. I had no idea what was going on, but something bad was happening for sure.

I took a taxi home, and then I got into my car and drove to a pay phone. I called Joe in San Diego and told him what had transpired. He went berserk. He refused to clue me in on the details about what was going on.

"Why don't you ever listen to me, Georgia?"

"Why don't you ever talk to me, Joe?"

"Why? Because of just what happened today. The less you know, the better off you are. There's a lot of shit coming down right now. Everybody's runnin' scared and they're makin' damn sure there's no loose ends. Mahoney is setting you up to get to me. Jesus," he said, absorbing the seriousness of the situation. "I should've never left you alone. If he puts the word out on the street that you were talking to Al, it won't be safe for you there. You and Toni get in your car first thing in the morning and start driving out here. We'll worry about your clothes later."

"Will you buy me some new clothes until mine arrive?"

"This is no time to be funny, Georgia."

"This is crazy, Joe, I don't know anything."

"You know a lot more than you think you do, honey, and besides, it's not what you know, it's what they *think* you know."

"Sammy would never—"

"Don't kid yourself, Georgia."

At five a.m. the following morning I brushed the snow off of my Chevy Masda and Toni and I headed for San Diego.

A week later all hell broke loose. Headlines shouted out death. The good guys and the bad guys were at war. The bad guys were killing each other off in order to insure that the golden rule of silence would not be broken.

"I really missed you, honey. I'm glad you're finally here," Joe said as he lifted his glass to toast me. "You're going to love California living."

"I won't love it if my hair frizzes up like this all the time."

"Give it a chance, Georgia. Look at the bright side of things for a change."

"Is there a bright side, Joe?" I asked doubtfully.

"You'll learn to like it," he snapped, his romantic mood suddenly changing.

Sitting in a wonderful restaurant on the ocean's edge, we drank our wine and watched the sun sink slowly into the ocean. The rhythm of the tide crashing against the rocks hypnotized me as I sipped my drink. California was a beautiful state, but I did not want to be there.

The waiter arrived with our meal as I took my last swallow of wine. Joe ordered another bottle and began cutting his steak as though it deserved it.

I watched in amusement for a while, then looked for my own fork. It wasn't there.

"Excuse me, sir," I asked the waiter as he passed our table, "would you bring me a fork when you get a chance?"

The next instant a fork was jabbed into my hand.

"Don't you ever do that again!" Joe said through a mouth full of meat. He swallowed and continued, "I'm the man, I'll ask for whatever you need. It's not your place to speak."

The pressure of the fork stayed constant in my hand as he reminded me of the rules. Involuntary tears sprang into my eyes. "Wipe your eyes before people see you," he demanded.

The waiter returned with a fork, unaware of the incident. "Thank you," I whispered as he walked away—not sure if that was allowed.

I sat toying with my food. I could feel his eyes daring me to show even a hint of a tear. Joe turned his head from side to side, and then he bent forward. "You got your damn fork—now eat!"

I looked up. "I'm not hungry anymore."

"Eat that fucking food or I'll shove it down your throat," he said through clenched teeth.

"I'm going to the ladies' room," I announced as I stood and reached for my purse.

"Leave your purse here."

"I need my make-up. I'm sure my mascara has smeared."

"Leave it."

I left my purse, but he knew, as always, that I was planning to run. I walked past the ladies' room and darted out the door. Not quite sure where the condominium was, I followed the beach and hoped I would recognize it. The seashore was dark and cold. California evenings were cool in January. The sound of the waves was somewhat soothing, but nothing could take away the emptiness in the pit of my stomach. I had no family, no friends, nowhere to turn. I was alone.

You're not alone. I'm here. You know, White, you're a lot smarter now. Don't let him take your independence away again. You know who you are. You've always known—but you let this jerk fill you with doubts. Don't let him do it again. Stand up to him. You have a lot to give, White. Don't waste it on him—he doesn't deserve you.

Toni was asleep when I returned. Joe had gotten there before me, paid the baby-sitter, and sent her home. He was sitting on the couch with a drink, looking remorseful as the reflected flames from the fireplace danced softly on his face.

"I fucked up again. I'm sorry—but dammit, Georgia, you know better than that," he said, trying to justify his actions.

Walking past him, I stood looking out the large sliding glass door at the moon-lit body of water, contemplating the words to express my anger. I cringed as I watched Joe's reflected image approach in the glass. Putting his body to my back he slipped his arms around me. "I'm sorry," he murmured, kissing my neck.

I pulled away. "I'm sorry, too. I'm sorry you will never be healthy. While you were gone I started living like normal people do." I turned to him and continued: "I forgot the sick rules, and ya know what? They're going to stay forgotten. I won't live like this anymore." I turned my back to him again.

He swung me around, pressing his long, thin fingers into my arms. Trapped in his pupils were the fire's flames, flickering as he spoke. "Oh, yeah?" he said, "and what do you think you're going to do?"

"I don't know..." I broke away from his grip and began walking toward the bedroom. He followed behind me, spewing his cruelty.

"Who do you think would want you with a kid? You're no prize, ya know."

You're gonna eat those words, Mr. Wonderful—just wait and see.

"When are you going to stop belittling me, Joe? If I'm such a stupid, undesirable woman, then what do you see in me? Why would you love such a worthless person? Can you answer that?"

He couldn't.

"You know," I continued, "I'm not nearly as stupid as you think I am, or should I say—as you'd like me to think. If you would just allow me to speak once in a while, you might find I have something intelligent to say. Or is that what you're afraid of? I'm a person, for God's sake, not your servant, not an instrument for your pleasure. I'm a human being! All I want from you is to be treated like one. Why can't I ask for my own goddamn fork in a restaurant?"

Go girl! That was good.

"Because it's not your place!" he screamed.

"It's not yours either!" I screamed back. "I have a mind of my own, Joe. From now on if I want a goddamn fork, I'll ask for it myself," I said assertively, but my bravado only served to convince *me*.

"You've been talking to your girlfriends again. I can see I've been away from you too long," he snarled.

"Do you really believe you think like a rational person, Joe?"

He inhaled deeply and when he resumed his voice was measured. "Look, Georgia, I said I was sorry. Now can we just start over and pretend this didn't happen?"

"Sure, Joe, I'll pretend. I'm good at that."

"What do you mean by that?" he snapped.

"Nothing."

The argument raged, then drifted off again. He tried to reach into my soul and soothe the wounds, but the fear he'd stuck in my heart over time had become too deep to be dislodged. I gave him a tired, indulgent smile and finally relented. But he was aware that inside my silence was a bucking bronco. It made him more determined than ever to tame me.

With the night between us, I lay in bed, lonely and homesick. The memory of the few short months I'd been away from Joe made living this way again unbearable. But for now, I had no choice.

Welcome to California...

In all the years with Joe, the next four months brought with them the worst mental abuse I ever encountered. I was a virtual prisoner. Having nowhere to run when he was out of control, I spent many nights hiding with Toni in the local theater, waiting for Joe's temper to cool so we could go home—that is, if I was lucky enough to get out with my purse. Other times, we hid outside in the cold night, clad in our pajamas, shivering from the dew-drenched grass beneath our bare feet and praying he would be calmer when we returned.

The more I stood up to him, expressing my thoughts, the more abusive he became. In the past, although I clung to my beliefs, I buckled under to Joe's ridicule and demands. Away from him for any period, I was able to think clearly. I had slowly become stronger, and my life with Joe became more intolerable. My tone changed. Rather than sounding as though I were pleading, I began speaking from strength. Joe was so extreme, so purposeful, so sure of everything, he made me want to fight him even if I agreed. I no longer wanted to tolerate looking at life through his eyes. He was losing control of me and it terrified him. His only recourse was to attempt to instill more fear, but I rebelled, regardless of the consequences.

Joe became so paranoid with my new attitude that I had to sneak to have lunch with my sister-in-law, Darlene. Even his own brother's wife was off-limits outside of our house. Darlene, a beautiful soul, was my only outlet for venting frustrations. Being in her company, if only for an hour, did wonders for lifting my spirits. Her husband Jimmy was nothing like Joe, but he too had his dominating ways. We could sit for hours and complain to each other, but only so many unguarded moments could be stolen.

An attractive mixture of Cherokee Indian and German gave Darlene a distinctive beauty. A sort of intelligent attractiveness touched with class. She worked as a representative for a cosmetic company. Her shoulder-length, honey-blonde hair and startling, direct green eyes enhanced her looks as well as her product. She always dressed tastefully; even if she simply wore jeans, she spent time in the planning.

Darlene never broke a rule in her life. She wouldn't even cross a street against the light. Her rigid lawfulness was a constant irritant to me, but that was Darlene. I could tell her anything. She always listened, wide eyed and animated. Always concerned, she put herself on the line by covering for me, keeping me out of trouble. This was a special feat for Darlene, being so damn rule-oriented. If she had to lie, she was usually a dead give-away, but she did it anyway.

I learned never to ask her opinion if I didn't want to hear the truth. Despite my hesitations, however, she spoke her mind without even being asked. During our many conversations, we often planned and schemed about how we were going to leave our husbands. To my surprise, Darlene acted on her threat and left Jimmy. Now she was *definitely* off-limits. It was impossible for us to have contact, and I felt lost and abandoned. My only outlet for sanity had deserted me. I wondered how I could survive without her.

If she could do it, so could I!

<hr/>

The day was finally here. Toni's class was bringing an end to the school year with a kayaking outing. She was so excited, she talked about it for weeks. We were in the bathroom trying out different hair styles. She wanted to look just right.

"Kevin doesn't like it in a ponytail, Mommy. Put a barrette in it and let it be straight."

"Who's Kevin?"

"Just a boy..."

"He sounds pretty special—"

Joe barged into the room, yelling. He had found the potato chips I had hidden under the bed. Because he was a health nut, we had to be too. He started pushing and shoving me and wouldn't let up. I ran from the house and down the 102 steps to the beach. I sat on the sand and waited until he had time to cool down.

I assumed Joe would take Toni to her event. He knew how much she was looking forward to it. When I got the courage to go back, the door was locked. I had to ring the bell several times before Toni finally opened the door.

She stuck out her lower lip and stared at me accusingly with teary eyes. I had let her down. Joe used her to get back at me for running by refusing to drop her off. I'll never forget that crushed look on her face. To this day, when I drive to San Diego on the 405 freeway and pass the place where she was supposed to go kayaking, a sick feeling fills the pit of my stomach, and I cry.

Joe entertained himself by playing tennis every day with a retired stock broker he befriended in the condominium complex. This allowed me some alone time. I sat on the cliffs and wrote poems in my head as I stared at the serenity of the sea. I walked for miles on the beach and thought of escaping the madness. How would I do it? Where could I go? How could I hide?

I'll help you, White. But you've got to make the first move. Once you're away from him and you can think clearly again, you'll wonder why you stayed so long. Trust me.

After one of my long walks on the beach at sunset, I came home to find Toni crying in her room.

"What's the matter, honey?" I asked, running my hand tenderly across her check.

Sobbing, she replied, "I didn't do anything, Mommy, and he made me go to bed. I was watching TV and he changed the channel and told me it was my bedtime. It's not even dark outside."

That bastard! Taking her into my arms, I could feel her body convulse as she clung to me. We held each other tightly and wept.

Wiping the tears from my daughters eyes, I coaxed, "Come on, honey, help Mommy with dinner. You're the bestest helper in the whole wide world."

"Okay, Mommy," she said, jumping from the bed, her face alive with a brave expression.

As we passed Joe on the way to the kitchen she avoided looking at him—afraid he would be upset that she was still up. Apparently we made more noise than he cared to hear. He shot us an irritated look.

This can't go on much longer. I'm really getting impatient with you now, White. You may take his shit, but what about her? It's just not fair!

I had no charge cards and Joe kept the money hidden. He always seemed to know what I was thinking even before I allowed a thought to form. He usually succeeded in deferring my plans, but the voice of my Shadow kept coaxing me.

Do it! Just do it! Remember when you were twelve and you hopped the freight train and ran away from home? You wanted to see the world and no one was going to stop you. You had such a thirst for life! You wanted to laugh. You wanted to live. You had spirit, White! What happened to you? You had no money then, you were just a kid! You jumped off the train when you got hungry and ate blueberries growing wild along the tracks. You used to say, "Where there's a will, there's a way." That was always your motto. You survived when you were twelve; you'll survive now, too. You used to have guts! You're a survivor, remember? Do this before there is no hope. If you can't do it, I will. Just get out of my way.

———◆———

Summer had started and Toni was out of school. If I didn't put a stop to this vicious cycle now, I never would. But where would I go? I hadn't made any friends in California. Joe made sure of that. I could have called my parents. They would have given me all the support I needed—but at the expense of their own emotional well-being. Tom, Toni's biological father, may as well have been nonexistent. He'd been a non-participant in Toni's life for ages—not that I could really blame him, under the circumstances. But he couldn't even get it together to pay the $15 a month in child support mandated by the court. Her future was in my hands, and mine alone. Another day went by, then another—and there I stayed. I found myself free-falling into a void once more.

You chicken-shit! You know, if you didn't need me so bad, I'd never speak to you again!

Sticks and stones can break my bones, but names will never hurt me.

Yeah, well why don't you start thinking about the broken bones! I'm not the one who's hurting you, you jerk!

"Mommy, can we go swimming today?"
"Sure, baby, let me get changed."
I held Toni's hand as we made our way through the beautifully-landscaped, winding paths that led to the pool. Swans stepped lazily aside, letting us pass. Toni let go of my hand and ran ahead. The breeze blew gently through her platinum blonde curls

as she chased ducks into the pond. The air was laced with the faint aroma of barbecue mixed with the clean smell of chlorine. As we crossed one of the many wooden bridges throughout the complex, we stopped to watch the fish in the rushing stream below. Toni parted with one of her crackers for the swan and we moved on. We arrived at the smaller of the two pools and I stopped to spread a towel on one of the many vacant lounge chairs.

"No, Mommy," Toni said, tugging my arm. "This is the baby pool. I want to go to the big people pool. Can we, can we? Please?" she pleaded.

"Okay, honey, but you can't go in the deep end."

"Why? I can swim and you'll be there to watch me."

As we entered the gate to the main pool, Toni spotted two little girls about her age and immediately took off in their direction. She was as starved for friendship as I was.

I spread my towel out on the chair, then looked down at the tennis court. Joe must have felt my presence, because he looked up at the same moment. He smiled and waved, then went back to the intensity of the game.

Joe played to win. He looked like a Greek God, especially in his tennis clothes. His jet-black hair falling casually in his eyes shrouded his interior. And his tall, lean, perfectly tanned body kept all the women in the complex competing for his attention. I couldn't blame them. From the outside, he looked like the ideal catch. I had felt that desire at one time too, but I no longer held the same fascination. Now I would give anything to be able to look in from the outside. But I was inside—and there was no way out.

We appeared to be the picture-perfect couple, the "mystery couple" everyone was curious about. We were often invited for dinner by the neighbors, but Joe would never accept. I wanted so badly to meet people. I needed others to talk to for a diversion, but Joe wouldn't hear of it. He had always been an extremely private person, and he was adamant that no one know anything about us. Avoiding people sitting around the big pool was difficult, so I always went to the smaller pool. No one was ever there.

People are naturally curious, wanting to know where you

came from, what brought you to California, and what you do for a living. Being evasive about everything only created more curiosity. If anyone asked, I was told to say that Joe was an independent investor. This was a strict, unalterable rule, maybe with good reason. The alternative was to avoid people and stay secluded in my own private, lonely world.

I lay in my lounge chair, separating myself from the rest of the women who were chatting together as their children played. Toni was enjoying herself. To see her laugh warmed my heart. Settling into the lounge chair, I put on my sunglasses, opened my book, and got lost in the story. I looked up frequently to check on Toni, but was careful not to make eye contact with those I felt looking in my direction.

The father of the children whose company Toni was enjoying joined his kids at play. The two little girls suddenly forgot Toni existed. They took turns jumping into their father's arms. Laughter and genuine affection were exchanged between them. The shimmering reflection of the water danced upon Toni's face as she sat on the edge of the pool and watched them play, feeling abandoned, yearning to be included.

Wet, straggly hair covered her features but failed to conceal her pain. The sadness I viewed was like peering into my own soul. I could tell by the way she moved that she was fighting to calm her breathing. She bit down on a quivering lip, trying not to cry. Then she looked over at me. When her eyes met mine my heart crumbled. In that instant we shared the unspoken knowledge of what lay deep inside both of our hearts. Toni wanted a daddy like those little girls. She needed love and affection. What she had was fear and emptiness. She didn't have a Daddy, any more than I had a husband. We had a dictator.

You don't have to live like this! Living in the car with Toni would be better than this—at least you'll have each other.

I didn't think, I just reacted. I rose from my chair, left my book and towel behind, and walked over to Toni. She reached up and took my extended hand.

As we walked to the gate, I looked down to see Joe still playing tennis with fierce intensity. Toni wanted to stop to feed the swan again, but my pace was so quick she had to run to keep up with me.

"Why are you walking so fast, Mommy?"

"Because we have to go someplace and we're gonna be late."

"Oh, you can't be late, Mommy, you know how mad Daddy gets when you're late."

"Do you think you can help me to not be late? I need you to help me carry some things to the car. Can you help me do that? We can pretend we're having a race, okay?"

I grabbed some of our clothes, with little thought as to what I was taking and what I was leaving behind. Fear replaced my ability to think. We made a few hurried trips and got into the car. My heart beat wildly. My hand shook so hard I couldn't get the key into the ignition. The more I panicked, the longer it took. The security gate seemed to move in slow motion as I sat waiting impatiently, looking over my shoulder, expecting to see Joe appear out of nowhere.

Deep breath...

Calm down, White. Act natural, slow down, you're doing fine. You'll make it. Remember, where there's a will, there's a way. You taught me that!

We exited the parking structure and turned down the hill toward the street. The next hurdle was to get by the tennis court without being seen. No chance. Joe's eagle eyes spotted the car filled to the top with clothes. Toni smiled and waved. He stood frozen. His dominating look told me to turn back if I knew what was good for me. I broke away from his paralyzing scowl. My foot, acting entirely on its own, pressed the pedal beneath it. Blurred images rushed past my window. I moved on pure adrenaline. I had no idea where I was going. The car drove itself, or maybe my Shadow had taken over.

I found myself on the 5 freeway heading north, without a clue as to how I had gotten there.

"Mommy, where we going?"

"I don't know, honey."

"What're we gonna do when we get there?"

"I don't know."

"I'm hungry, Mommy, can we stop at that McDonald's?" she asked, pointing at the yellow arches ahead.

I exited the freeway and drove to the drive-through window. Upon opening my wallet to pay for the food, I discovered I only had seven dollars. In a panic, I glanced down at the gas gauge. *Thank God!* It was full.

What am I doing? How far can I get on seven dollars?

Where there's a will, there's a way. You can't turn back now, White!

We arrived in Los Angeles during rush hour traffic. The HOLLYWOOD sign emerged through the smog. I didn't feel like I belonged. This was a far cry from the beauty San Diego had to offer. Swallowed in the size of the city, I felt lost and alone. And what was worse, there was no one who cared.

The traffic was bumper to bumper. Exiting the freeway, with no thought as to where I was going, I stopped at a phone booth. I stared blankly at the phone for several minutes.

Who can I call? I don't know anyone who lives in L.A.!

Don't panic, White. Think...you must know someone.

Jim! Jim Alquist—he lives here somewhere.

I opened the phone book and feverishly flipped through the pages. Thank God, he was listed! I dialed the number. *One ring...*

two...three...Oh no, he's not home. My heart began to sink. Then Jim's voice sounded, doing a pretty good impression of John Wayne on his answering machine. I left a message.

Looking in the phone book again, I jotted down his address and drove to the nearest gas station for directions. I had no idea how far Brentwood was from Hollywood. Driving on surface streets in rush hour traffic, I studied the faces in the laggard cars. They all had a purpose, a destination, a home to go to. Feeling rootless and adrift, I wanted to cry, but my Shadow wouldn't allow it. Toni sat quietly worried, her Bambi eyes wide with question. I conjured up an assuring smile, but she didn't buy it. Guilt over her and an incredible feeling of aloneness consumed me.

I found another phone booth and called Jim again. Still not home. Sinking into panic, I returned to the car. Sensing my alarm, Toni scrutinized my face with her inquisitive brown eyes. Her long, dark lashes fluttered anxiously. I hugged my little girl and tried to reassure her, but it was she who reassured me, giving me strength. As tired as she was, she was a little trooper. I drove around, searching for an inexpensive coffee shop in which to hang out until I could get a hold of Jim. When he hadn't answered by eleven o'clock, I rearranged the clothes in the back seat, making room for Toni to sleep. I dosed off periodically, but frightened of the uncouth-looking people prowling around the street, I didn't get much sleep.

"I'm hungry, Mommy," were Toni's waking words.

If I spent any more money, I wouldn't have enough left for the phone. I started the car and drove around until I spotted a 7-11. Leaving Toni in the car where I could see her from inside, I proceeded to steal a package of Hostess cup cakes and purchased a small carton of milk. I didn't care about the consequences. What could they do to me—chop off my hand for feeding my kid?

We wandered around in a park until the sun began to set. Calling every few hours, I was running out of change for the pay phone. I tried one more desperate time.

"Oh, thank God you answered, Jimmy."

"Georgia! I just got back from location and was listening to all my messages. How the heck are you?"

"Not great, Jim. I need to ask you a big favor—"

"Sure."

Elated I'd finally gotten hold of him, I began speaking rapidly. "I left Joe yesterday afternoon and drove up here from Solana Beach. I'm afraid I acted on impulse. I've only got thirty five cents to my name and I don't have a place to stay. I don't know what I would've done if you hadn't answered. I hate having to ask you this, but I don't know what else to do. I have my daughter with me and—"

"Slow down, slow down. Jesus, of course you can stay here, but it's only a studio. You and Toni will have to share the couch if that's okay."

"It's better than the car. Thanks, Jim. One day I'll repay you for this."

"Georgia, there is one condition: that the asshole never finds out I took you in. I put that bullshit behind me when I left Rochester. He hates my guts already. He doesn't need another excuse to come busting down my door in the middle of the night."

"Don't worry about that, Jim. He doesn't have any idea where to start looking."

"Okay, you're only ten minutes away," he said giving me directions. "I'll put some coffee on."

"Jim?"

"Yeah?"

"Thank you."

———————

The night air was cool and a thick fog had rolled in, obstructing my view of the street signs, taking us longer than the estimated ten minutes before we arrived. I could smell the coffee even before he opened the door. Jim's little bungalow was only one room with a small kitchen, but the sensitivity of his decor impressed me. I expected the typical bachelor's pad, but instead I entered a home. Warmth instantly enveloped me. Light from the fireplace danced on the walls. Near the hearth, an open book sat on the arm of a chair. A cowboy hat hung on the antique bedpost and his boots were neatly placed beside the bed. Western art decorated the walls. Indian blankets hung casually from the backs of the couch and chair. Jim had found peace in the private world he had created. The environment was exactly what I needed for my state of mind.

Joe had met Jim when he accompanied me to an industry party once. He hated Jim instantly. From that point on, I had to mislead Joe whenever Jim and I worked together. I hated to lie about silly things, but I learned to do it well. Jim and I worked closely at times, and the thought of this made Joe's skin crawl. I paid dearly when Joe happened to see Jim and me posing together in a newspaper or magazine ad. This was all the excuse Joe needed to have Jim's face rearranged. For Jim to open his door to me was exceedingly brave. Most men who knew Joe kept their distance.

Jim was soul-searching back in those days. Not unlike me, he married young and had children before he himself had grown up. With a burning desire to be an actor, he came to California to fulfill his dream, leaving his rocky marriage behind. Ann would always be his true love, but eventually he learned, as I would, that one can never go back.

When Jim left Rochester he sold all his worldly possessions. I bought his stereo for $500. When everything was gone, he hit the road for stardom. Jim never made it big as an actor, but he did make a living at it, which is more than can be said for most. When I see Jim now with a decent role on television, I always smile and think of the old days.

Toni immediately curled up on the couch and fell asleep. Jim and I stayed up for hours, talking in his tiny kitchen. He helped me considerably during that trying time, helped me to keep my sanity. He was a great listener, and I sure had some stories to tell. Our friendship continues to this day.

Jim was kind to let me invade his private world, but I couldn't take advantage of it. With a good night's sleep and a feeling of safety, I could actually think. I called my friend Fred Reed, who owned the Hair Zoo in Rochester. A few years earlier, he had asked me to do the commercials for his salon. He didn't have a big budget, so I did the spots at no charge. The commercials were a big success. Fred went on to open several shops on the East Coast. Time to call in a debt. Not that I needed a payback for Fred to help me—we had been good friends for years. He was another lifesaver when I needed a friend. I didn't even have to finish the sentence.

"How much do you need?"

"I don't know, five hundred, I guess," I answered, feeling uncomfortable with the vulnerability of my situation.

Fred wired me a thousand dollars the next day. At $80 per month, it took a year to pay it back. He'd said I didn't need to repay him, but my conscience wouldn't allow me not to. I'd always taken pride in being able to take care of myself. It gave me a feeling of independence.

I drove around for a few days and finally found an affordable apartment on Olympic Boulevard, near LaCienega. I was able to attain a fairly nice place for little rent. They call that area the Miracle Mile district. Boy, did I ever need a miracle. Ironically, Toni remembers those days as the happiest times of her childhood. Jim managed to find me a mattress and an old TV set. I bought a few plates and utensils at a garage sale and we set up house. I was amazed at how happy I could be with so little.

The old building resembled a small castle and only had four units. The architecture inside my apartment was very appealing, with rounded archways separating all the rooms. It had chocolate brown carpet, but with the many drapeless windows, the entire place was doused with sunlight so the carpet didn't make it dark. If only I had the money, I could have made the place into a little dollhouse. Wanting a real home for me and Toni made me more determined to make it—whatever it took.

———————

After settling down in the apartment, I hit the streets to find an agent. The well known agency of Wormser, Heldfond, and Joseph scooped me up on the first day out. I wound up staying with that agency for fifteen years. Janette Walton, my agent, was like a second mom. I've always had a strong sense of loyalty to those who proved to be friends in my times of need.

Not knowing a soul in Los Angeles except Jim, I had no choice but to take Toni with me on my auditions. Desperate for a job, I'm sure the hunger showed through. At first, nothing happened. The competition was stiff. At every audition, fifty to a hundred models vied for the same job. They flocked to L.A., all hoping to land that big part. Most of them would do anything for a shot at the big time. I was just another pea in a very large pod.

My ego wasn't hurting—my pocketbook was. I needed money. That was the bottom line. I knew it would be a matter of time before I'd get established, but could I make it for that long? I could survive more easily alone, but I had to feed Toni too. The pressure was on me, but I was determined.

After three weeks of pounding the pavement, I went on an audition for Fuji Film. The faces of the Japanese men lit up when I entered the room. I had this one. Toni sat quietly while they sifted through the pages of my portfolio.

"Hmm...You've done a lot of work for Kodak, I see."

Shit, I didn't even think about that.

"Uh, yeah...but that picture is at least ten years old, and that one is—"

"Ten years? How old are you, anyway?"

Put your foot in your mouth, White, then shove it down your throat, why don't you!

"Oh, I'm only 22...I started young."

And out of the mouths of babes...

"Mommy," Toni said, "you're not 22, you're 26!"

It's hamburger tonight, kid.

After an awkward moment of silence, I turned three different shades of red, smiled, and shrugged. The attention was turned toward this adorable little child and everyone burst into laughter.

"What is your name?" one of the men asked.

"Toni."

"And how old are you, Toni?"

"Six and three-quarters."

"Have you ever had your picture taken?"

"Lots of times."

Maybe all is not lost—but pray she doesn't say "Kodak."

"Can we take a picture of you today?"

"Can I, Mommy?"

Do you want to eat, kid?

"Of course, honey."

Hmm... beat out by a seven-year-old.

Toni charmed her way into their hearts—as well as their pockets. She was no stranger to the camera. She'd been only six days old when she'd done her first national ad for Kodak. With her platinum-blonde hair and dark brown eyes and brows, she was a photographer's dream. Needless to say, Toni got the job. We were able to eat for the next two weeks from the proceeds. Toni made me splurge and buy her a steak when the check came in.

We celebrated in our empty apartment. We didn't have a table, so we spread a sheet on the living room floor, lit a few candles, and toasted each other with wine glasses filled with milk. Then we ate as if it were our last earthly meal. Toni rolled with the punches well. We had each other, but, more importantly to Toni, she had me—totally to herself.

One month after Toni's lifesaving job, I finally landed one of my own—a brochure for the Sahara Hotel in Las Vegas. I took Toni with me and my cousin Mickey's daughter watched her while I worked. I was making $1,200 a day and the job lasted five days. Toni was already making out the grocery list. This job was our ticket to a less stressful way of life, but I had an unexpected set back—the production company went bankrupt and stiffed me for the money. Despite the pitfalls, I was getting a pretty good sense of my strength and I was more determined than ever to make a new life for my daughter and myself.

Then the inevitable happened: I answered the phone to hear Joe's voice on the other end. Under all that duress, I had forgotten to close my bank account in Solana Beach. Although I had opened a new account in L.A., it was with the same bank, and my statements were somehow mailed to the old address. I don't know if it was the bank's mistake or mine, but it happened. He had tracked me down through the rental agent. He didn't have the address yet, but it would be easy enough to find. I had to find another place—fast.

"Where are you, Georgia?" he asked calmly.

"L.A., where you called me," I answered.

"Where in L.A.? I'm in no mood for guessing games!"

"What difference does it make, Joe? I'm not coming back."

"I'm warning you for the last time, Georgia. Get your ass home now!"

Don't let him scare you anymore. Look how far you've come. You can do it.

"Not this time, Joe. I refuse to live that way anymore."

"Just come home, Georgia, and I'll forget this ever happened," he said, using his predicable nice guy approach.

"I can't."

"Why can't you?"

"Because it'll never end, Joe. You'll never change."

"I'll change. I've had a lot of time to think. I don't blame you for running, but you have to give me another shot. Let me prove it to you. Okay, honey?"

"Please, Joe, leave me alone. I need to be away from you right now."

"Do you love me, Georgia?"

"That has nothing to do with it, Joe. It just won't work. I'm so sick of being miserable. There's never been enough of me left to give Toni. How can I be a good mother if I'm always in mental turmoil? It hasn't been easy, but you know what? We're both happier than we've ever been. So please, if you really care about us, leave us alone."

"Let me come up there and talk to you."

"No, not now."

"I worry about you two by yourselves. Do you have any money?"

"I'm getting by."

"Do you have any idea what you put me through? Not knowing where the hell you are or if you're all right or not? You've heard about the Hillside Strangler, haven't you?"

"Yeah—so?"

"So? For Christ sakes, Georgia! You're all alone in that fuckin' city with a little kid. Do you realize what an easy mark you are? Honey, you need me more than you realize. Come home."

"I can take care of myself."

"Please, honey, let me see you."

"No."

"Goddamnit, Georgia!" he screamed. "Don't make me do this. Tell me where you are. You know I'll find out anyway, so why don't you make it easy on yourself?"

"See what I mean, Joe? I'm hanging up now."

"Don't you dare hang up! I'll—"

It's time to move on...

———◦———

Calling home to check in on the Rochester front, I learned that Sammy G had been indicted for Jimmy Massaro's murder, along with Gene DeFrancesco and a few others. The city was in chaos. Chief Bill Mahoney wanted the Mob so bad he'd sell his soul to get them. Eventually, he did just that. It would cost him his life. He escaped a violent death, although he came closer than he knew.

His heart gave out under the stress of the trials that followed.

It turned out that Mahoney fabricated evidence and coerced his detectives to lie on the stand, causing the murder charges to stick. He had the testimony of five of the "Big Boys" in exchange for their lives, or time in prison. But apparently his philosophy was: why leave anything to chance?

If he had just played by the rules, he would have gone down in history as a great cop. The result of the perjury would put Sammy Gingello and four other top crime figures of the Rochester Syndicate behind bars. Despite having F. Lee Bailey as his lawyer, Sammy went down hard.

All of Sammy's loyal supporters rallied to his cause with $1,000-a-plate dinners to raise money for his defense. He was guilty as charged, everyone knew it, but the point was they didn't have the evidence. So Mahoney *created* it. Amazing how many of the "tough guys" were turning state's evidence. Law enforcement was operating in the same way as the Mob.

In Rochester, the good guys and the bad guys had always been in cahoots. Having relatives on the police force, I grew up knowing quite a few of the "good guys." Most of the ones I knew weren't paid to close their eyes, but they did look in the other direction. I loved Sammy. Everybody did, including some of the cops. They knew Sam was getting the shaft. They helped him keep one step ahead by secretly providing him inside information.

I still have a mistrust for most cops. They have the power to play Hitler if they choose to do so, and the few bad ones have left me with negative memories of their corruption. With firsthand experience seeking help from a cop who had been bought off, I learned the hard way to work within my own world if I had a problem to solve. If nothing else, such experiences gave me the street sense I needed to survive.

With all that going on, Joe's fears had some validity. Still, not knowing who or what I should be afraid of, I kept my distance. My only choice was to tough it out in Los Angeles and somehow make it work.

CHAPTER NINE

"Excuse me, do you mind if my friend and I sit with you? There's a 45 minute wait for a table," the stranger said, fingering his watch.

The Red Onion in Beverly Hills was packed with the lunch crowd. At a table for four, I sat alone, pondering my future. I nodded, feeling a little grateful for the company.

"I'm Steve Zamett, and this is my partner, Mike Ruben," he said with mischievous eyes that danced while he spoke.

Steve had a warm smile and seemed to be pretty genuine—a rare thing in Los Angeles. A big, solid guy. His strong, round face was pleasant, complementing his personality. Mike was the opposite: a smaller, dorky kind of guy who hid behind his milk bottle glasses. Steve did most of the talking while Mike sat silently in his shadow. Steve was instantly likeable, and I felt comfortable in his company. I wasn't quite so sure of Mike. He seemed so businesslike, never cracking a smile.

"Where are you from?" Steve asked, patting down the mass of dark curls on his head.

"New York, originally. I moved here from Solana Beach a few months ago."

"Oh, really? We're from that area too—San Diego. Where do you live in L.A.?"

"In a small apartment on Olympic Boulevard, but not for long. I'm looking for a new place."

"Oh? Too small for you?"

"It's a long story," I answered, staring out the window, reflecting on my dilemma. Living on the run was getting old. "So what brings you two to L.A.?"

"We're in the construction business. We have a contract to build Lee Grant's house in Malibu," Mike said.

"Yeah, we're looking for a place to hang our hats for a while," Steve added, stealing the conversation from Mike. "We'll probably have a truck up here in a few days if you need any help moving."

"I may take you up on that. I don't have any furniture. Just a bed, a TV, some dishes, and a few clothes."

"Sounds easy enough," Steve replied.

"I should be going. I have an audition at two o'clock and I need to be back to pick up my daughter by three."

"Oh, how old is your daughter?" Steve asked.

"She's seven."

"I have a son that age, and a daughter, five. Where does she go to school?"

"In Beverly Hills. They have an excellent school system here."

"So I've heard."

I stood up, flung my purse over my shoulder, and reached for my portfolio.

"Where do we contact you?" Steve asked. He jotted my number down on a napkin. "Good luck finding an apartment," he yelled after me as I weaved through the tables toward the exit.

"Thanks, you too," I answered hurriedly over my shoulder. I really didn't expect a call, but I'd sure welcome help with the move.

———◆———

The audition went as had all the others. Masses of women, each one more beautiful than the next, filing through the door with their portfolios in hand. This particular casting was a monster cattle call. At 2:35, ten girls were still ahead of me on the sign-in sheet. I couldn't stay any longer. Toni would be getting out of school and I was at least twenty minutes away.

I fought the Hollywood traffic back to Beverly Hills. The temperature hit the 90s and, with no air-conditioning, my make-up had melted off my face. I probably wouldn't have gotten the job anyway. I had landed only a few jobs since arriving in Los Angeles. In Rochester, I had turned down more work than I could accept. The competition was a lot stiffer here, and my finances were looking grim.

Toni's face brightened when she saw my car pull up.

"Hi, Mommy," she said, bouncing into the car.

"Sorry I'm late again, honey. How was school today?"

"Okay, but that bratty Billy spilled ice cream all over my pretty dress in the cafeteria. Look," she said, scrunching up her face.

"That's all right, it'll come out in the wash. What did you eat for lunch today?"

"Nothing."

"What do you mean, nothing? I gave you lunch money."

"I know, but I didn't like what they had."

"Toni, you have to eat lunch. You're going to get sick."

"I didn't like it, Mom. What's for dinner?"

"Green beans and hamburger."

"When can we have steak again, Mommy? We always had steak when we lived with Daddy."

"Would you rather live with Daddy and have steak all the time?"

"No, I like hamburgers. I don't care if we have steak, really Mommy, that's okay. Hamburger is good."

I noticed a For Rent sign on the building directly across the street from the school. That would be great. Toni could walk home if I was running late. We parked and went to check it out. It would be more than I could afford, but I pressed the manager's button anyway. The apartment was on two levels. Off the only bedroom on the second floor was a large private balcony, giving a spacious, open feeling. The rent was $550 per month—$250 more than I was paying at the current apartment.

"This is nice, Mommy. Can we live here? Can we, can we?"

"I think it's a little too expensive for us, honey." Her excitement disappeared and she became quiet.

"The landlady may negotiate if you're really interested," the manager said. "Between you and me, it's been vacant for a few months. I know she's anxious to get it rented."

"Really? What do you think she'll take?"

Toni's face brightened again.

"Well, I don't know. Why don't you make me an offer and I'll see what she says."

"Ask if she'll take $400. I'll stop back in the morning."

Toni pleaded with me all the way home. The property owner came back with a figure of $450. I would make it work. I had to get out of where I was fast, and being right across the street from Toni's school made the apartment ideal.

Time to look for a real job. Getting established as a model in Los Angeles was taking longer than I anticipated. I hadn't worked for minimum wage since the job at the hot dog stand at Willow Point Park when I was a kid, but with no skills my choices were few. I answered an ad at a jeans store on Hollywood Boulevard called London Britches. Larry Armond, the owner, would accommodate me when it came to letting me off for auditions, and he allowed me to work around Toni's school hours.

Handicapped by my lack of apparel, chasing modeling assignments seemed futile. Larry offered to sell me clothes at his cost. Piece by piece, I slowly started rebuilding my wardrobe. I could make the rent, but that was all. I'd started accepting dinner dates just so we could eat. Ordering more food than I could consume, I took the leftovers home in a doggy bag. Deceitful or not—survival's what counted.

Steve did call, and the timing couldn't have been better. He and Mike helped me move to our new apartment. I was extremely grateful for the help, but the paybacks aren't always worth the favor. For some reason their apartment didn't materialize, and before I knew it, they were crashing on my living room floor on their frequent trips to L.A. But they always bought food, or took Toni and me out to dinner.

Eventually Steve asked, "When are you gonna get some furniture for this place?"

"As soon as I can afford it, I'm going to have my furniture shipped from New York."

"I have an idea," Steve said excitedly. "I'm taking my son to Philadelphia in a few weeks. Why don't you and Toni drive with us across country? I'll drop you off in Rochester and pick up a U-Haul on my way back from Philly. We can bring all your stuff back."

The more I thought about it, the better it sounded. I missed my stereo the most. I needed music in my life. I agreed to take Steve up on his offer. Jim Alquist's old stereo was going to make it to California after all.

The cross-country trip was actually fun. The kids had a great time. We camped at night, explored caves, and hiked the Grand Canyon. But I sensed Steve was falling for me. I had a lot of things to settle in my life and starting a relationship was not on my immediate list of things to do.

I learned a lot about Steve during those long hours on the road. He'd forgotten some things he'd told me, and when he retold a story, it was totally different from what he had said before. I discovered he was a pathological liar, and I began to surmise his past was a bit checkered.

He pretended to be someone he wasn't, trying to impress me with his importance. He lied about *everything*. He said he owned the San Diego soccer team. He actually did, but I later found out that he bought it with phony silver certificates. After a year, the bank finally figured it out. He was a serious con artist, and a good one too. The scary thing was, he really believed his own lies.

When we returned to Los Angeles, my better judgement told me to back off from continuing this friendship. At first I was polite, telling him there was no room in my life for dishonesty. I was moving through life cautiously, I told him, and was leery of his behavior.

"It's him, isn't it?" Steve asked from a phone booth somewhere in L.A.

"What are you talking about, Steve?"

"Your husband. You're still in love with him, aren't you?"

"Steve, this has nothing to do with Joe. I'm not ready for a relationship with anyone right now, but if I were, it wouldn't be with someone like you. I can't stand liars."

"If he was dead, would you give me a chance then?"

"What kind of a thing is that to say? I told you it has nothing to do with Joe. It's you, Steve!"

"Can I come over?"

"No, you can't come over."

"I want to show you something. Please..."

"What, Steve?" I asked.

"I want to show you my will."

"Why would I want to see your will?"

"Because I changed it," he said. "I'm leaving everything to you. Everything."

There's something very wrong here. Get rid of this guy—now!

"That's the most ridiculous thing I ever heard."

"No it's not, George. It proves how much I love you. I chose you over my children. I love you more than anything in the world."

"Change it back."

"What?"

"Change it back. If you can't see how stupid that is, then your problem is a lot more serious than I thought."

"If I can't have you, I don't want to live," he said, sounding weirdly sincere. "I want you to have everything."

"Steve, I strongly suggest you get some help. There isn't anyone worth taking your own life for."

"You are," he whispered.

"Oh, man, get some help," I said. "I've got to hang up now."

"Wait! Please say you'll just let me try. I know I can make you love me."

Nothing he could say was remotely interesting. He was relentless in his fruitless efforts at seduction. As I listened to him rant, I drew a stick figure on a notepad and added little pointed horns. "Steve, you're not hearing me. You haven't heard a word I said. There's no more point in talking. Good-bye."

"George—" he managed to squeeze in before the line went dead.

Ring, ring, ring, ring, ring, ring, ring, ring, ring, ring, ring, ring.

That's what I remember most about Steve: ring, ring, ring, ring, ring. I can still hear that phone ringing today. I'd hang up on him and he'd call right back. I'd turn on my answering machine and he'd talk until he used up my tape. I'd change my phone number and he'd manage to find out the new one. Ring, ring, ring, ring. I was beginning to lose it. He would show up at my door in the middle of the night, crying, begging me to let him in. I'd call the police and he'd take off. But he'd be back the next night with a different story.

One night he turned up bleeding.

"Please, please, open the door," he pleaded. "They're out there. They just stabbed me. Open the door, George, I think I need an ambulance. Look out your peephole if you don't believe me. I'm bleeding to death."

I didn't believe him; all his stories were "out there"—but when I looked through the peephole, he really was bleeding. He wasn't lying this time.

"What happened?" I asked with concern as I opened the door.

"I was parking in the alley and these two black guys jumped me. They stabbed me. Could you get a towel?" he asked, his body trembling.

"I'll call 911," I said after I got the towel.

"No, it's okay, I'll be all right."

He's lying, White.

"Steve, you're bleeding! You have to go to the hospital."

The police arrived before the paramedics. When they questioned him, the story was slightly different from the one he had told me. The police accompanied him to the ambulance, then returned to the apartment after Steve was driven away.

"This will sound crazy, officer, but I think he may have

stabbed himself," I voiced.

"Now, why would you think that?" the cop asked suspiciously.

"I believe he would say or do anything to get me to open my door to him. I've had this problem with him before. Your department has a record of all this. He's not a very stable person."

"We're aware of the problems here," the cop said, "but this is a far more serious situation. He claims your husband hired the guys who did this to him."

"What? Oh man, my husband doesn't even know he exists. In fact, he doesn't even know if *I* exist. This guy is a habitual liar. I *know* he stabbed himself."

"We'll still have to check it out. Where does your husband live?"

"No! I don't want him to find me. I won't tell you. Why can't you be as concerned about *my* safety? Do you know how many times I've called you for help? This guy is nuts. Why don't you believe me? Why don't you ever do anything about *him*?"

"Has he physically hurt you?"

"No, but—"

"We get a lot of calls from women complaining about their boyfriends, but if they haven't—"

"He's *not* my boyfriend. I keep telling them that. Does he have to kill me before you can do anything? The man is sick!"

"I'm sorry, miss, but if he hasn't actually hurt you, there's nothing we can do. Our hands are tied. Now about your husband..."

These cops are worthless. I thought you'd learned that by now. Maybe we should just take care of this ourselves.

"You *can't* contact my husband. I don't know who I'm more afraid of, this nut or my husband. Please, at least check out what I'm saying."

They did just that. They found, after checking with the hospital, that the stab wound was not substantial, and they were satisfied with my story.

All I had ever told Steve about Joe was that I was afraid of him and that he was connected with some heavy people. I never went into detail about my past. This was my new life; all that was behind me now and I wanted to forget it. Steve's vivid imagination had run wild, finding another arena for his sick mind to play in.

What if he contacts Joe and tells him where I am?

About a week later, after 300 phone calls, he showed up at my door again, this time claiming his daughter had been killed. He cried uncontrollably as I stood with the locked door between us. How could anyone lie about something like that? I started to feel guilty about shutting him out if there was a possibility that his story was true.

I opened the door. He looked like a total physical and mental wreck. I felt badly for making stand out there for so long. This story was true, I could tell by his demeanor. With the intensity of his gushing sobs he could hardly explain how it happened.

"She was only five, George," he cried. "How could God take my baby? She...oh, God."

"I know, Steve. Take it easy," I said, putting my arm around his shoulder.

"Be grateful your daughter is alive, George. The sight of her little body lying under that car, her bike all twisted, oh, God!" He put his head in his hands and cried uncontrollably.

I felt horrible. What can anyone really do to try to console someone who has lost a child? Not much.

"Oh, Steve, I'm so, so sorry."

"Will you let me stay here tonight? I just can't be alone, not tonight," he asked between sobs.

"Do you want a Valium?"

"One won't do it; give me twenty."

"Steve, stop it. You're being irrational."

"I am? My daughter is dead. You won't even talk to me. What reason do I have to live?"

"Just take this, try to get some sleep."

I gave him two of the blue pills that had been my pals during traumatic episodes in my life, then went upstairs to get him a pillow and blanket.

"Will you stay here until I fall asleep?" he asked.

I went to bed, but I couldn't sleep. I thought about losing Toni. My heart was sympathetic for Steve. It was too horrible to think about. The sun was beginning to rise when I finally fell asleep.

I opened my eyes to find Steve standing at the foot of my bed, looking as if he was in a trance. His eyes seemed to go far beyond what lay immediately in front of them.

"I have to leave now. There's a lot of arrangements to make. Thank you, George, for letting me stay here last night. Can I call you later?" he asked, his eyes still red and puffy.

Would it make a difference if you said no? I'm telling you, White, this man is going to be the death of us. He's playing on your sympathy now. Don't fall in that trap again. I thought you learned that lesson.

———◈———

I called Mike Ruben a few hours after Steve left. I hadn't seen or talked to Mike in quite a while. I had a feeling they weren't on good terms.

"What are you talking about, Georgia? They live right across the street from me. I'm looking at his daughter from my kitchen window as we speak. She's fine."

"What? Are you sure?"

"Of course I'm sure. Look, Georgia, that guy is bad news. He's got a screw loose somewhere. He just took me for eighty grand, and you know what? I'm walking away from it. I can't do anything legally anyway. He's not just shrewd, he's calculating and evil. If I pressed this, I think he'd do something drastic to my family. Take my advice—stay away from him!"

"Wait a minute, wait a minute. You're telling me his daughter is alive? A car never hit her? Are you sure that's her outside?" I asked, convinced he must have an axe to grind. There's no way Steve could have faked that scene.

"Georgia, I'm looking right at her. In fact, Steve is pulling into his driveway right now."

"What do you mean, *his* driveway? Does he live there too?"

"You didn't know he was married?"

"Married! He said he was divorced! Jesus, I can't believe

this guy."

"He may be divorced soon at the rate he's going. Carol thinks he's having an affair because he's in L.A. so much. Now that we're no longer partners, he can't use me as an excuse."

"Mike, how could he take his son across the country with us and not expect his wife to find out?"

"He probably made the kid lie."

"That's sick."

"*He's* sick, Georgia. I'm telling you, stay away from him."

This guy doesn't need a shrink—he needs a lobotomy!

Shock numbed me. From the way Steve had carried on it was hard to fathom that he'd lied. Even Steve himself had to believe what he had said. No normal man could act that well. I shuddered. A feeling of dread came over me.

I warned you, White! You've got to stop being such a bleeding heart. Don't let people take advantage of you like that. It's okay to be a bitch. It's called survival!

When Steve called, I was ready for him.

"Hi, George. This has to be at the top of my list as one of the most horrible days of my life. I wouldn't wish this on anybody," he said, sounding exhausted.

"Steve, I'd like to go to the funeral."

"Uh...I don't think that's a good idea."

"Why not?" I asked, enjoying listening to him squirm.

"My ex-wife is pretty upset, I just don't think—"

"You mean your *wife,* don't you, Steve?"

He suddenly went quiet, as if I had pressed a pause button. Then in a small voice he said, "What do you mean?"

"What I mean, Steve, is *if* your daughter was dead, then I guess your *wife* would be upset, but since she's not dead, do you think she might have something else to be upset about?" He was at a loss for words. "Don't you ever, ever call me or come around here again. Take my advice and get some help, Steve. Oh, and Steve, I want you to know I bought a gun. You have a nice little history with the Beverly Hills Police Department now. If you come anywhere near me, I'll kill you." I slammed the phone down.

Ring, ring, ring, ring. I walked drove to the nearest gun shop.

Way to go, White. Now you're getting the idea.

Before I could pick up the gun I had to wait two weeks—some kind of legal requirement. In the meantime, it was too damn quiet. The silence was more unsettling than the constant ringing of my telephone. He had to be up to something. Between working at the store and taking care of my other obligations, I began to look for *another* place to live.

Juggling my time was a real problem. One day, I was running late again from an audition. I arrived home at three-thirty, expecting Toni to be waiting patiently. She wasn't there. I walked over to the school, thinking she might be at the playground. It was deserted. Getting frantic now, I knocked on the neighbor's door downstairs. Toni liked visiting with Orna, the teenage girl who lived there, but Orna had not seen her. I raced back to my apartment to call the police. A feeling of dread hung heavily in the pit of my stomach. The phone was ringing when I entered. I prayed that it was Toni as I rushed to answer it.

"Hello?"

"I've got Toni," he said triumphantly.

"Where are you with my daughter, Steve?"

"I just took her for an ice cream. Why are you so worried?" I visualized him with a grin.

"Bring back my daughter, Steve. Right now!"

"Will you talk to me when I get there?"

"Yes, I'll talk to you, just get her back here—now."

Within ten minutes he was at my door with Toni.

"Hi, Mommy," Toni said, ignorant of being in the company of a highly unstable person. Steve stood behind her holding a long box.

"Honey, why don't you go downstairs and play with Orna for a little while."

"I don't have to do my homework first?"

"No, you can do it later."

"Yippee!" she cried as she shot out the door.

Turning my attention to Steve, I became hostile. "What the hell do you think you're doing, Steve? Why do you think you have a right to take my daughter without my permission? There's a name for that, ya know."

"I bought you a present," he said, ignoring my anger.

"I don't want presents from you, Steve. I want you the hell out of my life!"

He proceeded to open the oblong cardboard box. An emerging smile teased his face as he tore the tape off the side.

This guy just doesn't get it, White. He's even a bit too much for me to handle. You better call the police as soon as he leaves—again.

Hypnotized with fear, I watched as he sadistically pulled a double-barreled shotgun from the box.

"What are you doing?" I screamed.

"If I can't have you—neither can he," he said. His glazed, unseeing stare left no chance for negotiation. He pointed the gun at me and ordered me to walk up the stairs. Gripped with fear, I hesitantly started the climb to my death. With every step my mind raced at full speed. *How am I going to get out of this?*

"All I wanted was a chance. I know I could've made you happy, but you wouldn't give me the opportunity to show you."

I prayed Toni wouldn't come home.

"I didn't want to do this, but he can't have you. He doesn't deserve you. Before I kill myself, I'm going to kill him, too. I know where he lives. I've been watching him. He fucks everything in sight, ya know. I would never do that to you. I would've made you happy—if you'd only given me the chance.

Lie down on the bed. I'll make it quick, I don't want you to suffer," he said, tears streaking down his face.

Listen to me, White. We can get out of this, we've done it before. Just don't panic. Take control. You can't die now, we've come too far. Think!

My past experiences sprang vividly to mind. I remembered well how to trade the words "I love you" in exchange for my life, but maybe this was a different kind of sickness. I didn't know if it would work.

"Steve, lie down with me," I offered. "I owe you the chance to at least show me what I could have had." Teasing him with sensuous body language, I slowly lowered myself onto my back and unbuttoned my blouse, exposing my breasts to him.

In a retarded tempo, reality reentered his face. Startled by the transformation, I accelerated the tease, lifting my pelvis in slow seductive movements. His eyes wandered up and down my body, drinking it in. My act was working, as evidenced by the bulge in his pants. He shook his head as if waking from a dream. Cocking his head to one side, he hesitated. What I saw in his eyes, obscured by desire, was an irretrievable madness. But his hunger to have me sexually overpowered his desire to kill me. The cool steel grazed my leg as he laid the gun beside me. Straddling my body, he used both hands to fondle my breasts, then took my hand and directed it to his penis.

"Touch it."

The sensation of my hand gliding down his penis and my pelvic movement sent him into orbit. He rolled onto his side and impatiently began to remove his pants. I had the window of opportunity I was praying for. *Thank you, God.* I lunged for the gun. Catching him off guard, my finger quickly found the trigger.

We struggled for possession of the gun. It fired, blowing a huge hole in the wall. The roar stopped him cold. Taking advantage of his momentary shock, I sprang to my feet and ran like hell. I flew down the stairs to my neighbor's and pounded on the door. The blast of the shotgun still hummed loudly in my ears.

It seemed an eternity before the door opened. Frantically, I pushed my way in, locking and barricading the door while Orna called 911.

I'm proud of you, White. You handled that like a pro. Who said you can't take care of yourself? Where there's a will, there's a way...

The police took *another* report. Starring at them blankly as they wrote, I imagined what the next one would say: *The body was found lying face up...*

They couldn't help me, I knew that now. One can't stop a demented person from killing once he has it in his mind to do so. I had to leave. He'd be back, and I might not be so lucky the next time. The police waited as I packed my bags. I packed a lot, not knowing when we would be returning.

I held my daughter's hand and took one last look around as I closed the door and took my next step toward an unknown future.

———◆———

After all the futile attempts with the police, I came to the conclusion that my problem had no conventional resolution. There was just no way to stop this obsessive maniac. Well, yes...There was *one* way. The last resort, and now was the time. Hesitating, I picked up the telephone and dialed the number.

"Hi, Joe."

A long silence.

"Where are you?"

"I'm—"

"Where've you been hiding? I've been worried sick."

"I'm in Rochester."

"Rochester! Did you leave Los Angeles?"

"No...well...just for a while."

"What's the matter, Georgia?"

"I have a problem. I need your help. I don't know who else

to turn to."

He hesitated. "What kind of a problem?" he asked with concern.

"Well...there's this guy—"

His mood changed over the wire. I could feel his teeth clenching in the silence. The thought crossed my mind that I'd made a mistake, but I dismissed it. Aware I didn't really have a choice, I began to methodically work my way through the past months' events, carefully choosing my words. He listened without saying a word. He was so quiet. Had he hung up?

"Joe?"

"I'm here," he answered in a disgusted tone.

"You have to help me. He's going to kill me. He's just waiting for me to come back. My cousin Randy told me my apartment was broken into. Randy fixed the door, but he'll be back. I'm afraid to go home. Will you...will you help me?"

"If anyone's going to kill you, Georgia, it's going to be me. How do you get yourself into these messes? Do you see now why you need me? Who the hell else would do what I do for you? There isn't a day that goes by I don't think about you in that city, with all those nuts running around. I knew this would happen. Why don't you just come home—where you belong!"

"Joe, I called because I need your help, not to fight. Are you going to help me or not?"

"When are you coming back?"

"I'm not! If you won't help me then—"

"When are you coming back to *Los Angeles*, Georgia?"

"Oh. When I know I can...and be safe," I answered, still uncomfortable that I was giving him this opportunity to get to me.

"All right. Make your reservations, and call me back with your flight information. *Don't* bring Toni with you."

"Okay," I said, exhaling with relief.

After two weeks at my parents house, keeping a low profile, I had to do something. When was I ever going to feel safe? Joe hadn't actively pursued trying to find me, so I assumed he was beginning to accept my departure, or at least I hoped that was the case. I knew it was risky asking for his help. To open that door again, after months of managing to be away from his grip, was a chance I had to take. Hell, I was going to have to move again anyway.

An hour later I called Joe back with my flight information. He answered on the first ring.

"It's United, flight 227. I arrive LAX tomorrow at 8:30 p.m."

"Okay, I'll have someone there to meet you at the plane."

"How will I recognize him?"

"He'll find you. He has instructions to stay with you day and night until the problem is taken care of."

"What's he going to do?"

"You know better than to ask that kind of question on the phone. Don't worry, honey—you're in good hands. Nothing will happen to you. You've got one of the best in the business."

———

"Are you sure nothing's wrong, Georgia?" asked my father.

"Yes, Daddy, everything's fine," I assured him. "Will you please stop worrying about me?"

"I don't know...you haven't called any of your friends and you're acting so jumpy. Is there something you're not telling us?" he asked, deeply concerned.

"Daddy, I'm just a little stressed over money, but it'll be easier getting established without having to worry about Toni."

Handing me my carry-on-luggage at the gate, my father fought back tears and gave me a heartfelt hug. "Two weeks isn't enough time, but we loved having you home, honey. Call and let us know you got there safely."

"I will, Dad. Take good care of my baby until I can send for her. I love you," I said, blowing him a kiss from the jet-way.

Starring out the window of the jumbo jet in a trance, I watched the day meet the night, separated by a crimson streak. The dark against the light made me wonder what the evening's end might hold.

Arriving in L.A., I exited the plane and looked around. No one made contact. I waited until the last passenger had come out.

Still no one. I swallowed hard. *Don't panic.* I noticed a fat man seated alone in the waiting area. About 280 pounds lopped over both sides of the seat.

Could that be him? God, I hope not, he doesn't look like he could get out of his own way.

Then I spotted a rather large man standing near the pay phones wearing jeans and a sport jacket. His legs and arms were thick with solid muscle. He stood about 6'4", and his light brown hair had a hint of natural wave. His nose had been broken several times, and the scar on his left cheek spread three inches in length. No doubt, this was the man. Central Casting would have immediately hired him for the part he was about to play. As he walked toward me, his lips curved upward, displaying an easy smile.

"Hi, I'm Al. You're even prettier than your picture," he said, relieving me of my carry-on bag.

"Thanks. I was just about to call Joe. I didn't think you were going to show."

"I saw you right away, but I wanted to be sure you didn't have an unwelcome visitor waiting somewhere in the wings."

We watched as the bags came down the conveyor belt. "Why don't you get the car, Al, and I'll wait here?"

"Sorry, you'll have to walk. I can't leave you here alone."

"Walk?" I said, looking down at my luggage. *How the heck could we possibly walk with all this stuff?* As I had that thought, Al picked up my bags as if they were filled with feathers. For the first time in a long while, I felt safe.

We drove down Century Boulevard to the 405 freeway and headed north to Beverly Hills.

"So, tell me about this guy. What's the story?"

"Believe me, Al, when I tell you I've met some sick people in this world, I really have. I even know the Hillside Strangler who was just caught. He's been in my home in Rochester. But this guy tops them all. He's decided that if he can't have me, nobody can."

I continued to tell him of my bizarre encounters with Steve over the last few months. He listened intently.

"What does he look like?"

"He's not a bad looking guy. You'd never know to look at him that his mind is so warped. He's tall, about 6'1", black curly hair—a lot of it." Al hung heavily on my every word, nodding occasionally, storing the information. "Built pretty good for not working out."

"What's his nationality?"

"Jewish."

"He's a Jew? Does Joe know this guy's a Jew?"

"People are people, Al. There is another world out there that doesn't include Italians, you know. Are you Italian?"

"Yeah," he answered, as if insulted.

"Well, you could pass for a mayonnaise-face," I teased. "What's your last name?"

"You don't need to know," he said coldly.

"You're right—I don't."

"Does he carry a gun?" he asked, getting back to business.

"Yes, he has a .38 and a shotgun. He cornered me in my bedroom two weeks ago with the shotgun. I tried to talk him down by making him think I cared about him. When I thought I had him convinced, I grabbed for the gun. It went off—you'll see the hole in my wall when we get there. Thank God no one was walking by outside when it happened. I took off for New York the same day."

"Do you think he'll be around tonight?"

"I'm sure he's been checking the place daily. The minute he knows I'm back, he'll be there, no doubt about it."

We turned off Wilshire Boulevard onto South Elm Drive. Anything south of Wilshire was considered the slums of Beverly Hills. Quite a contrast to the mansions just one block to the north. Al drove past the apartment and around the block twice before parking in the alley. Leaving the luggage behind, I walked quietly up the stairs. Al followed close behind with a gun in his hand.

The door was slightly ajar. Stepping aside, I let Al enter first.

He cautiously pushed open the door. I turned on the light and closed the door. He walked slowly through each room. All of my plants were dead. Not wilted from lack of water—they were *dead*. An empty bleach container lay on the floor next to my big palm. That sick bastard had poured bleach in every potted plant in the place.

Al came back downstairs. "It's all clear, but you're not going to like it up there," he said, stuffing the gun into his pants.

I climbed the stairs, dread filling my belly. My closet doors were open and pieces of clothing were scattered all over the floor. Steve had taken one article of every suit and cut it into little shreds. One outfit was missing the pants, another was missing the jacket, another the vest. I wanted to cry. To build up my wardrobe again had taken forever. My pillows and comforter were slashed and feathers were everywhere. Pictures hung upside down on the walls. He had drawn mustaches on many of the photographs in my portfolio. He knew I'd be crippled without my tools. Above the shotgun hole in the wall, Steve had written YOUR HEART in red marker with an arrow pointing to the hole.

Al stood behind me, observing the scene. "This guy's one twisted character," he said, shaking his head from side to side in disbelief. "How have you managed to survive this maniac all alone? There's no doubt, this guy wants your blood. Jesus Christ," he said, still not able to wipe the astonished look off his face. "This is one job I'm gonna enjoy."

Rage built inside me. It had been suppressed by fear for too long. With Al to protect me, I felt safe. Now I could allow the rage to surface—and surface it did. Georgia Black took over.

That son-of-a-bitch is going to pay.

⊷⧫⊶

Al would not let me out of his sight for a moment. Together we walked outside for my bags. Again he carried them all. I carried his, a small duffel bag and a big, rather heavy briefcase. Then I ordered a pizza and rewound my answering machine.

Numerous hang-ups and a call from my agent.

"Hi, sweetie. This is Janette. I know you're in New York, but I think you'd better give me a call at home tonight. I got a very strange call from a guy by the name of Steve somebody or other. He said some pretty terrible things and if I didn't know you better, I'd take you off the active list. Point is, if he's making these kinds of calls to other clients of ours, we may have some problems. Oh, almost forgot. I have a juicy audition for you on Tuesday. Hope you're back by then. I'll give you the particulars when you call. Bye, sweetie."

Dammit! I was fuming. Al was now busy cleaning his guns. *That's why his briefcase was so heavy. There's a friggin' arsenal in there!*

It's about time you made a move, White. What took you so long? Who the hell did this jerk think he was dealing with anyway?

"This guy deserves what he's going to get," Al said coldly, continuing to polish his gun.

Fear and the sickening realization of what could happen momentarily eclipsed my anger. This was no game we were playing.

"What *is* he going to get, Al?" I asked, feeling the hair on my arms rise.

Fixing his green eyes on me, his face became serious. "What would you like him to get?"

"I just want him beaten badly enough to get the message."

Don't wimp out on me now, White.

"Are you sure this guy's going to get the message?"

I hadn't thought about that. But when it came right down to do or die, I couldn't play God with someone's life, even Steve's.

"Joe thinks he should be eliminated. To be honest with you, so do I. Guys like that never learn their lesson. You could put him behind bars for twenty years, and the day he gets out he'll be at

your door. Either you get him, or eventually he's gonna get you."
Simple but deadly logic.

After a long silence he added, "It's against my better judgment, but it's your call."

I stopped holding my breath and began inhaling normally again. The power was mine. Steve would live. Joe had clearly instructed Al to follow my orders, regardless of what he wanted to do. Joe saw my cry for help as his chance to get me back, hoping that if he played the knight in shining armor and rescued me, I'd gratefully return to him. If Joe had Steve "eliminated" against my wishes, or had Al take me back to Solana Beach by force, he knew he'd lose the battle. Knowing his pattern, he was in his good-guy mode.

The doorbell rang and we both jumped. Al grabbed one of the guns and quickly shoved the briefcase into the closet. He positioned himself behind the door and motioned for me to open it.

"Who is it?" I yelled through the door.

"Pizza delivery."

Al did not relax. Never having heard Steve's voice, he remained skeptical.

I opened the door to see a young boy holding a pizza.

"That'll be $8.56, ma'am."

"Wait here."

Walking to the kitchen table, I reached into my purse and pulled out a $20 bill. As I turned toward the door, the sight of Al standing there with a gun, and the boy, a few feet away and totally unaware, made me tremble. If Steve were to barge in at this very moment, this innocent boy could be pulled into this mess. Anxious to get the kid out of there, I gave him the twenty and told him to keep the change.

"Big spender, huh? I can tell who you've spent some time around," Al said.

"Maybe too much time," I replied, thinking out loud. A lot more had rubbed off than I thought ever would.

As we ate the pizza, Al instructed me on what to say and what to do when Steve showed up. The gun was never out of reach.

"Okay," Al said, "we'll do it your way. But if it comes to your life, or mine, it's gonna go down a different way. Understand?" He hesitated. "You better get some rest now. I'll need you to be alert."

I stuffed the feathers back inside the pillow and pushed it into a fresh pillowcase. Getting the extra blanket from the closet, I brought it down to Al. Standing in the dark, he looked guardedly out the window.

"See you in the morning, Al," I said as I started for the stairs.

"Georgia?"

I turned back to him. "Yeah?"

"Do you have any feelings for this guy?"

"Yes. I loathe him. The thought of him repulses me. I get nauseated when I dwell on him too long. Does that answer your question?"

"Yes, yes, it does. Goodnight, Georgia. Sleep well. Your life will soon be your own again."

What might that be like?

I slept like a baby. On the other hand, Al did not sleep at all. He was standing by the same window where I had left him the night before. Minus the sport coat, he still wore the same clothes. The dark, short sleeved t-shirt tucked into his jeans exposed his muscular arms and revealed his expansive chest. *I* surely wouldn't want to meet up with him in a dark alley. He heard me enter the room, but his attention remained out the window.

"What kind of a car does he drive?" he asked, peering out from behind the curtain.

"A '76 dark blue Lincoln Continental."

Turning to look at me, he said, "He drove by three times last night. He knows you're here."

"How do you know that?"

"When you left for New York, your drapes were open. How many of your neighbors are home during the day?"

"One."

"Which apartment?"

"The left front apartment downstairs, and the girl across the hall is out of town."

"Good."

"Are you hungry, Al?"

"Yeah, sure, I could eat."

"I'll have to run to the store. I haven't been here for two weeks."

"No. That's not a good idea. Are there any places around here that deliver?"

"Yeah, there's a deli I could call. Did you get any sleep, Al?"

"No, not really."

"I think you should, don't you?"

"Wouldn't be a bad idea," he said as the phone rang.

"Hello?" Click. "It was him. It won't be long now."

Hours went by and still no Steve. Al slept on and off. The phone rang again. Again he hung up. Day turned into night. The silence was getting on my nerves. I jumped when the phone rang the third time. Al stood at attention.

"Hello?" I could hear him breathing. "Hello?"

"I'm coming over," he finally said in a threatening voice.

"You bastard! You're not going to get away with this, Steve."

"I want to talk to you."

"There's nothing to talk about. Just stay the hell out of my life."

"I'm coming over."

"I'm warning you, Steve. Don't come here!" I slammed down the telephone.

"He'll be here in ten minutes."

He arrived in five. When the doorbell rang, Al took his position behind the door.

"Are you ready?" Al whispered, eyeing me for signs of weakness.

I was more than ready.

"Go away, Steve!" I shouted through the door.

"Open the door!" he demanded.

I opened the door as far as the chain lock would allow. He wore a suit and an absurd looking tie. Guess he thought I'd be impressed.

"What do you want with me, Steve?" I screamed.

"Let me in, I just want to talk to you."

"I don't ever want to see your face again. Now leave."

He pushed his weight against the door and broke the chain lock. The force knocked me to the floor. He was on top of me, his hands around my neck.

Al reacted quickly, kicking him in the head. Steve fell to the floor and reached for his gun. Al kicked it from his hand. I grabbed the gun and aimed it at him. My hand shook. *Dear Jesus! Could I kill him if I had to?*

Silently, I wrestled with Georgia Black.

"How can you do this to me, George? I love you!" Steve screeched, clutching his knee.

"I wouldn't want to see what you'd do if you hated me, Steve," I shot back.

He got to his feet and lunged at Al, pushing him into the wall. My finger, slick with sweat, tightened on the trigger. I didn't want this to end in death, but I mentally prepared myself to pull the trigger. Al quickly regained control, thank God. He smashed Steve's head against the wall several times. Blood was smeared all over the broken plaster. Dazed, Steve kept coming back for more.

The fight covered every inch of the room. Steve fell onto the coffee table and cut his head on the broken glass. Bleeding profusely, he rose again. Al punched him in the face, then in the stomach. Steve doubled over and Al kneed him in his face. I heard the faint crunch of Steve's bones breaking. Before, that sound would have sickened me. But Georgia Black had taken charge.

Steve went down for the last time. When he made an attempt to get up, Al kicked him. Every time he moved—another kick to the head. Al reached down and grabbed him by the hair, their faces inches apart. "This one's from Joe, motherfucker!" he snarled. He stood and kicked him in the head with all the force he could muster.

Steve lay still, his face a smashed-in mess. There was a moment of brooding calm. I felt as if I was standing outside of myself, watching. I slowly walked over to him, my adrenaline surging. Straddling his upper body, I bent down and pulled his head up by his ugly tie. I had no concern as the weight of his head dangled lifelessly beneath me. His eyes were open but he may not have been conscious enough to hear the ferocious vulgarity which came out of my mouth. When I was through, I let go of his tie and his head dropped to the floor in a puddle of blood.

Al stood a few feet away, casually smoking a cigarette, a slight smile on his lips. With admiration, he awaited the entertainment of my next move. To my own astonishment, I reached out, took the lit cigarette from Al's hand, bent down, and extinguished it in Steve's mouth. Looking back at Al, I was greeted with a conspirator's smile, stopping just short of a wink.

I thought about that moment for years after—the horror of how cold and demented I had been. To realize I was capable of such hatred, such brutality, was terrifying to me. Had I become so immune to this kind of violence that I was just like them? This man had pushed me to that point, but still...What I had done had been previously unthinkable to me.

"Let me end it for this fucking piece of shit!" Al said, holding a silencer to Steve's head.

Is this a game? Some kind of a fear tactic he wants me to play along with? If I play along, and he's serious—Steve's dead.

"No...Let him live," I said. "I want him to remember the price of loving me."

Steve couldn't move, but deep moans emerged from his throat. He was conscious enough to know that his life was hanging by a thread. If he could speak, death may have been his choice.

"Okay," Al said. "Back the car into the carport and we'll drag him down the back steps."

"Then what?"

"I'll take it from there."

He handed me a piece of paper with instructions to go to a hotel on Sunset Boulevard. I was to stay there until he called. I pulled Al into the kitchen. Keeping my voice low I whispered, "Al, you're not going to kill him, are you?"

"My instructions are to do whatever you want me to do. It doesn't make any difference to me if he lives or dies. It's your call."

"I don't want him to die."

"Okay, then he lives."

We dragged him down to the car. I ran back up the stairs, got some rags and a bucket of water and washed down the steps. I thought about cleaning the blood from the carpet, but there was too much of it. I gave the walls a quick wipe, grabbed my bags, and headed for the hotel in Hollywood.

In that shoddy place, I had lots of time to think. This was all like some scene from a movie. It seemed so unreal. What had I done? Surely I hadn't done any of that. Who was this person? Confusion and trepidation clouded my mind.

Steve is going to die.

How could you be so stupid? Of course he can't live. If he lives and he talks, Al will come after you. He deserves to die anyway, after what he's done to you.

Why am I in this sleazy hotel anyway? Maybe Al is coming back for me. Joe set me up, of course! It's always the one closest to you—the one you can trust with your life. How could I forget that?

Take it easy, White. You know I'm not going to let that happen. Have I ever let you down before?

My head swirled. Afraid to close my eyes, I paced while Joe's threats replayed in my mind:

If anyone is going to kill you, Georgia, it's going to be me. How do you get yourself into these messes?

Who is he, Georgia?

If you're lying to me, I swear, I'll kill you...I'll kill anyone that touches you. You belong to me.

I trusted you, Georgia.

Don't do this to me, Georgia. I'm giving you fair warning.

Don't do this...

You're gonna die, and so is the motherfucker you've been seeing.

Gotta get rid of that rug. No, I can't go home, he'll find me there. Call Joe! No, no—he's the enemy.

You're getting paranoid, White. If you'd just let him pull the trigger in the first place, you wouldn't have anything to worry about. Take a Valium, go to sleep—I'll take care of you.

Okay...

Georgia and sister Sharon in 1954.

Mom and Dad (Tony and Angela Durante), 1955.

Mom, Dad, Sharon, and Georgia on a weekend trip to Niagara Falls in 1953.

Georgia, posing practice for later; Florida, 1953.

*Sister Sharon with her first husband Dick at the
East Rochester High School Senior Prom, 1965.*

*Frankie Conti and Georgia at the Copa Cabana in
New York following the attempted murder at the
Sundowner and Frankie's release from jail, 1968.*

Kodak Summer Girl stand-up poster, 1969.

Georgia's first wedding, 1968. Tom's brother Babe (lower left), Joe Mugavero and husband Tom (lower right), cousin Keith Christopher (standing).

Jimmy Cristo's wedding was attended by some of the upper echelon of the Rochester Syndicate. Left to right: Rene Piccarreto, with his back to the camera; Joey Tiraborelli; Frank Valenti; Red Russotti; to his right, Sammy Gingello. Also pictured: wedding guests Norm Asito and wife Rachel, along with Sammy G's wife, Maryann.

Joe Lamendola's Caesar's II nightclub in Rochester, 1970.

Richard Marino and Sammy G at Jimmy Cristo's wedding, 1970.

Rochester models baseball team, 1970. Georgia is front and center.
Standing, second from left, "Susie Q" Michaelson.

*Sister Sharon, Georgia, and Joe Lamendola at
Sharon's second wedding, 1975.*

*Daughter Toni with Joe at the Solona Beach condo, taken the
week before the escape, 1976.*

Ex-sister-in-law Darlene (Joe's brother Jimmy's wife), Georgia and Richard Adray at their wedding in 1979.

Jim Alquist, Georgia, and cousin Randy Urich at Richard and Georgia's wedding at the Desert Inn Hotel in Las Vegas, 1979.

Billboard and magazine ad shot in New York in 1979 or 1980. After this shoot, Georgia just missed being on Flight 191 to Los Angeles that crashed on take-off in Chicago, killing all on board.

Reunion with the New York gang at a wedding in Manhattan, 1980.
Left to right: Flip, Frankie, Georgia, Billy, and Tommy Red.

Left to right: Gino Provenzano; Jimmy Cristo and wife Gail; Joey Tiraborelli
and friend. Seated: Vicky Cosco. Taken during a visit to Rochester, 1984.

Georgia posing for a Lipton Tea ad in Japan, 1984.

Georgia and friend Dennis Krieger, who was killed in a plane crash in Dallas in 1985.

Georgia behind the wheel at an SCCA race at Ontario Motor Speedway, 1986.

Georgia with Bobby Unser, Sr., both shooting auto commercials in Pikes Peak, Colorado in 1986. This meeting resulted in Bobby Jr. becoming a member of the Performance Two Driving Team.

Bobby Unser, Jr., Georgia, and Dar Robinson, "World's Greatest Stuntman," at team driving practice six weeks before Dar's death in a motorcycle accident during the filming of A Million Dollar Mystery, *1986.*

Georgia with son Dustin on a family ski trip to Vail, Colorado in 1987.

Toni's wedding, 1992. Georgia, son-in-law Barry, Toni,
and her father, Tom Mugavero.

Georgia Durante, Performance Two Driving Team, 1994.

Members of Performance Two during the filming of TV show, "The Exciting World of Speed and Beauty," which featured Georgia and her driving team, 1994. First row, second from left: daughter Toni. Right of Toni, cousin Debbie Urich. Georgia third from right.

Georgia (as stunt double) with Cindy Crawford, preparing for Pepsi commercial, 1995.

Ferrari crash, Bugle Boy Jeans commercial, early 1990's. Georgia is trapped inside car.

Seated: Quincy Jones. Standing: Georgia, Geraldo Rivera, and Kato Kalen at Drai's supper club in Beverly Hills, 1997.

Salvatore Reale, Jimmy Breslin, and Georgia at the Bel Air Hotel in Los Angeles, 1997.

Georgia's home in Southern California, 1998.

CHAPTER TEN

———◦———◉———◦———

The muffled sound of the telephone ringing could be heard as I turned my key in the door-lock of my apartment. Dropping my bag, I ran to answer the phone.

The voice on the other end was too faint to hear. I pressed my ear tightly against the receiver and said hello again. Steve was calling from a hospital bed, lying in traction with several broken bones and a broken nose and jaw.

"I still love you," the barely audible voice said. "I understand why you did what you did. It's okay. I still love you—I'll always love you..." Dial tone.

My God, it's not over.

You will never get rid of him. He'll never go away. You should have let him die!

My stomach turned as I observed the dark brown spots on my carpet and tried to think of a solution to my problem. What was the answer? Steve's obsession was going to be the death of someone, and by the looks of it, that someone was going to be me. My prior attempts for protection by the police had not worked. Seems that I would have to be pretty close to dead, or actually dead, before they could do anything.

Joe had allowed me to do it my way. The repercussion of this episode backfiring was my problem now. Any future involvement on Joe's part would only bring me back to another situation that was just as intolerable. If I had done things his way to begin with, I wouldn't be facing this dilemma now.

I had no choice. I started to carry a gun, and, this time, I had no hesitations about using it.

———————

A few weeks had passed since Steve's brutal beating. The aggravating hang-ups had started again, but other than that it was pretty quiet. I knew what the silence meant. I thought of calling Sammy G, but he was dodging his own bullets—from the Mob *and* the law. Unnerved, I called Frankie. I could always rely on him without a price attached.

"Of course I can fly out there, baby. I'll catch the red-eye tonight."

"How long can you stay, Frankie?"

"As long as you need me."

I picked him up at the airport the next morning and filled him in.

"Why didn't Joe just kill the motherfucker? You've got a bunch of fuckin' lightweights around you, baby. You should've just called me in the first place."

"I wouldn't let him, Frankie."

He rested his hands on my shoulders and all my worries seemed to fall away. "Georgie Girl, you gotta wake up. You have to harden your heart, baby," he said softly.

"Frankie, I'm so glad you're here. I feel so much safer now. This has been a nightmare."

"First thing we gotta do is find you another place to live."

"I found a place just around the corner from the school, but they want first, last, and security. I don't have it right now."

"Baby, I'll pay for it, don't worry about that. You gotta stop being so damn proud, too. You know anything I got is yours. All you have to do is ask."

I laughed. "Sure, that's easy to say when you haven't got anything."

"You haven't lost your sense of humor, I see," he replied with a wide smile.

"Is that a gray hair?" I asked, running my hand over his head, inspecting more closely.

"Yeah, baby. There's a lot of 'em. So we're goin' for the new place, right?"

"I suppose it's the wise thing to do. Thanks, Frankie, I'll pay you back."

"You even try an' I'll break your skinny legs. How's Toni Lee dealin' with all this?"

"She's in Rochester right now, but she's amazingly resilient. This is nothing new to her, Frankie. She hasn't had a very happy childhood. One day I'll make it up to her."

"Funny how life is," he said. "I let you go to protect you from the kind of life you wound up having anyway. I should've married you, baby. I've kicked myself more than once for being such a fool. There's never been anyone else like you. I keep searching for even a glimpse of you in other women, but it's never there. You're a cut above the rest, Georgie Girl. You deserve a lot more from life than what you've gotten so far. You're a winner, baby—and don't you ever forget that."

"Thank you for saying that, Frankie. I don't know if I believe it, but it's really nice to hear."

"You don't know if you believe it? You don't know? My God, Georgie Girl, what has that man done to you over the years?" he said with genuine sadness as he held me close, stroking my hair.

"I don't know which one I'd like to blow away more," he said almost to himself. We stood that way for several minutes without saying another word.

Frankie accompanied me wherever I went. To the bank, my auditions, even grocery shopping. Wherever my daily life took me, my temporary bodyguard followed.

Frankie and I became lovers again while he was in L.A., but I would not allow myself to think about a future with him. I was trying to get away from that old life. Too much time had passed. Too much of my innocence had been lost. Nevertheless, the comfort of our friendship would be there forever.

I liked having Frankie around. It had been long time since I had acted silly. Life had become so damned serious in recent years. The little girl inside me had not come out to play in a long time, and she was taking full advantage of it.

Even while we laughed and did crazy things, Frankie never lost sight of why he was there. He spotted Steve following us a few times during our outings, but he kept it to himself, careful not to alarm me. Steve was quietly moving into position, and Frankie was ready for him.

Finally, the silence was broken. Ring, ring, ring, ring. That old familiar sound.

"George, don't hang up! Listen, I'm leaving, I'm getting out of your life for good. That's what you want, isn't it?"

"Why are you calling me, Steve? What part don't you understand?"

"George, I'm getting out. I can't take any more. You made your point. I'm not mad at you. I've destroyed a lot of your things, and I feel bad about it. I know you don't have the money to replace them. I want to pay you for what I've destroyed. That's the only way I can leave without feeling like a total jerk."

"Okay, Steve. Bring the money over. Just put it by the door and leave."

"Oh no, I'm not falling for that again. Meet me at the bank. There's people all around. I can't hurt you there—I don't want to hurt you. Bring your friend with you for protection if you don't believe me."

"What friend?"

"The guy who's staying with you."

"How do you know anyone's staying with me?" I asked peeking out the window, feeling his eyes out there somewhere in the dark, haunting me. It gave him some kid of a perverse thrill to know he could follow my every move without my knowledge of it.

"I know everything you do, George, but I don't want to know

any more. I'm getting out of here—for good. Take the money. Let's part friends. What do you say?"

"Okay, Steve, I'll meet you at the bank at one o'clock tomorrow, but if you pull anything—consider yourself a dead man." I hung up at the same time Frankie hung up the extension.

"Georgie Girl, are you nuts? I can't pop him at a bank—in broad daylight!"

"Frankie, I don't expect you to. If he's serious about leaving and this will satisfy him, I'd much rather see it end this way."

Frankie and I drove to the bank an hour before the designated time. Steve was already there. We obviously had the same amount of trust in each other.

"This stinks, baby. I don't have a good feelin' about this."

"What can happen with all these people around, Frankie? You're here, and besides, I have the gun if I need it. Don't worry, I'll be all right."

"Somethin' ain't right," he said, scanning the bank with a trained eye.

Steve walked toward us with a cocky swagger, looking confident under the fading bruises. He was dressed in a dark blue suit, similar to the one that had been drenched with blood. He smiled as he extended his hand to Frankie and introduced himself. He acted as though he were giving a party and greeting his guests.

This infuriated Frankie. Veins bulged under his skin, throbbing as he spoke. "Give the girl her money, you fuckin' puke, and get the fuck out of this state if you know what's good for you."

At that moment I understood why Frankie never talked about the secret part of his life. He was two different people, and I did not want to acquaint myself with this Frankie. Steve didn't either. He quickly turned and walked toward the banker sitting behind the desk. We proceeded into the vault. Frankie waited outside, watching for anyone who looked the least bit suspicious.

The banker carried the box into a private room and left us alone. I suddenly didn't feel safe.

Steve proudly opened the box and displayed the stacks of cash, all $100 bills. "There's $250,000 here, George."

"Great, Steve, count out $3,000 and we're even."

"It's all yours. Come to Europe with me. We can be happy there."

"Steve, I want the $3,000 you owe me, and I want you to keep your promise about leaving," I said with the dreaded feeling that this was not going to end well.

"I know we can be happy," he said with desperation. "Let me just take you there until the money's gone. I'll show you the time of your life. Then if you're still not happy, you can come back. At least I'll be able to say I had the chance to try."

"Steve, look at me. *Listen* to what I'm telling you! If you persist with this fucking fantasy of yours, you are not going to live to see your next birthday. Do you understand what I'm telling you? You are not messing around with amateurs. Do not call me anymore, don't try to see me, just get on a plane and get the hell out of here. If you don't...Well, just take my advice, Steve."

"Will you just—"

I left him standing there and walked out of the bank, no richer than when I had walked in. No safer, either.

"Did you get the money?" Frankie asked when we got in the car.

"No."

"No! What happened?"

"He tried to bribe me with $250,000 if I'd go to Europe with him."

"And you said no?"

"Of course I said no! Are you nuts?" I answered, irritated that he might be serious.

"Hey, two hundred and fifty grand is a lot of dough."

"Knowing Steve, he either lied about the amount or it was counterfeit money. Frankie, he's not going anywhere. I should've known that by now."

"The fuckin' guy's got a death wish. We can make it come true," Frankie stated matter-of-factly.

"Let's stop by that apartment and see if I can get in there a little sooner. Maybe if we give the landlord some money he'll hurry it up."

I felt as if I was in a never-ending nightmare. I was so tired of moving and running and hiding. Frankie hired a moving company, and I was out of my apartment by that weekend. The new place was just around the block, but he made the trucker drive in circles for three hours to be sure we weren't being followed. He paid him well for his time and gas.

"I gotta teach you about living on the lam, baby," Frankie said, out of breath, as he helped carry a heavy ceramic pot up to the second floor. "Having all this stuff is cumbersome when you gotta move fast."

"I know, Frankie, but feeling like I have a home gives me an anchor. I need that." He cocked an eyebrow and gave me a patronizing smile as he continued up the steps.

———◦———

Feeling safer now that Steve didn't know where I lived, I started venturing out without my bodyguard. I went to the bank to retrieve some personal papers from my safety deposit box. As I exited the private room, two men in suits were standing there. Somehow I knew they were not bankers.

"FBI, Miss Durante," they said, displaying their identification.

"We'd like to ask you a few questions. Would you mind coming with us?"

What if they search me and find the loaded .38 in my purse?

Okay White, don't panic. Just get rid of the gun.

The thought never occurred to me that I could have declined. "Yeah, sure...but could I use the ladies' room first?"

"Sure, go ahead," said the tall one as he turned to lead the way.

Suspicious stares from the bank employees followed us as we walked toward the bathroom. *Please, let it be empty*, I prayed. It was. I buried the gun in the bottom of the wastepaper basket, took some deep breaths, and walked back out.

"I'm ready." Flanked by an agent on each side, I walked outside to a waiting car. "What's this all about?" I asked, feeling my composure slowly returning as the car pulled away.

"I think you know what this is all about, Miss Durante. Do you prefer Miss Durante or Mrs. Lamendola?" the agent asked, carefully monitoring my reaction.

"Neither," I answered stone-faced. "You can call me Georgia. Where are we going?"

"To the Bonaventure Hotel, downtown. It's safe there. No one will see you with us. Your safety is our first concern, Georgia. We're on *your* side."

As the elevator rose to the eleventh floor, I shifted nervously and stared blankly at the walls. Two more agents waited inside the suite. They stood as we entered, introduced themselves, and offered me a cup of coffee. What I needed was a drink.

We all sat down except the one named Nelson. He walked slowly to the window with both hands in his pockets, then turned toward me.

"We are prepared to protect you, Georgia," he said. "We can change your identity and relocate you in Europe, if that's your preference. Even give you enough money to start a new life for yourself. You'll be safe. But we need some answers—and we know you have them." He was cold and dispassionate; a touch of humanity might make him more convincing.

"Gee, I really need the money, and I'd love to live in Europe, but I'm afraid I don't know whatever it is that you think I know. Do you mind if I smoke?"

Nelson put up a hand to show he didn't mind.

"What do you know about the hit on Bompensiero?"

"Nothing," I answered, blowing out a puff of smoke.

"What about Joe Bello?"

"I don't know anything."

"Come on, are you saying you don't know Joe Bello?" Nelson thundered.

"Well...yes, I *know* him, but I don't know *about* him."

He swung a steely glare at me. "You have a selective memory. Is it your habit to be vague?" I shrugged and looked blankly out the window. "You were at a party in Bello's home on February 22, 1976, which you attended with your husband, am I correct?"

"If you say I was, then I guess I was," I answered, giving him a brittle smile.

The agent with the pointed features and a slick of smooth brown hair that I could tell was a rug sat silently studying my body language. He was getting on my nerves.

"Several reputed Mafia members attended that party. Did you overhear any conversations between any of these men that may be of interest to us?" Nelson continued.

"No."

"Why was Salvatore Reale there?"

My heart rate picked up. "I don't know the man."

They threw a picture on the coffee table of Sal and me at a restaurant called Separate Tables in New York. I glanced at the picture without expression.

"Anyone else you want to claim not to know?" Nelson asked as he threw out more pictures. There was Paul Castalano, head of the Gambino family; Tony Lee, Captain in the Gambino family; Sammy G and Joe Colombo at an Italian American Civil Rights dinner. "Nice guys you're friendly with," he said with a cutting sharpness.

These people had a better record of my life than I did.

"They're just old acquaintances—"

Nelson bent forward, placing both his hands on the coffee table. His eyes bore into mine. "Level with us, Georgia. We can help you."

Returning his intensity, I answered in an even tone, "I don't know anything."

After hours of getting nowhere, they were visibly losing their patience with me. Nelson paced, agitated by my reluctance to elaborate on my answers. Maybe he thought this was a case of the victim bonding with the oppressor. Maybe it was. I was immovable when flexibility may have served me better.

Nelson moved in front of me, a commanding figure in a gray suit, burgundy tie, and striped shirt. "I'm tired of sparring with you, Georgia!" he declared. "Now we said we'd protect you, but if you don't cooperate with us, I'm afraid we're going to have to leak your name out to the other side."

"We can't be responsible for what could happen to you," the tall one added in a surprisingly flat monotone.

"I'm confused," I said sarcastically. "Who's supposed to be the bad guys?"

They didn't answer. Instead they took out a picture of Al.

"Do you know this guy?"

I hesitated, but not long enough for them to notice. Inside, my anxiety ran wild. "No," I answered.

"Hmm. He's not a very nice man. In fact, he is what you would call a 'bad guy.' But I think you already know that, don't you?" He paused. "What do you suppose he would do if he knew you were talking to us?"

I lit a cigarette and glanced at my watch. "Do you mind if I use your rest room?"

"Go ahead," Nelson gestured, directing his arm toward the bathroom. "We're not going anywhere."

Upon closing the door, I rummaged through my purse in desperate search of a Valium.

Holy shit. Al and Joe are going to kill me for bringing this down.

Finding the Valium, I washed it down and took a few minutes to regain my composure. I checked my make-up, hoping it would buy me some mercy.

"Listen you guys," I said when I returned, "I don't know what you want from me. I don't know anything. I really don't."

"That's not what Steve's been telling us," Nelson said. "He says you know a lot," added the agent with the cheap rug.

So this is all Steve's doing. A wounded dog is a dangerous dog. Big mistake, White. You should've let him die.

"We can understand your fears, Georgia, but like we've been saying, we are prepared to relocate you and Steve and—"

"*What?*"

"Steve told us about the beating and the threats on your lives. If you two want any kind of life for yourselves, you're gonna have to be straight with us."

I laughed so hard it was almost impossible to speak. "I don't believe this! You guys must have an IQ three points below plant life! Let me get this straight: you think I'm in love with Steve, but Joe is putting a kink in it?"

"Well... yes. Isn't that the way it is?" Nelson asked.

"God, he's good. He's really good. Either that, or somebody messed up pretty bad when they let you guys into this agency," I said, enjoying the confusion in their faces. They didn't answer me. They just sat there passing silent glances at each other. "This guy Steve is a nut case! I'd rather face a fate with the Mob any day than with him. If you don't believe me, just call the Beverly Hills police department. I've filed several complaints against him. The man is obsessed with me! I can't believe you actually fell for that crap. Now, if you're really concerned about my life, you'll help me get rid of *him*. The so-called police can't seem to do anything about it. Why do you think I had to do what I did? There was nowhere else to turn."

Nelson's face was one big question mark. The seated agents' faces were tight and red. They all stared at me in awestruck silence. It was the most I had spoken in hours. Finally they believed me. It was apparent, however, that they had opened a door they could not easily close. The FBI had unwittingly played into Steve's hand. His strategy was brilliant.

It just so happened that Joe was the number-one suspect in a case on which they had been working for over a year. For them, this was perfect timing. What a break for the good guys. But Steve had no idea what he was stumbling into. Fortunately for Al, they wanted the bigger fish.

Nelson propped his glasses on the top of his forehead, leaned back in his chair, and rubbed his eyes in a circular motion. "Well, it looks like we've spent a lot of time here getting nowhere," he said, placing his glasses back on his nose.

The interrogation broke up shortly after, and they drove me back to the bank. As I got out of their car, Nelson had some words of advice: "We don't advise you to contact Joe about our little meeting, for your own safety."

"I won't," I answered, questioning his sincerity.

"Okay. Be careful."

I got in my car and watched as they turned right on Wilshire Boulevard. I went left. I drove around on side streets for about a half an hour until I felt sure I wasn't being followed. I remembered something Salvatore Reale had told me once: always make four right-hand turns to be sure no one is tailing you. I did that, then stopped at a phone booth—and called Joe.

"Hello?" he said in a foggy voice. I almost hung up, but somehow I got the courage to speak.

"Joe, you're not gonna like this," I said, and then started to blurt it all out.

"Georgia! What the fuck, haven't you learned anything by now? Don't talk on the damn phone! Were you at least smart enough to see if you were being followed?"

"Yes."

"Get in your car and get your ass down to San Diego right now. Don't stop at home."

"I can't. I—"

"Now!" He hung up.

I called Frankie and told him what happened.

"You gotta go to San Diego, baby. You gotta let Joe in on what's happening here."

Frankie hated Joe, but he felt a kinship in this situation. A code which Italians on the dark side live by was taking charge.

"If the FBI's been following you," he said, "they probably got a make on me by now. This is gonna bring down some heat on our friends in the East, and they're not gonna be happy about it. I gotta get back to New York and smooth this thing out before tempers start flaring, y'know what I mean?"

"A sit-down? But—"

"I didn't get permission, Georgie Girl. I can't explain it on the phone. You may have to come to New York for a few days. I'll send you a ticket if it comes to that."

"I'm afraid to go to San Diego, Frankie."

"Baby, you gotta go. You can't leave him in the dark."

"I know I have to..."

"I won't be here when you get back, baby. You got a place you can stay?"

"No," I said. Fear surged through me. I felt so alone.

"I'll leave you some money. Get a hotel for awhile until I can figure this out."

"I'll miss you, Frankie."

"Yeah, me too, baby. I don't like leaving you like this, but I have no choice."

"I know. See ya when I see ya, Frankie."

"Georgie Girl?...I love you, baby."

"I love you too, Frankie," I uttered, but he didn't hear me. The connection had already been broken.

—◈—

"It's all my fault," I said aloud, continuously checking the rear-view mirror. *If I hadn't asked for Joe's help he wouldn't be in this mess. He's probably working himself into a frenzy by now. Oh God, he's going to kill me.*

My nerves played havoc with me all the way to San Diego.

Walking up the path that led to the beautiful condominium on the cliff's edge, I stopped. The smell of fresh sea air and the sound of crashing waves against the rocks below gave me a surreal sensation. This had to be a bad dream. Would my life ever be as natural as the smells and sounds that filled my senses? Such calmness. However, when that door opens, it will be anything but calm.

My hand shook as I rang the bell. I braced for a predictable punch to my head. He opened the door and stepped back to let me in.

"I'm sorry Joe, it's all my fault. I'm so sorry. I had no idea—"

"Do you think you were followed?" he asked, dismissing my frantic attempts at explaining.

"No, I don't think so," I said, shaking as if from the cold.

Amazingly, he seemed composed. He poured us both a drink without saying a word. Thrown by his calm reaction, I struggled with my reluctance to relax. He handed me my drink and put both his arms around me, holding me tightly.

"Okay, sit down, and tell me everything from the beginning."

When I finished, Joe swallowed hard and ran his hands over his head. "Okay, this is what we're gonna do..."

It was four o'clock in the morning before we stopped talking. We were both pretty weary. As I knew he would, Joe tried to convince me once again how much he loved me. Suppressing feelings of love that I still harbored, I chose only to view the face of a batterer, an abuser, and a controller.

"Let's go to bed," he said, as if it were the natural thing to do.

"Joe, I don't think—"

"I just want to hold you, honey, we won't do anything, okay? Besides, you can't leave until you talk to Al. He's gonna need convincing that you know how to keep your mouth shut."

"They didn't seem to be concerned about Al, or the beating."

"Yeah, I know. He's small potatoes compared to where they're going with this, but they're gonna try an' squeeze him anyway," he said as we walked down the hall toward the bedroom.

"Do you have a t-shirt?" I asked.

"You don't need one."

"Joe."

"Don't worry," he assured me.

Sitting on the edge of the bed with my back toward him, I felt his eyes burning into my flesh as I unbuttoned my blouse. I quickly removed my clothes, leaving on my bra and panties, and got under the covers.

"It's nice to see you laying there again," he said, standing at the foot of the bed as he undressed. His desire mounted with each article of clothing that hit the floor. I closed my eyes, having only myself to blame.

I turned to my side with my back toward him as he slid his body next to mine. His smell was fresh and clean, with an undertone of cologne.

"Oh my sweet baby, you feel so good next to me. I've missed you so much." His hardness pressed against me.

I stiffened. "Joe, you promised."

"I know, I know. I love you, Georgia." I uttered no response. "Goodnight, my baby," he whispered tenderly.

"Goodnight, Joe."

The sun was pouring in through the large picture window when I opened my eyes. The condo was a far cry from the dungeon we had lived in above the club back in Rochester. In the morning stillness, the birds sang out in harmony. A calmness existed, as if life itself had been suspended.

Joe waltzed in with a tray of coffee and toast.

This is new and different.

We sat on the bed, Indian style, sipping our coffee as he mapped out my strategy for the day.

"Let's finish our coffee on the patio," he suggested.

Rising, I jumped into the shower. The welcoming hot water beat heavily on my body, releasing the previous day's tensions. My robe still hung in the closet, awaiting my return. Slipping it on, I walked out to the patio and joined Joe.

With his long, slender fingers wrapped around a coffee mug, he stared out at the sea. Breathing deeply, I took in the morning. Everything was so peaceful. Then my attention fell upon a woman sitting alone on the cliff, her quiet sobs lost in the wind... and I remembered.

So many days I'd spent sitting on that cliff, watching the endless rhythm of the ocean. It had been my salvation during the vividly painful times.

Joe sipped his coffee, put it down, and peered through his

lightly tinted sunglasses. His eyes became fluid as he spoke. "I love you, Georgia. I'm such a fool. You've made up your mind, haven't you?"

I didn't answer. It was hard for me; I loved this Joe, but I had made it too far to turn around now.

I drove to Al's house and knocked on the door. He looked shocked to see me. That was understandable, since he had no warning as to what he was about to hear. He displayed no signs of being agitated. His only remark, emitted with cold emotion, was: "I knew I should've killed the fucker." I shuddered.

He paced around the room as we discussed the course of action we would take, depending on the scenario. When he was satisfied, I left. *Phew, that was over.*

⚬

Entering the freeway, I headed north toward Solana Beach. As I approached the exit, red lights flashed in my rear-view mirror.

"Shit." *Just what I need, another ticket.*

Two men in plain clothes exited the unmarked car and approached. Putting a hand to my mouth, I gave them a guilty schoolgirl grin. It was a wasted effort.

With a stern demeanor, one of them asked, "Where are you going in such a big hurry?"

"Home."

"Where's home?"

"Los Angeles."

"Can I see your driver's license and registration, please?"

I handed him both and he walked back to his car, leaving me to speak with the other man.

"We clocked you at 102 near LaJolla. Took us this long just to catch up to you."

I had no comment. What could I possibly say to justify that?

"So, you're from L.A., huh?"

"That's right."

"What are you doing in San Diego?"

"I had a doctor's appointment."

"All the way from L.A.?"

"Well, I used to live here. I haven't found a doctor I like in Los Angeles yet."

That was quick thinking, White.

He watched me in polite wonder. "Hmm. All the way from L.A."

The second man returned and handed me back my license, his eyes constantly searching.

"Now you have a nice day and don't have such a heavy foot if you want to stay alive."

They turned and walked back to their car. Something was wrong. *Why didn't they give me a ticket?* They had me, no doubt about it. I didn't even try to talk myself out of it. I was baffled. I could understand if I was doing 70 miles per hour, but 102?

Ah...they weren't policemen at all. Don't exit at Solana Beach; just keep on going.

They followed me for a few miles and exited. When I was sure they were gone, I jammed on the accelerator and got lost in my thoughts on the two-hour journey back to L.A.

I arrived home at three o'clock, checking the neighborhood for signs of Steve before going in. The light on my answering machine was flashing. I pressed the rewind button and opened the refrigerator door. A horrified scream escaped from my throat. A dead rat lay next to a loaf of bread.

"STEVE!"

The tape playing in the background consisted of one hang-up after another, and then: "Hi, Georgia, this is your buddy Nelson from the FBI. Now that wasn't real smart of you. I thought we could trust you. Maybe you're right about us. Maybe we *do* have an IQ three points below plant life. Anyway, we're still looking out for you. It would be a real waste if anything happened to you. Be careful. We'll be seeing you..." Dial tone.

For the next three weeks they followed me everywhere. They

weren't even trying to be discreet. If they were, they weren't doing a very good job of it. I was sure my telephone was tapped. Secretly I felt safe, knowing Steve was still out there waiting for his chance to take me out, and knowing that Joe couldn't revert to violence with the FBI watching. Nevertheless, the surveillance played heavily on my nerves, forcing me to recall all the illegal activities I could be linked to. I even began to feel paranoid not making a full stop at an intersection. I had dealt with rogue cops before—justice is what they decide it is. If they wanted to get me, they would not be above fabricating evidence.

What the FBI knew for sure was that I was telling the truth about Steve. They knew they had to work quickly. The time and money put into this case could all be lost. They took a chance by exposing me to the knowledge that they were on to Joe and his friends. It backfired, leaving them with no alternative but to move fast, before they had all the pieces to the puzzle. Now they were hell-bent on getting the person whose name did not end in a vowel.

The phone rang. "Hi, Georgia, Nelson here. We think we can help you get rid of your little problem with Steve. Let's talk."

The secret meetings began. My code name became "The Black Widow." The gatherings took place at the Sunset Plaza Hotel—not as nice as the Bonaventure. Guess they were a little short of money. Wonder why?

"Before we get into this, gentlemen," I said, "I want to make sure we are all clear on one thing. I'm here to help you get Steve. Don't ask me anything about Joe or I'm out of here."

They glanced at each other briefly, then all nodded in agreement. They were sly, though, having some hidden agenda, but I played the game. It was my only alternative. As Al had said, "Either you get him, or eventually he'll get you." My instincts told me not to trust them, but they were serving a purpose for the time being.

The mind games were boggling. Who was screwing with whose head? I was going to have to mess with Steve's and that

THE COMPANY SHE KEEPS

was not exactly a smart thing to do with a person as off-the-wall as he was. Were they messing with mine? No trust was present with anyone involved in this intricate plot...a plot to get whom?

"Do you know where he's staying?" one of the agents asked.

"No, but he calls twenty times a day. You have my phone tapped—can't you find out?"

No reply.

"The next time he calls, tell him you'll meet with him. Make sure it's a place that is heavily populated. You don't want to be alone with him," Nelson warned.

"I think I'm more aware of that than you are," I replied.

"A suggestion. Nate & Al's on Beverly Drive would be a good spot. You may not have the choice, so use your head. Tell him you're afraid. Let him think we've leaked to the other side that you're cooperating with us."

"How do I know you haven't? As I remember, you said that was an alternative if I didn't collaborate."

"You're just going to have to trust us, Georgia. As we see it, you don't have a choice. Everything you told us about this fanatic is true. He is a danger to society, but the immediate danger is to you. We have our own reasons for wanting him, that's true. He cost us a few hundred thousand when he blew our entire investigation. In addition, of course, he made us look like fools in the process. But our first concern here is your safety."

"My safety, Nelson? Is that your first concern? You were ready to throw me to the wolves when I wouldn't answer your questions. Now you want to save my life. Why do I find that so hard to believe?"

"Look, we're doing each other a favor. You don't have a choice, lady, unless of course, you want to give Al a call—and spend the rest of your life behind bars. That is, if you live that long."

He was right, I didn't have a choice. If I did not cooperate, I would die by the hand of Steve Zamett. At this point, they were my only saviors. As long as the price tag did not include my cooperation in other matters, I had nothing to lose.

"Okay, so what's the plan?" I asked, placing my destiny in

their hands.

"Convince him there's a contract out on both of you. Let him think you're in this together."

"This better work, Nelson. I'm putting myself in a very vulnerable position with this maniac."

"We know that, Georgia. We won't let you down. We will keep you within our sight at all times. Just meet with him in places where people always surround you and you will not be in any jeopardy. We will do everything in our power to protect you. You have a gun—always carry it with you."

"How do you know I have a gun?"

"Because my IQ is only *two* points below plant life, not three. Do you know how to use it?" asked Nelson.

"Yeah, point and pull the trigger."

"Don't think we're giving you a license to kill. We want the pleasure of that ourselves," he said, half-kidding. "But if you should find yourself in a life-threatening situation, you'll have some protection."

I was getting more nervous by the second. "Do you think it may come to that?" I asked.

"We'll be there for you, Georgia. It's just a precaution."

"I hope your presence won't be as obvious to Steve as it was to me."

"I think you have a little more experience in these things than Mr. Zamett."

"No, I think you guys are just masters of the mind."

"Be careful," Nelson warned. "That statement puts us well above plant level."

"I take it back," I joked.

"Too late, it's already on the record. But I'll tell you one thing," Nelson said. He paused, putting his hands in his pockets and looking toward the ceiling, searching for the least embarrassing way to phrase his next words. "I've been in the FBI for more years than I care to count and this jerk...Christ, I still can't believe it. This jerk even conned *me*. We actually put him up in the Bonaventure Hotel, paid all his expenses, including a $600 telephone bill. He had us going—but he won't get away with it."

No, I don't believe he will. When these people want somebody, they get him, one way or another.

"Was he in the Bonaventure when you took me there?" I asked.

"Yes, he was in the room next to us. Here's something else," Nelson paused, and then continued. "Remember when he asked you to meet him at the bank?"

"Yeah."

"Remember the banker?"

"Yeah?"

"He was one of us. Where did you think Steve got the money he showed you in the vault that day?"

"I didn't know, and I cared even less."

"We gave him that money. We were convinced that once you saw the money and realized there was a way out for you, that you two could escape to Europe, you would talk to us. That money was yours—still is, if you talk to us."

I knew there had to be a catch. I stood up and walked to the door.

"Wait a minute," Nelson said, blocking the door. "Okay, I promised. I won't bring that subject up again." I hesitated, throwing him a distrusting look, and then sat back down. "Anyway," he continued, "we drove over to where Steve was hiding out. It was somewhere off Santa Monica Boulevard in West Hollywood. He pulled a gun on us. We should have taken the sucker out then, now that I think of it. I still don't know if he was really afraid for his life or if it was just another con game. He was pretty badly bruised, just got out of the hospital. At the time, I believed he was terrified of being taken out by some of your friends," he said, looking at me with an arched eyebrow.

"Nelson, what choice did I have?" I said, trying to conger up an expression of innocence. It worked.

"As a matter of fact," he continued, "he was so shaken he asked our man to drive his car. We followed behind in our vehicle. Later we found out our FBI man was driving a stolen car. Jesus, this guy has balls," Nelson exclaimed, shaking his head in disbelief.

I started to laugh. The FBI was now pulled into the same tragicomedy of errors I had dealt with, except that they had the power to act on their frustrations when this jerk went too far.

"I'm glad you shared that with me, Nelson. If the FBI can be deceived on the scale that you were, then I guess I'm not as gullable as I was beginning to think."

"That's precisely why I'm telling you this little story. He got us pretty good. We want him as badly as you do."

"How did he contact you in the first place?" I asked.

"Oh, that's another story. He didn't actually come to us directly. He contacted the IRS. Said he knew about all this mob money from New York going into MB Financial which, as you know, is Joe Bello's company. He wanted to make the ten percent of whatever they came up with based on his information. Just so happened the IRS agent was one of the guys we had working with us on our investigation. The agent called us. Wanted to know if we would like to talk to Joe Lamendola's wife. We couldn't believe the break! Out of nowhere!

"As I said, Steve had us believing you were terrified for your life. He said you would talk if you could be convinced that you and he could get safely out of the country. This was just what we needed to fit in the final pieces. Basically, if he could make it work, he'd get ten percent of God knows how many hundreds of thousands—plus the nice little pot we were prepared to part with, and you, all to himself. What more could a guy ask for?"

"You'd be surprised," I said, still trying to absorb it all.

"We were so close..." Nelson said, his gaze drifting out the window and his voice trailing off. "Then of course, the rest is history."

"I told you he was good. You wouldn't listen to me."

"Okay, you don't need to rub it in. Let's concentrate on how we're going to handle this. This isn't a game we're playing."

"No shit. Am I going to be wired?"

"No. We've learned not to underestimate this guy. He's too shrewd. He will be skeptical of your sudden change of heart, but more than anything he wants you. He'll want to believe you. We trust that you can handle that, or we wouldn't put you in this position. You're a survivor; we know that about you. You have been around some pretty tough characters in some interesting situations, some we know about, some we don't—and you're still around. You can do this. By the time this is over, you will have earned your code name. And, Georgia, it will be over, you can bet on it.

"You have to trust us, so I'll be straight with you. Yes, we want you to talk to us about other matters, but that is not a condition for helping you rid yourself of Mr. Zamett. We want him too. Our reasons are as personal as your own. I think you understand that now. So let's start with a clean slate and get this guy, okay?"

Sounds convincing, but be careful...

"Don't hang up! Please, just let me talk to you."

"Okay, Steve, talk."

Shocked that he had my attention, he was almost at a loss for words. "Uh...I'm sorry I talked to the FBI. I was angry and hurt. I love you, George."

"Sorry isn't good enough, you asshole. Don't you see what you've done?"

"What do you mean?"

"You've stepped in shit you know nothing about, and because of it, we're both going to die."

"What are you talking about?" he shouted in a panic.

"Steve, you messed with the big boys. They know I was picked up for questioning. I wouldn't talk, but those FBI bastards put the word out on the street that I cooperated with them. They know you were the one who brought the FBI down on them in the first place. You're an expert at digging your own grave, but now you've dug mine, too. There's a contract out on both of us. You should be happy—we can be together for eternity now. It's out of Joe's hands; he's powerless to help me. All he could do is warn me to get the hell out of town. I should've let Al kill you, you worthless piece of shit!" I slammed the phone down.

The telephone rang immediately. I picked it up and placed it back on the receiver without bothering to say hello. That charade went on for the next ten minutes. After about the eighth or ninth time, I finally spoke.

"What?!" I screamed.

His breathing was fast; he swallowed with a gulp. "George, Christ, talk to me. What do you mean there's a contract on us?"

"Is it that hard to understand, Steve? Bang, bang, we're dead—asshole!"

Click.

Ring, ring, ring, ring. I didn't answer. I had him now.

This man was just as stupid as he was smart. I knew his mind was running wild with thoughts of how he would meet his death. I avoided answering the telephone for two days. He didn't trust me enough to venture to my door. I reveled in his terror.

I'll teach you to screw with her, you lowlife scumbag.

"Good job, Georgia," Nelson said over his car phone. "Guess you know how to push this character's buttons."

"Yeah, I have a way with mentally deranged people."

"I tend to agree with you. What is it with you anyway? How do you attract these nuts?"

Good question, White. You ought to give that some thought.

"I don't know," I said. "I guess I'm too soft-hearted, but that's changing."

"I think it's time to take his next call," Nelson said.

"Do you know where he is yet?" I asked.

"No, you don't stay on the line long enough. And I want to speak to you about your language, young lady. Where did you learn some of those words that came out of your mouth? If I were Steve, I'd never call you again."

"Well, you're not Steve."

"You certainly have an Italian temper. I wouldn't want to be married to you," he kidded.

"Fuck you, Nelson."

He cracked up. "That's what I like about you, your gentle reserve."

He's getting a little too friendly, White. Keep your distance.

To my surprise, the telephone did not ring again. I went about my days, trying to find some normalcy in them, not quite sure what normal was. I missed my daughter, but she was better off where she was. This would soon be over and we could be together again.

When the phone rang, I was sure Steve's voice would greet me.

"Hi sweetie," said my agent Janette. "Can you make an audition today? I know it's short notice, but they asked to see you specifically."

"Really? Sure, Janette. Where is it?"

"The Holiday Inn at Sunset and the 405 freeway. You know, the circular-shaped building right at the Sunset Boulevard exit."

"Yeah, I know the place. What time?"

"Six o'clock. It's five now. You better get out the door soon if you're going to make it in time with traffic."

"Okay, Janette. What's the look?"

"Hmm...They didn't say. Just go casual."

"All right, I'll call you tomorrow."

"Oh, and sweetie, they said you should park in the back."

"Okay, Janette, I better run if I'm going to make it."

"This one's got your name on it, sweetie. Good luck!"

I dashed out the door after quickly checking the mirror and grabbing what had been salvaged from my portfolio. I raced through the heavy traffic, my thoughts on landing the job. I really needed a break soon. My credit cards were maxed out and the rent was due again.

I pulled into the parking lot with ten minutes to spare. I had one leg out the door when suddenly my passenger door flew open and Steve was inside the car. He yanked me back inside with one hand and held a gun to my head with the other.

I struggled, knocking the gun from his hand. Still clutching my arm, he bent to pick it up. His grip on me loosened and I was able to break free. I bolted from the car and ran across the nearly deserted parking lot to the hotel lobby. Finding a pay phone, I punched in the emergency number for the FBI. With my foot tapping impatiently and my eyes glued to the entry, I waited. *What is taking so long?*

An eternity passed before it was answered, or it seemed. "Put Nelson on the phone immediately!"

"Who's calling?"

"The Black Widow. Hurry! Please..."

"Nelson here."

"Nelson, where the hell are your men? Steve just put a gun to my head!"

"Calm down, where are you?"

"I'm at the Holiday Inn at the 405 and Sunset. He got in my car in the parking—Oh my God. He's in the hotel now!"

"Get safe, my men will be there in—"

The phone swung back and forth from the end of the cord. I bolted behind the desk and ducked safely out of sight. The young man working there would be a dead giveaway if he did not get that bewildered look off his puss.

"Please, just pretend I'm not here. Don't look down at me," I pleaded. "See that guy over there?"

"Yes, I see him," he said, looking straight ahead.

"He has a gun. Call the police...discreetly."

He did, but he never would have won an Academy Award for his performance.

"You can come out now," the young man said, his voice cracking from fear. "He just left."

"I'm not moving until the FBI gets here."

"The FBI? What's going on?"

"Is there a safer place I can wait, an office or something?"

"Sure, follow me."

I crawled to the office, too terrified to stand up in plain view. I was afraid that Steve was lurking around the corner, waiting for me to make a move.

I glared at the agents when they were led through the office door. "Where were you?"

"We're sorry, Georgia. You were driving so fast, weaving in and out of traffic...We lost you," they answered, looking like scolded children.

"That's obvious."

"It won't happen again."

"Where's all this sophisticated equipment you guys are supposed to have? Jesus Christ, if I can slip through, there must be a lot of murderers out there on the loose."

They stood there red-faced with their heads hanging. I continued being cool and hostile as they escorted me home. No one could help me. I was pretty much on my own. My only ally was Georgia Black. She had done a good job—so far.

I lay in my bed and waited for the tension to dissipate. Toni's face smiled at me from the photographs on the wall. I felt a sharp need for the sound of her voice.

Soon, baby. It will be over soon.

"Hello, is this Georgia Durante?"

"Yes, who's this?"

"You don't know me. My name is Shawnna. I was hoping you could help me. I found your number in Steve Zamett's personal phone book. He told me all about you. I hope you don't mind me calling, but I have to know the truth."

"I don't know what Steve has told you, but I'm sure whatever it is, it's not the truth. Where is Steve?" I asked, not sure if he had put this girl up to calling me. It had been three weeks since the Holiday Inn incident and I hadn't heard a peep from him.

"I was hoping you could tell me," she said timidly.

Her voice dripped with disappointment. Should I give credence to whatever she was about to say?

"I don't know what to believe anymore," she said. "He said your husband has a contract out on him. Is that true?"

"Who are you, Shawnna? What's your connection to this sick person?"

"I'm sorry, I guess I should explain. I met him at the bank. He started a conversation with me and I gave him my number. He said he could help me with some problems I was having regarding my house. Before I knew it, he moved in. I was a little uncomfortable with it, but he told me the story about your husband and said he needed a place to hide out for a while, so I let him stay. In the meantime, my house sold. He helped me to move into an apartment."

"Sounds familiar so far," I said with a tone of amusement.

"What do you mean?"

"Nothing, go ahead."

"Well, I have multiple sclerosis. It won't be too long now before I'm in a wheelchair. I desperately need the money from the sale of my house to survive on. Steve said he could invest it for me and triple the investment in a year. I gave him the money, and I haven't seen him or my Mercedes since. I have the sickening feeling I've been had. I was praying you would know something that may be helpful in getting my money back."

"Welcome to the long list of people who have been taken in by Steve. I am sorry this has happened to you, Shawnna, but all may not be lost. I think I can help. Can we meet?"

I met with the FBI in San Diego and we drove to the address Shawnna had given me. She told her story again in greater detail this time and the FBI was livid. They continued to be amazed by this guy's MO. They thought they had encountered every imaginable character in the book, but Steve broke all molds. He was in a class of his own, but they hadn't given it a name yet.

Shawnna was an earnest little thing with cropped brown hair and sparkling eyes. A trusting soul with a big heart, but she needed a "Black" of her own if she were going to survive.

The plan was for her to call the FBI when Steve contacted her, even entice him with more money to invest, but mainly to pin him down to a place he might be found. All we could do now was wait.

The call finally came about four days after we had our meeting. Steve told Shawnna that he had taken his kids out of the country for a while. He was on his way to drop them off and he would call her later. Shawnna played the sweet, innocent role, and Steve didn't suspect a thing. She called the FBI immediately, and Nelson called me.

"Well, how's the Black Widow today?" Nelson asked. "I got some good news for you," he added nonchalantly.

"You got him?"

"We sure did," he answered triumphantly.

"Oh, Nelson, what a relief! That is such good news. Now I can bring my daughter back. How did you do it? Don't leave anything out."

"We got a call from Shawnna. He told her he was on his way to drop off his kids. We didn't expect he would really do what he said he was going to, but he told the truth—for once. We had the place surrounded. When he pulled up, two of our agents jumped out of the bushes, aiming their guns at him. He was surprised, to say the least.

"You did an excellent job planting the seed. He pulled a gun on the FBI. Poor guy was confused. Thought it was the other guys," he explained with a chuckle. "It's just a good thing for him his kids were there. We didn't have the heart to shoot him in front of them. Now you've got the messy job of coming down here to San Diego to testify."

"Gladly, Nelson." I let out a sigh of relief.

"Just one more aggravating thing to add to this saga and it'll be over. I doubt the man will see the light of day for a long time—not if we have any say—and we *will* have our say, no doubt about that."

"Nelson, thank you," I said, feeling genuinely appreciative.

"The pleasure was mine. Maybe after your day in court you'll allow me to buy you dinner in celebration of our victory."

"I'll look forward to it, but I'm not waiting that long to celebrate."

That evening I splurged, bought a few bottles of champagne, and invited over my cousin Randy's girlfriend, Susan. Randy and Susan had not been in California that long, and they were trying to establish themselves on a shoestring budget. I couldn't be of much help. I also invited Sheila, a woman who lived in my apartment building, to join in the celebration. After we consumed the first bottle we were feeling pretty giddy. Sheila had a date with F. Lee Bailey and left early. Before she left, however, she called Pips, a private club of which she was a member, and left my name at the door. Susan and I continued the celebration.

We arrived at Pips around nine o'clock, and the party was in full swing. We stood in the crowded disco, looking for an open couch to sit on, when someone asked Susan to dance. They disappeared on the dance floor and I stood alone.

"Would you like to dance?" a man asked from behind me.

"Oh, no thank you," I answered, turning to face him.

"Would you like a drink?" he asked.

"No, thank you. I think I've had my limit for tonight. I haven't had anything to eat. One more drink and I'll probably fall on my face."

"You haven't eaten? Are you hungry?"

"No, I'm here with a friend...here she is."

"Hi, I'm Susan, who are you?" she asked jauntily, her long, tightly curled dark hair bouncing as she spoke.

"My name is Richard Adray. Are you hungry?"

"Yeah, I'm starved!" Susan answered without hesitation.

"Good, it's settled then, I'll get us a table."

I started to object but the music began again and my words were lost. I glared at Susan after he walked away. "What did you do that for?" I asked angrily.

"Lighten up, Georgia, he's just going to feed us, not rape us!" she answered, pushing a mass of hair off her freckled face.

"Our table is ready," Richard said upon returning. He escorted us through the crowded disco into the dining room.

I had no idea who he was, but he had some kind of influence, judging by the way the establishment catered to him. We had a lavish dinner in the elegant dining room filled with movie stars and wanna-bes.

Across from our table, Warren Beatty sat with three spectacular women, yet his eyes explored the room, resting occasionally in my direction. Frank Sinatra stood at the bar with Jilly, a character I had briefly associated with in New York City. Lucille Ball was absorbed in a Backgammon game in the adjacent room with Jim Rose, a director who lived in the building next to mine. Jim and I had met at a commercial casting and had become instant friends. I had taken refuge at his place a few times when I'd had a Steve sighting.

Richard's eyes darted around the room. I sensed he was in search of some recognition from his peers for the status we brought to him. He was nice enough, but a little too sure of himself when he lacked the goods to back it up. He was short with salt-and-peppered, curly hair and a round face. Not my idea of good-looking. At thirty five, he looked to be more in his late forties.

The dinner was interesting, but that was *all* I found interesting. We danced off the dinner in the disco and Susan and I headed home.

"I gave Richard your number," Susan confessed.

"Why did you do that, Susan?" I asked.

"I thought he was nice. You have got to start living, Georgia. It'll do you good to get out and have some fun for a change."

"He's not my type, Susan." I answered. I had an uninterested attitude about everything—except survival.

This episode of my life was now winding down, and I was weary. However, I was also struck with the bad choices I had made in my personal life. Though I had done some extensive living by this time, I really had no experience with a healthy man to distinguish the difference between what was normal and what was not.

Joe never let me out in the world to learn anything about life. I had to live it through his eyes. Now I was experiencing all the things he had warned me about. Not trusting my own choices, I was reluctant to accept any dates. I needed to get a sense of myself and my worth before venturing into that unknown territory.

Three days later, I drove to San Diego for my day in court. I was elated that Steve was safely behind bars and out of my life. Handcuffed, he was led into the courtroom wearing a yellow prison uniform. The color suited him. Canaries are yellow, aren't they? But it was my turn to sing this time. He stared at me with pleading puppy-dog eyes, but it was Georgia Black who returned the stare. There wasn't any compassion in the courtroom for Mr. Zamett on that wonderful yellow day.

Shawnna was the first to take the stand, then me, and finally the FBI. Steve didn't have a chance. When it was over he was led out of the courtroom. His eyes never broke connection with mine: *How could you do this to me, Georgia? I love you!*

Early that evening, Nelson and I had a celebration dinner at a patio table on the water's edge. Maybe it was just the light, but his eyes seemed as clear and blue as the sky behind him. FBI agents always look like G-men for some reason, and Nelson fit the mold to a tee. Nevertheless, this night he would shed his business face. He was a different person altogether. He left his professional mannerisms in the courtroom.

"Well, one down," he said, as we clicked our wine glasses together. *One down?* "You look exhausted, can I get you anything?" Nelson asked with concern.

I laughed dryly. "How about a new life?" I answered, taking a sip of wine.

"I already offered you that once. Are you reconsidering?" he inquired with renewed hope.

"No, Nelson, I'm not," I retorted tartly.

"What are you going to do with your life now, Black Widow?"

"Live it," I answered, "without fear, thanks to you."

"Do you think that's possible?"

"Anything's possible, Nelson."

"You're certainly proof of that," he replied, lifting his glass to me.

Nelson looked troubled. He spoke in layered words, but I could see where he was heading and chose to ignore it. He shifted in his seat as he contemplated moving the conversation into an area I was not willing to talk about. All I wanted to do was drink wine in the balmy air and enjoy the exhilaration of the victory. We ordered another bottle and I began to relax.

"You're really a beautiful woman, Georgia. I can almost understand Steve's obsession with you."

I sensed an intimacy he had not meant—or rather one he yearned for but hadn't meant to convey.

This is no time to relax, White. He's the enemy—pay attention.

"Thank you for the compliment, Nelson, but if you can understand that kind of obsession, I think we can reserve a cell for you right next to Steve's. Remember, you're the one who gave me my code name. If you want me to live up to it, keep it up," I said with a sly smile.

"What are you going to do about your other problem?" Nelson asked, slipping back into his business face.

"What other problem?"

"Joe."

"Oh, I think time is taking care of that. We've been talking. He seems to be accepting the fact that I'm not coming back."

"Come on, Georgia, I know you're not stupid. He's been laying low because of us. Now that we'll be out of the picture, I can guarantee you he'll change his colors."

"You may be right—"

"Georgia..." he hesitated, "we have reason to believe you're still not safe."

"What do you mean?"

"I wish you'd trust us. We've done everything we said we would do, haven't we?"

This is no celebration dinner. He's still working. Wake

up, White.

"Nelson, we had a deal. You lived up to your end and I lived up to mine. This is where it ends."

"Georgia, there are things going on that I don't have the authority to talk about. All I can say is, you're not as safe as you might think you are, lady."

"Well, Nelson, if that's true, then my life won't be much different than it has been, will it?" I stated sternly.

"Will you do something for me?" he asked.

"Probably not."

"Promise to call me if you need me. Even if you just need to talk. I'd like you to think of me as a friend. Forget about my job—I've grown to really like you over the past few months. My protective instincts for you go beyond my job."

Yeah, and my IQ is three points below plant life.

CHAPTER ELEVEN

Life was getting a little brighter. I was finally beginning to move forward. Things started to turn around for me in the modeling world. I got my first big break soon after my day in court—a national commercial for Toyota. I could easily bring Toni back now with no worries about her safety or supporting her needs.

I arrived on the stage at Raleigh Studio for what would be my first car commercial. The spot was entitled "Space." The vehicle was rigged with a sophisticated hydraulic system, allowing the car to appear to be floating in space. The last shot involved the car landing on a platform thirty feet above the ground. My action was to step out of the car, take off my helmet, and smile at the lens while shaking my hair. The $25,000 I made from that spot was like a million to me.

"I hope you're getting stunt pay for this!" said one of the crew guys working on the set.

"What do you mean?" I asked.

"You only have a foot up there of solid ground. You could easily lose your balance. Thirty feet is a hell of a drop. They should be paying you stunt pay for the risk," he answered, pushing his long, straight hair away from his face.

I was grateful just to be getting paid.

"I'm Jim Harkess, by the way," he said, extending his hand.

We shook hands. "I'm Georgia Durante. It's nice to meet you. What is your job here, Jim?"

"I own Two's Company. We do all the rigging for car shoots

and prep the vehicles for camera."

"Really? I never gave much thought to what's involved in a simple car commercial."

"Simple?" he replied with a small laugh. "Nothing is simple, but my job is to make it look that way."

As the director made camera angle and lighting adjustments, Jim explained how automobile commercials are created. By the end of the day, I had been introduced to a world I never knew existed. I began to watch car commercials more closely, with a behind-the-scenes understanding of the intricacies involved in obtaining the final version of the spot. I hadn't realized how many car commercials dominated the airwaves.

A light went off in my head. Someone was driving these cars. I'd always had a love for driving and a natural ability to which I never gave much thought, although people had told me for years that I should become a stunt driver. I was also told I should write a book—I never gave that much thought either.

From what Jim had said, professional drivers made residuals as if they were on-camera performers, even though their faces were never seen. Locked in with Toyota until my contract was up, I couldn't do another on-camera commercial for a competitive automotive company for 21 months. Wheels began to spin in my head. *If they never see my face, I could work for them all!*

I called Jim Harkess the following week and arranged a lunch date. I wanted to learn more about how to get involved in this end of the business. Jim suggested that I enroll in the Bondurant School of High Performance Driving, and he provided tips on people whom I should contact. My interest in a driving career was born.

Taking Jim's advice, I began moving in a new direction. The process was long and slow, however. Oddly enough, my biggest problem breaking into this business was my face. Not much credence was given to a woman in that world, especially to one who looked as I did. Only a certain kind of person was cut out for this type of work: one who understood the art of driving on the edge—and surviving it. I qualified, but directors dismissed the possibly that there could be more behind my face. What they

didn't know was that Georgia Black lived in there too.
Where there's a will, there's a way.

―――――◆―――――

It seemed as if a lifetime had passed as I anxiously looked out the airplane window. Viewing Rochester from above, the chaos in the city seemed distant and surreal. What a tangled mess. Nevertheless, for the first time in a long time, my future looked promising. I couldn't wait to see Toni again.

I tried to get in and out without seeing anyone—almost impossible in Rochester. I ran into Sammy G at the Flagship Hotel, as he lunched with F. Lee Bailey.

"Georgia!" Sammy exclaimed as he spotted me walking by. "Whatta you doing in town, kid?"

"Georgia?" Bailey said quizzically.

"Yeah, Lee. This is an old friend, Georgia Durante. She's living in California now. Left her old friends in the cold," he said with a wink.

I was only twenty-seven, and he was making me out to be ancient. But I guess fifteen years constituted being an old friend.

"Are you the same Georgia that's a friend of Sheila Sisco?" Bailey asked.

"One and the same," I answered.

Sammy's mouth hung open slightly as he turned his head back and forth between me and Lee. "You two have a mutual friend?"

"Yeah, Sam," I laughed, "you can't make a move without me finding out about it—even three thousand miles away."

"And vice versa, my friend," Sammy replied with a raised eyebrow. "Small world, huh?" he added.

"It's only small when you're living in Rochester," I stated.

"You got that right," Sammy said, sighing.

"Well, it's nice to finally meet you," said Bailey. "Sheila talks about you all the time."

I knew his attorney's fees had to be at least $500 per hour, judging by his appearance more so than his reputation. He was even more immaculately dressed than Sammy, and Sammy was tough to beat. Nevertheless, Sam insisted I stay and have a drink.

"Still drinking Scotch, kid?"

"No, Sam, now that I'm all grown up I've switched to wine. But I'll have a Scotch anyway, for old times' sake."

"How's Joe?"

"I don't know, I haven't seen him lately."

"Don't tell me—you left 'em?"

"Yep, I did."

"It's about time," he said with a wide grin. "Is he givin' you any crap?" he questioned, creasing his brow.

"Nah, he doesn't even know where I am," I lied. Sammy had enough problems of his own. He certainly didn't need to be concerned about mine. "What about you, Sammy, how's it looking?"

His smile disappeared. "Grim. That fuckin' Mahoney...lying bastard that he is. I wasn't even in town when he says the meeting took place to kill that slimy little prick. But I've got an ace in the hole—I have an alibi," he stated with a confident grin. "The desk clerk at the hotel in Florida where I stayed the night in question remembers me. I don't know how she could forget me—I left her a $200 tip!"

My mouth hung open in disbelief. "Why do I continue to be shocked at these crocked cops? I should know better by now. Anyway, it looks like your generosity served you well for once, Sammy," I said, noticing Bailey's somber expression.

For some reason, Bailey wasn't pleased with using this girl as a witness. I didn't know all the details, but I knew Sammy well enough to know that he was going to do it *his* way.

"It's a gamble, Sam," Bailey said. "I strongly advise against it."

"Not on this one, Lee, this one I gotta have," he said sternly.

Bailey shook his head and took a sip of his drink. He turned to me with a defeated shrug. "Can you talk any sense to this guy? He pays me a pretty hefty amount for my advice, and then refuses to take it."

"That's just Sam—a born gambler," I replied. "I've seen him

bet on two raindrops running down a window. He *always* wins. No matter which way the dice come up, Sam comes out a winner."

It was true. I hadn't really thought about that before.

"Sammy!" I blurted, "were you loading the dice all those years?" They both burst into laughter.

Interrupting valuable lawyer/client talk, I finished my drink and rose to leave. Sammy stood too. I didn't have a good feeling about his trial, but I displayed a positive attitude for his benefit.

"Good luck, Sammy. I'll be praying for you."

"Thanks, kid," he said, trying to appear unaffected by the severity of his situation. "You take care, and if you need anything, let me know. You can always reach me—no matter where I am."

I knew what he meant, but refused to acknowledge it. My eyes began to tear, so I quickly kissed his cheek and turned my attention to Lee. "Gotta run. Nice to meet you, Lee. I'll be in touch. Sam, I love ya."

I began to cry as I walked toward the stairs. I wanted to look back for a final wave and smile before disappearing down the steps, but I couldn't let him see me cry. Sammy was my closest connection to the world I had left behind, and I sensed that this would be the last time I would see him for a long, long time.

The truth came out a few months after the trial. Bailey was dead right about the witness from Florida. Mahoney had gotten wind that Sammy had an alibi, and his detectives were on it right away. He sent them down to Florida to do some "fishing." It turned out the girl's family was using their fishing boats to do a little drug running. As the story was related to me, they were told that, in exchange for a little altering of the truth, the heat would not be turned up. The woman took the stand—and she lied! Said she'd never seen Sam before. I wouldn't want to be in that girl's shoes if Sammy ever saw the light of day again.

The upper echelon of the Rochester Syndicate was now off the streets. In the ongoing battle between law enforcement and organized crime, the victory of the "good guys" in this case made history. Agencies from all over the country sent congratulations. I heard that the President of the United States personally called Bill Mahoney to acknowledge his achievement. The FBI was in line at the handshaking ceremony, but felt slighted that their participation was minimal. That was because Mahoney closed the door on them whenever he could find a legal way to do it. The FBI's suspicions, however, started the ball rolling with the investigations into Bill Mahoney and the Rochester Police Department.

The *Democrat and Chronicle* was having a field day as each day passed. The newsstands were sold out for the next few years. I wish I'd had stock in that newspaper back then.

It was only a matter of four or five months before the steel bars slid open and freedom was granted to the five convicted murderers. It was an incredibly bizarre twist of events. The Rochester detectives were found guilty of perjury and fabricating evidence and traded places with the mobsters behind bars. Even the people whose lives were never touched by the Mob were actually cheering for the bad guys, and rightly so. This could happen to any citizen. Right or wrong, everyone is entitled to a fair trial—even the Mob.

As little time as Sammy spent in prison, it was still too long. Those left behind couldn't hold the fort alone. The big guns weren't around for the reinforcement they needed. Frank Valenti's old pals were back on the streets. Little by little, they took over the gambling joints, the vending machines, the trucking. The juicy city construction contracts were all going into another pocket now. The same cops were getting paid to look the other way, but this time by the new regime. The newspapers labeled them "The B Team." Sammy G and his soldiers were called "The A Team." Nothing was really accomplished with all of Mahoney's efforts. Organized crime will *always* be.

Sam believed he could step right back in where he had left off. He did, but not without a fight. He managed to take back control of all the gambling clubs, but his enemies started to bomb them, one by one. After a while, patrons were afraid to go into the gaming haunts. Business fell off considerably.

Sammy G was a creature of habit. To plot his death wasn't difficult. He was bold and brazen, refusing to keep a low profile, living the flashy style that he had always known. He never walked alone those days, however, accompanied by his two trusted bodyguards, Tommy Taylor and Tom Torpey. Sam made a show of power by being blatantly visible. That was his style. Hollywood would have loved him.

—◆—

The lunch crowd at the Blue Gardenia had long since gone. Just a few stragglers remained. Sam finished his meal and was relaxing quietly with a drink. It was one of his favorite stomping grounds, and he could be found hanging around there on an average of three days a week.

Sammy G may not have been educated, but he was far from stupid. A sense about the guy standing at the phone booth made him stiffen. The man acted nervous. Catching Sammy's suspicious stare, he made a quick exit. Something was up. Sam weighed what he had felt and stood to leave.

He was halfway out the door when glass shattered as the bomb exploded. The blast threw him off his feet, and he landed in a snow bank six feet away. Miraculously, his injuries were minor. But his vengeance became severe.

This was the first of many attempts on Sammy's life. The enemy had now drawn first blood. Shaken but coherent, Sam knew what he must do. He never wanted it to come to this, but he had no choice. Sammy G called out his soldiers, and the retaliation was fierce. The war began.

One of the many to be riddled by bullets was Tommy DiDio. Hiding out in a secluded motel room near Exit 45 of the New York State Thruway, Tom DiDio violently lost his life. Tom came from the old regime—one of Frank Valenti's boys. He had gone underground for years, and hadn't openly surfaced until Sammy G and the rest of the upper echelon were securely behind bars. Unfortunately for him, he went underground again

—this time for good.

That day in The Overlook, the day I spied on DiDio for Sammy, did my findings cost any lives? I never fully realized how close to this world I was until I was removed from it.

In the end, Mahoney would visit Frank Valenti in prison, now old and bedridden, and ask him to stop the reign of death that Mahoney himself had started. Valenti would probably never see the light of day again, yet he still possessed the power to pull the strings from his prison cell. Bill Mahoney and Frank Valenti had been friends in the old days. Some speculated that Bill had started this entire crusade on behalf of Valenti to begin with, but that was never proven.

Richard Adray called shortly after I returned to where I now called home, Los Angeles. I could have killed Susan for giving him my number.

"Would you like to have dinner Friday?" he offered for the fourth time. He was persistent—I had to give him that.

"Thanks, Richard, but I don't have a babysitter."

"You don't need one. Your daughter is welcome to come."

I couldn't think fast enough to get out of it, so we went out to dinner with Toni in tow. Richard seemed to be a kind soul. My initial fears faded after a few dates which *always* included my daughter.

Richard was a short, stocky man, only 5'8" in height, but his money made him taller. He validated himself by the vast fortune he possessed. Only as I developed into a more healthy-thinking person would I begin to see this. Contrary to his Middle Eastern background, Richard's skin was light. His curly dark hair had far too much gray for his thirty-five years. His best feature was his blue eyes, the windows through which I had allowed myself to pass.

I found it nice to have a friend to talk to, and I began to look forward to our dates. I really didn't like the dating scene, mainly because I wasn't sure know how to handle it. Richard made my phobias disappear; he would go away happily at the end of the night without so much as a goodnight kiss. I felt comfortable with him, and Toni liked all the attention he showed her.

Then I got a call from Nelson.

"Hello, Black Widow. How's life been treating you?"

"Great, Nelson. I've got my daughter back with me. I'm working. It's going great."

"Well, I hate to burst your bubble," he said, "but our friend Steve is up to his old tricks again."

My heart sank. "Oh no. What now?"

"Well, fortunately, this time we were able to intercept, but I don't know if we'll be so lucky the next time."

"What? What's going on, Nelson? Is he out?"

"Oh, no. But he's playing his games from behind bars now. He was sharing a cell with an informant who was released this week. Long story short, he offered the man $10,000 to kill you." He hesitated, waiting for some reaction, but I was too numb to speak. "There's no danger to you at the moment, but I think you'd better start looking for another place to live—with an unlisted number and no forwarding address."

"When is it going to end, Nelson?"

"I'm always looking out for you, you know that."

"I think I could make the *Guinness Book* for the most number of moves in one year."

"Yeah, you probably could. Do me a favor. Save the Bureau some time and money and let us know where you land, okay?"

I found a cute little house just outside the Beverly Hills city limits. The white picket fence is what drew me. I'd always wanted to live in a house with a white picket fence. I still believed that life could be like Ozzie and Harriet. Even without the Ozzie, I wanted to create such an environment for my little girl. She had missed so much of her childhood due to my bad choices.

The rent was $1,200 a month, but the money was flowing now. I had paid back everyone who had loaned me money. Being debt free, I splurged on the house.

Shortly after I moved in, Joe called.

"Hi, honey," he said in a mellow, loving voice.

"Hi, Joe. How are you?"

"As good as can be expected, I guess. Are you okay?"

"I'm fine, just settling in."

"Are you sure you can afford that place?"

"I'm working."

"Why don't you let me help you? Christ, you're stubborn."

Yeah, I can see it all now. If he pays the rent, he's buying the right to control you again. You're smart enough to understand the "good guy" tactic by now. You don't need him.

"Thanks, Joe, but I'll be fine."

"My mother is coming out next week. She asked if she was going to see you. Why don't you and Toni come down for the weekend? She's planning on making Aunt Fannie's famous baked macaroni."

"Joe, we have to talk about the divorce. You need to stop avoiding the subject."

"Why? Are you dating someone?" he asked suspiciously.

"No, but we have to deal with this *sometime*."

"You better not be dating, Georgia. You're still my wife," he snapped.

"Joe, we have a legal separation. I can get the divorce without your consent after a period of time anyway."

"Then that's the way you'll have to do it. Are you going to come down this weekend or not?"

"Joe, I don't think—"

"Honey, don't make my mother suffer just because we have problems. You know how much she loves you and Toni. Let's just have a nice weekend while she's here, okay?"

"All right, Joe, I'll be there—but let's not get into any heavy dialogue, please."

I loved Joe's mother, Sue. She was the kind of mother-in-law women dream of having. Joe was on his best behavior, and the reunion was a good one. We laughed and reminisced—a rare, happy time. The smell of Sue's cooking brought back memories of being happy with Joe. How had it gotten so twisted? Joe showed no signs of the demons, but I knew they still lurked inside him somewhere. I had changed, grown strong and determined. Joe knew the old ways no longer worked. I was past the point of ever turning back. All I had to do was convince him.

While visiting her son, Sue was diagnosed with a brain tumor. The news devastated us both. Joe researched every possible cure, finally accepting that her death was inevitable. I spent the next three months driving to San Diego on weekends. Sue looked forward to my weekend visits. I washed her hair, helped her bathe, and shaved her legs. The simplest things brought her happiness. To do them for her made me feel good.

By the time Sue died, Joe and I had reached a whole new level of understanding. We both came away from that sadness as friends. Through his mother's death, Joe had painfully begun to learn how to let go.

I continued to date Richard. Toni had become quite attached to him by this time. He knew how to win over a child. He always brought her some expensive toy when he came to take us out. Slowly, he set the trap.

He'd point out people in restaurants, where Hollywood's finest hung out. "Look at all these people," he'd say. "None of them are happy. They're all chasing rainbows. Where it's really at is having a family."

A family, what a wonderful concept. That level of happiness doesn't exist in reality, White. Don't listen to him. He's full of crap!

Against my better judgment, I began to take Richard more seriously. Eight months had gone by and we had now graduated to a kiss at the door. I felt I was no prize for any man, and I was afraid to open my heart. That would be giving up all that I had struggled so hard to attain. But Richard kept pressing all the right buttons.

I was surprisingly happy, I had to admit. Richard treated Toni and me like royalty—an unfamiliar but welcome experience for us. I felt special being with Richard, as if I really did have something to offer. He was like a savior during an emotionally difficult period of my life. He knew about my past with Joe, was aware of the troubles I'd had with Steve, and he didn't seem to judge me.

Richard wasn't particularly attractive, and despite his wealth, he was uneducated. I figured his lack of intelligence explained why he wanted me—he didn't know any better. But he played his cards correctly, and he was patient. He saw what he wanted and was willing to play whatever game was necessary, because he knew he would win in the end.

After a year, the divorce became final. Joe did not contest it. What was his was his and what was mine was his. I asked for nothing. The divorce was enough.

My past was haunting, but it was also fading from my memory. I talked to Joe frequently, and I no longer feared him. We even visited some. I'd stop by if work brought me to San Diego, and he would come to L.A. on occasion. I never thought we would have this kind of relationship. In my mind there was no going back, but he held on to the hope that we would be together in the end.

On one of the jobs that took me south, I stopped by to see Joe with a purpose in mind. I wasn't quite sure if face-to-face was the way to deal with it. The sun was beginning its decent when I knocked on the door. Joe smiled when he saw me and poured us both a glass of wine. We sat on the patio watching the sunset as we had many times in the past.

"Joe, Richard has asked me to marry him," I admitted.

He almost choked on his drink. The shock faded and was replaced by concern. "You're not considering it, are you?"

"Well..."

"I don't believe this! How could you even *think* about sleeping with that sand-nigger?"

"He's good to me, Joe. He's good to Toni. We both deserve to have a life."

"I know I was a shitty husband and father, but come on. You're not really serious?"

I thought for a moment before continuing. "My answer was yes."

"It's the money, isn't it?"

"No, Joe, it's not the money."

"It can't be for his good looks and his intellect!" he retorted.

"You're right about that. But he was there for me when I needed a friend. I value that, Joe. He's good, he's kind..."

"Who you trying to convince—you or me?"

"Toni is a different kid. She laughs a lot. She's happier than I've ever seen her."

"Well, this is just wonderful news. Let's celebrate." He guzzled down his wine and filled his glass again.

"I'll never love again with the intensity and the depth I once loved you, Joe. But there are different levels of love. Richard doesn't even come close to that kind of love. That kind of love hurts too much. Once is enough. The kind of love I have for Richard is much different."

He felt better hearing those words.

"You know as well as I do," he said, "that when you're finished with whatever it is you think you still have to do, we'll be back together. I'm now the guy you always wanted me to be. I've changed a lot. You have to admit that, Georgia."

"Yes, you have changed, but not enough and a little too late. Joe, I made the decision long ago that you're not the person I want to spend the rest of my life with."

"And he is?"

"I'm happy, Joe. Let's just leave it at that."

"Bullshit! You may be able to convince *him* of that, but you'll never convince me."

"Let's just drop it, Joe. I thought I owed you the courtesy of telling you before I did it. I don't want to argue about it, okay?"

"When is this joyous event supposed to take place?"

"I don't know yet."

"Yes, you do."

"No, I don't."

"Well, when you *do* know—I want to know."

"I don't think—"

"I wish I could change all the bad things I did to you. Why was I such a fuckin' asshole? I still love you, Georgia. I'll love you till the day I die. I don't blame you for wanting a better life, but you have to make me a promise."

"What?"

"Don't ever cut me off from your life. If I couldn't at least hear your voice, I wouldn't want to live."

"I won't, Joe."

"You and Toni are all I have. You can't take her from me, too. I know I could never make up to you all that I've done to hurt you, but give me the chance to make it up to her. Please don't let her go through her life with bad memories of me. You've got to let me see her. Don't shut me out. Promise me, Georgia."

"I said I wouldn't. I'm not trying to punish you. I don't know how it happened, but it feels good to be where we are with each other right now. I never thought we could discuss something like this without—"

"Don't! Don't bring it up. As long as I can spend some time with Toni, and talk to you, I can live with this. I owe you that much."

"Thank you, Joe."

"Maybe someday you'll see I'm not such a bad guy after all. Maybe..."

He held me in silence for the longest time. His tears trickled down my neck. I cried too, for what could have been but could no longer be.

"Let me make love to you—one last time..."

I was just waking up when the phone rang. I hadn't had my first cup of coffee yet, but the news would call for a Scotch and water.

"Hello, Black Widow."

"Nelson! Are you still lurking out there in my life somewhere?"

"I told you I'd always watch out for you, didn't I?"

"What's the matter now, Nelson? What's he up to this time?"

"It's not Steve. I came to work early this morning and I got some news over the wire I think you'd like to know about, if you haven't already heard."

I paused, feeling a dull sinking in my chest. I inhaled deeply. "What is it, Nelson?"

"They got your friend last night."

"Which friend, Nelson?" I asked, closing my eyes and saying a silent prayer.

"They killed Sammy Gingello."

"Oh God...*Sammy!*" I cried, feeling like my stomach had dropped out. "How did it happen, Nelson?"

Every time I called home I'd hear about someone else who had been murdered. Just a matter of time. I immediately made some calls and spoke to people who had seen Sammy in different places during that fateful night. I pieced the story together from what I was told and from my own experiences when I'd been out on the town with him. In my mind, I traced the last steps of Sammy's life...

Defiantly, Sammy G strutted into the packed Club Car bar on Lyell Avenue with the confidence of the Don that he was. His bodyguards, Tommy Taylor and Tom Torpey, followed closely behind. They were his eyes as he walked through the crowd, shaking all the extended hands. An outsider would have thought the President had entered the room. The going was slow as he nodded and paused to exchange small talk with well-wishers.

"Good to see you back, Sammy," came a yell from the crowd.

"They should fry those rat bastards!" someone else offered, slapping him on the back.

"Keep your hands to yourself!" Tommy Taylor shot, quickly backing the man off with his icy stare.

"It's cool, it's cool," the man said, putting his hands in the air and stepping backward into the crowd.

Two detectives sat at a corner table watching the scene, wishing they could become invisible. Their colleagues had

295

changed places behind bars with Sammy and his entourage for fabricating the evidence that had convicted them for the murder of Jimmy "The Hammer" Massaro. "The Man" was back, but too much time had passed and too much money was at stake for Sammy G to easily resume the throne of the treacherous world of organized crime. The kingdom still belonged to him, but his loyal soldiers had switched sides in his absence. With loyalty the equivalent of power, it was hard to tell who the enemy might be.

A bullet with Sammy's name on it was out there somewhere. He could feel it, but he refused to lie low. Against the strong advice of the two big men who stood by his side, he would not wear the bulletproof vest. It remained in the back seat of the Buick along with the loaded .20-gauge shotgun. Hell, such an undergarment would spoil the effect of the expensive, custom-made silk suit that fit his body to perfection.

"Let's blow this place," Sammy said to the boys as he slugged down the last of his Scotch. "Let's see what's happening on the other side of town."

They went through the same charade on the way out as they had when they walked in. Taylor and Torpey gave the car a quick inspection before getting in. They drove down Lyell Avenue and considered stopping at Caesars II, now called Alexander's, but decided to pass. The place had lost the excitement it once had when Joe Lamendola owned the joint, and besides, that slimy little creep, Jimmy Massaro's brother, owned it now. Not a good choice.

The 747 Club would be their next stop. Sammy made a quick appearance there and moved on to the Encore Club, where he threw some dice in the dimly lit back room. He gave his winnings to the girl who stood beside him and whom he *thought* had brought him luck. Last stop: Ben's Cafe Society.

They didn't notice the light-colored Lincoln that followed in the shadows two blocks behind with its lights off as they hopped from bar to bar—a ritual Sammy had missed during those long days and nights behind steel bars.

Ben's—a place of many fond memories, laughter, and even a few tears. It was one of my favorite meeting spots in years past. I could still see the decor clearly in my mind's eye. The placement of the tables, the location of the piano bar...it was all familiar, as well as the smiles Sammy G encountered as he elegantly glided to the table which always sat empty, awaiting his arrival.

He noticed a girl alone at the bar, crying, and he sent her a drink even though she had already consumed one too many. It wasn't necessary to order drinks for themselves; three glasses of Scotch were waiting before they arrived at the table. Within minutes, four more shot glasses backed them. Torpey and Taylor sipped theirs slowly—they had a job to do.

While people approached the table to greet the king, Sonny Serpentino crept across the parking lot with the explosive device. Across the street in the Rascal Cafe, Chief Bill Mahoney sat unaware, staring into his empty glass and pondering his career. It all had gone so well. But now his world had changed. The good guys had suddenly become the bad guys. How could he have been so careless? The years he had given to the department in the name of the law would all be forgotten now. He would not go out a hero as he had hoped. He ordered another drink and tried to forget.

Drunken laughter spilled out toward the parking lot as the bar door swung open. Sonny's heart stopped as he cautiously retreated behind the 1978 Buick. He had to work fast. This was his last chance. Twice before during the course of the evening he had been forced to abort. It *had* to be now.

Inside, Murph Marciano approached Sammy. He had worked for the prosecution's office on Sammy's case. He and Sammy were boyhood friends. When they grew to manhood, Murph went in one direction—the right side of the law—and Sammy went in the other.

"Glad to see you again, Sam," Murph said with sincerity.

"Yeah, thanks for all the help," Sammy replied sarcastically.

Murph looked saddened and turned his face away. Sammy reached out and put his hand on his shoulder. Murph turned to Sammy with an obvious ache in his heart. He loved Sam. It wasn't his fault things had turned out the way they had.

"Ah, you did what you had to do, but you should've listened to me when we were kids. I told you those damn books were gonna get you in trouble. Gotta remember who your friends are, Murph," Sam said as he scrutinized his old friend's face. Murph held his breath. "I don't hold it against you, buddy," he added with a wink.

Murph sighed, grateful for being exonerated. Now maybe he could start sleeping again at night. He did his damnedest riding the fence, he really did.

Sonny finished the tedious job of planting the bomb, and then slithered to the alley where the Lincoln was parked. With his finger on the button and a smile frozen on his face, he waited.

Mahoney passed when they announced "last call." He paid his tab and left the bar, deep in thought. He took note of the gold Lincoln as he walked the block and a half to his parked car. Detail: that's what had once made him a good cop. Good or bad, he'd never stop being a cop. He'd been one too long to change his ways now. One too many drinks clouded his mind. Think about it tomorrow. He'd been thinking too much already tonight.

"Well, whatta ya say, boys," Sammy said. "Shall we hit an after-hours joint before we call it a night?"

"We might be stretching it, Sammy," Taylor answered.

"Yeah, you may be right."

They rose and began their departure. Torpey and Taylor snapped to attention. They had made it through another night without incident. Maybe tomorrow they would take the Rolls Royce.

"Thank you for the drink, Mr. Gingello," slurred the teary-eyed girl from the barstool as they passed.

"My pleasure," Sammy replied, adjusting his cuffs and straightening his tie as he continued to walk forward.

Maybe they all had just one too many. They were no longer paying as much attention to detail as they had when the night began. Sam opened his car door and casually got in. Taylor and Torpey had just opened their doors and begun to enter when Sonny could wait no longer. His sweaty finger pressed the button.

I could imagine Sonny's smile growing larger when he saw the bright orange flames. The glass and debris shot out over a

140-foot radius. The explosion threw Taylor and Torpey thirty feet from the vehicle. The blast could be heard three miles away on South Avenue.

Mahoney caught a faint sound as he drove toward his home, noted it, shrugged, and continued on.

Murph was the first one out the door. "Oh my God, they got Sammy!" he cried in disbelief. "Someone call an ambulance!" He ran toward the car, but the flames would not allow him to get close enough to try to save his friend.

The firemen were the first to arrive. Torpey and Taylor were walking around, dazed and in shock but otherwise unhurt. Flames from the burning car hid Sammy from the firefighters. They extinguished the flames, but two long minutes passed before he was visible. He was lying face up near the rocker panel on the driver's side, motionless, with his eyes wide open. Very little blood, although his right leg was completely blown off and the left one was hanging by mere strands of flesh. A few cuts and bruises marked his face, but his upper body was intact.

Presuming him dead, the firemen pulled Sammy from the smoldering wreckage and placed him on the stretcher. The mourning crowd watched in horror. Then he moved. He was still alive! He tried to raise his head to look at his legs, but didn't have the strength. Even in shock he was determined. With all of his willpower, he raised his upper body enough to see that he no longer had legs. He dropped back down on the stretcher and said nothing.

"Who did this to you, Sammy?" asked the detective on the scene.

Sammy looked at him, raised his right hand, extended his middle finger, and closed his eyes.

His arm dangled from the stretcher as they slid his mangled body into the ambulance. No one moved until the sound of the siren could no longer be heard, and even then no one was anxious to start their cars. An hour later, at The Genesee Hospital, Sammy G was pronounced dead from shock and blood loss.

The bloody war that followed Sammy G's murder will probably end up on the big screen one day, but for now it just lies in the memory of the few who survived. Not only was it the end of an era for the Mob in Upstate New York, but it was a turning point in my life as well—a crossroad long overdue. This was the only way it could end for Sammy. *Live by the sword, die by the sword.*

The cornerstone of my underworld past had fallen. It was the closure I needed to begin transforming my own life. Darkness would seek me out from time to time, to repay favors owed, but for the most part I moved forward with my life, trying not to look back at a world I no longer wanted to remember.

Good-bye my friend...Rest in peace...

———◆———

Today, organized crime is still doing business in Rochester, except all the players have changed. Nothing stays the same. Shadows of my past still weave in and out of my life, but mostly I only see mobsters on television now. The movie *Goodfellas* was an accurate portrayal of my perception of life in the Mafia. But that's in my past. Today my life and the people in it are very different. One thing will never change for me, though: I will always have the negatives—tucked somewhere in the darkroom of my mind.

Chapter Twelve

No invitations were sent. Only family members and a few close friends were present in a large suite at the Desert Inn Hotel in Las Vegas. This wedding wasn't setting well with Joe. He knew it was going to happen, but not when or where. Although we were finally on speaking terms, and he wasn't using the violent approach anymore to get me back, I still had to be cautious about his unpredictable personality. It was Thanksgiving Day, 1979. My new life was beginning on the same day that Jimmy Massaro's had ended six years earlier.

"I now pronounce you man and wife."

I expelled a big sigh. Time to sign the marriage certificate.

Darlene, once married to Joe's younger brother Jimmy, was my maid of honor. With pen in hand, she hesitated when signing her name as a witness. Darlene was easy to read. She worried that Jimmy or Joe would somehow find out that she was a willing accomplice in the "crime" I was committing, daring to remarry. When married to Joe, I wasn't even allowed to be friends with Darlene. Joe viewed her independent spirit as a bad influence on me, and here she was my maid of honor. Darlene never did well in handling the craziness of that world we had both come to know. I knew what she was thinking. A little "oh, God" escaped under her breath as she quickly signed her name in the appropriate place.

The photographer, anxious to capture the moment, tugged at Dar's arm. "Where you running off to? Let me get a shot of this."

Dar looked at me, rolling her eyes as she reluctantly moved

into position for the best shot. "This is just too bizarre," she whispered as the photographer went on to create more memories.

"Not as bizarre as our past, Dar," I whispered back, smiling.

With moist eyes, my mother and father took turns congratulating me. "We're very happy today, honey," my mother said. "Now maybe we can have some peace."

If she only knew the half of it.

"I wish Sharon could have been here, Mom. That would've made my day complete."

"You know your sister wouldn't get on a plane if her life depended on it," replied my Dad.

"I know. She misses out on so much of life."

"Georgia! Your sister's on the phone!" my new mother-in-law shouted crudely from across the room. Richard had a decidedly odd relationship with his domineering mother, and I was hoping I'd be able to handle this eccentric in-law without getting steam-rolled.

"Speak of the devil," I said as I crossed the room, shrinking with embarrassment.

"Congratulations, Sister."

"Thanks, Sharon. We miss you here."

"I miss being there. I hope this one works, Sis. You deserve to be happy. Is Toni excited?"

Standing beside me, Toni looked like a little princess. She was beaming. I bent down to kiss her as the photographer snapped a picture of the candid affection.

"Do I call Richie 'Daddy' now, Mom?"

"If you want to, honey. I think he'd like that."

I could hear Richard's mother from the other side of the room. She was ordering the hired help around with her loud, crass voice. If this was the worst of my problems, I'd learn to tolerate it. The champagne started to flow and the piano began to play. My new life was beginning.

I was standing at the bar and chatting with our guests when the door of the suite opened. All eyes followed the two men who entered. Everyone knew they were no ordinary men—one being so huge he had to duck to get through the doorway. I followed the stares to see Joey Tiraborelli and his bodyguard, Tommy Taylor, walking toward me. Joey donned an arrogant grin as he swaggered over. Tommy looked like "Mr. Clean" with his completely bald head and 250-pound, buffed-out body.

Joey Tiraborelli was Sammy G's sidekick, and also the guy who had brutally beaten Joe while I watched in horror on that long-ago night in an after-hours club in Rochester. Tommy Taylor was one of the bodyguards who was with Sammy the night he was murdered.

"Joey!" I gasped. I couldn't imagine what he and Tommy were doing here. I'd heard from friends in Rochester that since Sammy's death, Joey had lost power and was on the run. I'd also heard that he'd gotten heavily into cocaine and owed money to everyone in town.

With outstretched arms, he approached me; we embraced, and he kissed me on each cheek. I caught sight of Darlene as she watched from a corner of the room. She wasn't fond of Joey, and it showed.

"What are you doing here?" I asked, realizing the music had stopped playing.

Curiosity filled the room. Richard stood at the other end of the bar, his expression a cross between suspicion and fear.

"Have some champagne!" I said gaily to ease the tension in the suite. I looked at the piano player and said, "Play on." The music flowed, but the guests still looked uneasy, especially Darlene.

"I heard you were gettin' married and I happened to be in town, so I thought I'd surprise you."

"Well, you did. Who told you?"

"I ran into your sister last week," Joey answered.

"You make a beautiful bride, Georgia," Tommy said.

"Thanks, Tommy. I guess I must think so too, since I've been the bride three times now." We all laughed.

"So, who's the lucky guy?" Joey asked as he searched the room for a likely candidate.

I motioned to Richard. He walked over apprehensively.

Tommy Taylor had a powerful presence. His thick, bull neck and bald head continued to rivet the guests' attention. Taylor lit a cigarette as he watched Richard approach. His paunchy eyes became slits as the smoke billowed around his face. He gave Richard the once over. He wasn't impressed.

"Richard, this is Joey Tiraborelli and Tommy Taylor. They're old friends of mine from Rochester."

"Nice to meet you," Richard said, his eyes flicking nervously around the room.

An uncomfortable silence hung in the air. Then, without a hint of a smile, Joey seized Richard's eyes with his own. Holding him hostage with a steely gaze, he said gruffly, "You better be good to this girl."

The delivery of his words sent a chill up my spine. Richard got the message. The tension thickened. Tommy broke the ice by putting his arm around me and saying, "She's a very special lady, Richard. You're a lucky guy."

"Thank you, I know that," Richard answered, still not relaxed.

"Is there a place we can talk privately, Georgia?" Joey asked, ignoring Richard.

Richard pulled me aside and whispered into my ear, "Who are these guys?"

"Isn't it, like, *obvious*?"

"Yeah, and it is to everyone else, too. Get rid of them."

I excused myself from Richard, leaving him to entertain our guests. I led Joey up the winding staircase to the elegant bedroom, Tommy in tow.

"So what's up?"

"It's getting bad in Rochester, Georgia. Since Sammy G's been gone, there's been practically a murder a week."

"I know, I've been hearing."

"It's a freakin' power struggle, and I'm afraid we're not winning." Tommy nodded to every word.

"It's not my world anymore, Joey."

"It'll always be your world, honey. You can take the girl outta

New York, but you can't take New York outta the girl."

"You wanna bet? I've never seen you turn down a bet before, Joey. You want to lay a little down on that one?"

"George, I gotta go on the lam for a while," he said, changing his voice to a lighter tone. "I need five grand."

"Jesus Christ, Joey, this is my wedding day."

His upper lip curled, stretching tight across his teeth. "You think because you're married to a millionaire now y'can forget your old friends? I'll bet y'got more than that in that box down there."

"*He's* a millionaire, Joey, I'm not."

"I can think of a way to make you one real fast."

"Come on, Joey, don't kid like that."

"I'm not," he answered with a cold, penetrating smirk.

"What is this, a fucking shakedown, Joey?" I snapped.

His face relaxed. "Of course not, honey. We're friends. Friends helping friends. I'm desperate, George, or I wouldn't be askin'. If you want to see your old buddy alive five years from now, you'll help me. If ya don't, you're givin' me my death sentence."

"Don't lay that shit on me, Joey. I'm not giving you a death sentence. You did that yourself a long time ago."

"How many times did I save your ass from that piece of shit you were married to?" he pointed out.

Vivid pictures of Joey Tiraborelli making the sign of the cross on Joe's forehead with his own blood flashed through my mind.

"You didn't save my ass, Joey—Sammy did. And I never asked for the favor. Besides, you guys had your own agenda. Don't try to tell me that was all on my behalf. Now who's forgetting the girl's from New York?"

"If Sammy hadn't become 'The Man,' Georgia, you might not even be here to wear that pretty white dress right now—and you goddamn well know it. Who's kidding who here?"

Tommy stood silently by, watching our confrontation. His facial expressions stayed consistent. He neither smiled nor frowned.

"So what does that have to do with anything?"

"Everything! You owe me, honey," he snorted derisively.

"I don't owe you shit," I insisted, getting more agitated by the minute. How dare he speak to me like this, and on my wedding day! It was bad enough that these wiseguys had made an uninvited public display of themselves at my wedding, but to demand that I owe them? And to make thinly veiled threats towards my new husband—that was too much. Here was my old life literally and violently intruding on the new.

Joey sat next to me on the bed. "George, come on, honey," he pleaded, snaking his arm around my waist. "For old times' sake— give me the money. I'll pay you back."

Unmoved by his show of affection, I answered without empathy. "First of all, Joey, I heard you're into coke pretty heavy now. This money isn't going to take you to some far-off place for awhile until things cool off. If you can manage to get past the tables on your way out, you know damn well it's going up your nose."

"Since you brought it up..." He pulled a vile from his pocket, spooned out some of the white powder, and gestured in my direction.

"No, Joey, I don't touch that crap. If you keep that up, you won't have to worry about the Mob. If Sammy were still alive, he'd kill you himself," I said, as I watched him snort the cocaine. "I have to get back to my guests, Joey," I added disgustedly as I stood up. "After all, this *is* a wedding."

"What about the money?" he pressed.

The only way to get rid of him without ruining the entire wedding was to give him some money.

"Joey," I said, "gangsters walk around with $5,000 in their pockets. This is the real world. I'll get you a thousand, but that's as far as I go. For your information, this is coming out of *my* pocket. I'll have to pay Richard back. I expect you to pay me back someday...one way or another."

They followed as I descended the winding staircase. I found Richard and pulled him aside, telling him I needed a thousand dollars. He wasn't thrilled, but he didn't question it. I discreetly gave Joey the money.

"By the way," Joey said, "we heard Jimmy Lamendola's name being paged in the casino. Does Joe know you got married today?"

Darlene was within earshot. Sucking in air, she froze. Almost instantly, her face turned the color of her dress—pale green.

"No, he doesn't. I'm sure it's just a coincidence," I answered, more for Darlene's benefit than mine. "Needless to say, you haven't seen me."

They finished their champagne and left.

Fine beginning to my new life.

———

Shit! Jimmy was somewhere in the hotel. If it was that easy for Joey Tiraborelli to know where I was, then maybe Jimmy being around was not such a coincidence. I tried to enjoy what was left of the day, but every time the door opened my heart rate increased.

Finally the last guest left. Richard's father Andy still lingered at the bar. Not wanting to be impolite, I walked behind the bar, poured myself a drink, and joined him.

The open staircase curled up to a wide, railed landing that overlooked the entire lower floor of the suite. Occasionally Richard looked down, clearing his throat, a signal to his father that he had overstayed his welcome. Andy didn't take the hint. He continued to pour more vodka into his frequently empty glass.

Andy peered up at me with clouded, dark eyes. He resembled a Mafia kind of guy himself with his angry looking face, big nose, and dark complexion, but he was too short to intimidate anyone. Even I had three inches on him.

"Well, young lady," he said, slurring his words. "You do realize you just married a mama's boy, don't you?" he asked.

In his drunken state, he didn't realize how loudly he was speaking. Richard could hear every word. I listened without comment.

He had a wicked glint in his eyes as he continued. "You haven't just married my son, you married his mother too. That ain't gonna be easy. But if you give me a grandchild, I'll make it worth your while. You'll be set for life—whether you stay married to Richard or not."

What? Was this the way the rich lived out their lives? Everything done as a business—sign on the dotted line? I had already signed a prenuptial agreement, giving up my rights to everything I otherwise would have been entitled to. I really didn't care about signing those papers. What bothered me was that I felt as if I were entering a business arrangement, not a marriage.

I didn't marry Richard for his money. I married him for the promise of the storybook kind of life I never had. I married him to give my daughter the kind of childhood that I *did* have. I married him because I thought it was the sanest thing I had ever done—at least up to that point in my life. He was the light in the dark world to which I had become accustomed. This man couldn't play with people's lives as if he were playing Monopoly!

"Andy, Richard and I will have children if and when we decide to. I'm not an instrument to bear you a grandchild. The problem with people like you is that money is your god. You think you can buy anything with it, including people. Well, I've got a surprise for you: I can't be bought!"

The silence was broken by the sound of drawers slamming from the upstairs bedroom. Richard charged down the staircase, shooting us both a hateful look—an expression I had never seen before.

"I don't have to listen to any more of this bullshit," he barked. He stomped out the door, slamming it behind him.

I glared at my new father-in-law. The awkward moment stretched on. Finally, he rose from the barstool.

"Well, I guess I stayed too long," he mumbled as he staggered toward the exit. The door was closing behind him when he popped his head back in and said, "Think about it."

The door closed at the same time my glass smashed against it, shattering into a hundred little pieces.

Time to switch to Scotch. I poured a glass, leaving out the water, and sat for another two hours waiting for Richard to return. He never did. I carefully took off my wedding dress, thinking I might have yet another opportunity to wear it someday. I threw on jeans and a heavy wool sweater and headed for the coffee shop. As I passed the guard stationed at the front door, I recognized a hint of sympathy in his face and looked away. I tried paging Richard again—still no answer.

After a while I headed back to the honeymoon suite, avoiding eye contact with the guard. When I got to the door, I realized I had forgotten to take the key. The guard must have one. He did. We walked down the hall toward the room in silence. As he inserted the key and opened the door, he openly expressed his concern. Trying to be friendly, he commented, "Not working out, huh?"

"Obviously," I answered as I closed the door.

After staring at the ceiling for awhile, I finally fell asleep. The sound of a door slamming awakened me. Getting up, I looked down from the landing into the living room below. Richard noticed me watching him and began to curse me for losing his $40,000.

"I didn't tell you to gamble. What are you blaming me for?"

"You better not side with my father against my mother!"

"Richard, what are you talking about? I didn't say anything against your mother!"

After fifteen minutes of senseless arguing, he went to sleep—on the couch.

I slept alone on my wedding night.

———◇———

Miraculously, I became pregnant on my honeymoon. After the wedding-day confrontation with Richard's father, I wasn't as ecstatic as Richard was when I learned of the miracle inside me, but as my stomach grew, so did my feelings for Richard. Other than the problem of my mother-in-law, I couldn't remember ever being happier. I didn't quite trust the feeling, however, as though if I got too comfortable with it, it would be snatched away. There was hope, however, that such a promise of light could be permanent. I was actually living the family life I'd always dreamed about, and Richard's wealth only made it that much better. I slowly began to trust. Because I saw Richard as a deserving man, I opened my heart and began to give freely of myself.

I loved Richard when we first got married, but I wasn't *in* love with him. He wasn't all the things I had hoped for in a man; he was neither good-looking nor educated. But I didn't think anyone existed who could possess all these qualities and still give me that one treasured entity—an Ozzie and Harriet family. I settled, trading a portion of my personal desires for a real family existence, something I didn't want my daughter to grow up never having known. To my surprise, however, Richard whittled his way into my heavily-guarded heart.

Toni had an endless stream of friends coming to the house. She no longer had to worry about playing quietly or cautiously so as not to upset her step-father. Even my family was welcomed without malice. Richard was altruistic to a fault with all who touched my life.

Richard had Toni tutored and bought her all the latest designer clothes. He was very good to her. She was receiving the love of which she'd been deprived, and giving it back in return. Toni now had all the advantages of going through life never having to feel inferior, as I had felt while growing up.

Richard sold his business two weeks before we got married. It was a very successful wholesale appliance store called Adray's. That store grossed in the millions of dollars—monthly. The enterprise was the first of its kind; "Good Guys" and "Best Buy" have now taken over that market, but Richard was the pioneer. Volume was the key to the store's success. The profit on the merchandise sold was only six percent, but six percent of that kind of volume made him a very wealthy man. At thirty-six, he had all the money he could ever want or need, and, more importantly, the time to enjoy it. But time would turn out to be a curse.

I wasn't accustomed to Richard's culture. I had spent my life around fervent Italians, and the absence of physical affection within Richard's family bothered me. Richard's background was Lebanese and Romanian. Although he was born in this country, he had been brought up in the traditions of the Middle East, all foreign to me. I didn't understand the Muslim religion and didn't have any desire to learn. Toni and I turned up our noses at the dishes his mother prepared.

His mother practically lived with us in the beginning, and eventually did move in. He and his mother had joint checking accounts. I had my own separate account, into which Richard made monthly deposits. She accompanied us on every single vacation with our friends. She made everyone uncomfortable with her loud, dominant behavior, but Richard refused to see that. Because he was so good about including my parents in our activities, I tried to refrain from complaining. After awhile, though, my nerves became frayed. He acted as if he were married to his mother. I voiced my criticism of the unnatural relationship, but he cut me short by saying that he didn't deprive me of anything and refused to discuss it.

Richard decided one day that a Rolls Royce was in order. He had an inexhaustible appetite for toys. He already had eleven cars, but his playthings filled the gap in his self-esteem. He bought the Rolls, as he did everything: with cash. Only the best money could buy for Richard Adray and his family.

Richard, who would purchase anything on a whim, would quickly become bored with his material toys. He looked forward to the birth of our baby, but in the meantime he began to fill the hours of boredom with the recreational use of cocaine. I'd always thought having too much money brought out the evil in people, but I was about to see firsthand what the combination of money *and* drugs could do.

At times I was bored as well. I wasn't used to not working. Although I did do a few ads for expectant mothers when my pregnancy became obvious, for the most part my daily routine was slowed to a snail's pace. We had a live-in maid who did all the cleaning, washing, and cooking. With nothing for me to do, I filled my days lunching with friends, getting manicures and facials, and shopping for clothes that I knew would look great when my figure returned to normal.

Antsy for something to do with my time, I embarked on a major remodel of our already beautiful home in Beverly Hills. The house was 6,000 square feet and sat perched on top of a mountain overlooking the lights of the city below.

My creative juices were flowing. I had always wondered what I could do if I had the money to match my imagination. I had a beveled mirror installed at the end of the ninety-foot long hallway. It appeared to go on forever. Trying to add warmth to the expanded, empty space, I turned the hallway into a photo gallery and lined the walls with family photos and some of the thousands of modeling pictures I had stored in boxes. It worked.

When the remodel was finally completed, it was beautiful, but being such a large home it still lacked warmth. I settled for cool and elegant. I spent more on that remodel than Richard had originally paid for the house, but it now had my personal touch.

Four months into my marriage, Joe moved to Los Angeles, having no idea that I was pregnant and still convinced it wasn't over between us. The phone rang.

"I need you to invest some money for me. I can't have it in my name, and I don't want the cash lying around," Joe said from his new apartment in West Hollywood, only three miles from my home.

"I don't want any complications with Richard, Joe."

"What complications? Why does he have to know?"

"What about tax returns? It'll show up."

"Georgia, I'm sitting here with $150,000—in *cash*. Just come over and get it out of here. I don't care what you do with it, just invest it for me. Tell him it's your settlement from some property that we just sold. The government will never question you with all your millions," he said with a hint of sarcasm.

"Richard's millions, Joe, not mine."

"You're his wife now. This is California, honey, it's yours, too."

I never told Joe about waiving my rights to all those millions. He needed to believe money was the reason to allow the marriage to take place. If that meant no interference from him, I'd let him believe it.

"All right, Joe, I'll pick it up tomorrow," I consented to get him off the phone.

"Why not now?"

"Because Richard will be home soon for dinner."

"Let the asshole wait. How many times was dinner late for me?"

"Not many, as I recall. I'll see you tomorrow."

I hung up feeling unsettled. *Too close for comfort.* My life was too good—something had to ruin it. I had thought time would cure the problem with Joe, but his moving onto my doorstep would make time crawl, along with making me a wreck.

When I entered his apartment, he looked like a lost soul. He searched my face for a glimpse of what we had together, and what he hoped we might have again.

"Ya know what I miss most about you, honey?"

"What?"

He took hold of my hand. "Sitting like this, having our morning coffee together. I really miss that," he said.

I looked down at our touching fingers and gently pulled away. "I miss the view from the cliffs when I have my morning coffee. I don't see how you could leave that to live in Los Angeles."

"I've gotta start makin' some moves. I'm gonna need your help with a few things, and besides, I'll be closer to you and Toni this way."

"Joe, I'm married."

"What's that have to do with seeing Toni more often?" he said as he pulled out the duffel bag filled with $100 bills. "There's a hundred and fifty grand here. If anything happens to me, I want it to go to Toni. Y'can keep the interest."

"I don't need it. I'll deduct the taxes and send you the interest."

"I never did a damn thing for you when we were married, y'know that? I never even bought you a new dress. I was such a selfish prick."

"That's okay, I don't wear dresses anyway. My legs are too skinny."

"You don't have skinny legs, Georgia. I only told you that because I didn't want other men admiring what was mine. There's nothing wrong with your legs," he admitted.

"Really? I have nice legs?"

"You have beautiful legs, dear."

He answered with such sincerity that I almost believed him. A familiar look crossed his face. His thirsty eyes caressed my body, slowly drinking me in. It was time to leave.

"I better be going, Joe. I have to pick up Toni from school," I said, checking my watch.

"Oh, you mean you don't have a servant who does that for you?" he said sarcastically.

I shot him a disgusted look and he immediately tried to apologize. "I'm sorry, honey," he said, grabbing me by my waist and pulling me to him. "What's this? What's happened to your waistline? All that good living is going to the wrong places. See what happens when you haven't got me around to watch your diet?"

This is the time to break it to him.

"I'm pregnant, Joe."

"Pregnant! How the fuck did that happen?"

"It happened..."

"Why didn't you ever get pregnant with me? God knows we did it enough!"

"You gave me gonorrhea, remember?"

"I thought you needed an operation to get pregnant. Or was that another lie? You were taking the Pill, weren't you?" he accused.

"No, I wasn't. The doctor said my tubes might open on their own in time. I guess that's what happened. Besides, Joe, you were too selfish to have children. Don't pretend now that you wanted any. Maybe this is God's way of saying the time is right."

"You're not thinking of *having* it, are you?"

"Of course I'm having it, Joe."

"You can't do this to me, Georgia."

"Joe, I have a new life now. This is part of that life. Please let me be happy. I have to go, I'm gonna be late."

I left him sitting in a chair, his face distorted by the pain of the certainty that it could never be again. My heart broke to see him so devastated, but I was also relieved that the truth was out. We both needed to let go of the past—and a future that could never be.

——◈——

About a week later, Marina, my housekeeper, knocked on my bathroom door. "There's a man outside at the gate who wants to speak to you, missis."

I looked at the clock and wondered why the man I was expecting was so early. "Let him in, Marina. Take him to the billiard room, I'll be right out," I instructed.

"Yes, missis," she replied as she scurried down the hall.

I quickly dried off, threw on my raggedy old white robe, and ventured down the long hallway. I continued to the billiard room to greet the man with the samples of material for the new drapes.

When I entered the room, I stopped with a jolt. Joe had poured himself a Scotch and water and was playing pool.

"Do you always greet your guests like that?"

"What are you doing here Joe?" I said in a panicked voice.

"Nice place you got here. Yeah, you've come a long way from Lyell Avenue, haven't you honey?"

"Please don't start anything, Joe."

"I'm not gonna start anything, Georgia. I'm leaving. I'm going back to Solana Beach. Everything's packed in the car. I just wanted to say good-bye and see how my other half lives. Why don't you show me the place?"

He wasn't about to leave, so I quickly showed him through the house, excluding the master bedroom.

"Where's your bedroom?"

"It's at the other end of the house."

"I want to see it."

"Why?"

"Just show it to me."

I reluctantly turned and lead him down the hall. I opened the bedroom door and stood at the entry. He studied the room for a long time. Finally, he sat on the bed and patted the space beside him. "I want to make love to you in his bed," he said flatly.

"Are you nuts?"

He stood and approached me. "Y'know...I love the way you smell after you get out of the shower," he said softly.

He pulled open my robe, exposing my nude body. I quickly covered myself and backed away.

"It's time for you to go, Joe."

Marina appeared in the doorway. "Missis, there's a man here to see you."

"Thank you, Marina, tell him I'll be right out," I said, grateful for the interruption.

"Please, Joe, you have to go now. Richard could walk through that door any minute. Don't complicate my life."

"I love you, Georgia."

"If you love me, Joe, you'll leave right now."

Pressured, he reluctantly backed off. "I want to see Toni one weekend this month."

"Okay, I'll send her down on the train."

"Promise?"

"I said I would, now please...go!"

"Put something on before you go out there," he said, looking away, afraid he would betray the ache in his chest. Then he left.

Richard came home only ten minutes after Joe had walked out the door.

"What's the matter with you today?" he asked, sensing my uneasiness.

"Nothing."

"Who was here today?"

"No one. Why do you think someone was here?"

"Who was drinking Scotch in the bar?"

"Oh, I was."

"I thought you said you were only going to drink wine while you're pregnant? And why are you drinking in the middle of the day anyway?"

"Why do you do *drugs* in the middle of the day?" I snapped. "I found some more cocaine in your bathroom. I thought you said you stopped." Now I had *him* on the defensive—something I learned from Joe.

I began to relax now that Joe was back in Solana Beach. His only connection to me now was the money he had so proudly salvaged from the FBI, thanks to the prior warning from me that they were watching him. He hid it in the cushions of two of his barstools before they raided his condo. He laughed about how they tore the place apart and found nothing. The entire time they questioned him they were sitting right on top of the money.

I invested Joe's money and made him thirty percent the first year. After all those years of being told how stupid I was, making a profit on my choice of investments validated my intelligence, giving me great satisfaction. I was beginning to get a sense of who I was.

Positive people now filled my life. No more negativity clouded my head. With Richard I could feel, act, and think freely, without being afraid. He applauded my accomplishments instead of ridiculing them. I discovered my strengths because I wasn't fearful of showing them. Free now to expand on the riches life had to offer, I opened my mind to the hidden treasures I'd always possessed. I had made the right choice. Life could only get better as time went on.

I loved watching my stomach grow. I loved every minute of being pregnant. Everything was so perfect. I was happier than I ever remembered being. But lurking in the shadows, Richard's increasing use of drugs was promising to be a problem.

The birth of my son Dustin was one of the happiest days of my life. The hospital room was filled with flowers and balloons. Even Joe called to wish me happiness.

"What did you name him?" Joe asked.

"Dustin."

"Dustin! What kind of a name is that? Why didn't you name him Rocky?"

"Just be grateful it's not Mohammed," I kidded, and we both had a chuckle.

"Are you happy, Georgia?"

I smiled down at my newborn son and felt as if I was going to burst with joy. "Yes, I'm very happy, Joe. I have a healthy, beautiful baby boy, and my daughter. One of each. How lucky can I get?"

Marina's title graduated from housekeeper to nanny. She traveled with us everywhere. I could leave the house with peace of mind, knowing that Dustin was loved and cared for.

Richard's father was not happy when I had Dustin baptized, but that is where I drew the line. My son would be baptized a Catholic. When he grew older he could decide for himself, but for now he was going to be Catholic.

Toni loved having a new little brother, but the attention had now shifted to him. She had some trouble adjusting to the sudden switch in focus. She became quiet and withdrawn again. I tried my best to include her in the daily routine of caring for a baby, making her feel a part of it all, but I couldn't control the behavior of Richard and his family. For them, Dustin was the king.

I couldn't remember being this happy when Toni came into the world. Every little thing Dustin did was an event. His first step, his first tooth, his first word. Thirty was a good age to be a mother. Toni had been cheated by having a child for a mother, and I could see now how cheated I had been as well. But I was finally making up for some of the lost moments in my daughter's life. Life was good. I was happy—at last.

Chapter Thirteen

It didn't take me long to learn that being rich had nothing to do with money. All of the mink coats, diamond jewelry, and expensive toys could not bring me the happiness I so desperately wanted. The *family* unit was what I yearned to possess.

Still on cloud nine after returning home with my newborn son, I kept thinking life was too good to be true. Nine days after giving birth, I sat happily feeding my son in the living room when the phone rang. I picked up the extension at the same time Richard did.

"Hi, Denny," Richard said, keeping his voice to a whisper.

Curiosity kept me from hanging up. Why was he whispering?

"Listen, I can't talk now," he continued. "Call me at this number in an hour—and don't call the house again tonight. I'll explain it later."

I committed the number to memory and sat back down on the couch. Richard appeared a few minutes later.

"I'm going out for a while, honey."

"Where are you going?"

Nervously fingering his keys, he answered, "I'm going to meet Denny for a drink. I'll be home early."

"Would you buy some milk on your way home?"

"Sure, do we need anything else?" he asked, overly accommodating as he lovingly kissed me good-bye.

I waited the hour as he had instructed Denny to do before calling the number. My hand shook as I pressed each digit. I knew before she answered what the deal was going to be.

"Hello?" said a woman. It wasn't a voice I recognized.

"Can I speak with Richard please?" I said in a self-assured tone.

Evidently she knew he was expecting a call because she handed him the telephone without hesitation.

"Hi, Denny."

"This isn't Denny, you son-of-a-bitch! Where the hell are you?"

A dead silence, then the hum of a disconnected line.

My world was shattered. I looked over at my newborn son sleeping peacefully, unaware of how this moment would change his life. How could I have brought yet another child into the world who would grow up without a father? The memory of raising a child alone, with no money, flooded my thoughts. I was crushed, but more than that, I was angry. Angry that he could spoil my dream. We had a family. Three lives that would suffer—for what?

Toni was so settled and happy, it wasn't fair that she should be taken away from her new life and be forced to start all over again. It wasn't fair that Dustin, only nine days old, would never have a family life, with a mommy and daddy that actually lived together and had supper together. And lastly, it wasn't fair to me. I believed in Richard. Although I hadn't been in love when I'd embarked on my marriage, my trust in him had grown, and with that trust I had allowed my feelings for him to run deep. I had given him that part of myself which I was so afraid to let go of, and he had carelessly abused it.

So much for Ozzie and Harriet, White. I think you watched too much TV as a kid. Why didn't you listen to me? From now on, I'm calling the shots!

He was home within twenty minutes. I'd worked myself into a full-blown rage by then.

"I didn't fuck her!" he screamed in his defense. "I just let her suck my cock."

"Oh, that's all? How silly of me to be so upset. Get out of this house, Richard, and take your clothes with you!"

"This is *my* house, I'm not going anywhere."

"So it is. I'll start looking for a place tomorrow. In the meantime, which bedroom would you prefer?"

"Georgia, will you listen to me?"

"Stay away from me, Richard, I'm not in the listening mood. I'm really afraid of what I might do to you. For your own good, get out of my sight!"

He wouldn't do that. He persisted in trying to explain something that had no explanation, so I left before I lost control. There were no swords in the house, but there were guns.

I drove around aimlessly and wound up on Jim Alquist's doorstep. Fighting tears, I rang his bell and waited. Still shaking, I told him what had happened, but I refused to cry. No one would ever be worth my tears—ever again. Jim tried to comfort me, but the wound was too fresh.

"That fucking asshole! Doesn't he know what he's got?"

"What he *had*, Jim. I'm planning on looking for a place tomorrow."

"Are you really going to leave all that?"

"All that doesn't mean anything if I'm not happy. I refuse to live with a man who's blind to what's important in life. If he can throw it all away so easily, he isn't worthy of another minute of my time. I've wasted too much already. I wanted a family, not an instant replay of my past. There's no point in staying. I know from experience, it can never be the same."

"Don't be stupid, Georgia. Think about it for a minute. Where're you going to go? You don't have any furniture—you gave it all away. Your prenuptial agreement only allows you $30,000 if you leave now. How far can you go on that with two kids? That won't even pay a year's rent. Think about Toni. This is the first time in a long time the kid's been settled."

"I'm more aware of that than you are," I replied, reflecting sadly. "I hate him for this!"

"Well, I think a sudden move like that would be too traumatic for Toni. I don't think she could handle it. I'm not saying you have to live as man and wife, but Christ, Georgia, at least stay put until you have enough money behind you to make it on your own.

Have you forgotten how you struggled after you left Joe?"

"I know what you're saying, but right now I can't stand the thought of living under the same roof with him, much less in the same room!"

"It won't be as easy as you think going from princess to pauper. This'll be a tough transition for both of you."

"I just can't go back there."

"You don't have to decide anything right now. Stay here tonight. Tomorrow your mind will be clearer," he said as the phone rang. "Are you here?" he asked before answering it.

"Yeah, I have no reason to lie."

Jim answered and handed me the phone. "What do you want, Richard?" I asked calmly.

"I want you to come home. The baby needs you. How could you just walk out on him that way?"

"I walked out on *you*, not him. Take him to Marina's room, she'll care for him if you can't handle it."

"He wants his mother. What is it with you and Jim anyway? Is this the excuse you were looking for to have an affair with him, or have you already?"

"Drop dead, Richard!" I slammed down the phone.

"Why do all your husbands hate me?" Jim asked after I told him what Richard said.

We both got silly at that one. He broke open a bottle of wine and we spent the rest of the night drinking ourselves into a stupor.

They called it the "baby blues." I slid into a severe depression for a good month. The blood in my veins had turned to ice, and so had my heart. My protective armor was so thick it couldn't be penetrated. Georgia Black was in full command. I handed her the reins. It was over.

When the reality of it all set in, I realized Jim was right. I had to bide my time until I could walk away comfortably. I worked out like a madwoman trying to get my figure back so I could return to modeling and finance my departure. Soon I called my agent, telling her I was ready to pound the pavement again.

"Perfect timing," Janette said. "I got a request for you today."

"What's it for?"

"It's seven days on a cruise ship in Mexico. You'll be shooting print for a brochure, but they're also going to take the stills and turn it into a commercial. I know your husband isn't wild about long location jobs, but it's a good one, sweetie."

Fuck him. Who cares what he thinks? Look out for yourself, White. No one else is going to—you should know that by now.

"I'm in. When does it shoot?"

"Next week. I'll get back to you with the details. I'm glad you're back in action, sweetie."

"Me too," I answered.

I not only needed to build up my bank account, I needed to get myself out of my depression. Work was always a great escape. Our friends couldn't understand why the girl who had it all would continue with her profession. What more could she possibly want? Richard and I behaved civilly, like a happy couple, but we both knew the truth. Only those close to us were aware of a problem.

My parents were saddened to see my life take another solemn turn, but I continued to wear a smile and assured them it was really okay. Richard's mother was happy. She knew she'd soon have her baby all to herself again. But until then, I played the great pretender. We still went out to dinner a few nights a week and entertained at home. I'd worn this mask before—it was nothing new. I had the part perfected by now.

Richard's drug problem worsened. The more he indulged in cocaine, the more he drank. He didn't try to hide it anymore. He went from coming home late to not coming home at all. I never asked what he was doing; I only asked that he be discreet. He became predictable. I knew when he took out the Rolls Royce or the Clenét, it was Hollywood Boulevard night. He'd cruise down the boulevard shopping for hookers. As if that weren't bad enough, before he took them to bed, he took them to dinner at private clubs where we were members.

Richard's ego needed affirmation. He thought his improper actions made him the envy of all his friends. What he didn't know was that his peers were all laughing at him. They watched him pitifully destroy himself over a bunch of street girls and drugs.

Richard soon graduated to snorting coke with his morning coffee. By this time I realized the reason for the prenuptial agreement I'd signed. Richard didn't want a marriage, he wanted a child. Years later, I learned from a friend of his that Richard had boasted, before he'd even met me, that he was going to find himself the perfect woman, marry her, get her pregnant right away, divorce her, and keep the kid. But he had a big problem—the child was also mine. There were no papers to take that from me, at least not at the moment.

Not too long after the job on the cruise ship, I landed one for a German cigarette ad that was to be shot in New Zealand. Six models, three men and three women, made the trek to that faraway land. I had never seen such incredible scenery. Sheep snaked up narrow roads, surrounded on either side by lush greenery. Puffy clouds kissed the rolling hilltops. All of our shooting locations were in the deep backwoods, which we traveled to by helicopter and seaplane. From the air, the reflection of the mountains in the clear water was breathtaking. The mirrored effect made it difficult to distinguish which were the true mountains. I took a leave of absence from my emotional wounds to drown myself in this beauty.

Manfred, the German photographer, was an extreme perfectionist. He refused to shoot a picture if a cloud was in the sky. Consequently, we spent a lot of time having the helicopter fly us from lake to beautiful lake, and we fished for five days before shooting one frame of film. We had all the latest gear, compliments of the German wardrobe stylist. We were being paid $1,000 per day to go fishing in the most picturesque place in the world.

Sitting around the campfire drinking wine and eating fresh

fish, the other models and I had long, heart-to-heart talks. By day five we were old friends. All in our early thirties, we'd each been modeling for many of those years. The money was always sufficiently good so that we never thought of doing anything constructive with our minds. By smiling and looking pretty, it was easy to make the same amount of money a doctor or lawyer could make in a year. But we were all aware that age would soon dictate a change, and we had to be ready for it when it came. During one of the campfire talks, I expressed my interest in a driving career, and my unsuccessful efforts at breaking into the field.

Molly Lynn turned her head, and her long brown hair fell across her eye. "I know a guy who owns a driving team back in the States. I'll call him when we get back and set up a lunch so he can meet you," she said.

"I'm going to hold you to it, Molly," I replied.

"No problem. When this guy sees you, you're in. Trust me."

On the plane ride home, each of us was paid $10,000. The plane landed in Tahiti for fuel, and I decided to stay for a few days. I called my agent from the airport to put her mind at rest, letting her know we had received the money and that it had all gone well.

"I'm going to take a little R&R in Tahiti, Janette."

"No you're not, sweetie. You got that other German cigarette ad you auditioned for before you left. You have to be in Europe by Monday."

"That doesn't give me much time."

"No, it doesn't."

"How long is the job?" I asked.

"Ten days, just like this one."

Hmm...$20,000 closer to freedom.

"I'll see you at the agency sometime tomorrow," Janette said. "Sorry you can't stay in Tahiti. Maybe next time."

———◈———

After shooting the second German cigarette ad, I landed a third one. Not once was I asked if I had a conflict, and as a result, that year my face turned up on billboards, the sides of buses, and magazine ads all over Germany—all for different cigarette companies. I already had a campaign going for More cigarettes in the States. When that contract was up, I did another one for Kent Golden Lights. From there, I went on to beer and liquor ads, both in Mexico and in the U.S. Molly Lynn kept her promise, and I started shooting car commercials as well. I guess you could say it was a year of cigarettes, booze, and fast cars.

Wally Crowder, who owned Motion Research Driving Team, thought he had hit a home run when he took me on. Another pretty face he could flaunt before his clients. The shock was, I could drive.

The first job Wally booked me on was for Chrysler at the Laguna Sega Race Track near Carmel. The job called for two women drivers. I had no formal training from Wally and didn't know what to expect. I didn't have the slightest idea how to use the walkie-talkie, and the on-set lingo was like a foreign language. Damn Wally for not preparing me. I tried to fake it the best I could.

The other girl was in the same position. I had one advantage over her, due to my past racing experience: I knew how to handle a car. On the very first shot, she spun out on the track with the director in the car and came within inches of hitting the wall. She was sent home immediately, leaving me to finish the commercial on my own. The fact that the producers continued to trust Wally's judgment was, to me, unbelievable—but a lot of political games were being played that I was not yet privy to.

My real initiation was when I did my first conga line—six cars driving in a line about three inches apart from each other's bumpers. I concentrated intensely on the car in front of me. The director's voice came over the radio, asking me if I had white pants on.

"Yes, I do," I answered, taking one hand off the wheel to work the walkie. My eyes were still glued to the car in front of me.

"Get 'em off. They're causing a reflection in the windshield. Do it fast, we're losing the light!"

Embarrassed again. Damn that Wally. How was I supposed to know to wear black? We all came to a slow stop. I whipped off my pants from inside the vehicle and we began shooting again immediately. Little did I know they already had the shot in the can. The entire time, the camera car drove alongside my vehicle—filming my crotch! Never taking my eyes off the car in front of me, I was oblivious to this. Thank God I had underwear on. Watching dailies the following day, everyone got a good laugh, including me. But I learned not to be so naive after that.

I was never formally taught how to drive for the camera, but that's not really something one can be taught. It's a feel, an awareness of what the camera sees. I did take it upon myself to go to the Bondurant School of High Performance Driving. It looked good on my résumé, but mostly I learned from on-the-job experience. Being connected with a driving team gave me instant credibility, but with Wally that didn't mean you were properly prepared. Fortunately, I had a good on-camera look, which opened the door a little bit farther. There weren't many women in the business from which to choose, so most directors were patient with me when I messed up.

With every job, I learned more. When I was asked to jump a car, I pretended that I had done it a thousand times—and did it as if I had. I just went for it. Unlike the apprehensions in my personal life, I never lacked confidence behind the wheel. In this arena, *I* had control. The power of life and death was in *my* hands. My choices in the driver's seat had to be the right ones—no room for mistakes in this world. Shifting gears, I embraced my Shadow side with every intention of driving forward with my life. I was soon doing more car commercials than modeling assignments.

By this time, I had been married almost three years. As my money accumulated, so did the number of Richard's girlfriends. "Discreet" was not a word in his vocabulary. Come to think of it, there weren't many words in his vocabulary. It wouldn't be long now. I had almost enough money for a down payment on a house. Living with Richard under these conditions was wearing on me. We never argued, but the air was always thick with unspoken words.

Richard was out of town on my thirty-second birthday. I made reservations for dinner with some friends at Touch, a relatively new private club in Beverly Hills, exclusive to the "A" crowd. Touch was backed by Hugh Hefner and a few other partners. The price of the membership was set purposely high, excluding a clientele which lacked wealth or fame. The faces were all familiar. All the members from the Beverly Hills hot spot, Pips, had another club to frequent now.

After dinner my girlfriends departed and I went into the disco. O.J. Simpson and his girlfriend Nicole were seated on the cushy couches along with some friends. Nicole, as usual, was sucking on a lollipop. It was her trademark; nobody ever saw her without one. I walked over to say hello.

O.J. stood as I approached. "Have a seat. Help us celebrate my birthday," he said, greeting me warmly.

"It's my birthday too! I didn't know July 9th was your birthday," I said with surprise as the waitress approached.

"Are you all set here, Mr. Simpson?" she asked.

"Bring us another bottle of Dom Perignon," O.J. instructed.

"Right away, Mr. Simpson."

"So, have you been doing any near misses with people these days?" O.J. asked with a dry laugh.

"No, not since the Hertz commercial, unless you want me to count the times I wasn't getting paid to do it," I answered with a broad grin.

"I gotta admit, even though I knew you were all professional drivers, I was a little uncomfortable dodging those cars criss-crossing in front of me like that," O.J. stated.

"What do you mean, professionals? That was the first driving job for three of those guys," I kidded.

He almost gagged on his drink, then realized I was pulling his leg. Shifting my attention to the dance floor, I watched as a couple danced exquisitely to Michael Jackson's "Thriller." When the song ended, I noticed O.J.'s eyes had become transfixed as he sipped his champagne. I looked in the direction of his chilling glare to see a man staring at Nicole. She was innocently licking her lollipop, but this man plainly had another image in his head. O.J.'s disconcerting gaze, magnified by the strobe lights flashing eerily across his face, grew more intense. The familiar sight made me go cold inside. My mind immediately flashed to Joe. I had never seen this expression on O.J. before. It scared me.

Did Nicole have any idea what was in store for her? She was about the age I was when I first became involved with Joe. So young. So naive. What did *I* know at that age?

My fears were confirmed when I walked into the ladies' room. Nicole stood in front of the mirror applying make-up. The fluorescent lighting couldn't hide the bruises she was trying to conceal.

"Nicole, I know this is none of my business, but I think I understand what you're going through—"

"What do you mean?" she asked in an attempt to dismiss my suspicions.

"O.J. did that to you, didn't he?"

"Oh no," she replied. "I slipped by the pool and fell on my face. I'm such a klutz."

"Oh, is that all?" I replied with a knowing look.

No use in saying anything more. She was in denial, too blind with love to see. I remembered well. She wasn't ready to talk, but a feeling of helplessness churned in the pit of my stomach. I wanted to shake her, but I knew she would have to learn the same way I did...the hard way.

Richard and I had been leading separate lives. He left for the Las Vegas house one weekend with the kids. Despite the state of our marriage, he was good to Toni and he never left her out. When Richard had proposed to me, he'd expressed his desire to legally adopt Toni—another bit of bait for his trap. He did go through with the adoption, and it was finalized while I was pregnant with Dustin. Tom, her own biological father, had posed no objection.

Toni's life was now filled with dance and riding lessons, outings with friends, parties, and school plays—most of which Richard participated in. She felt she belonged, and was quite happy and content. Toni was the biggest heartache in my departure plan. How I agonized over her. But I couldn't live this lie for much longer. It wasn't healthy for any of us.

While they were in Las Vegas, I decided to throw a party for the New Zealand crew. I was feeling particularly lonely with the house empty and needed the company of good friends to take my mind off the hellish charade my marriage had become.

During the party I went looking for the pictures of our New Zealand adventure. It had been such a special time and we loved to reminisce. As I was searching, I came across a bag of cocaine in Richard's drawer. I had indulged in cocaine a few times with Richard, but stopped when I saw how seductive it was. The last time I had partaken was before I became pregnant. Looking at the baggie of white powder conjured up images of destruction. I was about to flush it down the toilet when one of the guests walked in.

"Hey, you going to share that?"

I hesitated and then handed him the bag.

"Here, have a party. Whatever's left is getting flushed."

When the coke was passed to me, I refused. But after a few more drinks, I indulged. When the party was over, I threw the remainder away and never touched the stuff again.

The next weekend, Fred Reed, my friend from Rochester, came to Los Angeles on his annual trip to the coast with his children. I had plans to take him to lunch. Richard came into the breakfast room while I was feeding Dustin. He sat down with his coffee and played with Dustin for awhile. His son was his pride and joy and my leaving was going to be tough on Richard.

"What're your plans for today?" he asked.

"Fred's in town and I'm taking him to lunch. Do you want to join us?"

"No, I'm going riding today. The horses need some exercise. Where you taking him?"

"I'm not quite sure yet. Somewhere in Beverly Hills. Maybe the Polo Lounge," I said.

"Where's Toni?"

"She left for the mountains with her friend Liz and her family for the weekend."

"Tell Fred hello for me," he said, as he poured the remainder of his coffee into the sink and walked out of the kitchen.

"Bye-bye, Daddy," Dustin said after him, but Richard was already gone.

By eleven o'clock the sun broke through the fog, putting a fresh new complexion on the day. Rather than sit in a stuffy restaurant, I decided to take Fred to the Marina. We sat at a window seat of a waterfront restaurant and watched the boats cruise lazily through the channel. Fred brought me up to date with the news from home. When the wine came, he lifted his glass and toasted me.

"Georgia, I've seen you through some pretty rough times. I'm so glad to see you're finally happy," he said with sincerity.

Maybe I should be an actress, I thought, as we clicked our glasses together. I took a sip of wine and looked away before Fred could read what was in my eyes. I'd spent years pretending to be happy. The last thing I wanted was to give satisfaction to anyone in Rochester who wished me ill. Getting wind of the fact that this marriage had become a nightmare too would surely create joy for my enemies. Fred was a friend, but he was still from Rochester, and I was always reminded of my vow to prove to the vicious gossips of my youth that I could be successful and respectable despite their expectations.

I gazed out the window at the serene view and then choked on my wine. Richard, piloting our boat, was cruising carefree down the channel with two trashy women by his side. From where I sat, it looked like they were snorting cocaine. One of the girls appeared to be drinking hard liquor straight from the bottle. They seemed to be having a wonderful time. His obsession with sleaze infuriated me.

"Are you okay?" Fred asked with concern.

"Yeah, it must have gone down the wrong pipe. Will you excuse me a minute?" I said. I walked in the direction of the ladies' room.

Richard was heading back to the slip. I jumped in my car and dashed over to the Marina City Club where we docked our boat. When I got to the gate, I discovered I didn't have my key with me. A Mexican guy was standing there sweeping the sidewalk.

"Have you got a key to this gate?" I asked with authority. He nodded affirmatively. "Open it!" I demanded.

As soon as the gate was open, I flew to the end of the dock and arrived just as the boat was pulling into the slip. The look on Richard's face was priceless. There was nowhere for him to go except forward. He was caught. The boat was halfway into the slip when I jumped on. I got Richard in a headlock and yanked on his neck so hard the captain's chair broke and he landed on the deck. Meanwhile, the boat was banging against the sides of the slip, unmanned for the moment.

"What are you doing to him?" screamed one of his shipmates.

I'd forgotten all about the girls in my rage, but now that they had called attention to themselves, my focus turned their way. In one sweeping move I pushed them both overboard. I kicked Richard one last time, jumped off the boat, ran to my car, and dashed back to the restaurant. A total of five or six minutes had passed. I calmly sat down at my table, picked up my wine, and continued my conversation with Fred as if nothing had happened. Yep, I would have made an excellent actress.

Fred and I continued to drink the afternoon away. Lunch had turned into dinner, and we still carried on. Sometime after midnight we called it a night. I was pretty blasted. When I returned home, I was appalled to open my bedroom door and see Richard snoring away in *my* bed!

Gotta give this guy some credit, White—he's got balls!

I immediately looked around for a gun, but anticipating my anger, he had carefully hidden all firearms—not wanting to have to replace all the windows in the house again. Georgia Black had surfaced frequently during recent times. On one occasion I had shot out all the windows in the house to vent my anger, but now

I wanted blood. I searched for another weapon. *Ah, the fireplace poker.* I walked back into the bedroom and smashed it with all my might against his back.

I'll teach him to screw with you.

"What the fuck!" he screamed.
"If you want to live to see morning, I suggest you leave now," I spewed in a controlled voice that even scared me.

Richard ran out the door in his pajamas and jumped into his Rolls Royce. He backed out of the driveway at high speed, scraping his prized possession on the half-opened gate as he fled. When he returned three days later, he was still wearing his pajamas.

The next day I began house-hunting and became extremely depressed. Compared to what I was used to, $300,000 homes in Beverly Hills and the adjacent areas were like shacks. They had small bedrooms, tiny closets, and no backyards. The San Fernando Valley posed the only solution if I were going to get any kind of a house for my money. The "Valley" was a foreign world to me. Although only ten minutes from Beverly Hills, it was the wrong direction from the world I had come to know.

Dust trailed the limousine as it sped the five miles to what seemed to be nowhere on the dry lake bed in El Mirage. Nothing was in sight except the black, sinister-looking vehicle. The heat waves rose from the vast, desolate surface of the desert's parched floor. Six drivers, five men and me, departed from the sleek machine. We were an impressive sight, dressed in identical black driving suits and helmets. Wally, our team leader, got a kick out of putting on a show. The temperature in the Mojave Desert was a blistering 120 degrees. With windows rolled up, no air conditioning in the prototypes, and wearing all black, I was going to earn every cent I made.

I had almost turned down this job, anxious to continue the search for a new home. Oddly enough, if I had not taken the job,

I would never have found the house in which I now live.

After a long, hellish, hot day, we returned to Los Angeles tired and haggard. Bob Schultz, one of the team's drivers, and I were both house-hunting and neither of us was having any luck. After describing what I wanted, he remembered seeing a place that fit my description. We happened to be close by, so he directed the chauffeur to the residence.

"This is it, Bob! It has everything I've been looking for. It's on a cul-de-sac. It has a guest house, a pool, and a big yard. What are they asking?" I inquired excitedly.

"Three hundred and eighty-nine thousand."

"If the inside is as nice as the outside, I'm going to make an offer on it," I exclaimed, trying to contain my excitement.

The next day I called my broker and had her make an appointment to see it. I walked through the house and instantly got a good vibe. Every room had a vaulted ceiling. The vertical space gave the house an expansive feel. Counting the guest house, it was 2,800 square feet, less than half of what I then lived in. It needed work to bring it up to my standards, but I was no stranger to remodeling. My offer was accepted, with a sixty-day escrow. Sixty more days of living under the same roof with Richard.

When the reality of my leaving set in, he became a real jerk.

"You'll take my son over my dead body!" he barked as he stormed out of the house, slamming the door behind him.

Then so be it...

Georgia Black came up with a plan. Richard had a bad heart. He'd already had a heart attack when he was only thirty-four years old. He'd actually died while being driven to the hospital. He was pronounced dead, but arrived in time to be revived.

You can kill him, White, and you don't even have to pull the trigger.

Richard was dining with one of his street girls at Pips when I made the call.

"I'd like to speak to Richard Adray, please."

"Uh, I don't think I've seen Mr. Adray this evening," said the bartender, recognizing my voice.

"John, this is an emergency. Try to find him."

Richard was on the phone immediately. I found my hysterical voice and screamed into the phone. "I just killed the kids! Now neither one of us can have them!" I hung up and immediately poured ketchup all over the foyer floor and walls, smearing it to look like blood.

This should do it.

He was home in five minutes. I sat on the couch in the living room, facing the entry so as not to miss the event.

No one is going to take your son away from you. I won't let that happen. No way.

His eyes bulged as he saw what he thought was blood. He ran into the kids' rooms and saw that they were fine. His entire body shook as he confronted me in the living room—but he didn't die.

Shit! It didn't work. What am I going to do now?

I'll think of something, White, don't worry.

My ever-increasing hatred for Richard knew no bounds. Once I was out of this marriage, I would never again allow another man to get close to me. The indignity of living with his infidelities had been bad enough, but his threat to take my son from me was an absolute declaration of war. Richard would *not* buy Dustin as though he were some material possession.

The house was big enough for us to avoid one another, except when we passed in the hallway. Most of the time I retreated into the sanctuary of my Walkman and pretended he was invisible. Richard and I communicated only through our lawyers now. Ron Litz, my attorney, was less than pleased with my latest outburst.

"Okay, Georgia," he said, "you've really done it this time. Now you're going to have to see a psychiatrist. We'll have to prove somehow you were under an exceptional amount of stress."

"Stress? Living under these conditions isn't stress—it's insanity!" I shrieked.

"After this episode, I tend to agree with you."

Life was stressful, but Georgia Black knew *exactly* what she was doing. All I wanted was to be happy. All Black wanted was revenge. But for now, I'd have to go along with the program.

Ron looked perplexed and shook his head. "What ever possessed you to do that?"

Black had possessed me, but he wouldn't understand.

"I wanted to kill him," Black answered out loud.

His eyes widened and he slowly let out a deep breath. "You're not making my job very easy. Do you think you can refrain from that kind of behavior?" he asked.

"I'll try, Ron, but I'm telling you right now, he's *not* getting my son. He thinks his money can buy anything. I'll kill him first."

My first session with the shrink consisted of taking a four-hour written personality evaluation test. A week after taking the test, I left to do a national Jeep commercial in Jackson Hole, Wyoming. After a long day of white-knuckled filming, I returned to my hotel room for some well-deserved rest. My message light was flashing when I arrived. The psychiatrist wanted me to call him at home immediately upon my return.

"What's up, Doc?"

"I just want to be sure you are going to keep your appointment next Thursday," he said in his heavy French accent.

"Yes, I have every intention of keeping my appointment. You called me just for that?"

"Well, yes, I have your test results back and we must speak."

"What's the problem, Doc?"

"We will discuss it on Thursday when you come in. I just

wanted to be sure you plan to be there."

"Well...okay. I'll see you on Thursday."

I was too tired to dwell on it. I washed my face and climbed into bed. Four o'clock in the morning came too soon to stay up and wonder. I'd find out on Thursday. I couldn't let my personal problems interfere with my job. I had four passengers riding with me in the picture car. One wrong move could mean disaster. The intensity of my work had gotten me through many painful times. I couldn't afford to think.

The next morning I arrived on location at the usual time for car commercials—before sunrise. We needed to reshoot some of the previous day's footage. Evidently, my passengers didn't look as though they were having too much fun. The look of terror was frozen in their expressions in full camera view.

"What can you do to try and make them more comfortable, Georgia?" asked the director, Dennis Gripentrog, while we stood by the catering truck sipping our first cup of coffee in the morning darkness.

"Why don't you hide the ambulance? That's an intimidating sight for them. These kids aren't stunt people. I think I remember suggesting to you before we left that we should hire professionals to be in the car. What do you expect when you stop ordinary people on the street and ask them if they want to be in a car commercial? Did anyone ever explain to them what they'd be doing?"

"They didn't have it in the budget to fly in four additional stunt people and pay them all residuals. The agency demanded we find local people."

"You mean to tell me these kids are working for just a day rate?" I questioned.

Dennis shrugged. "I guess so. I'm not involved with talent payment. That's not my department."

"Well, look what it's costing them now," I pointed out. "We lost a whole day yesterday. What it costs to reshoot everything would more than cover the cost of bringing in pros. And, at this rate, we still may not get the shot," I said crisply.

"Tell that to the bean counters in Detroit. Just do what you can to get them relaxed. We've got fifteen minutes before the sun comes up."

"Great."

The set designer had built these giant letters spelling out the words WAGONEER and CHEROKEE, the names of the vehicles we were featuring in the commercials. The letters were made mostly from chicken wire, covered with a material that looked amazingly like rock, matching our background setting of the real Grand Teton Mountains. They stood 20 feet high and 70 feet in length. The shot was to drive over the top of the letters in the vehicle with the same name. The surface on top wasn't flat, but indented with the natural curve of the letters and topped with various sizes of gravel, which created the hazard of slipping and sliding. The letters appeared as though cut out of the mountain. It all looked great. But my job would be a bitch.

I had gone over the specs with the designer before the sets were built and explained my requirements for a safe execution. He made a mistake in his calculations and left me with only four inches of solid ground on each side of the tires. It was workable, but didn't provide much leeway for error. With professional stunt people in the vehicle, we could've had the shot in two takes. With every take, the risk factor became greater. We had the long-shot in the can, but we needed the close-up to complete the commercial.

The fact that I was a woman made my passengers nervous. Their lives were literally in my hands. Just driving up the ramp onto the letters was scary enough for them. This was also a first for me. I hadn't driven up a ramp this size before. Of course, *they* weren't aware of that, and neither was the production company.

But I had no fears about doing it. The feeling is like being on a roller coaster—my only view the sky—with no visual reference points. I was driving totally blind, being guided only by feel and a lot of guts. To make it worse, the ramp was curved, rather than a straight shot to the top. There was absolutely no way to know where the curve started except by instinct. I not only needed to execute this with speed, but with the correct amount of it. Driving blind, I could only pray that when I came charging off the ramp and onto the letters, I was on my mark.

To top it off, my vision was restricted by the camera mounted on the hood of the Jeep. In addition, the windshield was covered with a translucent material. Its purpose was to shield the sun in order to properly light our faces from the cumbersome rigging inside. The amount of space to see out from at the base of the windshield was less than two inches.

The Wagoneer letters were the toughest. The spaces on top of the "W" were too wide. I had to have enough speed to get over it without the wheels getting stuck. That speed caused the Jeep to be airborne for an instant. When the tires made contact again, the vehicle naturally jutted from side to side, which made that four-inch margin critical.

Concentrating on all this was tough enough; now I was also expected to get these people to smile and refrain from clutching the seats. I gave them a little pep talk and got prepared for our first run of the morning.

"Action, Georgia," said the assistant director.

"You guys ready?"

"As ready as we're gonna be," answered my passenger in the front seat. His eyes instantly sprang open as I began to accelerate.

"Okay, here we go. Smile and act like you're having the time of your life."

I also had to think about my own on-camera face. Concentrating and smiling wasn't exactly easy. My personal problems never entered my mind. When I worked, my real life was a blank. I was in the moment. What a great escape.

"Back to one, Georgia, we'll go again."

We did it again.

"Stop here for a reload, Georgia, and go back to one. We'll shoot it again."

"Again?" asked one of the passengers.

"Hey," I answered, "it's up to you guys how many times we do this. You must not be smiling or something. I've been keeping the rubber side down, so I know it's not me."

We did it again.

"Ah, Georgia, could you get out of the vehicle and come up to us? The director would like to speak with you. Over."

"Ten-four. Be right there, Gary."

At the video monitor, the director and the ad agency guys stood in a huddle. They moved aside, making room for me to look at the playback.

"See the one in the back? Now watch him in the next take. His lips are curled upward, but look at those eyes! Did you ever see such fright? Fast forward to the third take, Rick. Okay, now look. The guy in the back looks more relaxed, but the guy in the front is looking out over the edge. What can we do?" Dennis asked frustrated, like I had some magic formula.

"Let's show them the video," I suggested. "If they see it for themselves they'll be more aware."

After the local talent viewed the video, Dennis gave them some direction, trying to keep his composure as he spoke. Dennis was not known for his patience in dealing with incompetence. Financially, he also had a lot riding on this commercial. The commercial had to be shot and edited and ready for airing by the following week. To breach his responsibility would be disastrous for his reputation and for securing of any future work from the Jeep clients.

We returned to the vehicle, buckled ourselves in, and headed for our number one position.

"Listen you guys," I said to my passengers, "I'm going to let you in on a little secret. Did you see how visible you were on camera?"

"Yeah. We didn't think they were going to see us in the car."

"They probably didn't think that you'd be as recognizable as you are either, but now that you are, do you have any idea what that means to you? You'll be upgraded to principals."

"We're going to be famous!" they replied gleefully.

"Not only that, but this will earn you about forty grand. Around here, you could probably buy a house with that kind of money."

They were dumbfounded.

"Well, I'm estimating of course, but from what I've heard, they're cutting this into several spots and they plan on running the hell out of them for an extended period of time."

"What does that mean?"

"It means that every time they show this on television, you'll get a residual check in the mail. From my experience, I'd calculate that to be around forty thousand in a year's time."

The excitement on their faces was what we needed when the camera rolled.

"But it probably won't happen," I added for effect.

"Why not?" they all asked together.

"We're running out of time. If we don't get this shot in the next few takes they'll have to scratch it. We have four more setups to do before we lose the light today. It's not in the budget to add another day onto the schedule. The only way to do it is for all of you to look happy. If any one of you looks scared, they can't use the shot."

That did it. Money *can* buy smiles. We got the shot in the next take. We did it twice more, just for a variation to give the client a choice. Dennis was ecstatic.

"What'd you say to them?" he quizzed.

"Nothing," I answered innocently. "I thought you directed them brilliantly. But I did tell them if they didn't get it right, I was going to show them what it felt like to land head first in the dirt in a brand new Jeep!"

Dennis chuckled. After a total of twenty-seven takes in two days, the passengers were released and we finally moved on to the next shot.

We finished the shoot on Saturday and had the traditional wrap party that night. Sunday morning we traveled back to L.A., where my personal dilemmas waited. By Thursday, the spot was on the air. I caught it just as I was leaving for my appointment with the psychiatrist. To the viewing audience it looked so simple. The five of us driving along, laughing casually as we bounced over the letters. It took only three seconds to show that scene. A smile crossed my face. *If they only knew.* Running late for my appointment, I flipped off the television and hurried out the door, anxious to find out what was so important about not missing this session.

———◆———

He sat behind his desk smoking a pipe. I waited for him to speak, but he just kept staring at me. He pulled at his hairy chin with his free hand, searching his brain for the right words to begin.

"Well?" I asked impatiently.

After a few more moments of nerve-racking silence, he finally spoke. "I must tell you...I've been a psychiatrist for over twenty years. I have given this test to all of my patients. This is the first time I have ever gotten results back like this," he said, still studying my face.

"Well, what did it say?" I asked with growing frustration.

"First, let me explain. This is an extremely accurate test that places people in categories according to the way questions are answered."

"Yeah, so?"

"You do not fall into any of these categories."

"So what you're saying is...I don't have a category? That's it?"

"That is correct."

"Well, hell, Doc, I could have told you that!"

"The people in Minnesota are very confused by this. They would like to fly you out there, at their expense, of course, to further test you."

Don't even think about it, White. That's exactly the ammunition he'll need to get Dustin from you. Just be glad that the test results are too inconclusive to do him any good.

"I'm sorry if I messed up their perfect testing. I guess they have some work to do. Sounds like there's a category they overlooked. There must be. I'd sure hate to go through life without a category."

"Are you saying you won't go to Minnesota?"

"That's what I'm saying. I don't have time for this. I really didn't want to come here to begin with. I'll let you in on a little secret though—I *know* I'm a little outside the dots. It's the people who don't have a clue that you have to worry about. You can rest assured, Doc—I'll let him live."

Back to the drawing board. There were only thirty more days before I was to be the proud owner of my very own home, but details of the divorce needed to be worked out.

"I don't want to go to court, Ron," I said to my lawyer. "I just want to get on with my life."

"Do you realize what you're giving up? What about child support? I can get you thousands a month. I can't believe you're going to settle for $250 a month per child. That's ludicrous."

"It is, but going to court isn't worth the mental toll it will take on me. Richard has agreed to split custody. If I took him to court, I wouldn't have a chance against his millions and I'd risk losing my son in the end."

"But the judge will laugh him out of court with that kind of an offer," he persisted. "Georgia, stop and think about this for a minute. He's adopted Toni; you've had a son together. The judge is going to consider the style in which you're all accustomed to living. There is no way you'll ever have to work again with the kind of money that will be awarded to you, especially after you tell the court about his drug habit and the hookers."

He just wasn't getting it. If I didn't accept Richard's offer and I took him to court, I'd come out a loser. I'd seen firsthand what money could buy, and I wasn't about to lose my son.

"Ron, why are you arguing with me? It's settled."

"I'm your lawyer, that's why. It's my job to do the best I can for you and make you aware of exactly what you're entitled to."

"Okay, so you've informed me. Now draw up the papers the way I asked you to."

He threw his hands in the air and stood up. "Okay," he said, "but I'm going to have to make you sign a paper for me, too."

"What kind of a paper?"

"One that states that I tried to talk you out of this, so a few years down the road when you realize what a mistake you made, you can't come back and sue me for malpractice."

"Sure, I'll sign it."

"You're one of a kind, Georgia. I've never met anyone like you before. You're in a category all your own," he said, shaking his head.

"Yeah, someone told me that."

Dustin's third birthday, August 12, 1983, would be my last day at the house. Joe's brother Ronny and his wife Ninfa were visiting Joe in Solana Beach. I was a little concerned about the move going smoothly, so they came up, spent the night, and helped me move out the next day. Having my ex-husband's brother stay overnight at my soon to be ex-husband's house felt strange. But I'd been known to do stranger things.

There wasn't a lot to move. All I had were my clothes and the few things I'd brought into the marriage. I could have kicked myself for selling Jim Alquist back his stereo—at half the price he sold it to me. But who would have thought I'd ever need it, having married the appliance king of Los Angeles? Furnishing a new home from scratch, along with the extensive remodeling that had to be done, put a new stereo at the bottom of my priority list.

I was taking the pictures off the wall in the long hallway when Richard came out of the bedroom.

"I've decided I'm going to give you the car," he said, as if making a big sacrifice.

"That's really big of you, Richard, since I've got ten thousand of my own money in it."

"Yeah, well, I'll finish paying it off, but you better take care of it. It'll be the last nice car you'll own."

I laughed out loud. "You don't know me very well, do you, Richard? Do you really think it's downhill for me from here? I've always taken care of myself. I don't need you. I never did. If I want a new car every year, I'll have it. Don't underestimate me, Richard, it's not good for your heart."

"Just make sure you take all the pictures you're in," he said tartly as he proceeded to walk toward the breakfast room.

He came back an hour later and saw all the pictures stacked

up on the floor. Quite a sight looking down that long hallway with nails sticking out of the wall, stretching the entire length of both sides of the hall.

"You're taking all the pictures!" he gasped, staring at the bare walls—except for the one 8 x 10 photograph of him standing next to one of his expensive exotic cars.

"Well, you said to take all the ones I was in. You know something, Richard? This wall sort of tells the story of your life. You have your beautiful cars, your beautiful homes, your boats, your horses, and all your other toys, but like this wall, your life is empty."

Those were my final words...and I walked out of his life.

Chapter Fourteen

———◦———◉———◦———

I gained a lot from my marriage to Richard. The time I spent wasn't completely wasted. I had been released from all the confusion and fear that had once imprisoned me. During our courtship and through the first nine months of our marriage, before everything fell apart, I gained strength in the discovery of who I really was.

There is a lesson to be learned from every aspect of our lives. With Richard, all my attributes were acknowledged, helping me to build my previously crippled self-esteem. All of my husbands contributed to the totality of who I am. With Joe, I learned to be a survivor. With Tom? I guess I walked away knowing what I *didn't* want from life. I took what I had learned from my experiences and tried to carry the knowledge forward.

Looking ahead with excited anticipation, I began to follow the light. The tranquility of the world had always appeared distant. Now I was touching it, embracing it, determined to defy life's hidden hazards.

———◦———

Thank God for Darlene, my ex-sister-in-law. She moved into the house with me shortly after I bought it. Our friendship was the only thing that survived our marriage to brothers. We had bonded long ago, united by our grief. It was so good to have a friend close by who knew my history so intimately. With Darlene, I had an outlet to confide my innermost thoughts without fear of my words showing up in the gossip section of the *Hollywood Reporter*. I'd spent the last year in seclusion, remodeling my house. Having Dar to fill the gap, I didn't feel so cut off from the rest of the world. Adjusting to the sudden change in lifestyle was difficult.

Toni had an even tougher time. Her world fell apart, through no fault of her own. She blamed me silently, but her actions validated that she held me responsible. She became rebellious—not so unusual at fourteen—but our history revealed that her self-destruction had far more depth. Dustin really didn't notice the difference; he was still a baby. Toni continued attending Beverly Hills High School. At least that part of her life wasn't disrupted, but getting her over Coldwater Canyon in rush-hour traffic took us nearly an hour. The traffic moved faster in the covered wagon days. We were both frustrated.

I exhausted myself trying to provide my children with the kind of home and lifestyle to which they were accustomed. Now, more than ever, I was relentless in striving to make it on my own. The experiences with the men who occupied the pages of my life fueled my determination to rise above them. The time had come to cast my own shadow. No more illusions of a knight in shining armor. Having had a taste of life on a higher plane, I refused, for myself and for my children, to live any other way. Only *I* could make it happen.

Where there's a will...

<hr />

The Tippler bar was crowded by four o'clock in the afternoon. Most of the skiers were already down the mountain, checking out what dinner dates or parties were in store for the evening. Aspen was becoming an annual trip for me at Christmas time. I had spent my first Christmas here the year before, in celebration of my divorce from Richard. But now, almost a year and a half later, I was finally beginning to emerge from the unhappy places where I had spent most of my life.

Five girls crammed into a one-bedroom condo. The skiing was great, but the party was the attraction. The winter of 1984 was the year they had to truck ice cubes in from Denver. The party was nonstop.

The millionaires and the movie stars vied for the title of "best party of the year." Who could have the best band, food, and beautiful people? Who had the most outrageously beautiful home with the best view? They constantly tried to outdo each other. The parties were the most lavish in the world.

I slid through those open doors as if I'd been there all my life—except that life had changed in the years I had spent in the dark. Drugs now ran rampant, as well as the decline in sexual morals. Shielded by my marriages, I now had a new set of dilemmas to encounter. I wasn't totally naive about what was going on, but didn't have to deal with it personally.

The single life was not compatible with my personal values. My biggest challenge was making a dinner date and figuring out how *not* to be dessert. I was extremely friendly, but aloof. I kept my personal life private—something I had learned to do when I was married to Joe. It just came naturally now.

I was not conscious of all that I was at that time, partly because my protective walls were so impenetrable. Anyone inching close to me had to deal with Georgia Black first. No one was allowed to cross the threshold of my heart. She left nothing to chance. But I was slowly regaining the spirit misplaced so long ago. Life was again becoming an adventure.

After spotting Darlene and my girlfriends at the bar, laughing with some rather good-looking men, I left my window table to join them. Pushing my way through the crowded lounge, I heard my name being called. Searching over the sea of heads, I spotted a tall, slim woman waving a gloved hand in the air. As I got closer, I recognized her: Darrien Earle.

"Hi, Darrien," I said, joining her table. "How've you been?"

"Great. This year's skiing couldn't be better, or maybe it just seems better when you're in love," she said, looking admiringly over at her male companion. "Honey, this is Georgia Durante, and this is Dennis Krieger."

"Nice to meet you, Dennis," I said, extending my hand. I was not as impressed as Darrien seemed to be. "Do you have a daughter named Jennifer who goes to Beverly Hills High?" I asked.

"I do," he answered with a warm smile.

"I thought the name Krieger sounded familiar. Our daughters are classmates."

"Are you the same Georgia who's a friend of Ann Feldner?" Dennis asked, trying to connect where he'd heard my name before.

"That's me. How do you know Ann?"

"I met her at the Bistro Garden in Beverly Hills about a month ago," he explained. "She told me about your adventures in New York City. I can see how you two would be trouble out on the loose."

I smiled. Darrien didn't.

"We're skiing Snowmass tomorrow. I reserved a table at Krabloonik's at one o'clock. Why don't you join us?" Dennis offered.

Sensing his interest, I refrained from intruding on my friend's interlude. "No, thanks. I know how that is. I want to ski, and I don't think I'll make it back on the slopes once I settle in there with a few bottles of wine. But I'll try catching up with you guys before the week is over."

The week flew by. It had been another memorable ski trip, but the time had come to leave and to face the realities of life once more. I was home about a week when my phone rang.

"Hi, Georgia, it's Ann."

"Ann Feldner, what have you been up to, girlfriend?"

"Just checking out the L.A. scene."

"I'll say you have. New York has taught you well. I ran into an acquaintance of yours in Aspen. You don't waste any time, do you?"

"That's why I'm calling you. Dennis called me after he got back. He wants to know if he can have your number."

"Absolutely not. What is it with these guys? He's dating a friend of mine."

"Well, it looks like that relationship is winding down. He thought you were something else. He's called three times already to ask if I've talked to you yet."

"Ann, if they're truly breaking up, tell him to do it before he goes out with other women. I hate that."

"So, can I give him your number?"

"No!"

Three weeks passed before I heard from Ann again.

"Hi, Georgia, how was your trip?"

"Which one?"

"To Detroit. Didn't you say you were going back there on your annual PR trip with the advertising agencies?"

"Oh, it worked out fine. I managed to be in the right place at the right time and landed a job for Jeep. I just got back from a five-day shoot in Lake Tahoe."

"Great, that should help recoup your expenses from the Aspen trip."

"It certainly helps."

"Georgia, Dennis has been calling—he's not giving up. He broke up with Darrien. Why don't you just have lunch with him?"

"Ann, he's not my type."

"You and I are supposed to have lunch, so what if Dennis just comes along?" she persisted.

"Since when have you become cupid, Ann?"

"Since I can't get Dennis off my back. I'm his only connection to you. How's Wednesday at the Bistro Garden?"

Ann wasn't taking no for an answer. I reluctantly agreed.

———◆———

Wednesday just happened to be Valentine's Day. As I was getting dressed for our lunch, the doorbell rang. Dennis had sent two dozen long-stemmed red roses. What is it about receiving flowers that opens the door to a woman's heart?

When I arrived at the restaurant, Dennis and Ann were already seated on the patio. I loved the Bistro Garden. The women, as well as the men, were always so elegantly dressed. I was a people-watcher from way back, and the Bistro was an exceptional treat for my eyes. Seated under the umbrella-tables and listening to piano music on a warm sunny day was a wonderful way to pass an afternoon. It was *not* the place to come for lunch if in a hurry. I always wondered what all these people did for a living that they could linger so long over a glass of wine in the middle of a workday.

Ann greeted me as she held her drink with both hands, toying suggestively with the stem of her glass. I wondered why Dennis was not attracted to her. Ann possessed an irresistible, wild sort of charm. Untamed and unattainable.

Dennis stood and pulled out my chair, bumping into the woman behind him as he did. The lady turned and gave him a thin-lipped, uptight, rich-woman-being-gracious smile. He politely apologized and turned his attention back to me, immediately seizing me with his charm.

No question, Dennis was a decent man. He was known for his cutting wit, and I found myself drawn to his sense of humor. He was an investment banker and looked the part. He wasn't at all the kind of man to whom I was usually attracted. Not that he wasn't a good-looking guy—he was—but not the kind of good-looking that made my head turn. Physically, Dennis was as American as you can get, complete with the stuffy banker look. His light brown hair was cut short, but it suited him.

I found myself captured by his magic, of which he had an abundance. What I really loved was his outgoing personality, a contradiction to his banker appearance. His dress was understated, yet he still perpetuated wealth. Dennis was so full of life, he obviously would not allow a day to go by without enjoying it to the fullest. It was a quality I sought. At the hub of the Bistro Garden crowd, his presence drew people to him like bees were drawn to honey. People approached our table in a steady succession all throughout our lunch.

Pleasantly impressed, I accepted a date with him. Despite my reservations about Darrien, the fact remained that they had completely broken up. I had been divorced for almost two years, and this was the most charming man I'd met in ages. I couldn't believe how differently I felt from my first impression of him.

We could not have been more different. My friends were all

in advertising or the movie industry. And, of course, my friends in the stunt business were in a category all their own. His friends were all wealthy business tycoons. Our dates usually consisted of dinners with business associates and black-tie functions. If we continued to date, I had a lot of shopping to do. Where he got all of his energy was mystery. He ran circles around me, and I was ten years younger.

Dennis always had a phone glued to his ear. He was constantly making deals. He had a home in Palm Springs, but the difficulty was in finding the time between our busy schedules to take advantage of weekend retreats. His business day spilled into our evenings together, but that didn't stop him from celebrating life. Lunch at the Bistro Garden became a Friday afternoon ritual.

This man needed a woman who could blend in with his lifestyle. To my amazement, I slipped into his world with ease. Previously avoiding relationships, I had consumed myself with work. But Dennis was changing all that. He was becoming a priority, with surprisingly no effort on my part. The very thought that I was falling in love intrigued me. My Shadow endeavored to sabotage my relationship with Dennis, but those efforts were met with defeat. Dennis and I were good together. The essence of our relationship was laughter.

I never expected to fall in love with Dennis. I was appeasing a friend by having an innocent lunch. I had never dated a friend's ex-boyfriend before. Guilt about Darrien stabbed me because I knew she was still in love with Dennis, and he felt guilty, too.

Through my persistence, I made him call her and take her to lunch, hoping it would heal both their wounds. Darrien began to work on Dennis, using his guilt as her weapon. Georgia Black sensed trouble brewing and began to make a move, but not without a fight from Georgia White. I could not remember the last time I had felt this way and was reluctant to let go so easily.

Darrien was a social butterfly. She needed to be with a man who could bring her social status. In the end, she wound up exactly where she strove to be. She married Lee Iacocca. Life with him gave her all that she required.

On a hot Sunday in July, about a week before Dennis left for Florida on a business trip, we spent the day at the Jonathan Club, a private beach club in Santa Monica. Sitting under an umbrella on the sand, we watched the surf, both deep inside our own private thoughts. Dennis looked relaxed for a change. For once, a phone was not growing out of his ear.

Breaking the silence, Dennis said, "Whenever I fly, I always think about that flight I canceled at the last minute. The plane crashed, and I never quite got over the fact that I was supposed to be on it."

"I know the feeling—that happened to me, too."

"Really? What happened?"

"I flew to New York to shoot a magazine ad for More cigarettes. I called my mother when I got there. When she found out I was in New York, she insisted I come to Rochester to see her. I was anxious to get back, but my mother was really hurt that I could be so close and not stop to see her. I finally agreed. I told her I'd call her back and let her know what flight I would be on. Since I was no longer in a rush to catch my flight, I called some friends in the city and met them for lunch. I did a little shopping, then caught a cab to the airport. Unbeknownst to me, my connecting flight back to Los Angeles had crashed on take-off in Chicago—"

"Chicago! Was it American Airlines, flight 191?"

"Yes, it was. The one that lost the engine—I think it was in '79 or '80."

"This is incredible! That's the same flight *I* was supposed to be on!" he exclaimed.

"You're kidding! What are the chances of that? We didn't even know each other then, and we were both supposed to die on the same flight. I wonder what that means?"

Maybe I'm wrong. Maybe God has a hand in this...Nah, I don't think so. Let's not get carried away.

Astonished, he replied, "This is unbelievable!"

We continued talking as we dragged out beach chairs into the sun. "What's really strange is what happened when I got to the airport. I was standing in line to purchase my ticket. I hadn't yet called my mother to give her the flight information. The agent behind the counter was on the telephone, and I heard him say my name, so I stepped out of line and walked up to him. I told him who I was and he handed me the phone. I was confused. I couldn't imagine who'd be looking for me. It was my mother! When she heard my voice she got hysterical. She had heard about the crash and hadn't heard from me yet. She thought that I had decided to go back to L.A. without stopping in Rochester. She found me! Can you believe it?"

"That's really amazing," Dennis said, shaking his head.

Neither of us could get over the coincidence. We baked in the blistering sun and talked for a few more hours.

"Have you had enough sun?" he asked, patting the glistening beads of sweat on his face with the edge of his towel.

"I'm ready if you are," I answered, rising lazily from the comfortable beach chair.

"I have a surprise for you," he said mischievously.

"Oh...Can I wear it?"

"No."

"Can I eat it?"

"No."

"Well, tell me."

"It won't be a surprise then, will it?"

"I hate it when you do this, Dennis. Tell me!" I demanded.

"You'll find out in about fifteen minutes," he said, smiling coyly.

We drove down Pacific Coast Highway to Sunset Boulevard. As we zipped up the winding road, I remember feeling so happy and carefree. The warm summer wind blew through my hair as we drove. The salty air and the smell of suntan lotion filled my nostrils. The anticipation of the surprise churned within me. I never knew what Dennis had up his sleeve; he was always full of wonderful surprises. He turned onto Stone Canyon Road in Bel-Air.

"Where are we going, Dennis? I can't take the suspense!"

He looked over at me with a big grin and continued driving without a word. Then he turned into a large circular driveway.

"This is a beautiful house. Whose is it?" I questioned, looking over at him with wonder.

"Mine."

"What?" I exclaimed, snapping my head back toward the house and taking a longer look. It reminded me of a slightly smaller version of a stately European palace.

"Yep, I put an offer in on it last week, and they accepted. It's in escrow," he said proudly, admiring the property.

"You're kidding! This has to be a $4 million house."

"You're right, but it was a steal."

"Dennis, this is an incredible house. No, this isn't a house, this is a mansion!"

"Wait till you see the inside," he said excitedly, grabbing my hand and leading me to the front door.

As we walked from room to room, I was open-mouthed. It was breathtaking.

"What do you think we can do with this room?" he asked, gesturing toward the vast space.

We? What is he saying?

"This would make a great exercise room," I replied, recovering. "I'd mirror all these walls and put hunter-green carpet in here. There's certainly enough light to carry it."

"I like that idea," he said, eyeing the room, imagining what it would look like with the changes.

Still awestruck, I said, "I can't believe you bought this house."

"I couldn't pass up the deal."

My creative side was bursting with excitement. My mind was running wild with what I could do with this place. I stood at the large picture window and looked out at the expansive grounds. "I hope you realize your friends are going to be living here because of that tennis court."

"That's what it's there for, to enjoy."

"Does this mean I have to learn to play tennis?" I asked.

"I think you should. You'd really like it. With your athletic ability, I'm surprised you don't play."

"I did play at one time...with my ex-husband Joe. But playing with him gave me a bad taste for the game. I was never good enough for him," I said, reflecting momentarily.

"I'll get you a private instructor when you're ready."

"Do I get to choose him?"

"Have you got someone in mind?"

"Yes...about 6'2", evenly tanned, thick dark hair, gorgeous blue eyes—"

"*I'll* choose the instructor," he said, pulling me passionately into his strong arms. Neither of us wanted to say it out loud, but Dennis had clearly bought this house with the idea of living in it with me.

Back off, White! This can't work. You know whenever it's too good to be true, it usually is.

But this one's different!

What about Richard? He was different too—or so you thought.

We walked out to the back of the house to admire the landscaping. I struggled to wipe the negative thoughts from my mind. Georgia Black was beginning to annoy me.

I recognized the house next door. "See that house over there?" I said, pointing out the property next to his. "That's James Caan's house. His backyard is unbelievable."

"How do you know him?" Dennis inquired.

"He's a good friend of a friend of mine. You should try to get his landscape person to work on this place. He has a stream with beautiful waterfalls and bridges that run all through the property. It feels more like a park than a backyard. You could do something like that here—although the tennis court kind of takes up a lot of space," I said, eyeing the layout more closely.

Dennis's relaxed face became serious. With an arched brow he said, "Don't get any wild ideas about taking it out."

I laughed. "I think I can find enough here to keep me busy for awhile without ripping out the tennis court."

"Are you going to have time for all this?" he asked as we walked along the side to the front of the house.

"You got the money, honey, I got the time," I answered with a playful smile as he opened my car door.

We chatted as we drove to Beverly Hills to pick up my son.

"Isn't it funny how just seven months ago we didn't even know each other and our lives were running parallel," Dennis said.

"What do you mean?"

"Well the plane thing for one, and our daughters being friends. Don't you think that's quite a coincidence?"

"As strange as it may be, it's almost normal for me."

"How is Toni anyway?"

"Her grades are dropping and her attitude is getting out of hand. I don't know what to do with her lately."

"Jennifer tells me she's been hanging around with some kids who are a little rough around the edges. You'd better keep a close eye on her."

Toni was a handful with both eyes open.

While we drove in silence, I thought about the merger Dennis had just precipitated. I'd bought the stock the day it became available to the public. He was one of two principals in the company. This was a pivotal move in Dennis's career. It was his baby. Years of work went into ironing out the intricate details of the merger. This venture would make him wealthy beyond belief, but his pride was the more valued commodity. Dennis had come from a wealthy oil family, but he had made his own fortune. Money was never his God—*making* it was.

Everything Dennis touched seemed to turn to gold. He was brilliant in his field. Taking his advice, I invested every cent I had in the stock. But doing so cleaned out my savings account and left me with no backup. The memory of the days when I first arrived in L.A. created an obsession with seeking and attaining financial security. That fear served as my incentive never to return to that place in time.

"Dennis, how soon do you think it will be before the stock goes up?"

"It went up a quarter of a point every day last week. It's moving nicely. Are you worried?"

"No. I just want to be able to sell some if I should need to, preferably at a profit, so I can have a cash flow."

"Do you need money?"

"No, I was just asking a question."

"Are you sure?" he asked, looking at me skeptically.

"Yes, I'm sure," I answered reassuringly.

"If you need anything, I hope you'll tell me. As far as the stock is concerned, try to hang on to everything you've got. You're going to come out of that a very big winner."

"You really think so?" I asked.

"I know so. I got the inside scoop, remember?"

———◆———

After spending a delightful day with Dennis on Sunday, I started out my week in a pleasant mood.

"Mommy, take me to the arcade. Please, please, please," Dustin begged.

"Your dad always takes you to the arcade. Don't you ever get tired of it?"

"No, I wanna go to the arcade."

"Why don't we take our bikes to the park?"

"No, I hate the bike at your house. The one at my dad's is better. Can we go get it?"

"No, Dusty. I'm tired of driving up and down that hill every time you want a special toy. There's nothing wrong with this bike."

"The one my dad bought is better. I want that one or I don't want to go," he whined, crossing his arms in a determined fashion.

"Well, I guess we don't go then. You can't always have what you want when you want it," I replied, holding firm.

I hated having to be the bad guy, especially with the short

time I had to spend with my son, but Richard obviously never said no. If I didn't destroy this facade of life as Dustin knew it, he'd never have a chance of surviving in the real world.

"Why not? Daddy gives me everything I want," he persisted.

"Yes...and you're really getting spoiled, too. Why don't you call your friend Mark and you boys can help me make chocolate chip cookies. Won't that be fun?"

"Yeah..." he answered, giving up any hope of getting his way.

After cleaning up the mess in the kitchen, Dustin and Mark went outside to play in the tree house. When Frankie had visited a few months earlier, I was in the process of having a deck built. He paid the workers on the sly and surprised us by having the tree house built.

"Every kid should have a tree house," he said, reflecting on his less fortunate childhood.

Frankie secretly got more pleasure from the tree house than the kids did. They'd all stay up there for hours. I'd have to bring up their lunch when they couldn't stop playing long enough to come down to eat. When Frankie played, he really got into it. He always had to be the Indian so he could paint his face. Such a big kid. He cracked me up. The thought of him made me smile.

With the kids busy at play, I sat alone in my kitchen, enjoying the temporary silence. A shaft of sunlight streamed through the skylight, trapping slow convections of dust. The shrill ring of my telephone disturbed the calmness of the moment.

"Hello, Miss Durante?

"Yes?" I answered, setting my coffee on the counter.

"This is Mrs. Louis from the Beverly Hills High School."

"Is Toni all right?" I asked, feeling a sudden jolt of fear.

"Oh, yes. I'm just calling to inform you of Toni's absenteeism." I relaxed. "It has come to our attention that she's been cutting classes quite frequently over the past three months of school, and she didn't show up for summer school again today."

"Three months? Why haven't I been informed of this sooner? This is July!"

"Well, Miss Durante, this is a very large school. We have a lot of students here. It sometimes takes a while for the paperwork to catch up," she explained.

"Well, if the school can't be on top of that kind of a problem, then maybe it isn't the right school for my daughter," I replied, feeling let down by the school's laxness. "Do you know of an educational consultant I can speak with?"

"Why, yes, we have an excellent educational consultant we work with. Her name is Dr. Katherine Kendall. She's also an excellent therapist, if you should find you have a need for that service," she added.

"Are you suggesting that I might?" I asked, anxiously scribbling down the number.

"Well, more often than not, when children start this kind of behavior it's a good indication drugs are the cause. It might be wise to look into that possibility," she answered in a tone that confirmed my fears.

Dennis's warning about the friends with whom Toni was spending time came to mind and filled me with a dreadful foreboding.

"Thank you for your concern, Mrs. Louis," I said, feeling uneasy. "I'll give Dr. Kendall a call right now."

I set up an appointment for that afternoon. I took Dustin to Mark's house to stay for a few hours and left to meet with the therapist.

—◆—

I told Dr. Kendall about Toni's behavior over the past few months. Aside from the absenteeism I'd just learned about, and the uneasiness I felt about her new friends, her attitude towards me had been steadily deteriorating. She was hostile and rebellious, more so than the usual teenager. I knew the divorce was hard on Toni, but I'd always been able to reach out to her in the past. Lately my instincts told me that she was lying to me; she was sneaky and secretive about the smallest things. Besides, she was sleeping far longer than usual.

After discussing the situation for over an hour, Dr. Kendall finally said, "You know, Miss Durante, I can find a private school for Toni, but she'll most likely be expelled. When you finally admit to yourself that your daughter has a drug problem, then I can help you. From what you've told me, I'm convinced. I see these kids every day; it's the same pattern."

"What do you suggest?"

"First, let's get Toni in here and see if she can clean up her act on her own. If not, there are some good programs I can suggest that I've had very good success with. These programs require a big commitment on your part. You may get a call at three o'clock in the morning and be asked to get on the first plane to Montana. If you don't go, it won't work. The participation of the parents is an essential part of why these programs work. You'd be wasting a lot of money if you didn't live up to your commitment."

"How much does the one you have in mind cost?"

"It's $40,000 a year and they would like a two-year commitment," she answered casually, as though everybody had that much money just lying around.

"Forty thousand! What do people do if they don't have that kind of money?"

"They go to funerals," she answered simply.

She hit home with that statement. Where was I going to get that kind of money—and in a hurry? At that time in my life, I was struggling to keep my head above water with the exorbitant expenses that came with being a new homeowner. Every cent I made went into my house.

Shocked, I sat thinking, trying to come up with a solution. "Well...I guess I could sell my house," I said, feeling a knife-like jab in my heart. "Do they need to have all the money up front?"

"They'd like at least ten thousand before she arrives. I'm sure they can set up some kind of payment schedule for you, maybe five thousand or so a month, until it's paid up."

Dr. Kendall explained how the program worked. It was a wilderness survival program, sort of like Outward Bound. If Toni entered the program, she would arrive at the site in the wilds of Montana, and would immediately be sent on an eight-day "solo" journey. She would be in the woods, seemingly alone, although always followed by trained counselors. They would see her, but she wouldn't be able to see them. She would be expected to find her own food, sleep in the woods, and basically survive all alone.

After the eight-day solo, she would spend 21 days surviving in the wilderness with a group of other teens. Dr. Kendall reassured me that the counselors wouldn't let her starve to death, but it definitely wouldn't be a picnic. Drug abuse was a serious problem, and this was a serious solution. Once Toni made it through her solo and group journey, she would be housed with other teens in a rustic camp area. She'd have to partake in group therapy sessions as well as daily chores in a communal living environment.

At the suggestion of Dr. Kendall, I spoke with other parents who had children in the program and they raved about the results. I felt reassured that this was the right thing to do. We made an appointment for Toni the following day and I left with a migraine headache.

"Toni, your mom can't deal with you anymore," Dr. Kendall said, explaining the options to her. She would be given certain rules to follow; if she broke the rules, the consequence would be that she would have to leave home immediately and participate in the survival program. Dr. Kendall explained the program in full.

"Here is a list of things your mother would like you to adhere to in order to be able to stay at home," she continued. She went on to itemize them: hang up the phone when you are told, make your bed in the morning, pick up your dishes from the table and put them in the dishwasher, and so on. "These don't seem like tough demands. Do you think you can do this for the privilege of living at home?"

"Yes."

"Are you absolutely sure?"

Looking extremely bored, Toni rested her elbow on the armchair and chewed on a clump of her hair. Without looking up, she answered, "Yes, I'm sure." Her voice was low and even.

"Are you willing to sign your name to this and honor your word?"

"Yeah," she said, attempting a weak smile.

Dr. Kendall leaned over her desk and handed Toni a pen. Toni ran a hand through her wavy blonde hair, pulling it away from her thin face. She leaned forward and signed matter-of-factly, then slumped back in her chair as if to say, 'Okay, I played your silly little game. Can we go now?'

"How old are you, Toni?" Dr. Kendall asked.

"Fifteen," she answered, raising her Bambi eyes, now even more beautiful than when she was a child. Her eyes were dark, mysterious, and alluring. Like myself at her age, Toni looked older than she was. Unlike me, her Italian heritage was unmistakable. I looked like the girl next door; she possessed a stunning, exotic look. If she ever acquired my gutsy attitude, it would be a lethal combination. As it was, she had a wildness to her beauty that most older men were finding addicting. At fifteen, she kept me acutely on my guard.

"If you want to see your sixteenth birthday, you'd better wake up now, young lady," Dr. Kendall retorted. "If you break your promise on any of the above rules, you're out of here. Your mother is standing firm on this, so don't think for one minute you're going to slide by on this one. Do you understand what I'm saying?"

"Yes," Toni answered, rolling her eyes.

⸺◈⸺

By Friday, Toni had broken a rule. It was not a rule on the list, but it was certainly important enough to command attention.

Her bedroom was in the guesthouse, separate from the main structure. Dustin and I had fallen asleep on the couch while watching television. It was close to midnight when I woke up and carried him into his bedroom. For some reason, I decided to check on Toni.

Her light was on, so I walked over to the guesthouse. The door was locked. I knocked, but she didn't answer. I knocked harder—still no answer. I ran back to the main house, got the key, and let myself in. What I saw made me go cold inside. Toni was lying on the bed, sound asleep, with a lit cigarette between her fingers. It had been burning for a while, judging by the long curl of the ash. As if in slow motion, it rolled out of her hand and onto the bed at the precise moment I entered the room.

"Toni!" I screamed, scaring myself with the shrill pitch of my own voice. She didn't budge. "Toni!" I screamed again, trying to shake her awake.

She didn't move at all. I thought she was dead. I continued to shake her violently, screaming her name.

"Please, Toni, wake up! Please God, let her wake up!"

Toni began to moan and my heart's quickened pace began to slow. She mumbled something as she opened her glittering, stoned eyes. She was alive! She must have taken a downer of some kind. I forced her to her feet and made her walk. She responded satisfactorily. Thank God, she was going to be okay. What if I had not walked in when I did? She would've burned to death!

"You made a stand, Georgia, you have to stick by it," Dr. Kendall said firmly. "She has to know you mean business. You're going to learn firsthand the meaning of 'tough love.' I know it's not easy." Dr. Kendall hesitated. I could feel her trying to read me, wondering if I'd be able to withstand the heart-wrenching circumstances of the journey we were about to embark upon. "I'll call the school to make the arrangements and get the plane reservations. You'd better get busy shopping for the things she'll need," she instructed, handing me a list. "Plan on leaving tomorrow sometime. I'll call with your flight information as soon as I know it."

My mind raced wildly. This was so quick!

"Georgia... you're doing the right thing."

Chapter Fifteen

The reality of my daughter being out in the wilderness overwhelmed me. Was I really doing the right thing? My stomach did flip-flops. I had to trust that Dr. Kendall knew what she was talking about and that this was the best thing I could do for her. But it was so hard.

I dropped Dustin off at his father's house. The plane would not be leaving until five o'clock. Toni had no idea that she was going. We had made previous plans to go to a psychic fair that next morning. I stuck to the agenda, wanting to make her last day at home a good one to remember. At the fair, I accompanied Toni into the makeshift tent while she had her psychic reading.

The reader studied each of the Tarot cards as she slowly turned them over. She spent time with each one, going back to the first card each time. Finally, she raised her head and looked at Toni.

"Fire..." she said. "I see fire around you."

Hmm, this is interesting.

After a silent, creepy evaluation of Toni, she continued. "It's the kind of fire from an explosion—like a plane crashing or something. Are you planning a trip in the near future where you may be taking a plane?" the physic asked.

"No," Toni answered, unaware that she would be on a plane in less than six hours.

Oh, God. We've got to get on a plane now! Should I cancel?

Oh, come on, you don't really believe this stuff, do you?

We came home and I put our bags in the car without her noticing. As I was walking to the bedroom, I passed by the door that led to the backyard and saw a huge white owl perched on the pool ladder.

"Toni, look at this—quick!"

She ran from the living room and joined me at the window. "Wow, where did that come from, Mom? I thought owls only came out at night," Toni said, not able to take her attention from the extraordinary sight.

"They do."

"What's it doing here?"

"Darned if I know."

It was about two and a half feet tall and at least half of that wide. It was immense and completely white. I had never seen anything like it before.

"Mom, don't owls mean someone's going to die?"

"Well, that's what they say, if you choose to believe it," I answered, feeling uneasy. I wanted to shrug it off, but the reality was right in front of me. I couldn't ignore it.

"What's it doing out in the middle of the afternoon?"

"I don't know, Toni."

A fluttering in the pit of my stomach persisted. I didn't like the idea of flying after what the psychic had said, and now this. This was too weird. But I wasn't about to let superstitions run my life. We had to leave, and I wouldn't allow myself to find irrational reasons to back out. The phone rang, and I left Toni at the window, watching the owl in awe.

"So what's the deal?"

"I'm leaving for the airport in about an hour, Dennis," I answered, trying to keep my voice to a whisper.

"Does she know yet?"

"No, I'll tell her on the way."

"Are you okay?"

"Yeah, I'll get through it. I just hope she doesn't try to run away when she realizes where she's going."

"Call if you need me," he said. "I don't have to leave for Florida until Wednesday. Will you be back before then?"

"I don't know, I have no idea what it's going to be like until I get there. I want to hang around and check it out for myself. I'm not sure how long it will take for me to feel comfortable with it."

"Do you have a number?"

"No. From what I understand, they barely even have electricity. I'll try to call in at least once a day for my messages. Just call my service if you need to get in touch with me. I can be beeped."

"I think you'd better call me tonight, if you can. This place doesn't seem too...I don't know, it just sounds strange," he said.

"I'll try. Dennis, as soon as I get back I'll have to sell some stock. I need $10,000 within two weeks."

"Don't sell the stock. I'll lend you the money."

"What if the stock takes a dive and I can't pay you back? No, I'm selling the stock."

"It's not gonna take a dive. Will you stop worrying!"

"Dennis, I'm selling the stock," I insisted.

"Let's not talk about it now. We'll talk about it when I get back from Florida."

The trip to the airport was surprisingly uneventful. Toni seemed to expect what was coming and she went without a fight. I think she was at a point where even she realized she needed help. Despite reassurances from Dr. Kendall and the parents I had spoken with about the program, I was upset and uneasy about taking this step. I don't know if I could have held up and gone through with it if Toni had put up a major fight.

The plane landed in Spokane, Washington, where we proceeded to rent a car. The journey was far from over. We still had a three-hour drive ahead of us, not counting the time we spent getting lost. We drove through Idaho into Montana. It was not quite dark yet, and we enjoyed the beautiful landscape until night descended upon us. Misty clouds hung low over the expansive land. Lovely old farmhouses sprinkled the countryside. We hurried past, trying to make up for lost time.

The farther we traveled, the deeper into the backwoods we got. Soon, no more farm houses were visible. Darkness fell, and miles now spanned between us and civilization.

"I don't think you're going to run away from here, do you, Toni?" I said as we drove through the heavily wooded terrain. "There's nowhere to run for miles."

"I don't think so," she answered, looking out the window into the endless black forest.

"Toni, you need to understand something. This is not a form of punishment. I'm trying to help you. You can't seem to help yourself, or you don't want to."

"This isn't going to help. You're just wasting your money," she said, still staring blankly out the window.

"I'll take that chance," I responded. "Don't you want help with this problem?"

"I don't have a problem," she answered. "I don't know what you're making such a big deal about."

"You don't think you have a problem? What do you call almost burning yourself to death?"

"I just took some downers so I could sleep, that's all."

"Toni, what are you running from that you find yourself unable to sleep? Something's bothering you. Why can't you tell me what it is?"

She looked as though she wanted to talk, but had second thoughts. She turned her face to the window and stared out into the dense forest. Toni had an old soul. She carried a heaviness in her heart, too heavy for such a young person. My heart was heavy too, wanting to reach out to her, but not knowing how.

We saw a sign that read SPRING CREEK COMMUNITY. Toni began biting her nails as we turned onto the narrow dirt road leading to the log cabins that would become her home after her

28 day experience in the wilderness. Anticipation of the unknown danced on both of our faces.

A faint light glowed in the distance as we tentatively approached the trailer that served as the office. The trailer door swung open, revealing the silhouetted figure of a man. He held the door and stepped aside. He didn't look at all like the mountain man I expected to see, but more like a college professor. Too thin for his height, he stood tall and straight, wearing horn-rimmed glasses and a stern demeanor. But a gentle glint in his eyes told me that a soft, caring side of the man existed.

"Hi, Toni, my name is Steve Cawdry. I'm the headmaster here. You're safe," he said as he hugged her. "Go into the bathroom and wash that make-up off your face," he added firmly.

While Toni was in the bathroom, Steve introduced me to another man who appeared to be in his late twenties. After saying hello, he proceeded to go through Toni's luggage. He pulled out a few articles and stuffed them into a duffel bag. When Toni returned, her already large eyes grew twice the size.

"Kiss your mom good-bye," the headmaster instructed.

"Wait a minute. Can't she stay the night and leave in the morning?" I asked, beginning to feel panicky.

"No, she must leave tonight," Mr. Cawdry answered with authority.

Toni hugged me, fighting back tears, and followed the young man out the door. I watched as they disappeared into the blackness.

"I love you, Toni!" I shouted after her into the still night. Silence and the sound of crickets were the only replies.

I turned to Mr. Cawdry with uncertainty. Had I just led my young to the slaughter? He placed a gentle hand on my shoulder and asked me to sit down.

"What are your concerns, Miss Durante?" he asked softly.

"Did you see what my daughter looks like?"

"Yes, I saw a very mature-looking little girl."

"That's right, and she's going out in the wilderness with that young man—alone!"

"Let me tell you something, Miss Durante. We have over three hundred applicants per year seeking this position. Do you know how many we hire? Two. We check them out back to their grandmother's underwear. I can assure you, your daughter is safe."

"I'm sorry if I can't share your confidence. I'm just not comfortable with this. Why couldn't she leave in the morning?"

"We have our way of doing things here. That's what makes our success rate so high. There will be many things that will concern you about the way we run this program, but it works. That's what's important. We must have full rein with our decisions. Toni needs to stay separated from the rest of the school until she comes back from her 21 days with her group, which will be forming eight days from now. What she is doing right now is what we call a solo."

"What is the principle behind not giving them food for three weeks? Or, as I see it, in Toni's case, four weeks?"

"That's not altogether true. They have to learn to rely on themselves for survival. When they get hungry enough, they'll find ways to eat. They can spear a fish or trap a rabbit. But they have nothing with them for preparing a meal—no matches to start a fire, that kind of thing."

"How do they cook what they catch?"

"They have to use flint and rub two sticks together. If they aren't lucky enough to catch an animal, they end up eating ants, or lizards, or whatever they can find. They have none of the comforts of home. They use leaves for toilet paper. We have them hike uphill ten miles a day. At the end of the day when they are tired and vulnerable, they sit around the campfire and the therapists start pushing their buttons. It's amazing what they spill out after a grueling day in the woods. They have no sleeping bags, only a tarp to put on the ground."

"What if it rains?"

"Then it rains on them."

"What if they get sick, or break a leg?"

"The therapists are never out of radio contact. We have a rescue team in town with a helicopter for emergencies."

"Have you ever needed it?"

"Yes, on occasion. We've had kids physically hurt themselves just to get out, but that's rare. We've had a few cases of hypothermia. We watch very closely for that."

With every word he spoke, my head spun faster. "I can see you don't pull any punches."

"No, we don't. You will get a good taste of it the first time we ask you to return. You will experience what we call the 'hot seat' in a group session, and you won't be treated with kid gloves, I can assure you of that," he said with a slight smile. "Where are you staying?"

"I haven't made any reservations."

"There's a nice little inn in town, about three miles down the road. I could call—"

"How would you feel about my staying in the dorm with the girls?"

"Well, it's—"

"Mr. Cawdry, I'm really not so sure about all this. I'd like to get a better sense of this place. The only way I'm going to be reassured that I'm doing the right thing is by seeing and hearing from the kids who have already done their time out there in the wilderness."

"Well, I don't see a problem with that, but I can't guarantee you a good night's sleep. If you're ready now, I'll lead you up to the cabin. Oh, and please, call me Steve. We're not that formal around here."

I followed Steve up the hill to the cluster of cabins. The only light was from the swarm of stars in the endless sky. I couldn't remember ever seeing such a luminous body of space.

Steve knocked on the door and three girls yelled out, "Come in."

"Hello, girls. This is Georgia Durante. She and her daughter Toni arrived here tonight. Toni is out on a solo right now and Georgia isn't feeling very comfortable about it. She asked if she could stay here and talk to you all."

"Cool," said one of the girls from the far side of the room.

"Guess I'll leave you to chat. Goodnight, ladies."

I watched as Steve disappeared into the night and then I turned to the girls.

"So, what's she in for?" asked a hard-looking young lady.

"What you're all here for. Drugs," I answered.

"Not me! My mom just hates me—can't deal with me. That's why I'm here," one of the girls offered.

"Oh Karen, cut the shit," another girl said abruptly. "I thought you were over that my-mother-hates-me bullcrap. You're one of the biggest druggies in here! Who you kidding?"

"This is no place for your daughter. If you really love her, you'll get her out of here ASAP!" Karen squealed, ignoring her attacker.

"Come on, Karen, you're gonna make this lady think this is some kind of a prison or something."

"Well...*isn't* it?"

"You know damn well this place is straightening up your act. You just admitted that in group yesterday, remember?"

"Well, it doesn't do me any good to fight it, does it?" Karen retorted.

"Don't mind her, Georgia," the other girl said. "We've all been on her case today. Each of us have our chores to do and this is Karen's week to cook for the entire group. There's thirty-eight of us altogether, counting the boys. She didn't live up to her responsibility, so none of us ate."

"I didn't feel good," Karen retaliated.

"That's bullshit, Karen. It was my job to cut the wood today. What if I didn't do it? You wouldn't be lying around here when the nights get cold feeling nice and toasty, would you?"

"Yeah Karen, we shouldn't have to suffer because you're so damn lazy!" another girl added. "You're gonna have to pull your weight around here if you want to have any friends."

I thought the girls would never tire of talking. I was exhausted. As I lay on the small, cramped cot, I couldn't stop wondering if Toni was cold, or if she was frightened. Overwhelmed with it all, I had forgotten to call Dennis.

I had only been asleep five minutes, or so it felt, when a bell sounded. It was one of those triangle bells they use on farms to call the family for dinner. The girls were all filing out the door, half-awake.

"What's going on?" I mumbled, trying to focus.

"There's a problem somewhere. We gotta have a group session and work through it," someone answered flatly in the dark.

I glanced at my watch. "At four o'clock in the morning?"

"It doesn't matter what time it is. We have to deal with it at the time that it happens and no one gets to go back to sleep until the problem is settled."

I quickly put on my jeans and followed the girls out to the main cabin. Everyone sat in a circle and waited to be told what the problem was. No one looked particularly excited about being there.

Finally a short, good-looking man with gentle eyes and a full beard appeared. He was exactly the kind of guy you would expect to find in the woods. In fact, he was the mountain man I had anticipated when I met Steve, the headmaster.

"Hi, I'm Little John. You must be Toni's Mother," he stated pleasantly.

"Yes, I am. It's nice to meet you," I replied, shaking his hand. He introduced me to the boys and then proceeded.

"Well, let's get this over with so we can all go back to sleep. Jeanie was caught sneaking into the boys' dorm. This is the second time this month." Little John peered over at the scrawny looking girl defeatedly. "So what are we going to do about this problem, Jeanie?" he asked compassionately.

Jeanie just shrugged, looking totally bored.

Little John turned his focus to a tall thin youth with surfer blonde hair and deep blue eyes. "Robbie, what do you have to say?"

"Well, shit," Robbie replied, "what would you do if you were sound asleep and a girl woke you up by stroking your dick? Wouldn't you go for it?"

Jeannie eyes were wide with insult. "You knew I was coming over. Don't try to act like Mr. Innocent!" she retorted.

"Jeanie," Little John said, "why don't we talk about this need you have for sex. Where do you think that comes from?"

"Don't *you* have a need for sex, Little John?" she asked.

"Yes, I do, with someone I love. You don't care who you're with. You're gonna go through the entire community before you leave here."

"She already has," responded another girl sourly.

I surmised from the girl's tone that Jeanie had slept with a boy she was sweet on.

"Fuck you, Sandy!" Jeanie shouted.

"Jeanie, don't you think Sandy has a good reason to be angry with you?" another girl inquired with a less accusing voice.

"Maybe..."

"Maybe shit, you little tramp!" Sandy yelled.

"Sandy, let's try to help Jeanie with this problem," Little John suggested with an even tone. "You all have your own shit to deal with. Let's consider Jeanie's problem right now and help her to see why she has the need to continue with this behavior."

"Maybe she just likes it, did you ever think of that, Little John?" one of the boys asked innocently.

"Do you think that's true, Jeanie? Is it just the sex you love?" Little John asked in a gentle voice.

"No," she whispered, picking fuzz balls off her socks.

"Then what is it, Jeanie?"

"I don't know."

"Yes, you do," he pressed.

"No, I don't!"

"Come on, Jeanie, get it out, whatever the hell it is, so we can all go back to bed!" a boy in the group blurted out impatiently.

"Jeanie, how do you feel about your dad?" Little John asked, expertly knowing which buttons to push.

Jeanie looked at him with surprise. "What do you mean?"

"You know what I mean, Jean—"

"I know what he means," interrupted the short, dark haired girl. "Your father sexually abused you...didn't he?"

"NO!"

"Who are you protecting? Just tell the truth, Jeanie. Get it out," probed Little John.

"YES! YES! My father abused me!" she screamed, bursting

into tears. "It wasn't my fault!"

"We know it wasn't your fault, Jeanie, but you're blaming yourself every time you sneak into the boys' dorm. You're punishing yourself for something you had no control over. It's the reason you take drugs too. We are all your friends here, Jean. You're safe."

Everyone got up and surrounded Jeanie, taking turns hugging her, even Sandy.

"Okay kids, good work. We'll continue this session tomorrow. Now go and get some sleep," instructed Little John while holding back a yawn.

The group dispersed, anxious to get back to bed. I was too exhilarated to sleep. *That was great!* I was beginning to understand how it worked. After that night I was pretty comfortable with the program. I could have left feeling that everything was going to be all right, but I was fascinated with the whole process and elected to stay for another five days.

I had my chores. I chopped wood and took my turn at cooking as well. We did plenty of hiking and rock-climbing in the following days. I took a few of the girls out on a deserted dirt road and taught them how to perform one-eighties with my rented car. I got to know all the kids and their problems before I left. Each of them admitted that this was a good place for them. I even had my turn on the 'hot seat' a few times in the group therapy sessions.

"When are you going to start dealing with your pain, Georgia?" Little John asked in group.

"What pain? I'm fine, I'm happy."

They all burst into laughter, as though they knew something I didn't. They did.

"What do you feel when you think about your three marriages?"

"Nothing."

"That's the point. You have never dealt with your own pain. How can you teach your daughter how to deal with it, when you don't have a clue how to do it yourself? Don't you want to let that little girl come out of the dark and let her have her cry? How long has it been since you cried?" Little John asked.

"I can't remember."

"Of course you can't. You can't remember a lot of things. Don't you think it's time?"

They all took their turns, poking at me until I finally did cry. Then, one by one, they took turns hugging me. I couldn't believe how good crying felt. It was good practice for what was about to come.

The day before I left, I joined the kids on a trip to the lake. We loaded inner tubes into a beat-up old pickup truck and we all piled in. It reminded me of how I had grown up. My childhood had been filled with adventures like this—a simple life, a good life. I thought of Toni and wished she could be sharing this with me. By now I understood that wherever she was and whatever she was doing, the outcome could only be positive.

The kids all knew I made my living doing stunts and dared me to jump off a nearby bridge. I had never backed down from a dare when I was a kid, but I wasn't a kid anymore. The setting took me back to another place in time, and the last thing I acted like was an adult. The child in me came out to play as I climbed the rocks up to the bridge.

Jesus, it hadn't looked this high from down there.

From a height of some sixty feet, I was having second thoughts. Then I felt a faint rumble and soon I heard the train approaching. I looked down at the water, then back at the train. *Closer.* The train whistle blew. *Gotta go.* I jumped.

That day, I gained the respect and the confidence of all those troubled kids. Thank God for the train.

I had some problems adjusting to city life in L.A. after breathing all that fresh air and experiencing the beauty of the mountains. The warm, starry nights of the Big Sky and sitting around the campfire were etched in my mind. Why does life take us so far from what's real?

I answered my own question as soon as I picked up the phone to hustle up work so I could pay for the school. Being married to Richard had caused me to shun big money. It changed people somehow. But I had to have at least enough to buy us freedom.

Back to the grind.

"What's the deal?" Dennis asked when I answered the phone.

"Dennis! I just got back."

"Yes, I know, I've been calling every day. How did it go?"

"I'm sorry, phones just weren't a commodity out in the woods."

I told him everything that had happened. He sounded relieved. We both had been a little skeptical in the beginning.

"Well, my deal went great, too," he said with excitement. "I'm going to celebrate tonight. Now I have something else to celebrate as well. It sounds like that place is going do it for Toni. I sure hope so."

"When are you coming home, Dennis?"

"I'm leaving in the morning. Do we have a date tomorrow night?"

"We better have a date," I answered.

"You pick the place. I'll be at your house at seven. I miss you."

"I miss you too, Dennis. See you tomorrow."

Dennis called in the morning with a change in plans. He had stayed out a little too late, had drunk a little too much, and had missed his flight. He was taking the next one out, bringing him in later than expected.

It was a beautiful August day. Darlene and I sat around the pool sipping margaritas and soaking up sunshine. She was such a joy to have around—always there to lend an ear when I needed to vent. When the phone rang, neither of us wanted to move from the comfort of our lounge chairs to answer it, but curiosity got to Darlene. She forced herself up and sauntered over to the terrace. After talking a moment, she placed the receiver on the outside patio table and walked back toward the pool.

"It's Darrien!" she whispered.

"Oh Christ, she's probably calling to complain about Dennis again. Frankly, I'm getting sick of this." I marched over to the phone. "Hello, Darrien," I said impatiently.

"Who was that who answered the phone?"

"That was Darlene, my ex-sister-in-law."

"Is she still there?"

"Yeah, why?"

"Because I have something to tell you, and I don't think you should be alone." Remembering the last time someone had said that sent a chill through me.

"What's wrong, Darrien?"

"Dennis...Dennis is...he's dead Georgia."

"What are you talking about, Darrien? I just spoke to him. Why would you say something like that!"

"Georgia...his plane crashed. He's dead!" she blurted and burst out crying.

"NO! You're lying to me! Darrien, say that's not true! Please! Oh my God...say it's not true! Oh, no! No, no, no, no..."

"What's the matter, Georgia?" Darlene kept asking as she paced in front of me.

I couldn't say it, I just could not say the words: *he's dead.* All I kept saying was, "NO!" Darlene picked up the receiver. Never having seen me in a state like that before, Dustin got scared and started to cry. After Dar heard the news she immediately called Richard and asked him to come over to pick Dustin up.

I turned on the television and we watched the horrifying image of the plane burning. Dead bodies were being pulled from the wreckage.

"Wait...someone's alive...that man is alive! Maybe it's Dennis, Dar?"

"Georgia, this is not live footage. Darrien said he was positively identified. She spoke to his brother."

"Maybe they made a mistake!" I shouted, refusing to give up hope.

Darlene took me by the shoulders, forcing me look directly at her. "Georgia...Dennis is gone, honey."

Stunned by the reality, I painfully turned back to the TV, trying to absorb the truth.

"Did you hear that, Darlene?"

"Hear what?"

"Dennis *is* dead."

"Did they say his name?"

"No."

"What did you hear?"

"The flight number."

"What about it?"

"It was flight number *191.*"

"So what does that mean?"

"It means...he's dead."

Eyeing me strangely, Dar poured me a very strong drink. Consumed with tremendous grief, I couldn't pull my thoughts together to try to explain. Vivid pictures ran through my mind: the white owl, the psychic who saw the fire from a plane crash. It was all coming together now. We were both supposed to die on flight number 191. We had escaped that fate once, but it would be too much for Dennis to escape it twice. *It was in the cards.*

<hr>

On August 5, 1985, when Dennis's plane crashed in Dallas, my spirit crashed too. I thought I'd already seen the worst of life's sorrows, but I was wrong. I don't know how I got through the funeral. I was in a daze that entire week. None of it seemed real. Soon, I'd wake up from this horrible dream, I was sure of it.

A phone call soon brought me back to reality.

"Hello, Georgia?"

"Yes?"

"This is Dr. Kendall. I just got a call from Spring Creek school. They said they have not yet received the $10,000. They were supposed to have received it last Monday."

"Oh, Dr. Kendall, I'm sorry, I completely forgot about it. I've had a difficult week—I just wasn't thinking. I'll make arrangements to sell my stock today."

I called my broker and found that the news of Dennis's death had driven the stock down to a point where I could not sell it without taking a terrible loss. I hadn't even thought of the effect his death would have on the stock. What was I going to do? I had to keep Toni in that place somehow. Selling my house was the last resort. I opened my jewelry box and began adding up the value. I must have had at least $50,000 in jewelry. If I could get ten for it, I'd be lucky, but ten was what I needed. I put some feelers out and prayed I'd get a buyer soon.

The next day I met with Dr. Kendall regarding Toni's progress. I was gone for an hour. When I returned I found my house had been broken into. The carpet had just been vacuumed and fresh footprints led directly to the jewelry and back out the door. Nothing else had been taken. I had no rider on my insurance for the jewelry. I sat down at my kitchen table and put my head in my hands. What more could happen?

Toni was not yet aware of Dennis's death. The school didn't think the timing was right to tell her; they were getting close to breaking some ground. She was out in the wilderness and I couldn't even speak to her. I felt a horrible separation. I wanted to hold her so bad.

None of Toni's friends knew where she had gone. It had all happened too fast. Then I got a call from Toni's best friend, Angie.

"Hi, Georgia. This is Angie. I've been calling Toni all week on her line but she never answers. Is she home?"

"No, she's in Montana, Angie"

"Montana? What's she doing there?"

I explained what had taken place and told her about the program at Spring Creek. She started to cry.

"Oh, Georgia, I'm so glad you got her to a place like that. I know you have no idea about this. Toni will probably never speak to me again for telling you, but you have to know..."

"Know what?"

"I don't know how to say this..."

"Angie, just say it! What?"

"You know how she's been going to Solana Beach on weekends sometimes?"

"Yes, go on."

"Well, Joe...Joe's been...he's...he's been molesting her."

My heart stopped.

"I'm sorry, Georgia, but I had to tell you. Toni's been getting worse and worse with the drugs. I was so afraid she was going to overdose. She's trying desperately to put it out of her mind," she sobbed.

My whole body began to shake. If he were there, I would have pulled the knife from my heart and stuck it into his.

"Angie, how long has this been going on?" I asked, trying to keep my voice from trembling.

"I guess about a year."

"A year! Why didn't she tell me?"

"She just confided in me a few months ago, and she tells me everything."

"Thank you for having the courage to speak up. You did the right thing by telling me, and you've helped Toni more than you know. You're a true friend, Angie. I'm going to call the school right away and let them know. This will save a lot of time, trying to dig for the problem. Angie, I can't talk anymore. I think I'm going to be sick."

I hung up the phone and threw up. My head was spinning. I realized why she had never told me. He was using the same technique he had used with me: fear. *That bastard!* Of all the things Joe was, I never in my wildest dreams thought he'd step over this line. My daughter. That bastard!

In a white-hot rage, I picked up the phone and punched in his number.

"You son-of-a-bitch!" I screamed at the top of my lungs.

"What are you taking about?"

"You know goddamn well what I'm talking about, you bastard! You weren't satisfied just destroying me, you had to destroy my daughter too, you sick motherfucker. I can't believe I felt sorry for you—and all the while you were molesting Toni. Joe... *I'm going to kill you!* You better look over your shoulder because I'm not gonna rest until you're dead. I'm gonna blow your fucking brains out. I should have done it years ago. I was afraid of you then, but now *you* better be afraid of *me!*"

He started to cry. "Georgia, don't you see why? I know I must be sick, but I closed my eyes, and...she was *you*. She's the closest thing to—"

"Don't you *dare* try to use me for your excuse. Is your mind so twisted that you actually think that makes it all right? If you do, you're sicker than I thought. Joe, you have finally destroyed the only two human beings on this earth who ever cared whether you lived or died. Now you have nothing. No one! Maybe I should save myself the jail time and just let you do it yourself—you will, you know. I predicted long ago you would die a sad, lonely old man, by your own hand. When you finally have the guts to look at yourself and see how you've lived your life, and all the people you've hurt so cruelly, you'll do it. Maybe that's the best revenge after all. All I know is I *hate* you. Don't you ever call this house, do you understand that? I don't ever want to see your face or hear your voice again."

"Georgia, *please* listen to me," he pleaded.

"You've got nothing to say that I want to hear. Don't call this house, Joe. If you do, I'll have you arrested. In fact, I'll have you arrested anyway. Where the hell is my head? You had me so brainwashed about calling the cops, the thought just occurred to me. You raped my daughter! I'm going to fucking have you arrested, you no-good bastard!"

"Please, Georgia, try to—"

"I'll see you in court, Joe—if I don't kill you first!" I screamed as I slammed down the phone.

I took a few minutes to stop shaking and pull myself together, and then I called the school and spoke to Steve, the headmaster.

"You have to get him here, Georgia. It's extremely important that Toni confront him. If she cannot confront him face-to-face and tell him how she feels about what he did to her, she will always have a problem with men. It's the only way she can truly get well. Can you get him to come?"

"I don't know. He's an extremely private person. He would never deal with the 'hot seat,' I can tell you that right now. His pride will kill him someday. I just don't think I'll be able to make that happen."

"It's essential to Toni's mental well-being. Tell him you won't have him arrested if he comes, then have the jerk arrested anyway."

"Okay, Steve. I'll do my best, but I have to wait 'til tomorrow to call him again. I'm out of control right now."

"I understand."

"I'll call you after I speak to him."

"You try to get some rest, we'll handle Toni. Georgia...maybe you should talk to Dr. Kendall. You're under an unusual amount of stress. Frankly, I don't know how you're holding up under the circumstances."

"I'm okay."

"You're not, really, you're numb. Talk to Dr. Kendall. By the way, we still haven't told Toni about Dennis. I know how you feel, but we think it's better that we don't for now."

"I suppose you know what's best."

I lay in bed, my stomach churning. I tried not to think, but I couldn't stop. The pictures were all too vivid in my imagination. I remembered the times the subject of child molesters had come up around Joe. He'd get so angry, he'd say they should hang them by their balls. I thought his beliefs were strongly against that kind of thing. But now I could clearly see how he had twisted my thoughts in an effort to cloak his deception. *How could I have been so blind?* I felt as if I was being separated from reality.

How sorry I'd felt for him after he lost his mother, after he'd lost me. His life had seemed so sad and empty then, and when he'd asked me to send Toni down to Solana Beach for visits, I thought it would help heal both of them. He had seemed so changed, so much gentler, and I wanted Toni to see a better side of him. He had wanted to make up to her for the trauma he'd caused in her childhood. And I thought seeing Toni would bring a little light into his life, too. What a fool I'd been. Again, my soft heart had been my downfall, and now it was Toni's, too.

This betrayal was too much to cope with. I walked into my closet and took the gun down from its hiding place. I stared at it for awhile and contemplated driving to Solana Beach and putting a bullet into Joe's head.

You can't kill him, White. You need him. As tempting as it is, you can't do it. Wait until after he goes to Montana.

What if he won't go?

He'll go...I'll make sure of that.

I put the gun back, took two Valiums, and waited for sleep to take me away.

Joe called the next morning.

"Georgia, don't hang up, please let me just—"

"Joe, I don't want to hear your excuses. The only explaining you need to do is to the police."

He started to cry again. "I know I'm sick, I need help. I guess I can't blame you for never wanting to speak to me again. I've lost everything—you, Toni, my mother—everything. There's nothing left for me if I can't even hear your voice again, and it's all my fault. I don't want to live anymore. How could I have been so stupid? God, help me."

"I don't think God can help you, Joe, but before you kill yourself, you could help Toni. Don't leave this earth without trying to mend what you've managed to destroy."

"What do you mean?"

"Toni's going to need extensive therapy because of what

you've done to her. But it won't work unless she can look you in the eye and confront you. She needs to tell you face-to-face how she feels about it."

"I know how she feels, she doesn't need to tell me."

"You're wrong, she does."

"So what am I supposed to do?"

"Go to Montana. Face up to what you did."

"What's that going to do?"

"Keep you out of jail!"

"How do I know you won't turn me in anyway?"

"You don't. If you ever wanted to do anything positive in your life Joe, it's this. If you care about Toni's mental health, you'll do it. I see it as serving two purposes: it will help her, and it will keep you out of prison. The choice is yours."

After a long silence, he finally agreed. "When do I leave?"

"In two weeks, when she gets back from her survival trip."

"Georgia...I know it'll be the last time I ever see the two of you again. That's the punishment for my crime, but someday I hope you'll understand that I'm sick. I don't know why I've done the things I've done to you. I've banged my head against the wall many times, trying to understand. I'm so sorry for all the pain I've caused you over the years. I guess you'll both be better off without me in your lives. I've been selfish, and—"

"Save it Joe. There's no more forgiveness in my heart for you."

He burst into tears one more time. "I'm *sorry*...I'm *so sorry*..." he proclaimed between sobs.

I placed the phone in its cradle and sat on the edge of my bed. What had happened in his childhood that made him who he was? When he'd been drinking, he had told me some disturbing stories. His father used to tie him up in the cold, dark cellar. He would beat Joe and keep him there for days. Joe described the fear he had lived with in vivid detail—when the rats had crawled near his feet and how he screamed for his mother to rescue him. He told me how she would sneak him food and pray she wouldn't get caught.

The little he had told me about his childhood had been

distressing enough, but I knew even more anguish and suffering hid behind the anger and hatred with which he lashed out. Maybe because he had been helplessly controlled as a child, he felt the need to control and dominate. I don't know. Until Joe had the courage to unlock the doors to that ugly past, no one would ever know what motivated his outbursts. But somehow, without ever knowing, I knew. I understood, without really understanding.

Joe did go to Montana. He didn't have a choice. His excessive pride made it the hardest thing he'd ever done in his life. By the time Little John and the woman therapist, Gay, had finished with him, there was nothing was left of him that even remotely resembled a man. Toni, though, was still afraid and couldn't confront him with her deeper feelings. I found it pitiful to watch her struggle with her emotions.

Georgia Black was with me on that sweltering Montana day. And she wasn't hiding in the shadows. We sat in an open field and tore into the darker depths of Joe's mind. Without Black, I couldn't have handled the pain of all that came from that altercation.

By the afternoon's end, distinguishing the tears from the sweat was impossible. I didn't know it at the time, but Joe had warned Toni that if he were ever found out, he would kill himself. He had manipulated her adolescent mind with fear. I reflected on my own days of fear. Not until this moment did I understand how the game was played.

His pride was shattered. He would never recover from the embarrassment of that confrontation. He fled to Rochester shortly after returning from Montana, afraid of my wrath, leaving a life in California he had grown to love. No more tennis everyday, no more beautiful sunsets to feast his eyes upon. No more Joe Lamendola. Funny, the years I ran in fear...now *he* was running from *me*.

At that point I was still moving Joe's money. I had over $100,000 in my name. Fifteen thousand of it was rightfully mine, but I'd never entertained the thought of asking for it. I cashed out all the investments, deducted fifteen thousand and sent him the balance, putting an end to any future contact. In retrospect, I probably should have taken it all and given it to Toni for the irreparable damage he had done to her mind.

Using my portion of the money, I was able to make the down payment for the school. What he had done to us both was the ultimate betrayal. I never uttered a single word to Joe again.

I came away from that experience at Spring Creek wondering how many more lessons I had in store before I could be granted peace. I continued putting one foot in front of the other, having no idea where I was going—except that it was forward.

CHAPTER SIXTEEN

---◦—◄◉►—◦---

While Toni was away at Spring Creek, I desperately tried to balance my budget. I worried about not being able to keep up with the school payments. My need to work and to earn money gave me something on which to focus other than sadness and grief.

I had professional obstacles to overcome, too. Wally Crowder was dating a new girl. He was pushing jobs in her direction that should have been mine. I had to take control of my own destiny.

Jim Harkess called for our annual lunch. Our birthdays were a few days apart, and somehow we always managed to celebrate together over lunch. He picked me up at ten o'clock the next morning.

"Are you sure we aren't going to have breakfast?" I asked. "Why so early?"

"You'll see," he answered with a smile.

We pulled into a small private airport in Burbank. I thought maybe he had to pick something up before we went to lunch, but instead we drove directly to a sleek-looking midnight blue Lear jet with the name TWO'S COMPANY painted on the side.

"Is this yours?" I asked, looking at the plane in awe.

Jim looked like a remnant of the sixties. He was dressed in blue jeans, and his thinning hair hung just above his shoulders. A thick, graying beard covered the signs of years of alcohol abuse. Hard to believe by his appearance he could be so successful.

"Yes," he answered proudly. "We're branching out into

aviation now. There's a camera system built inside the belly of the aircraft, but today it's for pleasure. Where in the world would you like to have lunch?"

"Wow, you should've given me a day to think about this. Why don't you just surprise me?"

He whispered to the pilot, put on some music, and came back to the cabin with a bottle of champagne. We toasted my 36th birthday and his 38th.

"I can't believe I'm sitting here in my own private jet with Georgia Durante. Do you know how long I've dreamed about this day?"

"No."

"Since the day I met you on stage for that Toyota job, ten years ago." He paused. Fingering his beard, he looked everywhere but at me. "I fell in love with you then," he admitted shyly.

"You could have fooled me."

"I was married, but I was secretly in love with you all those years. The day you married Richard, I wanted to do what Dustin Hoffman did in *The Graduate*. That's why I didn't come to the wedding. I remember coming to that big house on the hill after you were married, to drop off some pictures for you. I realized I would never have a chance with you unless I was as wealthy as he was. That's when I began dreaming of having the jet. Now it's a reality. You're really here, Willie Nelson is playing "Georgia" on the stereo—exactly like I dreamed it would be."

"Jim, I can't believe you felt like this all these years and I never knew it."

"Well, you know it now."

"I'm flattered that I had something to do with you reaching your goals," I said, "but it's not money that attracts me. I've learned to run the other way from people who place too much value on wealth. Don't let your success go to your head. You're too nice a person to let it destroy you. Aren't you still married, Jim?"

"Yes, but we're getting a divorce soon."

"Does it have anything to do with your being so driven to be successful?" I asked.

"No, not really," he said. "You know how this business is. We're always on the road. It's tough on relationships. If you're not in the business it's hard to understand."

"What a great birthday," I said, wanting to change the subject. "Where are we going, anyway?"

"Lake Tahoe. Do you want to sit in the cockpit for the landing?"

"That would be fantastic. I'd love to learn to fly this thing."

The plane landed and we drove to a nice little restaurant and continued the celebration.

"Why don't you leave Motion Research?" Jim asked. "You don't need Wally Crowder. Christ, all the clients you have you've gotten on your own anyway. If you left, they'd all follow you."

"You really think so?"

"Hell, yes. I've been telling you that for years. You've got a good reputation in the business. They know when they call Georgia Durante for the job it's going to get done professionally. They never know when they call Wally what kind of bimbo they'll end up with. It astonishes me how he stays in business with all the crap he's pulled."

I said, "You know what I found out last week? I ran into a producer from Detroit. He said he called me for a job and Wally told him I was booked. So Wally sent him this girl he'd just started dating. She'd never driven for camera in her life. If she hadn't ended up crashing the car I probably would never have found out about it. I wonder how many clients I've lost because of Wally's little games?"

"Plenty. I think it's time for you to move on."

"You know what really aggravates me? I spend my money flying to Detroit. I take the clients out to dinner on my tab, promoting Wally's company, and when a job does come in, because of *my* efforts, he gives it to a fly-by-night he's trying to bed down."

"So what are you going to do about it?"

"Well, I've been thinking. An all-women driving team would really be unique. There's a need for good women drivers. If I did some research and came up with six or seven dynamite-looking girls who could drive the hell out of a car, and trained them in precision driving, I think it could be a winner."

"If you need an office, you can have a space in my building." He paused. "You know, that's not a bad idea. If you moved into my building we could be a full-service company. We would be separate entities, but we could use each other's services when we needed to."

"Hmm, let me think about it," I replied. "This could be very interesting."

"Your clients and my clients are the same. If you're there, you'll see everyone coming in and out of the building on different projects, but more importantly, they'll see you. You'll have the opportunity to land a job before a production company even starts the bidding process."

Now in a business mode, my fingers began tapping a drum solo on my knee. "Good point," I said. "If you're really serious about this, I'll start moving on it right away."

———◆———

That night I called Tony Santoro, Wally's partner in Motion Research. I told him I was planning to leave the team.

"I'd like to join you," he said. "I'm fed up with Wally's bullshit, too."

"Well, I was thinking of an all-girl team. You don't quite fit into my plan," I answered, surprised he felt the same way.

"So, you can have a women's division. You know there's a lot more demand for men. I think you'd be better off having both. You and I would make a dynamic team. They always pair us up on shoots. This could really work, and if Harkess is serious about what he's saying, this could be big, Georgia. I'd really like to be your partner. Whatta you say?"

"It sounds good," I said, "but we have to work fast. We're in the middle of the busy season. The timing couldn't be better. We have to think of a name so I can design a logo, order the stationery, business cards, t-shirts—"

"Slow down, George, we can do all that in time."

"Tony, it has to be done immediately. We need to send all our clients a letter to let them know we've formed a new company. We can't do it on plain white paper. It has to make a statement."

"What do you think it'll cost?"

"About five thousand each."

"That's a lot of money."

"It's not a lot of money to start up a business. If you want to make money, you have to be prepared to spend some."

"Guess you're right."

"I think the name should have the word 'performance' in it."

"Yeah, that sounds good. What about Performance Two, since the company consists of you and me?" Tony said.

"Yeah...and it works into the Two's Company thing that way, too, in case we end up in business with them down the road. I'll get working on the logo right away. You think of some good drivers we can bring in. Plan to have a drivers' meeting at my house two weeks from today, so we can weed them out and see what we've got. I'll find the women. You're not much better than Wally in that department," I said laughing, but he knew I wasn't kidding.

"I don't think we should say anything to Wally until we're ready to make the transition, Georgia. No sense in losing any work that may come through in the meantime."

"I've already got my summer booked with my own clients," I said, "but in your case, you're probably right."

A week later, Tony and I left for Moab, Utah, on a $6 million project for Chevrolet. We worked well together. We *looked* well together, which was the reason agencies paired us off. Tony stood about 6'1". Salt and pepper hair didn't seem to keep him from getting work—his strong chiseled face compensated. Tony was a man's man, but women, too, were taken by his unique charisma. His phone never stopped ringing.

Tony was Sicilian so our Italian heritages gave us a connection right from the beginning. He had the kind of physical look which attracted me, but I wasn't looking. Our relationship was strictly a professional one. I couldn't believe, after having had two Sicilian husbands, that I was actually considering one as a partner. And having a partner is nearly the same thing as a marriage.

After Moab, we continued the shoot in Pikes Peak, Colorado. Tony and I were flown down a day ahead of the rest of the crew so we could test the road before we started filming. We made the mistake of getting off the plane and driving directly to the top of Pikes Peak before acclimating ourselves to the altitude. The peak rose to 14,000 feet. We had reached 12,000 feet when Tony pulled over, his handsome face absent of color.

"You take it from here. I can't breathe. I feel like I'm gonna have a heart attack. I don't know if I can do this, George."

He walked around to the passenger side. I watched him with amusement, even though I felt lightheaded as well.

"You're lucky, all you had to do is slide over," he said, as he fell into the passenger seat, totally out of breath. "I know a driver who lives in Colorado Springs. I'm gonna have him replace me on this portion of the job."

"Tony, get a grip. You can do it. We shouldn't have driven straight up here without getting used to the altitude first. They said they would have oxygen in the cars for us tomorrow. It won't be so bad with the oxygen. You'll be fine."

"Don't you feel lightheaded?"

"Yes, but you're panicking. Just calm down and breathe slowly."

"I don't think I can do it," he insisted.

"Tony, come on, get a handle on it. I suggested you for this job. If you wimp out, I'll look like a jerk. This is one of my biggest accounts. Don't screw it up."

"They're not paying us enough for this."

"On the contrary, Tony, they're paying us more than double what the contract calls for."

"Those narrow dirt roads with the 300-foot sheer drop-offs we just drove in Moab make the job worth more than that."

I had lived on the edge most of my life. The edge of a road

couldn't put the same kind of fear into me as dying the kind of violent death I had come close to so many times.

"Just lie back and relax," I urged. "I'll take it to the top and it'll be over with for today. When we get to the hotel you'll see it's not all that bad."

"I don't know..." he said as he lowered the seat back and concentrated on breathing normally.

A tough shoot, even with the oxygen. The thin air made our reaction time slow as Tony and I raced up the mountain, he in a 1986 Beretta, and I in a 1955 Chevy. My foot took forever to go from the gas pedal to the brake. The sensation felt strange, as if I were moving in slow motion.

An Audi commercial was filming in Pikes Peak at the same time. During the day, we sometimes had to give way to the other film company for the use of the road. Tony was quite happy about that. It gave him a chance to *breathe*. The two separate crews broke for lunch at the same time.

Bobby Unser, Sr. was the driver for the Audi commercial. He set his food tray next to mine and sat down. My business sense, which I wasn't even aware that I had, took over. A name such as Unser, which had been associated with racing for years, would make the industry take note of Performance Two right from the start—cutting in half the time it would take to build a company such as mine.

I told Bobby a few of my ideas and captured his interest. He invited me to fly to the Phoenix Raceway where he was going to be a commentator for an Indy race the following week. He was interested in hearing more about my ideas.

I flew into the Phoenix airport, where Bobby Unser, Sr. was waiting for my arrival at the gate. We had dinner and discussed the business opportunities his involvement might bring to his career as well as to Performance Two. The next day he picked me up at my hotel and we drove to the track. In all the years of being in the stunt business, I had never had a ride quite like that. I was in the hands of one of the best drivers in the world, but this was real traffic. There were no cops holding vehicles, allowing us to go beyond the limits of safety, and I wasn't being paid to put my life on the line. When we got to the track he introduced me to his son, Bobby Unser, Jr.

"I'll meet you back here after the race. I'll take you back to Los Angeles in my private plane," Bobby Sr. said.

"Uh, no thanks, Bobby. If you fly anything like you drive, I'd rather take my scheduled commercial flight."

"Are you sure? I have to go to L.A. anyway."

"I'm positive."

"I'll give you a call from L.A.," he said, and rushed off.

"You made a good choice," said Bobby Jr. "Even I won't fly with him. If you think he's bad on the road you haven't seen anything until you've experienced the stunts he pulls in that plane."

Bobby Unser, Jr. took a great interest in the business I was there to discuss with his father.

"This sounds like something *I'd* like to do," he said.

"It is an interesting business, for sure. There's a lot of people who'd like to do it, but there aren't many who qualify."

"Do I qualify?"

"If you drive as well as your father does—on the track that is—you do, but precision driving takes practice, Bobby. It's a different kind of driving than what you're used to. It takes a lot of discipline as well as concentration, which I'm sure would come naturally to you once you got the hang of it. I'd expect you to fly into Los Angeles once a month to practice with the rest of the team. Just because your last name is Unser you won't be treated any differently than the rest of the drivers. It's going to take a lot of work on the part of all the drivers to achieve the kind of team I'm striving for."

"I'll fly in. I'll do whatever needs to be done," he answered anxiously.

Bobby Jr. drove me back to the Phoenix airport, and the experience was almost as bad as it had been with his father. I chalked it up to his age, but then that didn't give his father much of an excuse. If Bobby wanted to make it on my driving team, he'd have to learn fast.

"I'll give you a call in a week or so to let you know when to come in for the first practice. You'll need to rent a car at the airport, and don't forget to take out insurance."

"Oh...that may be a problem."

"What do you mean?"

"They won't rent cars to an Unser."

"I can't say I'm surprised," I laughed. "We'll work it out. I'll give you a call."

Mission accomplished. I returned to Los Angeles with an Unser on the driving team. The world's greatest stuntman, Dar Robinson, also signed up at the drivers' meeting. After reading automobile magazines, I contacted the best-looking female race car drivers with good performance records. They joined us. Now all we had to do was train them to work together to form the best driving team in the country.

In August 1986, one year after Dennis's death, Performance Two Inc. was born, and once the flag was dropped we were out in front. We started with sixteen drivers, both men and women, and for a while we didn't think we would have enough drivers to meet the demand.

It took a lot of work on my part to get the business off to a good start. Tony always seemed to be too busy to help with all the tedious chores. Women occupied most of his time, so I was pretty much the driving force behind the business. He wasn't happy with Bobby Unser, Jr. Bobby took the wheel in practice as if he were born for the business and Tony saw him as a threat. I had to fight him all the way to keep Bobby on the team. Eventually, Tony began to like Bobby. They had a lot in common. Tony was in his late forties, but he hadn't quite grown up either. Before long, they were prowling around together outside the job.

The business was doing well, but when we started to make some money, Tony wanted to pocket it all. I wanted to put it back into the business. The only time he made an appearance at the office was when he came to complain. I loved him dearly, but he had no concept of business. He was never around to see for himself what it took to run a company.

I did all the scheduling of the drivers, ordered all the business supplies, and took the clients to dinner. I answered the phones and ironed out the problems that occurred on the set. Tony was just another one of my drivers out in the field, having no idea how much effort it took to maintain the momentum. I didn't mind doing all the work, but being criticized was tiresome, especially when I deserved a pat on the back. The bickering between us began to get ugly. Neither of us would back off. We almost came to blows a few times.

One day he came to the office to be part of a meeting I'd set up with clients from Detroit. The purpose was to discuss an exclusive contract to do all of the driving for their commercials. I got there early to prepare for the meeting. The guard opened the gate when he saw me approach.

As I pulled in, I glanced in my rear view mirror and saw Tony behind me. The guard closed the gate before he could enter. I poked my head out the window and yelled to the guard, "It's okay, he's my partner."

The gate swung open and the guard motioned him inside. I opened the office door thinking that if the meeting went well I'd need to find more drivers to fill the demand. Tony followed me, complaining about the guard.

"Tony, since the guard didn't even recognize you, don't you think we should start thinking about dissolving this partnership?"

"I want fifty thousand to get out."

"Get serious, Tony. I'll give you what you've put into it."

"It's worth more than that."

"If it is, it's because of my efforts, not yours. I'm trying to be fair with you, Tony. If you don't accept it, I'll just dissolve the corporation and start another one and you'll end up with nothing."

"You'll have to give up the name that way. What about all the promotional stuff you just spent a small fortune on?"

"Performance Two will only be one now. It would only make sense to change the name anyway. Don't be stupid, Tony, take what I'm offering you."

"I'll think about it."

"I don't like what this has done to our friendship, Tony. We argue worse than if we were married. I know you're worried about what will happen to you without a team to call your home. You can stay on as a driver. In fact, no one even has to know you're not a part of the company. I just have to be free to make business decisions the way I see it, without a constant battle."

I don't know if Tony purposely sabotaged the meeting, or if his lack of business sense got in the way, but we didn't get the contract. Knowing the curtain was coming down, he didn't make any positive action to clinch the deal. We had one last job to do together for Oldsmobile, and then we were in the lawyer's office. The partnership had only lasted a year. Tony signed over his stock in the company. I kept the original name and signed a check for what he had put in.

Tony's Sicilian pride didn't want me to succeed without him. He filled Bobby Unser's head with lies, saying that I was telling everyone in the business that Bobby was an alcoholic. Tony was an excellent driver, but he just didn't know how to do it on his own. Unfortunately for Tony, neither did Bobby.

Wally joined the bandwagon to try to obliterate Performance Two, even though he had to swallow his pride and become friends with Tony again. *I* was the force that needed to be destroyed for them to hang on to what accounts they had left. They were all determined to put me out of business. My other competitors were doing their part to chip away at me, too. I was a woman in a man's world, fighting alone through this treacherous jungle.

Finally the competition resorted to attacking me the only way they could—on a personal level. They said that I was getting the work by sleeping with the clients. Women are always vulnerable to this kind of warfare. Sharp-edged tongues are hard to fight. But I pressed on, making my mark in the wonderful world of automobile commercials.

The doors that open to beautiful women are deceiving. I was a beautiful woman in a male-dominated world, where doors automatically opened for me at every turn. They weren't necessarily doors to truth, knowledge, or awareness. No, those have to be pried open at great cost. The doors I passed through were easier, more seductive, more elegant, more dangerous. Doors that were perfectly suited to my keen sense of adventure. Doors to wealth, power, and glitz. Every man I met had a smile and wanted to help me. Only time would teach me what was behind those smiles.

Before I had my company, I had never dealt with men on this level. I walked into every business meeting thinking they were seeing *me*, that person who lives inside. But in the advertising world they saw women who looked like me all the time. These women teased and manipulated. I never came from that angle, but because of their jaded view, I was punished for it.

The punishment was the withholding of work. I couldn't understand it at first, but a producer told me how men in the advertising world saw me. He said, "You don't understand just how much heat emanates from you, and how much invitation smiles out of your eyes. You underestimate your powers. They see plenty of Georgia eyes and they learn to trust nobody." He said that he himself had felt that way about me until he got to know me.

Women producers were another problem, but this I could understand. I have dealt with jealousy all my life, but these women have the power to punish because of looks. How I am perceived by others never ceases to amaze me, because I perceive myself so differently.

I have managed to connect with some directors and producers on a human level in business. These are the people with whom I make my living today. They are people who go beyond ego and know how to look into the soul.

So, yes, doors do swing open when you're a beautiful woman. I took those doors for granted, never giving them much thought, simply because they were always open. I'd never experienced

THE COMPANY SHE KEEPS

anything else to know the difference. The trick is, how do you keep them from slamming shut?

I became a hard-driving woman, determined to succeed until nothing was left of my fearful, vulnerable side. I learned how to tap into the more positive aspects of my Shadow: strength, power, and self-preservation. As I took on the business world with a vengeance, people began to cling to me for my strength.

My determination made things happen, but I was giving away my soul, the one thing that made me inwardly beautiful. To win, I had to play hardball.

I had carved a new world, learning more about myself as I pushed forward. With every roadblock I crashed through, I became better acquainted with my strength. Fear no longer controlled me. I laughed in its face. Even today, with my reputation preceding me, I still run into men from the Stone Age. Discrimination against women will always exist, but I now find it impossible to tolerate. My Shadow will not allow it.

With Toni away at Spring Creek, my life revolved around my six-year-old son. No one was allowed to invade our precious time. We only had every other week together so I always tried to make it special. It was not enough time to instill the values my son so desperately needed, but I tried.

I cleared my busy schedule and planned a camping trip with Jim Alquist and his two sons in the Big Bear Mountains. Jim was now a member of my driving team. He made more money in his first year with me than he'd made in all the years he'd been struggling as an actor. No one can ever say I don't repay my debts.

Jim and I drove our Jeeps and we raced off-road in the mountains. Dustin, wide-eyed, loved every moment. Unlike Toni, he had my daring spirit. His father would have freaked out if he could have seen us. Richard was so overprotective he would not even let Dustin play baseball. It was up to me to expose my son to a variety of things or he was going to grow up to be a wimp.

The next morning, Dustin and I packed a lunch and went off on

403

a long hike. The silence of the forest spurred a soulful conversation.

"How come Dad doesn't do stuff like this with me?" he asked.

"Your dad doesn't know how to have fun unless he can buy it, honey. It's really not his fault. No one ever showed him how."

An expression of anger flashed across Dustin's face. Scrunching his eyebrows, he uttered, "All he ever says is, yes, yes, yes! He never says no!"

"I thought you liked it when he buys you everything you want."

His face softened. "Well, I do...but I think I would like it if he said no, too, sometimes. You always say no."

"I do not."

"Do too," he said, pushing his lips into a pout.

"I only say no when I'm trying to teach you that you can't always have everything you want. Life isn't like that, Dustin. I just don't want you to have a rude awakening one day. I'm only trying to prepare you, that's all.

"Dad says it's 'cause you're cheap."

"Yeah, he would say that. He just doesn't understand stuff like that, Dusty. But I hope you'll be smarter than that one day."

"Can we go fishing now?" he asked.

"Okay, but only if you put the worm on the hook."

"How come you drive so good and act like a silly old girl about stupid worms?" he questioned.

"Ehh, they're just so slimy!" I answered, twisting my face up.

"You're funny, Mom," he said grinning as he stuck his hand in the container of worms to display his manhood.

"I love you, Dusty boy," I said, mussing up his hair.

"I love you more," he said as he stuck a big worm on the hook.

"How much more?"

"All the way up to the sky, past the moon, past the stars and all the way past ET's house," he answered, gesturing widely with his arms. "That's how much."

"Well, guess what?"

"What?"

"I love you way way past that!"

"No way," he answered, refusing to be topped.

When our time together came to an end, I dropped Dustin back at his father's house and had the usual pang in my heart as I drove through the gates and headed home. Six was such a precious age. We were missing the day-to-day interaction most mothers and their children shared. But how could I change things?

———◆———

When I returned home, Darlene was entertaining a friend. They sat on the living room floor sipping wine as Jay read her Tarot cards. Darlene was heavily into all that psychic stuff. Jay was a musician and looked like one with his long, mousy brown hair. It was too thin to be worn long, detracting from his relatively handsome face. He had a good stage presence, moving his tall, slender body with the beat as he sang, but his voice was just average. Making it big in the music world would be an unattainable dream, but Jay was a dreamer and he never stopped droning on about his career. He began stopping by the house often and we soon became good friends.

Jay was a soft and caring person. We would talk for hours when he visited. I found myself drawn to his sensitivity. He thought more like a woman than a man. Because he was ten years younger than me, he had not grown up with the same kind of beliefs as men and women of my era. The younger generation's way of thinking was refreshing to me.

Jay's presence in my life, with his invigorating, youthful innocence, gradually helped to open some doors to my inner self. To my own surprise, I began revealing painful events of my life to him. I had always kept my feelings buried, but the group therapy sessions at Spring Creek were helping me deal with some of my deeper hurts. Jay and I talked extensively about Toni's problems regarding Joe. I felt very comfortable discussing my concerns about Toni's mental well-being with Jay. His understanding nature made me feel sheltered.

Gradually, our friendship evolved into a relationship. It shocked *me* more than people who knew me. This was very unlike me. However, considering my state at the time, I was ripe.

Georgia Black allowed this association because I needed someone who understood my emotional traumas. Besides, it was *safe*. No way could this man ever come close to breaking down the thick walls surrounding my heart, not in any long-term sense. For the moment, yes, I enjoyed and needed the closeness I had with Jay, but he was far too young and inexperienced for me to entertain the thought of any kind of future with him.

We were both aware that the relationship was temporary. We had been open about it from the beginning. When the time came, we parted and remained friends. Jay continued to stop by frequently just to say hello, or to take Dustin out for an ice cream. Dustin had become very attached to Jay and Jay to him. He remained near the outer edges of my life for several more months.

—————

The long awaited day came when Toni was ready to leave Spring Creek.

"Georgia, I just spoke with Little John," Dr. Kendall said. "He seems to think Toni has risen above her problem with drugs, but he feels she has never fully dealt with what happened with Joe. They warned me that she will probably repeat an unhealthy pattern with men if she doesn't resolve it."

"What do you mean, pattern with men?"

"It's the way Toni will unconsciously deal with future encounters with men, due to the trauma of her involvement with Joe. She most likely will not be able to obtain a healthy relationship and will continue to make the same mistakes repeatedly. Toni's reality in regard to men may be distorted and could cause her a great deal of emotional pain."

"So where do we go from here, Dr. Kendall?"

"The school is aware of your financial condition. They are willing to let her come home, but with the understanding that she continues with therapy. As far as drugs are concerned, they strongly recommend that she not return to Beverly Hills High School. I think a small boarding school close to home would be best for now."

"What about Ojai?" I suggested. "She went to summer school there one year and really liked it."

"I couldn't have thought of a better suggestion. Yes, that is ideal. It's only an hour away—close enough to come home every weekend. And it's small enough to keep an eye on her. I could see her on Saturdays for her therapy. That would work great. Shall I call and see if we can get her in?"

"Yes," I answered, excited that my daughter was coming home.

Toni attended Happy Valley School in Ojai. She began to help Dr. Kendall with other kids to recognize their drug problems. I was proud of her progress.

Somehow, on Toni's weekend visits at home, she and Jay connected. They began to see each other secretly. When I found out, I was infuriated. Toni viewed my behavior as jealousy. My real concern was the pattern with men that I had been warned about. But she was in love and could only see it from her perspective. I turned my anger on Jay since he was ten years older than Toni and had some understanding of her emotional problems. The hours we'd spent discussing my fears about this topic didn't seem to play a part in his agenda. What kind of a man would do this? Had I been that wrong about his character? Obviously, I had.

Georgia Black took charge and verbally ripped Jay apart. This only served to create strong resentment in Jay and to push Toni further away from me. In the aftermath of the venomous confrontations, I became the enemy. For him to have created that kind of disruption in my relationship with Toni was totally irresponsible. To me, it was *major-league* betrayal. Even having been educated as to Toni's state of mind, I still couldn't help but feel betrayed by her, too. How could this have happened? I blamed myself for being so stupid as to become involved with someone Jay's age—another of the many bad choices I had made.

I refused to have any contact with Toni until Jay was out of her life. She had to take some moral responsibility. If I didn't stand firm on my position, I would be condoning her actions. Perhaps I was wrong in the way I handled this situation, but the whole thing just wasn't right in my eyes.

One of the ways I punished Toni was to take away her car. Jim Harkess had me flown to Ojai in his helicopter to retrieve car. I landed unannounced on the high school football field. It was a bit dramatic, but I made my point. It didn't do any good, though— I'd forgotten how strong the force of love could be.

"Mom, how could you take my car?" Toni protested from her dorm a few hours later.

"How? If you're going to carry on with Jay against my wishes, then why should I supply you with the wheels to see him?"

"That's not going to stop me, Mom. I love Jay."

"Well, let's see how far you go on love, Toni."

"Why can't you let us be happy? You're just jealous," she cried.

"Jealous? Toni, can't you see how wrong this is? I don't care about Jay! I care about you."

"I love him, Mom, and I'm going to keep seeing him," she said with conviction.

"It's your choice, Toni, but you're making a big mistake. You can always get another boyfriend, but you can't get another mother."

In the meantime, I still had Dustin at least every other week. I had told Richard repeatedly that a week here and a week there was not working. When Dustin was a baby it had been fine, but since he had started school the constant back and forth was becoming disruptive. I wanted to change the arrangement to three months and three months, or six months and six months, with the other parent having him on the weekends. Richard refused. He was so hell bent on hurting me that he couldn't see what was happening to Dustin.

Finally, the Buckley School called. We were asked to come in for a conference.

"Dustin is a very bright child, but we feel he's not working up to his potential," said Mrs. Tabocco. "We've noticed he's confused. He never seems to know which bus to get on—the one that takes him to his mother's, or the one to his father's. We feel this is causing some emotional stress and it's getting in the way of his ability to concentrate on his school work."

I looked at Richard to see if he was blocking it out. He probably thought I'd put them up to saying that, but he was listening.

"Do you think you two could work out something where Dustin can be in one household for the school year?"

Now that the school had confirmed my fears, Richard was willing to make the changes that were in Dustin's best interest. We decided that we would change our arrangement to six months and six months. We were almost into June and approaching my busiest time in the commercial season for automobiles, the time of year that most of my work was done on location. Richard took him for the first six months, and I had him every weekend.

We planned to make the switch in January, which was a good time for Dustin as he would be starting a new semester. It was also a time when I would be home more consistently. But when January came, Richard refused to make the switch.

"We like it the way it is, I'm not giving him back. Take me to court," he spewed in a superior voice.

Knowing my financial stranglehold, he probably never thought I would do it, but I was in the lawyer's office the following morning. The resultant nightmare would consume my life for the next year and a half.

CHAPTER SEVENTEEN

Richard, who was retired and bored silly, now had a new game to entertain him. He needed to win the custody battle at all costs. He even went so far as to marry a girl he met in France (and knew for only six days) so he would appear to the court to be the better-suited parent. She couldn't even speak English. After the proceedings, he paid her $30,000 and sent her back to France. The poor girl had no idea what was happening. But worst of all, he twisted Dustin's young mind and turned him against me just to reach his ultimate goal—to win. His motivation infuriated me.

Richard stopped at nothing. He fueled the fire that existed between my daughter and me. He used our strained relationship to his advantage, condoning both her and Jay's behavior and making himself their ally—someone with whom they could seek refuge and feel exonerated. He took them on trips and bought them gifts. He was an expert at using people and manipulating them to do his dirty deeds. He made large donations to Dustin's school and showered the administration with gifts.

It broke my heart to see my son being pulled away from me. I'd never felt more alone. Richard did a good job of poisoning Dustin's vulnerable mind. When I would pick him up, he was scared to look happy to see me.

"What's the matter, Dusty? Don't you love Mommy anymore?" I asked.

He looked out the car window and waited until he could no longer see his dad's house.

"I love you, Mommy," he answered, wrapping his arms around my neck. He wiggled as close to me as he could get, and rested his head against me. Then, suddenly, he jerked his head up and looked at me. "Don't tell Daddy I kissed you...he'll be mad."

My heart broke. "It's not wrong to love your mom, Dusty."

"Don't tell him, don't tell him!" he pleaded.

"Okay, okay...but why are you so afraid?"

"'Cause."

"'Cause why?"

"'Cause he won't buy me the remote-control truck."

"That's not a very good reason to pretend you don't love your mom."

"I know, but he doesn't like it when I love you. He always says bad things about you. When I tell him he's lying, he gets mad at me, and then he doesn't buy me stuff."

"You shouldn't ever have to pretend like that, Dusty."

"Sometimes it's not pretend."

"What do you mean?" I asked, feeling another jab to my heart.

"How come you always have to take me on weekends? That's when my dad does all the fun things—and I can never go."

"Your dad shouldn't plan things on our weekends together. He does that on purpose, Dusty, so you won't want to come to my house. We have fun at my house too, don't we?"

"Yeah, but you don't got all the neat toys like at Dad's house."

When we arrived at my house, Richard called—as he normally did. He persistently worked at trying to turn Dustin against me.

"Put my son on the phone," he demanded.

I gave Dustin the phone and went into the bedroom and picked up the extension.

"Someone wants to talk to you," Richard said.

"Hi, Dustin, this is Patrick. I just got here with my father. Are you coming on the boat with us tomorrow?"

"No, I gotta stay at my mom's house," Dustin answered disappointedly.

"Okay, here's your dad..."

"Dust, is it okay if Patrick and his friend play with your

Nintendo? They wish you could be here. It's no fun for them when you're not here, but we're going to have a lot of fun tomorrow. If you didn't have to stay with your mother, you could have fun, too."

"I wanna go," Dustin whined.

"Wish you could. Well, I gotta go now. I have to set up the Nintendo for the kids."

After Dustin got off the phone, he had a temper tantrum. Exactly what his father had in mind. *Damn Richard!* He did this all the time, and each time he did it, Dustin's resentment toward me grew. It was such a cruel thing to do a child's mind—all for the sake of winning. I finally had to get a court order to keep him from calling the house when Dustin was with me.

On Dustin's birthday, he wanted a go-cart that an acquaintance of mine had for sale. I offered to pay the fifty dollars she was asking. Richard found out, and when I went over to pick it up, it was gone. He had gotten there before me and offered to pay her $100. He didn't want me to have anything that might be a lure. The sad thing was, Dustin couldn't even ride the go-cart at Richard's house. He lived on a hill, so Dustin was confined to the driveway.

My son would have to talk to the judge at some point and tell him with whom he preferred living. Richard had a whole year to work on my child's gullible mind. He succeeded in making Dustin resent me in countless ways.

Richard claimed that I had relinquished custody of Dustin to him, then had changed my mind six months later. When I went to the school to ask them to verify what had really happened, they turned their backs and said they did not want to get involved. Involvement, of course, meant a loss of revenue.

All this turmoil took place while I was establishing my business. I was busier than I had ever been. I had the responsibility of sixteen drivers, their training, and putting together press kits in an effort to secure work for everyone. All this required my time— the endless phone calls, dinners with clients, and putting out the endless fires. I slept on a plane more than in my bed. Between bookings, I'd fly to Detroit, Chicago, and New York in an effort to promote my service. Business was booming, but the money was all going back into the company for advertising and promotional items. Between the business, the exorbitant upkeep of my home, and lawyers, nothing was left over.

My diligent efforts landed me the Oldsmobile account, bringing plenty of commercials to go around for the entire team. In the first spot in the series I doubled for Priscilla Presley, although her daughter Lisa was being featured. Oldsmobile went all out on this new campaign, sparing no expense. They hired a Lear jet to fly the talent to the shooting location in Washington State. I was used to being flown first class, but this was a step above that.

Priscilla was a pain in the butt, refusing to fly in anything but a Gulfstream. They reluctantly gave in to her request. Being given an inch, she went for a foot—demanding the same top-of-the-line personal vehicle which Lisa had been given. The advertising agency drew the line. They did part with a car, but a model of lesser value than her daughter received. I could never understand why stars had to act in such a manner, but even more unclear to me is why the people who pay the tab put up with it. Even so, the escape from my personal life's irritants was refreshing.

I didn't have to deal with Priscilla all that much. I worked mostly with Lisa in the car. We drove in and out of the surf with a helicopter filming closely behind, above, and in front. Beach driving can be tricky. Being where a chopper needs me to be and concentrating on not getting swallowed by a wave is a true test of ability. The surf was deceiving and unpredictable, causing me to make sudden changes in direction. In making those sudden moves, I was constantly cautious of the helicopter—just feet from the vehicle. Lisa was nervous at first, but after the first day she became more comfortable and began having fun.

When the job ended, I once again concentrated on the strategy of making my son a more permanent part of my everyday life.

It took about sixteen months to finally bring the custody case to trial. It was the most heart-wrenching time of my life. I was cut off at every turn, as Richard always got there first with his wallet. With every day that passed, Dustin was being pushed further and further from me. My only weapon was to simply love him.

Toni and Jay had moved in together after she'd graduated. Toni and I hadn't spoken, but Dustin told me he saw them at his father's all the time. Richard had managed to steal both my children. Heartbroken, I put on my public face and went about my life like a robot.

A court date was *finally* settled on. That is, if Richard didn't file for *another* continuance. I had lost a great deal of income turning down work, thinking each new date would be the real thing.

Before we were set to go to trial, I got a call from my past.

"Hello, Georgia. Recognize the voice?" he asked.

"Salvatore Reale! How's it going?"

"Great. How's your business doin'?" Sal asked.

"It's doing well," I answered.

"Good. Always knew that'd be your ticket, you're pretty good behind the wheel—for a woman," he added with a laugh.

"Still a chauvinist I see, Sal."

"Not really. I'm calling because I need your driving expertise."

"Oh?" I answered, wishing suddenly that I'd let my answering machine pick up.

"I need you to transport something from Vegas to New York for me. There's fifty grand in it for you."

"Reale, I stopped transporting bodies in the sixties."

He laughed, "No, it's nothing like that."

"What else could be worth $50,000?"

"I'm sending you a ticket. Meet me in Vegas next Tuesday. The name of the hotel will be with the ticket. And you know the name I'll be registered under."

"Sal, I have a job next week, I—"

"Not one that pays fifty grand. Be there." He hung up.

The ticket arrived the next day. I had to go. Resolving this over the phone was out of the question. $50,000 would make a pretty good dent in my attorney's fees, but losing my son wasn't worth the risk. *Now, how do I convince Sal?*

When I arrived at the designated place, I knocked on the door. I heard shuffling inside, then a gruff voice saying, "Who's there?"

"It's me, Georgia."

The door opened slightly, enough for Jerry Pitzitello to peek his head out and look both ways down the hall. He had dark circles under his eyes and his face was unshaven. He opened the door just enough for me to squeeze inside.

Armed with an Uzi and dressed in clothes that looked as if they'd been slept in, Jerry said, "The years haven't hurt you a bit. You're looking pretty damn good."

"You look like shit."

"Thanks," he answered, not sounding the least bit insulted.

"Jesus, Jerry, what are you guarding in here, Fort Knox?"

"Sal's in the other room, he's been waiting for you."

When Jerry opened the door to the adjoining room, I couldn't believe my eyes. They *were* guarding Fort Knox. $4.5 million, in stacks three feet high, covered two queen-size beds. The $100 bills were bound with rubber bands in $10,000 bundles.

Sal stood next to the bed, immaculately dressed, as usual, and enjoying the expression of awe on my face.

Knowing I was asking a stupid question, I blurted out, "Where did all this money come from?"

Sal raised a suspicious eyebrow and didn't answer. "We rented a car for you. Tomorrow you—"

"Wait a minute, Sal. First tell me what the deal is with this money," I interrupted.

"It's clean. That's all you need to know," Sal answered.

"How clean can it be if you're paying me fifty thousand to transport it? Come on, Sal."

"Okay, the money's mine. I need you to transport it because I can't take the risk of gettin' stopped. The IRS, you know the dance."

"Yeah, but where's the risk, Sal? For fifty grand, I know there has to be one."

"You may have a problem getting through the check-points.

But with your face, who'd ever suspect? We've already checked it out. At midnight they have a shift change. The guards are busy checking in and out and they wave all the cars through. The timing's gotta be exact. But if you should have a problem...that's where your driving ability comes in. This isn't chicken feed y'know. We're trusting you."

Sal was not your regular kind of wiseguy. He was voted Man of the Year for Queens county in 1978 and had served as campaign manager for Geraldine Ferraro when she ran for Vice President of the United States. He had his hands in the pockets of many New York politicians, from the Governor's office on down. He possessed a smart business sense and had invested his money well over the years. It wasn't inconceivable that this money was really his, but I smelled more to the story than he wanted to reveal. It was true that the less I knew the better off I was, but this was not the old days. I was wiser now.

"I realize that, Sal. But there *is* a risk, and I can't take that risk right now." Sal's face turned hard, sending a chill up my spine. He could be extremely treacherous if you crossed him. I'd made the mistake of calling on him a few times for a favor. Wrong thing to do with a guy like Sal. He was now calling in the debt and expected me to pay up.

I continued while I still had the momentum. "The timing is all wrong. I'm going to trial soon for custody of my son. If anything happens, it'll cost me. Although I could really use it, no amount of money is worth it. I'm sorry, Salvatore, I just can't take that chance."

"That problem can be easily eliminated. Fuckin' sand-nigger should be whacked—"

I cringed. Behind Sal's gentlemen-like facade was a heartless killer. "Yeah, well, there's no one who hates that man more than I do, but he's still my son's father."

Sal swore under his breath in Italian and paced around the room. "What happened to your balls? Has Hollywood softened you up?"

"C'mon, Sal, give me a break. Jesus, this is all I need right now."

"I'm really not happy about this, Georgia..." He thought for a moment. "Ehh, shit. Okay, you're off the hook, but goddamnit you'd better remember—you owe me one."

I took a flight back to L.A. a few hours later, sighing with relief. The phone rang the following night, waking me from a deep, dreamless sleep. The green glow from my alarm clock read 2:23 a.m.

Groping for the receiver, I mumbled a sleepy hello.

"Georgia...I got a serious problem," Sal announced, sounding as if he'd just finished running a 10K.

"Oh shit..." I sat up in bed and turned on the light. "What happened?"

"They got us at the Sierra Blanca check-point near El Paso."

"Oh my God."

"Yeah. We were a little early for the midnight shift change so we stopped for coffee about twenty minutes from the check-point," he explained, speaking rapidly. "When we pulled back on the highway, I opened the window a crack to let out the smoke. That's when I heard the helicopter, but it didn't register. As we approached the check-point, the Border Patrol stepped out in front of the car. It was pitch black out there, but my headlights illuminated his face pretty good as he stood directly in front of the car. He looked down at my plate and then his eyes slowly rose up over the hood, lookin' me square in the eye. I knew we were dead. My fuckin' stomach fell out."

"Oh, God, I know how you must have felt," I said.

"No, you don't. Anyway, I was thinkin' about squashing him when outta nowhere, ten of 'em, DEA and Customs agents, carrying shotguns and wearing bulletproof vests, surrounded the car. They already knew our names. How do you suppose they knew that, Georgia?" he questioned suspiciously.

Am I still asleep? Did he just say what I thought he said? My heart started racing. "What are you saying, Sal? You think I blew you in?"

"I hope not, for your sake. Only three people knew about this besides me, you, and Jerry. I do trust you, but right now you're highly suspicious. I hope J.G. didn't discuss this with anyone. Maybe it was bad phones, I don't know. I can't take a chance of making contact right now, so until we see how this thing washes, watch your back."

"Where are you now, Sal?"

"At a gas station, about twenty miles down the road from the check-point."

"Where's the money?"

"They got it in a wooden shack back there at the check-point. Guy by the name of John Hopkins, some big shot with the DEA, gave me his card and told me to call him in a few days. Said they needed time to count it. Ha! They'll be there a fuckin' week. We're lucky they didn't take us in."

"Sal, this isn't making sense. They didn't cuff you. They let you go. Where's the crime? This is beginning to scare me. I have a feeling if you head down that road another ten miles there's going to be a road block. And ya know what? You're not gonna make it out of there alive. They're going to say you tried to run. That's $4.5 million you left back there. Now that they have their hands on it, do you really think you're ever going see it again? I don't know what's clouding your brain, but you'd better get your ass back there—pronto!"

The dead sound of silence rang loudly in my ear, and then Sal said, "Jesus Christ, you're not too dumb for a broad. I think you hit it right. I'll call you back." He hung up abruptly.

A mix of emotions surged through me. I felt exceedingly grateful that I had been able to get out of doing the job. I was also fearful for Sal and Jerry, and scared the death that I wouldn't have the chance to be proven innocent. I wanted to run, but if I took off now, I'd only look guilty. I wiped the dust from my gun and slipped it under my pillow. How could I allow myself to think this chapter of my life could ever be over?

The next day I had visitors. The good guys, thank God. An FBI agent, a Customs agent, and an IRS agent. Walking up to my front door, they looked as if the British were coming in their $39 suits from J.C. Penney's and loafers that looked like they'd been resoled several times. Between the three of them, there was probably enough retread for a new tire.

By this time, I knew my rights. I didn't have to talk to them. But they had done their homework. The first thing they said concerned my impending child custody trial. They threatened to subpoena me if I didn't talk, not only making the judge in my case aware of my involvement, but also informing the rest of the country. All could be kept quiet, however, as long as I cooperated. I had nothing to hide and I really didn't know where the money came from. I let them in.

The IRS agent plopped down on my couch and it sagged down five inches. The chalk-faced FBI agent sat beside me and laid a picture on the table.

"This look familiar?" He waited while I looked at it. Even in a photograph the money was an awesome sight. "What can you tell us about this money?"

"I can't tell you anything. I know about as much as you do. Nothing."

"We know you were offered fifty thousand to transport it. We've got it on tape. We want to know where it came from, and the reason you didn't do it, which, by the way, was a smart move. We had a beeper in Mr. Reale's car, been tailing him ever since he and Pitzitello left New York."

"I didn't do it because I didn't want to," I answered flatly.

Playing good-guy/bad-guy all by himself, the FBI man thundered, "You know that's the skim money from Vegas to John Gotti and the Gambino family! We have you tied to that family from the late sixties so don't try to bullshit us."

"Is that a weekly or a monthly take?" inquired the IRS agent. I shrugged. "Beats me."

"Or maybe it's the missing money from the Lufthansa Heist? Your friend Salvatore organized the unions at the JFK airport during that time. You remember that, don't you?" the FBI agent asked in a way that told me he had more pieces to the puzzle than he cared to divulge.

"That money was never recovered," the Customs agent added. I was wondering if he could speak. He had been sitting there the whole time, staring at me with a trained eye, studying my body language. He was getting under my skin.

I walked to the fridge and took out a can of soda. "Ya know what?" I said, irritated that I'd been dragged into this mess. "If you've been keeping tabs on me, you should know what my movements have been over the past ten years. Try investigating your own government agencies if you *really* want answers. I wish all you guys would just let me get on with my life."

"Well, let's see...In 1985 we have pictures of you at Sparks Steak House on E. 46th Street with John Gotti and two other Captains of the Gambino crime family. That was during the week they were playing musical chairs and the pianist, Paul Castalano, was shot. Before that, we can place you at the infamous 14-hour lunch at Altadonna's restaurant in Queens. They're still writing about that in the *New York Times*. Your elusive presence in this world has long been a mystery to us. You may not get around too often, but when you do, it's a pretty major event. And these are just a few of the things we know about."

I remembered that night well. I was meeting Sal to go to an after-hours club. Upon my arrival at Altadonna's around 2:00 a.m., I noticed a blue van with exhaust coming out of the muffler parked across the street. After bringing this to Sal's attention, the meeting ended abruptly.

The night Paul Castalano was murdered, I was in a bar in Manhattan with Sal when we saw the news broadcast announcing his death. Sal had a broad smile on his face as he watched the news commentator. Sal had been acting sort of edgy, insisting that I spend the entire day with him. Now I understood why. He knew what was coming down and needed an alibi. He asked me to join him at a hidden farmhouse in Vermont that the mob often used after a publicized murder had taken place. I refused. This was a red-hot happening that I wanted no part of. The eighty-eight acres of wilderness was owned by a New York City police lieutenant. This law enforcement official was responsible for setting up a safe haven for the mob. He put the tie together with "Shoot 'Em In The Back" Donnelley, the local Sheriff of the small Vermont town. Being on the Mob's payroll, Donnelley tipped off the Mobsters whenever the Feds came snooping around. It had been an interesting week.

I ignored the agent's sarcasm and flopped into the oversized leather chair stationed near the fireplace. "My presence both times was perfectly innocent," I answered, unshaken.

"Yeah, sure it was. What kind of business does a guy like Salvatore Reale have for fourteen hours with Commissioner Sedowski, Board of Elections; Pete Presioso, Head of Intelligence; John Santucci, District Attorney for Queens; and Lieutenant Doyle of the 106th precinct?"

"If three grand juries couldn't find out, why would you think I'd have the answer?" But I did have the answer. It was never made public, but the purpose of that meeting was to use the Mob's influence to get Pete Presioso elected as the new Police Commissioner.

The FBI agent leaned back on the couch and ran a hand over his closely cut, reddish hair. "We're still baffled. Only two calls were placed at that meeting. Why would they call Tip O'Neil in Washington and Mayor Koch at home?" The agent seemed to be asking the question more to himself than to me.

I tried hard not to grin. "Beats the hell out of me," I said, popping the top off my can of soda and taking a long swig.

"We know for a fact that you know more than you're telling us. If you want to win your custody case, I think you'd better start talking."

"What's so unusual about Sal being with a bunch of politicians? He was elected to the National Convention for Nixon for the 38th assembly district, for Christ sake!" I retorted.

"Yeah, we know about that. And it turned out to be the most politically corrupt clubhouse ever under Reale's leadership. Maybe even worse than when Carmine DeSapio ran Tamanny Hall."

"I don't know anything about that."

"Your friend Salvatore is quite a colorful guy, a real gentleman. Now tell us about this money," he pressed.

They grilled me for a little longer. The FBI agent finally stood to leave, giving me an unsatisfied grin. Leading the way, I opened the door and they all filed out.

"We'll be in touch..."

I did not hear from Sal for another week. The story broke over the news and in the papers, so I at least knew they were alive. The headline read: "Gotti's Pal, Sal, Picked up With 3.8 Million." *3.8 million? A mistake? I don't think so.* God, how close I had come to those headlines bearing my name. Sal told me in shocking detail what had happened. Maybe not so shocking to me—I had dealt with crooked authorities—but the scale to which this corruption existed was truly amazing...

When Sal and Jerry walked back into the guard shack, only seven of the original ten men were still there. The agents, still hovering over the money, were shocked when they turned and saw that the two Mobsters had returned. An awkward silence filled the room while the agents cautiously eyed one another.

The money was neatly laid out on two eight foot long tables. A 4'x 4' empty space immediately signaled foul play. Sal nonchalantly scanned the money, quickly adding it up in his head. Ten bundles high, $100,000 per row...that meant a total of $700,000 missing, along with the three agents. Recognizing the greed in the eyes that watched him, Sal knew that if he accused them, he and Jerry would be dead. He resolved to let them keep the $700,000 and he'd walk away. But it wasn't that easy.

By daybreak the next morning, the Border Patrol and the other agents were still counting the money. It was a long, exhausting night. Sal began to look a bit disheveled. Jerry remained unchanged. They were sitting on a bench outside of the shack, smoking a cigarette from their fifth pack, when they heard the faint roar of helicopters approaching. As the sound grew louder, they could make out three birds in the sky, flying in an echelon formation. *Closer.* Heat waves rose from the hot desert road, creating a surreal mirage effect as the flying machines came into focus. *Closer.*

The military-type choppers circled overhead, preparing to land. Adrenaline shot through both Sal and Jerry as the helicopters descended, creating a dust storm from which there was no escape. Sal said an odd thought crossed his mind; he wondered if the dry cleaners could get the dirt out of his $400 silk shirt. Knowing Sal, I didn't find that thought so odd.

The helicopter blades were still spinning when the doors slid open and men in black jump suits, armed with machine guns, came out. Not until the dust settled could Sal and Jerry tell how many there were. An army of men, some forty in all, arrived via helicopters, government vehicles, and state police cars.

John Gleason and George Stamboulitis from the New York Organized Crime Strike Force were flown in during the night in a private jet. A siren was heard and a speeding car pulled up to the scene carrying a U. S. Attorney from Texas. A round faced, gray-haired FBI agent by the name of Reynolds and the Chief of Border Patrol came in from Washington.

No camaraderie existed between the government officials. Each perused his own self-important path to fame. With proud smiles, they took turns posing for pictures standing next to the money. Before long, heated arguments flared between them over who would be getting the money. The FBI argued that it had initiated the investigation. Customs declared its claim, as it was the their illegal alien check-point where the money was confiscated. The DEA argued that it would be proven to be drug money and therefore should belong to them.

As the officials all huddled, another car pulled up. Four men in suits exited the vehicle. One of them, carrying a white piece of paper, walked directly over to the money and slapped the paper on top of it, saying, "This is an IRS matter." His credentials revealed that he was the Head of Intelligence Division for the

IRS. Sal noted that the look on the other faces was almost as pained as his own expression had been eight hours earlier.

The FBI man, Reynolds, eventually walked over to Sal, asking him to sign a release for the money. Sal looked at the paper, which read $3.8 million. He handed it back to the agent saying, "I'm not signing that, it's the wrong amount. There's supposed to be 4.5 million. They stole $700,000 when they released us."

Reynolds let lose with a roaring laugh and hollered over to John Hopkins, "Hey Hopkins, wanna hear a good one? This guinea says you released him."

The room fell silent. Hopkins eyes darted nervously from face to face."Hey, well, what's the crime? We didn't find any drugs. The money could be theirs for all we know. What could we hold 'em on?"

Reynolds' eyes narrowed. "You know he's a top O.C. guy. We knew about it, you knew about it—who you kidding?" Reynolds turned to Jerry, still not believing that any law enforcement officials would be stupid enough to let the suspects out of their sight. "Did you leave the scene?"

"We came together, we left together," Jerry answered.

"Where'd you go?" Reynolds asked with great concern.

"To a gas station down the road."

Reynolds glanced at John Hopkins with a disgusted look, and then turned back to Jerry. "You use the phone?"

"Yeah."

Reynolds panicked. He yelled out to the other agents, "We're gonna be taken down! Get the money out of here—NOW!"

The helicopters started up. Men disappeared in the dust storm with bags full of money. Each helicopter took off with $1 million and one man from each government agency. The $800,000 left over was divided between seven vehicles. In a matter of five minutes, the place was evacuated.

The remaining lawmen jumped into the waiting cars and turned on the flashing lights. With sirens blaring and speeds exceeding 100 miles per hour, they headed for the Federal

Building sixty miles away in El Paso. Jerry turned to Sal after they were placed in the car and said, "Gee, now I know what John Dillinger must-a felt like."

Upon entering the Federal Building, Sal and Jerry were taken to the fifth floor. Awaiting their arrival were eight Secret Service agents who had been flown in earlier from Washington. Their job was to check the money for counterfeit bills. So far, Sal and Jerry were clear of any wrongdoing, except perhaps evading taxes.

Sal smelled it coming. He took Reynolds aside and whispered, "Listen, Fat Face, you stick a phony bill in there and believe me, I'll scream plenty. I'll start from the President on down. I'm sure the American public would find it interesting why the CIA had members of the Gambino crime family standing by in the background in France when President Bush met with Ollie North on the Iran Contra matter. And that's just one example." Reynolds understood.

Sal was eventually charged with a probation violation for unauthorized travel and served five years in prison. Jerry was released. The money was never returned, nor did Sal ask for it back. And I got back to my problem at hand.

One good thing did happen that week. The stock I'd bought from Dennis took an upward turn. I sold it, making the profit Dennis had promised I would. Now I had all the ammunition I needed to fight Richard. God always provides. It saddened me that Dennis was not around to see how his vision had materialized. I invested my profits at a high rate of interest with a man who owned five banks. I was prepared to spend every dime to get my son back.

CHAPTER EIGHTEEN

The custody trial began. A reputable person in the psychology field took the stand on Richard's behalf. I had never met this woman, yet she testified that she had been in my home. From what she had observed, Richard was the better parent. I was appalled at what the power of money could buy. I learned a lot about the judicial system. Every little detail was twisted to look like a major flaw in my personality. The things I could have said in my defense were not allowed. I could only answer yes or no, without explanation. The days turned into weeks and the questions were grueling.

"Do you know a man by the name of Dan Whitman?" Mr. Anton, Richard's attorney, asked.

"Yes, Dan is a friend of mine," I answered.

"Where is Dan presently?"

"Dan is in prison presently," I said, knowing exactly where he was going with this line of questioning.

"And what is Mr. Whitman doing time for?"

"I don't know. It had something to do with ticket scalping or something."

"Isn't it true Dan Whitman is in prison for conspiracy to commit *murder*?"

"I object!" my attorney interrupted. "I'm not going to allow my client to answer that question. That has nothing to do with this child custody case!"

Seymour Winston was my attorney. I had sought his legal

assistance on the advice of Dan Whitman, as Dan had known Seymour for years. He respected him as much as I did. Dan was not the criminal they were trying to make him out to be, or at least, the Dan I knew wasn't. He had been involved with the Rams' owner's husband, selling tickets to the Super Bowl. Tax evasion and other accusations prompted his arrest. I don't know all the details of the case, but evidently they had enough evidence to convict him.

"I think it has everything to do with this case, counsel. It establishes the kinds of characters your client associates with," Anton retorted.

"Well, excuse me," I interrupted. "Dan Whitman happens to be very close and very good friends with Ronald Reagan. If he's good enough for Ronnie, I'd think he'd be good enough for me."

Mr. Anton looked lost for words. Seymour looked surprised and a little self-satisfied. A slight grin broke out on his face as he waited for the opposing counsel's comeback. Mr. Anton wasn't prepared for what he'd heard; he paused for a moment, collecting his thoughts.

"Well, that's a matter of opinion," he said, and immediately changed the subject.

By the lunch break a few hours later, we looked to be in the lead. Richard and his attorney sat a few tables away in the courthouse lunchroom.

"Does Dan really know Reagan?" Seymour whispered.

"No, but what are they going to do, subpoena him?" I answered with a coy smile.

Seymour burst into laughter. Richard and his bald-headed attorney looked over at our table curiously.

"You really threw him for a loop. Whatever made you think of that?"

"I just thought about Dan. He does walk with royalty. Just think of all the people he associates with, Seymour. He's tight with many of the stars from his producing days. He's college-educated and well-respected. That jackass was trying to convince the judge that he's a lowlife criminal. It just got to me. You know as well as I do that's not who Dan is, but how do you make the judge see that? I don't know, Seymour. It just came out."

"Well, keep it up and we'll win this case."

"Do you really think so?"

"It's different today than it used to be, Georgia. The court always used to lean toward the mother, but today they look more at the whole picture. The judge will analyze your lifestyles. Richard is married. He's retired, which means he can be in the home all the time. He can afford the private schools and the tutors. You, on the other hand, are on location a lot. You're not married. Right now Richard appears to be the more stable of the two of you. We have to prove otherwise."

"Seymour, many single mothers work. We *have* to work. I don't have anybody paying my bills. How do I provide a home for my son if I don't work? The judge certainly has to take that into consideration."

"You should've gone to court when you divorced Richard. I can't believe you walked away from that situation with nothing. Do you realize you probably could have gotten ten thousand a month in child support? You wouldn't have to be a working mother right now. I amazed you didn't go after it."

"Seymour, we've already gone over that. I just wanted to be happy. A court battle would only put my life on hold. I didn't care about Richard's money. I knew I could survive; I always have. I didn't need him or his money."

"But look what it's costing you now. It's a catch-22. I don't know how it's going to come out. All I'm saying is they're leaning more and more toward the fathers these days, especially in California. I just want you to prepare yourself emotionally if it goes that way. In the meantime, you need to think about his history with drugs."

"Why do these kinds of trials always have to get dirty? Just the simple fact that Richard's mind is warped is reason enough for the judge to see my son is better off with me. Richard just gives Dustin money and lets him do whatever he desires. He doesn't spend quality time with him, whereas I take him camping, I take him fishing, I get him involved in sports. That's usually the kind of things dads do. I may work, but my time with Dustin is quality time. I give him *me*. Richard gives him *money*. Richard doesn't know how to love. He buys people, he buys love—that's all he knows. The judge has to see that."

"I know you'd like to keep this clean, but it just can't happen that way. You saw what they were trying to do to discredit you. He's insinuated you're an alcoholic and a drug addict; he'll try to use that to counter his own affliction. Is there anything he can say in that regard to give his accusations any merit?"

"No. I can't do what I do for a living and take drugs! I'm a believer in living on the edge, but that's a good way to drive over it. I rarely drink as much as a glass of wine when I'm on location, Seymour. It's absurd!"

"Well, the film business is known for heavy drug users. Have you ever been in the company of these people when drugs were in use?"

"No...Well, there was one time that did happen."

"When was that? I want all the details. I don't want to be caught off guard."

"It was around midnight when I got to the Santa Monica airport. The production company had chartered a jet to fly us to the Bonneville Salt Flats in Utah—"

"What were you filming?"

"A commercial for Volkswagen."

"Was that the one where the car blasts through the paper barrier and does a three-sixty?"

"Yes."

"I remember that one. So then what happened?"

"There were about nine of us in the crew who weren't flying commercially. We waited in the plane until two o'clock in the morning before the director finally showed up. I was getting impatient. I'd worked all day and planned on getting some shut-eye on the plane. We were scheduled to be shooting by sunrise."

"You've got a pretty unusual occupation. Why were you leaving at such a late hour?"

"Some key people, including myself, had other obligations we had to fulfill. With the conflicting agendas, it was too late to catch a commercial flight and make it to the Volkswagen location on time. The director's shoot lasted longer than anticipated, leaving us all with no time to rest before we had to start working again. I was going to try and get at least an hour of sleep. That never happened."

"Is this where we get to the incriminating part?"

"Well, it's not really incriminating, Seymour, but you wanted to hear the extent of any drug history with people in the business."

"Is Richard aware of this incident, or does he know anyone who was there?"

"I don't know. He might."

"Okay, go on."

"As soon as the director boarded, he put the stereo on full blast, making it impossible to sleep. He pulled a bottle of vodka from his bag and began pouring everyone a drink. He was sort of a rebel—not your typical director. I had never really dealt with that kind of behavior in the film business before, believe it or not, at least not to that extreme."

"Go on."

"Well, after everyone was pretty inebriated, the cocaine came out. I couldn't believe I was watching them all snorting this stuff like it was going out of style. It turned into a frenzy. They were dancing in the aisles."

"What were you doing all this time?"

"It was impossible to sleep, and I couldn't beat 'em, so I joined 'em."

"You indulged?"

"Not in cocaine, but the director refused to take no for an answer with the vodka. He poured me a drink and I nursed it the whole way. And that's about the extent of it, Seymour."

"How the hell did these people manage to work after that?"

"They couldn't. It was a total disaster. We got off the plane and went directly to the location. When the sun came up, the heat really intensified their hangovers. The camera never rolled; it was a wasted day. We had to hustle like hell the following day to catch up. There were still a few shots we never got to."

Seymour looked at his watch. "We'd better get back."

———◆———

"Miss Durante, do you take drugs?" Anton asked.

"No, I don't."

"Have you ever taken drugs?"

"Yes."

"And when was the last time you took drugs?" he prodded.

"I can't give you an exact date, but it was before Dustin was born, and he's eight now."

"You never took drugs with Jay Willard?"

"Absolutely not! I don't touch drugs," I answered.

"Miss Durante, do you work with helicopters?"

"Yes."

"Do you feel this is dangerous?"

"No."

"So, you don't think what you do for a living is dangerous?"

"No, I don't."

"Was Dar Robinson one of your drivers?"

"Yes, he was."

"Was? Would you like to tell the court what happened to Mr. Robinson?"

"I object! It's irrelevant," Seymour interrupted.

"Your honor, I'm trying to establish that Miss Durante has no regard for her own life, so how could she care for a child when—"

"That's ridiculous!" shouted Seymour.

"Overruled. Answer the question," the judge instructed.

"Repeat the question?" I said, stalling for time, trying to figure out where he was going to take this.

"You said Dar Robinson *was* one of your drivers. Does that mean he is dead?"

"Yes, Dar is dead."

"How did he die?"

"He died in a motorcycle accident."

"Was he working when he died?"

"Yes, he was."

"What was he working on?"

"A movie called *Million Dollar Mystery*."

"Will you explain the circumstances surrounding his death?"

"Well, I wasn't there, but Pat told me—"

"Who is Pat?"

"Pat McGroarty, another one of my drivers who was working on the job with Dar."

"Okay, what did Mr. McGroarty tell you?"

"He said that they had already done the shot and they were—"

"What do you mean? What was the shot?"

"It was a chase scene."

"Is that driving at fast speeds?"

"Not necessarily. They can undercrank the camera to make it look like they're driving faster than they actually are."

"Was that the case here?"

"I don't know. I wasn't there."

"Okay, continue."

"They had already passed the camera, from what I understand. They were slowing down to return to their number one position to shoot another take. For some reason, Dar must have hit the soft shoulder and lost control of the bike. No one knows for sure since he was the last in line. No one actually saw what happened. He went over the embankment and was impaled on a sagebrush limb."

"Was there an ambulance on the set?"

"There was earlier, but they had released it."

"Why was it released?"

"Because they had done a stunt earlier in the day and didn't feel it was needed for the remaining shots. Dar didn't die doing a stunt. It was a simple shot."

"Do you often have ambulances on the set?"

"Yes, at times."

"Why would they have an ambulance there if you don't think what you do for a living is dangerous?"

"It's part of our contract; it's mandatory."

"Well, Mr. Robinson *died* doing a *simple* shot. I find it hard to believe doing something so simple could cost you your life. Do you care about your life, Miss Durante?"

"Yes."

"Can you explain *why* you have chosen your occupation?"

"No, it's just what I do."

"Was your company contracted by a Japanese oil company to shoot a commercial?"

"We've worked for several Japanese companies. Which one are you referring to?"

"The one where the A-4 jet crashed less than a quarter of a mile from the crew and the picture-vehicle."

"Yes."

"Was the pilot killed on that job?"

"...Yes."

"No more questions."

I was completely drained by the end of the first week. The unwarranted character assassination and the inability to defend it was unbearable. Every detail was distorted, leaving me exasperated. Most frustrating of all were the rules that had to be adhered to. I couldn't bring up Richard's fascination with hookers or his problems with drugs. No, that was five years ago. The court was only interested in today.

What I could tell about the present was considered hearsay. I knew he was still doing drugs; I had lived with it long enough to know the signs. But that didn't count—I had to prove it. I did not keep up with his life or his friends in order to be able to shed any light on his present shenanigans. Five years before, I would have had no problem proving it. Only now did I regret not going to court when we were divorced.

"Miss Durante, did you leave your son when he was a few

months old and run off to New Zealand?"

"I object!" Seymour blurted.

"Sustained. Rephrase the question, counsel."

"Did you leave Dustin and go to work in New Zealand when he was only a few months old?"

"Yes, but he was well cared for."

"Oh? And who took care of him while you were gone for two weeks?"

"Richard and our housekeeper, Marina."

"Can you tell me then, Miss Durante, why you think Richard is such an unfit father, when you can go off for two weeks and leave Dustin in his care? Didn't you allege he was heavily into drugs at that time?"

"Marina was quite capable. I didn't have to worry with her."

"Your Honor, I'd like to call the next witness," Anton announced.

The pain in my heart was agonizing as Toni walked into the courtroom. She avoided making eye contact with me as she took the stand. Picking at her lips—a nervous habit she had acquired when she was younger—she waited for Anton to begin.

God! Richard is so unbelievably shallow. Winning is all that counts! Can't the judge see through this?

Between Richard's and Jay's contemptuous attitudes toward me, Toni was being sadly manipulated. Jay sat in the back of the courtroom, giving her moral support. He was on the list to testify, too. Seymour brought this fact to the judge's attention and he was asked to leave. Toni stiffened and shifted in her seat. Her eyes flickered all over the courtroom, not knowing where to focus.

I was faced with a choice: which of my children do I save? No mother should ever be in that position. Seymour could tear her apart on the stand, if he were to do his job, but how could I let that happen? I flashed back to my day on the stand after I had been raped. They had tried to turn it all around and make me look at fault—not so much different than what was happening now. I could not let that happen to Toni. Too much damage had already been done to her psyche. Whatever it was she was coerced to say would just have to be. All I could do was hope that the damage could be repaired. The pain of this moment was too much for me to bear. I hid out in my Shadow. It was all happening to Georgia Black, not to me. I was safe now.

⸻◆⸻

"Toni, how long has Richard been your legal father?" asked Anton.

"Since I was nine or ten, I guess."

"How old are you now, Toni?"

"I'll be eighteen in October."

"Has Richard been a good father to you?"

"Yes."

"Is he a good father to Dustin?"

"Yes."

"Have you ever seen Richard use drugs?"

She looked over at Richard. "No."

"That's a lie, Seymour," I whispered to him. "She used to steal cocaine from his drawer. That's how she got hooked to begin with! I can't believe she's doing this."

Toni still had not looked in my direction. I glanced at Richard and caught him nodding at her in encouragement.

"How old is your boyfriend, Jay?" Anton continued.

"Twenty-seven."

"Isn't it true that Jay was also your mother's boyfriend at one time?"

"Yes."

"Do you know if Jay ever spent the night at your mother's home when Dustin was present?"

"Objection. That's hearsay," Seymour interrupted.

"Sustained," replied the judge.

"Toni, is it true that your mother's second—or was it the first husband? How many times has your mother been married?"

"Objection. That's been asked and answered."

"Sustained."

"Did your stepfather, your mother's second husband, molest

you, Toni?"

"Yes...he did."

Tears began to well in her eyes. As soon as I began to react, Georgia Black took charge, and I was quickly under control.

"How old were you when that took place?"

"Fourteen."

"Was your mother married to Richard then?"

"Well, it was toward the end. They were still living together... but I don't know if you would call it a marriage."

"How did you see your stepfather Joe? Did your mother drive you there?"

"She used to send me down there on the train."

"Did Richard know about your visits with your stepfather?"

"No, Richard didn't want me seeing Joe."

"Do you think Richard was trying to protect you by not letting you go to San Diego?"

She paused and looked at the ceiling. Shrugging, she answered, "I don't know."

"Why do you think your mother would send you there against Richard's wishes?"

"She said Joe was all alone since his mother died...and I guess she felt sorry for him."

"Did you ever tell her you didn't want to go?"

"Yes."

"And she sent you anyway?"

"Yes."

"Do you feel as if your mother didn't protect you, Toni?"

"Yes," she answered, sobbing.

"That's all the questions I have. Your witness," Anton said, directing his attention to Seymour.

Seymour rose and slowly approached the witness stand, deep in thought. He reminded me of a big teddy bear. He was about seventy years old, I'd guess, and was short and stocky with a head of thick white hair. He appeared to be a gentle old soul, but I knew a ferocious lion lay under that exterior.

"Hello, Toni. I'm Mr. Winston. I understand how hard this is for you," he said sympathetically. "Would you like a glass of water?" he asked, handing her a tissue.

"Okay," she answered, wiping her tear-streaked face.

"Toni, I'm going to have to ask you some questions that may be difficult for you, but I'll try to make it as easy as I can." Seymour hesitated for a moment. "When you were going to San Diego to visit your stepfather Joe, you were fourteen you said?"

"Yes."

"How often did you visit Joe?"

"Once every couple of months. Sometimes a little more, sometimes less."

"When you told your mother you didn't want to go there, did you tell her why?"

"No."

"Why not? You weren't a child. You knew right from wrong, didn't you?" Seymour asked with a gentle tone.

"I guess so," Toni answered, looking pained.

"And weren't there times you *did* want to go?"

"I NEVER WANTED TO SUCK HIS COCK!" she shouted, surprising even herself with her outburst.

A sudden stillness filled the courtroom. The shock of hearing Toni's pain and anger shot through my heart like a thousand arrows. The agony she had buried so deeply inside made me want to run to her. I wanted to put my arms around her and comfort her as I had when she was little. Her pain was my pain. But we were in a courtroom, not a living room.

When the judge studied my face shortly after, he saw only Georgia Black, who protected and concealed my emotions. That was her job. My emotional side needed to surface now to save my son, but Georgia Black had held the reins for too long and I no longer knew how to act on my own.

"Seymour, get her off the stand," I pleaded. "She's much too fragile to take this."

"We have to counter this somehow. It's not looking good."

"It is what it is. I can't lose them both."

Seymour pondered my request for a moment. With a defeated

demeanor, he approached the witness stand. "No more questions, Toni. You can step down."

Toni looked briefly in my direction as she rose from the witness stand. She was as twisted inside as I was. My emotions were a jumble of pain, anger, and hate. Pain for Toni. Anger for Richard. Hate for Joe.

Joe had done a hell of a job destroying my life, even long after he was out of it. He had messed up my head and now the evil cycle would continue with Toni. And, finally, I might even lose my son.

<hr>

After lunch, the defense had yet another trick up its sleeve. They rolled out a video machine and monitor and began to set it up. Seymour looked at me with wonder.

"What do you think they're going to show?"

"I have no idea, Seymour."

"If you can think of anything you haven't told me, Georgia, now is the time."

Oh my God, did the FBI have me on tape? Nah, they didn't go away uttering any threats. What could it be?

"There's nothing I haven't told you. I can't imagine what this is all about."

When the videotape was played, a gasp was heard in the courtroom. It came from me. On the screen was a scene from the New Zealand party. All eyes were glued to the television set as the camera focused in on a close-up of my face. There I was, bigger than life, spooning cocaine into my nostrils. I had totally forgotten about that isolated incident. Every eye in the courtroom had converged on me. Silence.

And when was the last time you took drugs?

I can't give you an exact date, but it was before Dustin was born, and he's eight now.

Did you leave Dustin and go to work in New Zealand when he was just a few months old?

Richard's attorney had executed his job flawlessly. I guess you get what you pay for. Only the best for Richard Adray.

439

The judge looked into my eyes and did what judges are paid to do—he judged me. Seymour's face was a sympathetic mix of disappointment and defeat. I wasn't trying to hide it; I had completely forgotten about it. But what could I say in my defense now? Nothing. Who would believe me? No one. My credibility was destroyed. The judge's expression said it all: *if she lied about this, then she probably lied about everything.*

Richard leaned back in his chair, grinning triumphantly at me. His attorney, a sickening smirk on his face, stood next to the television with his arms folded. I don't really know what I did; Black handled it.

We all lost a chunk of our lives in the courtroom that day. Richard may have thought he walked out a winner, but life will prove him wrong. When the emotional well-being of children is involved, there are never any winners—only losers.

Chapter Nineteen

Four long years passed without any contact with my daughter, and I only saw my son every other weekend. My heart never ceased to ache for Toni when I thought about her outburst in the courtroom, but it didn't change the fact that she had betrayed me on the stand. Her lies had shielded Richard and contributed to the loss of my son. Toni needed to take responsibility for her actions, despite what she had suffered. My door was open to her, but not while Jay was still a part of her life. It killed me, but not once did I attempt to call her during those four years.

I did a lot of soul-searching during that time. Maybe I wasn't such a good mother. Toni had always been a quiet child, keeping her fears and dreams to herself. Maybe she was hiding out in her own Shadow. She ran with me, she hid with me, but we never talked about it. I'd always thought she just kind of *knew*, but I'd never shared with her my fears and my incredible hurt. I had tried to protect her from all that, so how was she to know what was going on? All she knew was that I wasn't there. Why hadn't I ever looked at it from her perspective before? Of course she harbored resentments—she didn't understand.

When I'd finally escaped from Joe, I had tried to recapture all I had missed out on. I always felt as though I was going to die before I had a chance to live. I felt so cheated. Why didn't I think about how my daughter had been cheated? I was so wrapped up in my own pain, I didn't think about hers. Any good mother would have. Maybe I put too much blame on Joe for Toni's drug problem. It was time I took some responsibility for the shambles I had made of my own life.

The sad thing was, God had given me a second chance: he had given me Dustin. I was thirty years old when he was born, ready to be a mother, but I never fully had the chance before he was stolen from me. Was this one of God's lessons? Was this my punishment for Toni's lost childhood?

I again focused my energies on my work. I didn't want a relationship. It would only end as always—in betrayal, pain, and hurt. The only affair I had going was with Mac—my Macintosh computer. Georgia Black held the power, protecting me from potential heartbreak. The minute I came near the possibility of a meaningful relationship, Ms. Black jumped in and, like a vampire, sucked the life from it. She reduced everything to an emotional zero. She created and maintained distance. Distance equalled safety.

My heart became hardened and I was driven to succeed. The loving Georgia was nowhere to be found. But it wasn't all in vain. I learned my capabilities, I understood my strengths, and my determination was unrelenting. I finally believed in who I was.

Toni lived with Jay during our time of estrangement. We both fought the temptation to call each other. My mother, bless her heart, was sick over what had become of the relationship between Toni and me. She had broken up with Jay and my mother invited her to my house on Christmas Eve without my knowledge. The four years of indescribable hurt vanished as we hugged and cried in each other's arms. In time, however, the outpouring of love would be shadowed by the resentments we both harbored.

Toni knows I love her and I know she loves me, but the process of healing when the injury is as deep as ours takes time. There is no deeper hurt, except for the death of a child, than being betrayed by a child. I am trying to get past my hostility to better understand the reasons for Toni's actions. We are both working at taking responsibility for our past behaviors and trying to put the pieces of our lives back together.

About six months after our reunion, Toni brought a nice young man named Barry over for dinner. We sat on the deck in my backyard, enjoying the warm summer evening. I thought it odd the resemblance Barry had to Joe, but at least his name didn't end in a vowel. He was seven years older than Toni. I could see in my daughter's eyes that same sparkle I'd had in mine when I looked at Frankie. Toni and Barry held hands and climbed the ladder to Dustin's infrequently-used tree house. It was there that they kissed for the first time.

"What do you think of him, Mom?" Toni asked when Barry went into the house.

"I like him."

"Oh good! Can I keep him?"

I smiled. How wonderful it would be to feel that way again. But only in youth is a heart allowed to be so vulnerable.

------◆------

Toni and Barry were married in May of 1992. They picked a date that didn't conflict with my heavy work schedule. Bridal fairs were fun, and I enjoyed advising the kids on tradition, decorum, and taste. Toni asked her real father, Tom, to give her away. Even though Richard had adopted her, she knew she meant nothing to him—another hard fact for her to come to terms with.

Toni had not seen Tom since she was seven years old. He had never even bothered to send a birthday card. A year before the wedding, however, while visiting Rochester, Toni had contacted him and they had bonded. Tom told her he had to think about it. I could sense her disappointment, so I called him myself.

I hadn't seen or talked to him Tom years. After he got over the initial shock of hearing my voice, I asked if he was going to give Toni away at her wedding.

"I don't know," he said. "It's awfully expensive. I don't think I can afford it."

"It's six months away. You can't pull $400 together by then?"

"I don't know. If you could see the way I live, you'd die."

"What do you mean?"

"I live in a tiny room in a shabby motel," he said.

"How much does that cost a month?"

"$400."

"That's crazy," I said. "You can get a nice apartment in Rochester for eight hundred. Why don't you get a roommate and split it? For the same amount of money you can live like a human being!"

"Yeah...but I don't have any furniture."

"Jesus, Tom, how you can live like that?"

"Georgia, will you answer something for me?"

"What?"

"Why did you leave me? I've been wondering about that now for twenty-two years. I'd really like to know."

"Well, I was pretty young then, but I guess...even as young as I was, I knew that I didn't want to live in a motel room when I was forty years old."

"I always thought you left me for that guy Frankie from New York, but when you didn't marry him, I couldn't figure it out. Now I know."

"Listen, Tom," I said, determined to get back to the purpose of my call, "if you start saving now, I'm sure you'll have enough money for the plane ticket. I have a guest house you can stay in, so it won't cost you anything for food or lodging. This is important to Toni. You've never sent her as much as a card for Christmas, her birthday, or graduation. You haven't acknowledged *any* special event in her life. I think you owe her this."

"Yeah, you're right," he said. "I'll see what I can do."

Time to deal with Richard. I took a deep breath and called him.

"Toni told me you offered to pay for her honeymoon," I said. "I have a proposition for you."

"Can't wait to hear it," he responded, sounding bored.

"The airfare to Mexico at that time of year is pretty expensive. With hotels and car rental it'll probably cost you about $4,000. It would really help me out if you would contribute that money to some of the wedding expenses, and I'll pay for the honeymoon. I have some free air miles and car-rental certificates. I can also get 50% off on the rooms. What do you think?"

"Well, I've thought about it since I made that offer. Toni owes me a thousand dollars. I'm just going to give her a card and write her a note saying she doesn't have to pay me back."

"That's real generous of you, Richard."

"Hey, she's not my responsibility. And besides, I may be in Europe when she gets married."

"You mean you're not going to her wedding? How could you do that to her?"

"My mother will be there."

"Big deal! You know you really are a piece of shit, Richard—"

He hung up on me.

———◆———

The wedding day finally arrived and Toni looked radiant. I'd never seen her so happy. I was bursting with pride. Dustin was an usher, looking so grown-up. Where had the time gone? Tom did come, and he even managed to give Toni $1,000 for a wedding gift. His hair was pretty much all gray now, but he was still a handsome man.

The ceremony took place in the formal gardens at the Greystone Mansion in Beverly Hills. The grounds were similar to an elegant European castle estate, set on a mountaintop overlooking the city. The temperature was perfect, but then, it usually was in Southern California. Harp music played softly while the guests were being seated.

I was busy checking on the photographer, trying to make sure everything was running smoothly, when I heard...

"Hi, baby."

"Frankie! You came!"

"Of course. I wouldn't miss little Toni Lee's wedding for anything," he said, a huge grin on his face.

"I'm so happy you're here."

"Where's the little monster?" he asked.

"He's with the wedding party. Wait till you see how big he's gotten. He'll be so happy to see you. So will Toni. She asked if you'd responded."

"I wanted to surprise her. Is Dustin too big now to take him to the Lost World?"

"I love the way you work a child's imagination, Frankie," I said, thinking of how he'd opened my mind when I was young. "Only you could turn a backyard into a Lost World. But to answer your question, I'm having my doubts that he's still a virgin."

"You're kidding."

"No, I'm not.

"Well I'll be a son-of-a-cockroach," he exclaimed, and we both burst out laughing.

"You'll never guess who's here, Frankie."

"Who, baby?"

"Tom."

"You're shittin' me. Really? You mean we're gonna meet after all these years? Hey, you didn't give him my room, did you? I'm really gonna be pissed off if you did, Georgie Girl."

"Well, I did, but then some relatives came in, so I moved him to the couch."

"I can't believe you let him sleep in my room!"

We both got silly. We never lost the magic of laughter.

Frankie sat beside me as Toni walked down the aisle on Tom's arm. She was beaming. Seeing her so happy after all the sadness she had suffered in her young life brought tears to my eyes. I couldn't help remembering walking down the aisle with Tom twenty-four years earlier, wishing it was Frankie. As if reading my thoughts, Frankie squeezed my hand, and I realized for the first time that our moment in time had really been a lifetime.

Everyone was there. Even my sister managed the courage to get on an airplane. It was such a happy day.

"Well, honey, I never thought your dad and I would live long enough to see this day," my mother said, teary-eyed.

"Going through life with you was enough to put anyone into an early grave," my dad added with an endearing smile. "Business must be doing well—this is some affair you're putting on here. Don't you think you should give your old dad ten percent of all your action? I paid dearly for that driving education if you'll recall."

"How could I forget? I don't know how you ever put up with me, Dad."

"You were worth every minute of it. Look at you now. I don't know where your courage came from, but we're so proud of what you've done with your life, honey."

"Thank you, Daddy. I couldn't have done it without all your love and support. I love you guys."

The reception was held at the Marina City Club. Richard's clout got us access to the room, as he had been a longtime member. That was the extent of his obligation. After the reception, we went back to my house. I collapsed on the couch, exhausted from the months of preparation. The result was well worth it; the wedding was a beautiful, memorable event. Frankie poured a glass of wine and sat down next to me. Tom made himself a drink and sat on the couch across from us.

Frankie said out of nowhere, "Georgie Girl, are you *sure* Toni's not mine? Y'know, she does have my eyebrows."

I couldn't believe he said that! It had been so civil so far.

"I never worried about that, Frankie," Tom retorted. "I always thought she was my brother Babe's child."

"What! Why in the world would you ever think that, Tom?" I asked, more shocked by his remark than by Frankie's. Frankie was kidding but Tom was serious.

"My brother hated me. It would be like him to do something like that to me, but I know she's mine now."

"What makes you so sure?" Frankie asked, egging him on.

Jesus, Frankie, will you leave it alone?

"I think we should change the subject," I said, but no one paid attention to me. They were politely venting twenty-four years of unspoken hostility.

"Yeah, Tom, 'of all the gin joints in all the world, she had to walk into mine.'"

"You know what, Frankie?" Tom said. "I actually came to New York looking for you once."

Frankie raised an eyebrow in mocking amusement. "Yeah? Well, it's a good thing for you that you didn't find me," he answered, half-serious.

"Wasn't it a beautiful wedding?" I interrupted, feeling like a referee.

"Yes, it was a beautiful wedding. You did a nice job, Georgia," Tom said. "By the way, how come your asshole ex-husband wasn't there?"

"He's in Europe. That was more important, evidently."

"Not *that* asshole, the other one."

"I'm really tired, you guys. I think I'll go to bed," I said, avoiding the subject.

"Where am I sleeping?" Frankie asked.

"Right where you're sitting," I answered, and I brought them both pillows and blankets. "Goodnight guys. Don't stay up all night talking now."

I walked into the bathroom and washed off my make-up. Looking in the mirror, I studied my face and wondered where the time had gone. The fine lines around my eyes reflected an intelligence enhanced by time. That smile—the same smile of my youth, the one that opened the door to trouble when I was unaware of its power, the smile that had brought so much pain and joy. Only *I* really knew, behind my misleading smile, that I had never been happy or free.

I lay in bed that night thinking back on my life, back to Toni being born. A lot had happened in my short forty-two years. I wondered: if I had the chance to do it all over again, what I would do differently? Nothing. Well...almost nothing. Life *is* what it *is*. How we deal with it is what matters. We all have peaks and valleys. My lows were extremely low, but my highs were extremely high. I've been uncommonly blessed with all the highs in my life. Most people never come near those heights, so I guess my lows had to be lower than most in order to compensate.

There are still lessons to be learned—there will *always* be lessons. I don't define my life by my losses, it's the gain from those losses that I measure. I have never viewed my life as an undeserved punishment. I learned to survive. Being a survivor is nothing more than attitude and determination, and, most importantly, believing in yourself. I've always known what I *don't* want, but now I have the courage to say so.

Getting on with my life was something I had never really gotten around to doing, at least not on a personal level. I began moving forward ten months after Toni's wedding.

Richard married and divorced for the third time. Then, instead of marrying them, he began to move women in and out of the house with increasing frequency. With each new fling, they decreased in age. The most recent was only nineteen. That kind of atmosphere is what I'd always feared for Dustin. I was sure his values would become warped, being unprotected from the exposure to distasteful women and the evils of wealth. I kidded with him one weekend while he and his friend were having breakfast in my kitchen.

"Gee, Dustin, pretty soon you'll be vying for the same girlfriends your dad has."

"Why not *now*?" his friend retorted.

I burst out laughing at his serious expression, realizing at the same time that my son was not a child anymore. No, Dustin was becoming a young man. His lanky body was surpassing me in height. He looked more like me than Toni did. His delicate features complimented his sandy colored hair and sensitive brown eyes.

In a voice changing from that of a boy to that of a man, he said, "I hope I don't turn out like my dad," and he rolled his eyes.

At that moment, I felt my diligent efforts had been rewarded. I had managed to ingrain some values in my son. Despite all the obstacles, Dustin was developing into a decent human being. Miracles *do* happen. Like me, he was willful and independent, and had a mind of his own.

Joe had become a recluse. He became his own judge and jury and sentenced himself to a life of imprisonment. He drove his car into his brother Ronny's driveway, and it sat in the same spot for seven years. He made himself physically sick. He developed some kind of a bone disease that limited his movement, and then he was diagnosed with emphysema. He gave up on life altogether and waited impatiently to die. At the age of fifty-seven, he could barely walk or breathe and the demons in his head continued to haunt him. My prediction about what the end of his life would hold for him surely rang loudly in his ears on the oh-so-long days he spent alone with himself.

You're going to be a sad, lonely man in the end, with no one left to love you—or care whether you live or die.

When death refused to take him naturally, he finally took the gun that had mysteriously disappeared from my house, put it to his head, and drove the demons away once and for all.

Not many fond memories or nice words were said in the wake of Joe's passing. The world had not suffered a great loss. Toni and I sat across the table from each other, teary-eyed, silently reflecting on our past.

"Isn't it funny, Mom? We're the ones he hurt the most, and we're the only ones mourning his death."

"I think it's time we both went to therapy, Toni."

"I think you're right, Mom."

Until Joe's death on March 10, 1993, I was still a prisoner because I still held the negatives. His death allowed me the freedom to develop those negatives in my mind. Georgia Black had been living my life. Somewhere along the way, Ms. Black completely took over, running my business *and* my personal life. She too had eventually stolen my spirit. The mask I was wearing became who I was.

The wheels of life have taken me on quite a journey. I am now taking control of the wheel and I'm focused on driving in forward gear. In comparison to my past, running in Hollywood's fast lane is like a slow waltz for me. I have grown and I've accomplished a lot. Yes, I am willful. Yes, I am independent. And yes, I have a mind of my own. I have truly begun to be free. But at what cost?

As I continue the inner work I need to accomplish in order to become whole again, I realize more and more that I need not give up my Shadow to be a loving, feeling human being. I can choose to conquer with hate, but I prefer to conquer with love. It's an ongoing process, but the light and the shadow of my psyche both have something to offer in creating the totality of who I am. In the love and intimacy of my inner light, there is joy. And in the strength, determination, and self-preservation my shadow side provides, there is safety. At moments I have understood that in that synthesis—that beautiful paradox of feeling protected by living with an open heart—there is true empowerment. This is the path I am on, and this is the ultimate freedom I seek.

Reflecting once again on my childhood, back to a time before life became cruel, I could see my face as it once had been. I remembered the look in my eyes. I had such a wild spirit, full of hunger for adventure and exploration. There was love and human dreams. They weren't dreams of wealth or power. No, I was in search of spiritual dreams—of closeness, family, security, and peace. It's the me that never quite was and still ought to be—loving and completely free.

There's one more thing I must do before I can achieve my goal...

Dear Joe,

My life has been filled with anger and hate for you these past years. You are gone now. You suffered in the end. I knew you would, but it didn't make me happy. I'm sorry you suffered, as I know that part of that suffering was your penance for the pain you caused us. We must all pay a price...it's in the cards. I know that you were not given the power to change your life. The devil really had a hold on you, didn't he? I have finally found it in my heart to forgive you now. Maybe because you don't reside with us anymore, it's easier. But I have let go. In doing so I can now begin my life. I only hope God has forgiven you too and you have found peace. Oh, and Joe, please stop visiting me now. I believe you are sorry, okay?

May God have mercy on your tormented soul...

Georgia

What matters today is where I drive my life from here. The merry-go-round is slowing down and when it stops...will anything be waiting for me?

It's time. Time to burn the negatives. The lights are flickering now. There's a curve up ahead and I'll go off a cliff if I don't slow down and turn on the lights...

The Ferrari entered the turn. I geared down but still had too much speed to take the curve. The vehicle went off the cliff and rolled three times, coming to rest upside down on a steep bluff.

My lights should have been snuffed out for good. It should have been a wrap.

But instead—the lights turned on... And my life was just beginning.

EPILOGUE

The writing of this book has taken me on quite an emotional journey. It has forced me to examine myself as never before. Through this therapeutic process, I was able to unravel the origin of an extraordinary tangle of neurosis and buried trauma in search of the woman at the center. I like what I found.

After setting my pen aside, I began to take lighter steps through my life with opened eyes and an open heart. Then, out of nowhere, he came into my life. His name is Jim Henderson. We met at Dan Tana's restaurant in Los Angeles. I was with a date and Jim was a guest of my date's friend. Jim called me the following week on the premise of asking me to decorate his house—and it went from there.

We share the kind of love I've written about, but never thought I'd attain. And I couldn't have, without the knowledge and insight I gained from writing this book, along with the wisdom acquired from my life's experiences.

Jim began his law career in 1972 in Washington, D.C. with the United States Justice Department. During the course of his service, he was appointed Chief of the Strike Force for Organized Crime. He battled in court with the top crime figures in Chicago from 1975 until 1978. He was then assigned to Los Angeles where he succeeded in breaking up the West Coast Mob with the conviction of Los Angeles Mob Boss Dominic Brooklier. In the Brooklier case, Jim supervised and handled the development, debriefing, and nation-wide trial testimony of Jimmy "the Weasel"

Fratianno, until recently the highest-ranking organized crime figure to ever become a government witness. Following the Brooklier trial, Jim was assigned to try its companion case against New Orleans La Cosa Nostra Boss Carlos Marcello, which also resulted in conviction.

In Jim's sixteen-year career with the Justice Department, he handled more than 100 organized crime prosecutions and directly participated in 100 others, earning him the title of having convicted more organized crime figures than any other U.S. Attorney in history. He was undoubtedly the one prosecutor the Mob feared the most.

At this point in my life, nothing shocks me. I guess I am destined for the bizarre. Jim is probably the last person on earth I would have expected to fall in love with, and I'm sure some of my acquaintances on the darker side feel the same. Though we had the law between us, our lives ran in a paralleled course over the years. In fact, they almost overlapped when he prosecuted my friend Dan Whitman, to whom a few pages of this book were devoted.

We recently took Dan out to dinner. He tried to pick up the check, but Jim snapped it away, saying, "Do you really think I'd let you buy my dinner after I put you away for nine years?"

Dan replied, "Well, look at it this way. you've paid for my dinner for nine years. It's my turn."

To my surprise, Dan has the utmost respect for Jim. He readily accepts that Jim had a job to do and appreciates that he carried out his duties with integrity and without malice. Unfortunately, some of my other acquaintances do not share Dan's view. In fact, we hesitate before starting our cars.

Jim is now in private practice as a Federal Criminal Defense attorney. Subsequently, I am surrounded once again by the same cast of characters who have always paraded through my life. Guess it's in my cards. Ironic as it may be, I think this common bond is what strengthens our relationship. By the looks of it, Jim may very well be my final chapter.

Who ever said three strikes and you're out?